John Ruskin was born in London on February 8, 1819. The only son of a wealthy wine merchant, he was educated at home until the age of 15, an education shaped by an emphasis on religion and morality. After graduating from Christ Church, Oxford, where he won the Newdigate Prize for poetry, Ruskin began the travels and study that led to his volumes of art criticism, *Modern Painters*, which appeared from 1843 to 1860, and his notable work on architecture, *The Stones of Venice* (1851-53). Increasingly convinced of the intrinsic relationship between the quality of art and the nature of society, Ruskin became one of the Victorian era's most eloquent champions of economic and social reform. While his public life was marked by growing renown, his private life was marred by an unconsummated marriage, a scandalous divorce trial, an unhappy love, and growing mental instability. The last decades of his life were spent in virtually complete retirement. Ruskin died on January 20, 1900.

S E L E C T E D

P R O S E

O F

John Ruskin

EDITED
AND WITH AN INTRODUCTION BY
MATTHEW HODGART

PREPARED UNDER THE EDITORIAL SUPERVISION
OF HAROLD BLOOM

A SIGNET CLASSIC from
NEW AMERICAN LIBRARY
TIMES MIRROR
New York and Scarborough, Ontario
The New English Library Limited, London

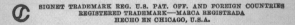

SIGNET TRADEMARK REG. U.S. PAT. OFF. AND FOREIGN COUNTRIES
REGISTERED TRADEMARK—MARCA REGISTRADA
HECHO EN CHICAGO, U.S.A.

SIGNET, SIGNET CLASSICS, SIGNETTE, MENTOR AND PLUME BOOKS
are published *in the United States* by
The New American Library, Inc.,
1301 Avenue of the Americas, New York, New York 10019,
in Canada by The New American Library of Canada Limited,
81 Mack Avenue, Scarborough, 704, Ontario,
in the United Kingdom by The New English Library Limited,
Barnard's Inn, Holborn, London, E.C. 1, England

FIRST PRINTING, JUNE, 1972

PRINTED IN THE UNITED STATES OF AMERICA

Contents

Introduction   vii

Biographical Profile   xxi

Selected Bibliography   xxv

Modern Painters, Vol. I (1843)   29

Modern Painters, Vol. II (1846)   55

The Seven Lamps of Architecture
(1849)   59

The Stones of Venice, Vol. II
(1853)   91

Modern Painters, Vols. III
and IV (1856)   158

A Joy for Ever: The Political
Economy of Art (1857)   198

The Two Paths (1859)   232

Modern Painters, Vol. V (1860)   254

Unto This Last (1860)   280

The Crown of Wild Olive (1866)   294

Time and Tide (1867)   313

English Art (1870)   324

The Eagle's Nest (1872)   327

Fors Clavigera (1872 and 1873)   329

Notes on Prout and Hunt (1879)   335

Praeterita (1885–89)   338

Introduction

John Ruskin was a prophet, in the sense defined by William Blake: "Every honest man is a prophet; he utters his opinion both of private and public matters. Thus, if you go on, the result is so. He never says, such a thing will happen let you do what you will. A prophet is a seer, not an arbitrary dictator." Ruskin did not begin as a prophet, but as one deeply in love with the physical world, and with the art of painting, which captures and recreates the glories of that world. From there he went to the study of architecture, the most social of the arts, and the one which best symbolizes man's harmony with nature; and from there to an examination of society itself, both of the good society which had served as a matrix for art, and of the bad society, as he saw it, of his own day which made good art, or at least good architecture, next to impossible. Thus he became an explicitly political prophet, and in that role he was both unpopular and influential in his prime. At the end of his long life he was venerated but misunderstood, a common fate of prophets. As a political thinker his radiance has dimmed: his vision had become cloudy even in his lifetime, as he fell into eccentricity and madness; and today it is perhaps untranslatable into terms that can apply to the complexities of modern society. Nevertheless Ruskin's great moments of insight spoke to the imagination of thousands, perhaps of millions, and can still speak to us, as in parable.

He remains the first and greatest prophet of the natural world's ruin, and as such is the patron saint of conservationists. He taught his age that the world was beautiful down to the minutest details of its structure, but was in immediate danger of spoliation and destruction. We may find Ruskin's thunderous denunciations exaggerated when applied to the actual conditions of Victorian England—a few railways through Derbyshire, after all, did no great harm to the landscape. But today, when the whole of little England and even much of great America is in danger of terminal blight, the import of Ruskin's sometimes wild and whirling words is clear. Again, his lecture called "The Storm Cloud of the Nineteenth Century" (1884), in which he produced a theory that the weather had irrevocably deteriorated, is meteorologically absurd if taken literally: there were some wet summers about that time, but no evidence of a real change for the worse. But today, when we are told that the vapor trails of jets and rockets and the heat discharged from the cities may produce irreversible changes in the atmosphere, we may think that Ruskin saw something real, if through a glass darkly. That may be speculation; but there is nothing speculative about this: uncontrolled industrial plants had turned, he said, "every river of England into a common sewer, so that you cannot so much as baptize an English baby but with filth, unless you hold its face out to the rain, and even *that* falls dirty." And now, if the drinking water is purer, the cities of the world are rapidly becoming uninhabitable from pollution, and the seashores that Turner painted are infested with sewage and oil. We may reject Ruskin's hostility to technology as obscurantist, and his version of the deteriorationist myth as fantastic. For example, he saw not only architecture and society as declining from the Middle Ages, but also nature itself in decay: he noted that the glaciers were retreating in his beloved Alps, and many places were free from snow for the first time in living memory, and as a result of the melting snow there was an increase in what he called the "deadly maremma," i.e. in the malarial marshes around Pisa and Venice. As a matter of scientific fact this is not precise, and put in Ruskin's moral and theological terms, with the implication that these climatic events were a symbol of divine displeasure at man's wickedness, it is absurd; but it remains true that many parts of the natural world are in decay, thanks to human greed and indifference, and it is a matter of urgency to save what is left.

If Ruskin's thinking ranged over too wide a field for any one man to grasp, it began and ended in the accurate observation of nature. He took up the defense of Turner against his critics, claiming that Turner saw the shapes and colors of the world more truly than any other painter of landscapes. Whether this claim was true or false need not be discussed here (nor whether Ruskin was justified in his attacks on great painters like Claude and Constable): it was important that he felt he had to back up his claim by an enormous labor of observation and learning. He began this in the first volume of *Modern Painters* (1843) and had not finished it with the fifth and last volume of that huge and untidy Gothic cathedral (1860). His program included making an exhaustive study of the shapes of clouds, mountains and trees: it was not enough to prove that Turner could render perfectly the appearances of such phenomena, he had to prove that Turner had an intuitive mastery of their underlying structure. This led Ruskin to the quasi-scientific study of meteorology, geology and botany; and from these into the minor branches of mineralogy and ornithology; all of which he expounded passionately until the end of his career. Nothing in nature is too small for the painter's attention: the bands of an agate are just as important as the storm clouds over the Matterhorn. To take mineralogy first (since this is the Ruskinian topic of which I am least ignorant), he made several collections of semi-precious stones and rock specimens, studied the structure of crystals and chalcedonic layering minutely, and before giving his collections away with characteristic generosity, catalogued them in some of his least-known but most-striking prose. "87. Agate, a portion of an amygdaloidal nodule with jasperine bands of exquisite beauty, illustrating nearly every phenomenon of folding and crystalline interference. The minute cones of quartz locally traceable with a lens along the white, and the finely-veined innermost bed, exactly like the tents of a camp in the desert, are extremely rare" (Catalogue of a series of specimens in the British Museum [*Natural History*] *illustrative of the more common forms of native silica*). This kind of thing must not be dismissed as collector's folly, or the aberrations of a literary genius, for on just such obsessive enquiries Ruskin based his most impressive theories. So with the many pages, some magnificent, others too technical for most readers, on the folding of mountains in *Modern Painters;* and so with his exact descriptions of the ways branches grow out of trunks. Ruskin was a devout Wordsworthian, and learned from his master how to describe clouds; but in his patient and profound analysis of natural shapes he went much further than Wordsworth or indeed any other poet of the age. His greatest disciples in this field are Gerard Manley Hopkins and Marcel Proust. Hopkins's journals, with their attempts to catch the "inscape" of a scene by combining bold metaphor with microscopic precision, are the most notable examples of Ruskinian word-painting in the nineteenth century; they are surpassed only by Proust's marvelously exact description of the hawthorns. When Hopkins praises God for "dappled things" and for nature's "veined, stained variety," he is expressing just what Ruskin loved most: the veins of silica in a pebble, the stained look of jasper, the capillaries of a leaf, the dappling of clouds. In asserting dogmatically that the painter's eye must seize every quality of his subject, Ruskin had to prove that his eye was keener and his patience in observing greater than the painters he despised, and approached the level of the masters that he praised. He could not or would not learn to paint in oils; but his drawings of flowers and trees, and above all of architecture, are masterly and have an intimate relationship with his finest prose.

This prose, at its best, strikes a perfect balance between descriptive science and poetic evocation. Ruskin is concerned with explaining how things are on the surface and below the surface—how nature works—and with re-creating the total experience of an observer. When he strays too far to one side or to the other, the magic of his prose vanishes. Throughout *Modern Painters* there are deliberately purple passages, when he pulls out all the stops as climax to an argument; and then he is sometimes betrayed by his oratory into sentimentality or even vulgarity. A mark of his failure on these occasions is a tendency to lapse into blank verse: e.g. "the silver lichen-spots rest star-like on the stone; and the gathering orange stain/ upon the edge of yonder western peak/reflects the sunsets of a thousand years" (*Modern Painters,* Vol. V, Part 5, end). Pseudo-Wordsworthian cadences like "sharing the stillness of the unimpassioned rock" are happily not too common; and Ruskin's powers of describing scenery are the greatest in the English language. When on the other hand Ruskin moved toward pure science he often failed in a different way. He had certainly some astonishing intuitions: in his early discussions of plant growth he was groping toward an understanding of the Fibonacci numbers (1,1,2,3,5,8,13 etc.), which have since been shown to be important in the structure of shoots and branches. His detailed analyses of agate formation are valuable; while, as Herbert notes, when Ruskin put forward the theory that a glacier was a moving river of ice, he was right and his professional opponents wrong. On the other hand, he disliked Darwin's theories and tried to refute them, but was ill-equipped to tangle with the greatest naturalist of the age. The energy with which Ruskin threw himself into the study of various sciences was vast; but he could not submit to the discipline of any particular one, insisting rather that his was the only right way of seeing things. Some of his incursions into natural history were beautiful, others bizarre, as in the ornithology of *The Queen of the Air, The Eagle's Nest,* and *Love's Meinie.* James Fisher, a leading expert, quotes a striking sentence from the first of these: "We will take the bird first. It is little more than a drift of the air brought into form by plumes; the air is in all its quills, it breathes through its whole frame and flesh, and glows with air in its flying, like a blown flame; it rests upon the air, subdues it, surpasses, outruns it;—*is* the air, conscious of itself, conquering itself, ruling itself." Fisher finds himself unable to decide whether that sentence was "based on a poet's intuition or a scholar's knowledge of the intricacies" of the inner pneumatic system of birds; but concludes that Ruskin's influence on nature-lovers was finally confusing as well as illuminating: "Even when I was a boy, bird-watchers and butterfly collectors were looked down on with Ruskinian scorn by over-educated teachers and scholars on the English literature side, who subconsciously still deemed animals as beings capable only of being understood through literary mysteries . . ." (*The Shell Bird Book,* 1966, pp. 198-99). To quote another expert opinion (Wilfrid Blunt, *The Art of Botanical Illustration,* 1950, p. 231), "Ruskin's *Proserpina* [1874-86], in spite of its untidy diffuseness, its irritatingly didactic tone and its ill-digested science, remains the most stimulating book ever written about flowers." His drawings are nearly as fine as his prose descriptions, although he refused to use a microscope to pry into the sexual mysteries ("with those obscene processes and prurient apparitions the gentle and happy scholar of flowers has nothing whatever to do").

The didactic tone is always there, especially in Ruskin's earlier works. In his approach to science as to art, he emphasizes the moral element: everything in nature has a purpose and everything that is beautiful has a lesson to teach us. This was the result of his early Evangelical training; and it caused him to get involved in philosophical problems that neither he nor any other writer on aesthetics has been able to solve. For it is impossible to prove that nature is teleological or that it has anything to teach us about how to conduct our lives. Ruskin called his treatise on mineralogy *Ethics of the Dust,* but, dust, alas, even diamond dust, has nothing to say about ethics. Morality intrudes into all his art criticism, causing almost as great a degree of confusion as in his scientific digressions. He was unable to show, though he asserted it strenuously, that good art proceeded from high moral qualities in the artist, or caused any ethical improvement in the viewer; and these propositions remain today a matter of hope rather than of fact. After his "deconversion" in middle age, when he lost much of his Evangelical intolerance, Ruskin gave less emphasis to morality in his criticism; and even in one passage, intended for a later edition of *Modern Painters* but never printed in his lifetime, he came near to the doctrine of "Art for Art's Sake." The voice of the preacher is always ready to interrupt his finest descriptions and explanations. When he turned from nature and art to politics, which *is* closely connected with ethics, there was no longer the old confusion between fact and values: his moral arguments and his eloquence as preacher and prophet served a wholly proper end.

Besides its emphasis on morality and on truth to nature, Ruskin's art criticism contains a vast number of profound insights and technical comments, if no very systematic theory. It must not be supposed that Ruskin advocated mere fidelity: truth to nature demanded of the artist, as we have seen, both the mastery of surface appearances and the grasp of the underlying structures, but Ruskin went further than this. The true painter, having these at his disposal, must apply a set of transformations to his material, to produce a composition that approaches the ideal both of abstract patterning and human truth. The power by which he is able to do this is the imagination: and Ruskin's account of the imagination is extremely lucid and realistic. In Dante, Scott, Turner and Tintoretto, it does not mean a voluntary production of new images, but an involuntary remembrance, exactly at the right moment, of something they had actually seen: "Imagine all that any of these men had seen or heard in the whole course of their lives, laid up accurately in their memories as in vast storehouses, extending, with the poets, even to the slightest intonations of syllables heard in the beginning of their lives, and, with the painters, down to minute folds of drapery, and shapes of leaves and stones, and over all this unindexed and immeasurable mass of treasure, the imagination brooding and wandering, but dream-gifted, to summon at any moment exactly such groups of ideas as shall justly fit each other: this I conceive to be the real nature of the imaginative mind" (*Modern Painters*, Vol. 24, 1900, p. 33). That explains why the muses are the daughters of Memory, and can be restated in modern terms: the mind of a great painter or poet is an outstandingly efficient system of data retrieval. It is the imagination that puts natural phenomena in direct relation to humanity, and thereby transforms them into fit subjects for art. Ruskin also stressed the purely formal aspects of painting, with exquisitely described examples and much practical advice. His theories of color anticipate the Impressionists; and his discussion of "ornament," i.e. design and texture, is also wholly original. As Herbert says, he "based his life's work upon visual sensations, and provided the twentieth century with the most compendious discussion of the 'abstract' components of art."

Ruskin came to politics through the arts, but above all through architecture. The questions he raised can be put simply, although the answers are obscure: What are the social conditions necessary for good art? Is a good society a precondition of good art? Ruskin was never able to solve the problems raised by the painters he loved most, Titian, Veronese and Tintoretto. He detested what he took to be the economic and social culture of the later Renaissance (capitalism, individualism, false religion and so on), but had to admit that these painters flourished in a moral dunghill. He thus grants tacitly that painting is a private enough art to thrive in adverse social conditions; but clearly he could not say the same of architecture, because of the vastly greater degree to which patronage, corporate funds and the labor of many hands are involved. He answered the question by asserting simply that all Renaissance and later architecture, including all Baroque and neo-classical, was inferior to the Gothic or positively bad. He then set up the Gothic architecture of the thirteenth and fourteenth centuries as the absolute standard. Nothing has equaled Ruskin's descriptions and sketches of this architecture, but in trying to explain why it was so great he was on insecure grounds. He had to make ill-founded assumptions about the nature of medieval society; for example, that Venetian life in the thirteenth century was more "communal" and less capitalistic than it became two hundred years later, or that the building of the great churches was a spontaneous expression of the people's will—views which were given a romantic elaboration by his disciple William Morris. In fact, if a society is judged by the extent to which it provides a reasonable standard of living and security for the majority of its population, that of the Middle Ages does not deserve high praise. To illustrate his theories, Ruskin confined himself to the arts of classical Greece and Rome and of Western Europe; but today most art critics would, I think, prefer to survey the world from China to Peru before arriving at any conclusion. So much is now known about the architecture and other arts of the Orient and ancient Egypt (much of this was still undiscovered in Ruskin's time) that it may seem impossible to generalize about art and society, beyond noting that some great architecture has been produced by societies that have been not only unjust but, like that of ancient Mexico, even horrible. Indeed, Ruskin came to abandon his earlier theories for the simpler and more sensible one that he outlines in his inaugural address to the Cambridge School of Art: "There's no way of getting good Art, I repeat, but one—at once the simplest and most difficult—namely to enjoy it. Examine the history of nations, and you will find this great fact clear and unmistakable on the front of it—that good Art has only been produced by nations who rejoiced in it; fed themselves with it, as if it were bread; basked in it, as if it were sunshine; shouted at the sight of it; danced with the delight of it; quarrelled for it; fought for it; starved for it; did, in fact, precisely the opposite with it of what we want to do with it—they made it to keep and we to sell."

The last phrase is of course the key. If Ruskin could not prove a positive connection between good art and the good society of the past, he could at least point to a real decline in the architecture of Victorian England, and of the other decorative arts; and he could plausibly argue that this decline was caused by the expansion of a laissez-faire capitalist economy. The two faces of Victorian architecture were the hideous workers' dwellings run up by speculative builders, and the pompous villas and town halls that were the status symbols of a new class of Philistines. Ruskin's best critique of the latter is his lecture "Traffic" (*The Crown of Wild Olive*), which is also his finest piece of satire. He had been asked to speak to the prosperous citizens of Bradford about a new Exchange they were planning to build, and startled them by saying:

In a word, then, I do not care about this Exchange—because *you* don't; and because you know perfectly well I cannot make you. Look at the essential conditions of the case, which you, as business men, know perfectly well, though perhaps you think I forget them. You are going to spend £30,000 which to you, collectively, is nothing; the buying of a new coat is, as to the cost of it, a much more important matter of consideration to me, than building a new Exchange is to you. But you think you may as well have the right thing for your money. You know there are a great many odd styles of architecture about; you don't want to do anything ridiculous; you hear of me, among others, as a respectable architectural man-milliner; and you send for me, that I may tell you the leading fashion; and what is in our shops, for the moment, the newest and sweetest thing in pinnacles.

Ruskin argues that you can't get good architecture like that: on the contrary, it is "the expression of national life and character; and it is produced by a prevalent and eager national taste, or desire for beauty." We need not follow him in his analysis of various periods of architecture and of the way in which they reflected public morality and religion; but he is surely right when he says what the real religion of Victorian England is: "the ruling goddess may be best generally described as 'the Goddess of Getting-on' or 'Britannia of the Market.' . . . She has formed, and will continue to form, your architecture, as long as you worship her, and it is quite in vain for you to ask me to tell you how to build to *her;* you know far better than I."

Ruskin had arrived at this point in 1864 after his special study of craftsmanship in *The Stones of Venice* (1849-53), which is summarized in his chapter "The Nature of Gothic." The characteristics or moral elements of Gothic are Savageness, Changefulness, Naturalism, Grotesqueness, Rigidity and Redundancy: and he sees these as the expression of the free Northern character, which he illustrates in a great prose poem. The most important aspect of Gothic architectural decoration and sculpture is "roughness," that is, the avoidance of a perfect finish or "servile ornament." The slave-culture of ancient Greece had produced such a finish; it is contrary to the spirit of Christianity and of the North; and it is abhorrent to the free craftsman. Ruskin's view that all medieval stonework was designed by working craftsmen may be based on a misunderstanding—like his disciple William Morris he is probably taking a masterpiece like the Chapter-house of Southwell Minster as the norm instead of the exception. But this does not matter: what is vital to his argument is that the semi-mechanized carving of his own day was of poor quality, and this was caused by the decline of the craftsman and "the degradation of the operative into a machine." He had written earlier in *The Seven Lamps,* "I believe the right question to ask respecting all ornament is simply this—was it done with enjoyment—was the carver happy while he was about it?" The industrialized workers of Victorian England were unhappy, and that meant the ruin of design. He gives the first classic description of mass production, in this case of glass beads: "The men who chop up the rods sit at their work all day, their hands vibrating with a perpetual and exquisitely timed palsy, and the beads dropping beneath their vibration like hail." As satire on this topic, that has only been equaled by Chaplin in "Modern Times": Ruskin, like Chaplin, and like Swift, has a gift for the unforgettable image. That these beads were used for handsome beadwork designs did not placate Ruskin; it was enough that they had been made by virtual slaves, and so he admonished his readers never to "encourage the manufacture of anything that is not necessary, in the production of which invention has no share." He attacks the notion of the "gentleman designer" as based on two errors: "the first, that one man's thoughts can be, or ought to be, executed by another man's hands; the second, that manual labour is a degradation when it is governed by the intellect." Both the gentleman and the worker should work and both should think; but as it is today, "the mass of society is made up of morbid thinkers, and miserable workers."

After his attack on mass production as the enemy of art, Ruskin began to consider it as an evil in itself; and from the denunciation of contemporary society as the matrix of the arts, he turned to purely social questions. In this he spent many years of his career, from *A Joy Forever: The Political Economy of Art* (1857) to the installments of *Fors Clavigera* (1871-84). At one moment he wrote, "For my own part ... I have seceded from the study not only of architecture, but nearly of all art, and have given myself, as I would in a besieged city, to seek the best modes of getting bread and water for the multitudes, there remaining no question, it seems to me, of other than such grave business for this time" (*The Study of Architecture*). The articles in which he expressed this sense of urgency most eloquently were published in the *Cornhill Magazine* in 1860, arousing a storm of hostile criticism, and collected in 1862 as *Unto This Last;* more concrete details of his political program may be found in the letters of *Time and Tide* (1867).

The greatest issue for Ruskin was the poverty of a large part of the English nation. He was too nationalistic or provincial to think in terms of the poverty of the world's population, which remains today as at least the second greatest issue (the greatest being that of the population explosion); but much of what he wrote about England can still be applied to the world. The booming economy of Victorian England, led by vigorous engineers and entrepreneurs, left millions below the line of tolerable housing, food and education. The apologists for this economy, who included the liberal theoreticians, believed that technical progress, the growth of industrial plant, and the spread of trade would of themselves cure all social ills: meanwhile nothing must be allowed to interfere with free enterprise, which had achieved such spectacular results. Ruskin's response to the brutal facts of human misery was intuitive and uttered in moral terms. He violently attacked the dogmas of orthodox political economy, and put forward the plea that the state had the duty to intervene in all economic affairs, since this was the only way of overcoming poverty. "I hold it for indisputable that the first duty of the State is to see that every child born therein shall be well housed, clothed, fed and educated, till it attain years of discretion. But in order to the effecting this the Government must have an authority over the people of which we now do not so much as dream" (*Time and Tide*, Letter xiii). Although Ruskin advocated the intervention of the state to ensure these basic minimum requirements, he did not believe in the destruction of the private sector. Business men must be guided by social morality: they must think of themselves as soldiers in the service of the nation; the state's final authority need not be called on, if the capitalists do their duty. On the theoretical economists who stated that the capitalists had no duty except to buy, manufacture and sell as profitably as possible, without regard to the welfare of the poor, he poured out his contempt. "You have founded an entire science of political economy on what you have stated to be the constant instinct of man—the desire to defraud his neighbour;" whereas "the real science of political economy, which has yet to be distinguished from the bastard science, as medicine from witchcraft and astronomy from astrology, is that which teaches nations to desire and labour for the things that lead to life." The key sentence of *Unto This Last* is the conclusion Ruskin had drawn from his earlier studies of nature and the arts: "Government and co-operation are in all things the laws of life, anarchy and competition the laws of death."

Ruskin is rightly regarded as the father of the Western European Welfare State, toward some form of which all advanced countries have been compelled to move. For his attack on classical nineteenth-century capitalism he has been acclaimed by many socialists and reformers of different kinds—for example, he seems to have provided the main inspiration for the British Labour Party in its infancy—but he was not a socialist in any recognizable modern sense, and he was no more of a liberal in the political than in the economic field. It is often and conveniently forgotten that his criticism is an attack on the two faces of liberalism: on the one hand against laissez-faire economics, on the other against political permissiveness, which he saw as leading to anarchy. If he was anti-liberal, it did not mean that his thought was out-and-out reactionary, looking back to the feudal past with nostalgia, or totalitarian, looking forward to an iron future. Reaction is founded on a dream, totalitarianism, whether Fascist or Communist, on a lie; and Ruskin, despite his eccentricity, rejected both the dream and the lie. He was unsentimental about the *ancien régime;* the aristocracy had lost political power, entirely through their own fault, and now he considered that their only useful function was to be custodians of their ancient properties. "Do you want her [England] to be nothing but a large workshop or forge, so that the name 'Englishman' shall be synonymous with 'ironmonger' all over the world, or would you like to keep some of your lords and landed gentry still, and a few green fields and trees" (*Time and Tide,* Letter iii). This is an anticipation of the English National Trust, which has now saved for ever many country houses and tracts of land. Ruskin, a royalist and anti-republican, tended to favor the more conservative governments of France and of the rest of Europe; but he did not regard any of them as having solved the problems of poverty and human misery. The modern state, not just in England but everywhere, is a ship where "on the deck the aspect is of Cleopatra's gallery—under hatches there is a slave hospital."

There are aspects of his thought which have attracted totalitarian thinkers, especially his fragments of a blueprint for a new society, which are scattered throughout *Time and Tide* and *Fors Clavigera.* It has even been said that Chairman Mao has been influenced by these: and Ruskin's proposal for an extended tutorial sytem, whereby a "bishop" or overseer should be in charge of every hundred families and should write reports on every individual, has an unpleasantly Chinese ring. But if we discount some of his concrete proposals and his practical ventures, like the Guild of St. George, as products of his insanity, there remains a fairly consistent and sane body of thought, which is not totalitarian, but certainly paternalistic and authoritarian. Ruskin believed firmly in obedience to authority whether in business or in politics; and in the necessity of government's intervening in critical matters and exacting this obedience. For example, he condemned large families "as indeed the very Malthusians teach." He was not prophet enough to see that the control of population would become the most urgent issue in the world; but he could see not only that it was important but that it could be ensured by positive enforcement. Although a natural preacher, he could see that exhortation was never enough. Ruskin did not share the optimistic view of human nature that underlies all liberalism: he saw man as a dangerous animal, whose destructive impulses have always to be kept in check. This is, of course, the normal outlook of the satirist: and Ruskin was a potentially great satirist who exercised his gift only too rarely. If this means that his approach is often reductive and simplistic, and that he refuses to understand the complexity of the political matters he discusses, it also means that, like Swift, he sometimes looks through to the heart of the matter, pointing to "the imminent danger to which we are now in England exposed by the gradually accelerated fall of our aristocracy (wholly their own fault) and the substitution of money-power for their martial one; and by the correspondingly imminent prevalence of mob violence here, as in America . . ." (*Time and Tide,* Letter xiii). Ruskin, in glimpses such as that, shows an intuitive understanding of the unstable and potentially anarchic nature of all modern societies, especially of large urban communities. Mob violence is once again an outstanding feature of Western life, and threatens the fabric of all democratic societies; and as violence and crime increase, so does the permissiveness of liberal intellectuals, whether by negligence or by conviction. The malaise of certain universities, caused by violence and permissiveness in harness, is a warning of the possible suicide of ordered society. If Ruskin was wrong in his hostility to science and technology, he was surely right in his conviction that government means life, and anarchy, death.

Biographical Profile

John Ruskin was born in London on February 8, 1819, the son of a wealthy wine merchant of Scottish origin. He was privately educated: his mother, a devout evangelical, gave him lessons in the Bible, which remained his greatest literary influence; he was also taught drawing, and early became a lover of the painting and drawing of Turner. He traveled a great deal with his family in France, Switzerland and Italy, and came to acquire early his remarkably wide knowledge of European scenery and monuments. At the age of seventeen, Ruskin went up to Christchurch, Oxford, as a gentleman commoner; his studies were interrupted by an attack of tuberculosis, and he did not proceed to the bachelor's degree until 1841. With a large allowance from his father he was able to work at home on the first volume of *Modern Painters*, which he published anonymously (by "A Graduate of Oxford") in 1843. In 1845 he made his first tour of Italy without his parents, and gained a new understanding of Italian art; from then on he spent some part of almost every year in Europe, studying and sketching architecture.

In 1848 Ruskin married Euphemia Gray, a distant cousin; the marriage was not consummated and was annulled six years later. The miseries of this married life are well documented, and in recent years more thoroughly discussed than Ruskin's writings themselves. Between 1849 and 1852 the couple spent most of their time in Venice, where, interrupting the continuation of *Modern Painters*, he began *The Stones of Venice*. From about 1851 his falling away from the strict evangelical faith began, and his interest in social questions also dates from about this time, stimulated by his friendship with Carlyle.

In 1854, after his marriage had ended, Ruskin began to lecture on art at the new Working Men's College, and for many years proved an extremely successful lecturer. He worked on many projects simultaneously with fanatical energy, and in 1855 he had one of the illnesses which were to recur until the end of his career: sometimes described as insanity, they have never been convincingly diagnosed as psychotic, and may have had a physical origin. When he was nearly forty he fell in love with Rose La Touche, a girl of ten: this obsessive love tortured his life until Rose died insane seventeen years later.

In 1860 Ruskin completed the last volume of *Modern Painters* and turned to questions of social reform. His four essays on political economy in the *Cornhill Magazine*, later reprinted as *Unto This Last*, caused a storm of protest. In his forties he continued his great series of social tracts and became as famous a reformer as art critic. In 1864 his father died and Ruskin inherited a large fortune; this he got rid of in a few years, by means of charitable gifts and mismanagement; by the end of his life he was living entirely from the royalties of his books, which were fortunately very large. In 1869 (now fifty) he was appointed the first Slade Professor of Fine Art at the University of Oxford. He lectured intermittently, sometimes to enthusiastic audiences but with increasing incoherence, until his resignation in 1877. At the same time he was publishing the installments of *Fors Clavigera* and undertaking experiments in social work, such as founding St. George's Fund and directing his students to mend a road near Oxford. He bought a house on Lake Coniston in the Lake District in 1871 and made this his home until the end of his life. A group of brilliant but uneven books on various sciences and arts appeared in this decade. In 1877 he was sued for libel by Whistler and lost a farthing in damages; this absurd lawsuit was disastrous for his reputation.

In his sixties Ruskin was ill for much of the time. In his periods of health he resumed his professorship (1883-85), wrote *The Bible of Amiens* and a few other works, concluding with his beautiful autobiography, *Praeterita*. When he was seventy he had his most serious illness and thereafter wrote no more, and lived in retirement. He died on January 20, 1900.

Since Ruskin insisted on the primacy of the eye, it is appropriate to end with a visual impression of the man, and since he insisted on the revelatory powers of the imagination, such an impression should show something of the author's mind. The most famous image is Millais's "Portrait of Ruskin at the Waterfall," painted when the subject was in his thirties. It shows a dandyish figure, too well dressed for a country walk, the hair long and reddish-blond; the brow and eyes somber and brooding; the mouth stubborn yet humorous; the whole face ready to spring into energetic movement. The waterfall does not give the scale of this neat and tonic frame; but we may learn of that from W. S. Kennedy's description of him in his fifties at Oxford:

> Professor Ruskin is emotional and nervous in manner, his large eye at times soft and genial and again quizzing and mischievous in its glance, the mouth thin and severe, chin retreating, and forehead prominent. He has an iron-grey beard, wears old-fashioned coats, sky-blue neck-cloths, and gold spectacles; is rather *petit*, about five foot five in height; his pronunciation as broad as Dundee Scotch, and at times "as indistinct as Belgravia Cockney." He is one of the most popular lecturers in England, and his influence over the students at Oxford is said to have been such that, at one time, he purposely avoided (in a measure) their society that it might not be thought that he was doing an injustice to his fellow-professors.

The last pictures show a placid patriarch, the flame extinguished.

For this selection, I have chosen not the most striking of Ruskin's short descriptions or reflections, but longer passages, mainly from his earlier works, where his argument is prolonged throughout enough pages to present a coherent aspect of his thought. I have not tried to emphasize his theoretical and applied art criticism, nor yet his literary criticism, since there are excellent recent anthologies of these; but I have tried to show the general scope of Ruskin's mind.

Selected Bibliography

WORKS

Collected Works:

The Works of John Ruskin, Library Edition, edited by E.
   T. Cook and Alexander Wedderburn, London (1903-
   12)

Principal Books:

Modern Painters, Vol. I (1843)
Modern Painters, Vol. II (1846)
The Seven Lamps of Architecture (1849)
The Stones of Venice, Vol. I (1851)
The Stones of Venice, Vols. II and III (1853)
Modern Painters, Vols. III and IV (1856)
The Harbours of England (1856)
A Joy for Ever: The Political Economy of Art (1857)
The Elements of Drawing (1857)
The Two Paths (1859)
Modern Painters, Vol. V (1860)
Unto This Last (1862)
Sesame and Lilies (1865)
The Ethics of the Dust (1866)
The Crown of Wild Olive (1866)
Time and Tide (1867)
The Queen of the Air and *The Cestus of Aglaia* (1869)

Lectures on Art (1870)

Fors Clavigera (1871-84)

Aratra Pentelici (1872)

The Eagle's Nest (1872)

Love's Meinie (1873)

Val d'Arno (1874)

Mornings in Florence (1875-77)

Proserpina (1875-86)

Deucalion (1875-83)

St. Mark's Rest (1875-84)

The Bible of Amiens (1880-85)

The Storm Cloud of the Nineteenth Century (1884)

Praeterita (1885-89)

Selections:

Frondes Agrestes. Readings in "Modern Painters." Orpington, George Allen, 1875.

Selections from the Writings of John Ruskin. Ed. W. G. Collingwood. Orpington, George Allen, 1893.

Selected Writings of John Ruskin. Ed. Peter Quennell. London, Falcon Press, 1952.

The Lamp of Beauty: Writings on Art. Ed. Joan Evans. London, Phaidon, 1959; Garden City, N.Y., Doubleday, 1959.

The Genius of John Ruskin. Ed. John D. Rosenberg. New York, George Braziller, 1963.

Ruskin Today. Ed. Kenneth Clark. London, John Murray, 1964; New York, Holt, Rinehart and Winston, 1965.

The Art Criticism of John Ruskin. Ed. Robert L. Herbert. Garden City, N.Y., Anchor Books, 1964.

The Literary Criticism of John Ruskin. Ed. Harold Bloom. Garden City, N.Y., Anchor Books, 1965.

Biography and Criticism:

Bell, Quentin. *Ruskin.* Edinburgh, Oliver and Boyd, 1963.

Cook, E. T. *The Life of Ruskin,* 2 vols. London, George Allen, 1911.

Evans, Joan. *John Ruskin.* London, Jonathan Cape, 1954.

Harrison, Frederick. *John Ruskin*. New York, Macmillan Co., 1902. (The best short introduction.)

Hough, Graham. *The Last Romantics*. London, Gerald Duckworth, 1949.

James, Sir William. *The Order of Release*. London, John Murray, 1948; title in U.S.A. *John Ruskin and Effie Gray*. New York, Scribner's, 1948.

Leon, Derrick. *Ruskin: The Great Victorian*. London, Routledge and Kegan Paul, 1949. (The best long biography.)

Painter, George D. "Salvation through Ruskin" in *Proust: The Early Years*. Boston, Little, Brown, 1959.

Proust, Marcel. "Days of Pilgrimage: Ruskin at Notre-Dame d'Amiens" and "John Ruskin" in *Marcel Proust: A Selection from his Miscellaneous Writings*. Trans. Gerald Hopkins. London, Allan Wingate, 1948.

Quennell, Peter. *John Ruskin: The Portrait of a Prophet*. New York, Viking Press, 1949.

Rosenberg, John D. *The Darkening Glass: A Portrait of Ruskin's Genius*. New York, Columbia University Press, 1961.

Wilenski, R. H. *John Ruskin: An Introduction to Further Study of his Life and Work*. London, Faber and Faber, 1933.

Modern Painters
(Volume I)
(1843)

If it be true, and it can scarcely be disputed, that nothing has been for centuries consecrated by public admiration, without possessing in a high degree some kind of sterling excellence, it is not because the average intellect and feeling of the majority of the public are competent in any way to distinguish what is really excellent, but because all erroneous opinion is inconsistent, and all ungrounded opinion transitory; so that, while the fancies and feelings which deny deserved honour, and award what is undue, have neither root nor strength sufficient to maintain consistent testimony for a length of time, the opinions formed on right grounds by those few who are in reality competent judges, being necessarily stable, communicate themselves gradually from mind to mind; descending lower as they extend wider, until they leaven the whole lump, and rule by absolute authority, even where the grounds and reasons for them cannot be understood. On this gradua victory of what is consistent over what is vacillating, depends the reputation of all that is highest in art and literature; for it is an insult to what is really great in either to suppose that it in any way addresses itself to mean or uncultivated faculties. It is a matter of the simplest demonstration, that no man can be really appreciated but by his equal or superior. His inferior may over-estimate him, in enthusiasm; or, as is more commonly the case, degrade him, in ignorance; but he cannot form a grounded and just estimate. Without proving this, however, which would take more space to do than I can spare, it is sufficiently evident that there is no process of amalgamation by which opinions, wrong individually, can become right merely by their multitude. If I stand by a picture in the Academy, and hear twenty persons in succession admiring some paltry piece of mechanism or imitation in the lining of a cloak, or the satin of a slipper, it is absurd to tell me that they reprobate collectively what they admire individually; or, if they pass with apathy by a piece of the most noble conception or most perfect truth, because it has in it no tricks of the brush nor grimace of expression, it is absurd to tell me that they collectively respect what they separately scorn, or that the feelings and knowledge of such judges, by any length of time or comparison of ideas, could come to any right conclusion with respect to what is really high in art. The question is not decided by them, but for them; decided at first by few: by fewer in proportion as the merits of the work are of a higher order. From these few the decision is communicated to the number next below them in rank of mind, and by these again to a wider and lower circle; each rank being so far cognizant of the superiority of that above it, as to receive its decision with respect; until in process of time, the right and consistent opinion is communicated to all, and held by all as a matter of faith, the more positively in proportion as the grounds of it are less perceived.

But when this process has taken place, and the work has become sanctified by time in the minds of men, it is impossible that any new work of equal merit can be impartially compared with it, except by minds not only educated and generally capable of appreciating merit, but strong enough to shake off the weight of prejudice and association, which invariably incline them to the older favourite. It is much easier, says Barry, to repeat the character recorded of Phidias, than to investigate the merits of Agasias. And when, as peculiarly in the case of painting, much knowledge of what is technical and practical is necessary to a right judgment, so that those alone are competent to pronounce a true verdict who are themselves the persons to be judged, and who therefore can give no opinion, centuries may elapse before fair comparison can be made between two artists of different ages: while the patriarchal excellence exercises during the interval a tyrannical, perhaps even a blighting, influence over the minds, both of the public and of those to whom, properly understood, it should serve for a guide and example. In no city of Europe where art is a subject of attention, are its prospects so hopeless, or its pursuits so resultless, as in Rome; because there, among all students, the authority of their predecessors in art is supreme and without appeal, and the mindless copyist studies Raffaelle, but not what Raffaelle studied. It thus becomes the duty of every one capable of demonstrating any definite points of superiority in modern art, and who is in a position in which his doing so will not be ungraceful, to encounter without hesitation whatever opprobrium may fall upon him from the necessary prejudice even of the most candid minds, and from the far more virulent opposition of those who have no hope of maintaining their own reputation for discernment but in the support of that kind of consecrated merit which may be applauded without an inconvenient necessity for reasons. It is my purpose, therefore, believing that there are certain points of superiority in modern artists, and especially in one or two of their number, which have not yet been fully understood, except by those who are scarcely in a position admitting the declaration of their conviction, to institute a close comparison between the great works of ancient and modern landscape art; to raise, as far as possible, the deceptive veil of imaginary light through which we are accustomed to gaze upon the patriarchal work; and to show the real relations, whether favourable or otherwise, subsisting between it and our own. I am fully aware that this is not to be done lightly or rashly; that it is the part of every one proposing to undertake such a task, strictly to examine, with prolonged doubt and severe trial, every opinion in any way contrary to the sacred verdict of time, and to advance nothing which does not, at least in his own conviction, rest on surer ground than mere feeling or taste. I have accordingly advanced nothing in the following pages but with accompanying demonstration, which may indeed be true or false—complete or conditional but which can only be met on its own grounds, and can in no way be borne down or affected by mere authority of great names. Yet even thus I should scarcely have ventured to speak so decidedly as I have, but for my full conviction that we ought not to class the historical painters of the fifteenth, and landscape painters of the seventeenth, centuries together, under the general title of "old masters," as if they possessed anything like corresponding rank in their respective walks of art. I feel assured that the principles on which they worked are totally opposed, and that the landscape painters have been honoured only because they exhibited, in mechanical and technical qualities, some semblance of the manner of the nobler historical painters, whose principles of conception and composition they entirely reversed. The course of study which has led me reverently to the feet of Michael Angelo and Da Vinci, has alienated me gradually from Claude and Gaspar; I cannot, at the same time, do homage to power and pettiness—to the truth of consummate science, and the mannerism of undisciplined imagination. And let it be understood that whenever hereafter I speak depreciatingly of the old masters as a body, I refer to none of the historical painters, for whom I entertain a veneration which, though I hope reasonable in its grounds, is almost superstitious in degree. Neither, unless he be particularly mentioned, do I intend to include Nicholas Poussin, whose landscapes have a separate and elevated character, which renders it necessary to consider them apart from all others. Speaking generally of the elder masters, I refer only to Claude, Gaspar Poussin, Salvator Rosa, Cuyp, Berghem, Both, Ruysdael, Hobbema, Teniers (in his landscapes), P. Potter, Canaletto, and the various Van somethings and Back somethings, more especially and malignantly those who have libelled the sea.

It will of course be necessary for me, in the commencement of the work, to state briefly those principles on which I conceive all right judgment of art must be founded. These introductory chapters I should wish to be read carefully, because all criticism must be useless when the terms or grounds of it are in any degree ambiguous; and the ordinary language of connoisseurs and critics, granting that they understand it themselves, is usually mere jargon to others, from their custom of using technical terms, by which everything is meant and nothing is expressed.

And if, in the application of these principles, in spite of my endeavour to render it impartial, the feeling and fondness which I have for some works of modern art escape me sometimes where they should not, let it be pardoned as little more than a fair counterbalance to that peculiar veneration with which the work of the old master, associated as it has ever been in our ears with the expression of whatever is great or perfect, must be usually regarded by the reader. I do not say that this veneration is wrong, nor that we should be less attentive to the repeated words of time: but let us not forget that if honour be for the dead, gratitude can only be for the living. He who once stood beside the grave, to look back upon the companionship which has been for ever closed, feeling how impotent *there* are the wild love and the keen sorrow, to give one instant's pleasure to the pulseless heart, or atone in the lowest measure to the departed spirit for the hour of unkindness, will scarcely for the future incur that debt to the heart, which can only be discharged to the dust. But the lesson which men receive as individuals, they do not learn as nations. Again and again they have seen their noblest descend into the grave, and have thought it enough to garland the tombstone when they had not crowned the brow, and to pay the honour to the ashes which they had denied to the spirit. Let it not displease them that they are bidden, amidst the tumult and the dazzle of their busy life, to listen for the few voices, and watch for the few lamps, which God has toned and lighted to charm and to guide them, that they may not learn their sweetness by their silence, nor their light by their decay.

In the 15th Lecture of Sir Joshua Reynolds, incidental notice is taken of the distinction between those excellences in the painter which belong to him *as such,* and those which belong to him in common with all men of intellect, the general and exalted powers of which art is the evidence and expression, not the subject. But the distinction is not there dwelt upon as it should be, for it is owing to the slight attention ordinarily paid to it, that criticism is open to every form of coxcombry, and liable to every phase of error. It is a distinction on which depend all sound judgment of the rank of the artist, and all just appreciation of the dignity of art.

Painting, or art generally, as such, with all its technicalities, difficulties, and particular ends, is nothing but a noble and expressive language, invaluable as the vehicle of thought, but by itself nothing. He who has learned what is commonly considered the whole art of painting, that is, the art of representing any natural object faithfully, has as yet only learned the language by which his thoughts are to be expressed. He has done just as much towards being that which we ought to respect as a great painter, as a man who has learnt how to express himself grammatically and melodiously has towards being a great poet. The language is, indeed, more difficult of acquirement in the one case than in the other, and possesses more power of delighting the sense, while it speaks to the intellect; but it is, nevertheless, nothing more than language, and all those excellences which are peculiar to the painter as such, are merely what rhythm, melody, precision, and force are in the words of the orator and the poet, necessary to their greatness, but not the tests of their greatness. It is not by the mode of representing and saying, but by what is represented and said, that the respective greatness either of the painter or the writer is to be finally determined.

Speaking with strict propriety, therefore, we should call a man a great painter only as he excelled in precision and force in the language of lines, and a great versifier, as he excelled in precision and force in the language of words.

A great poet would then be a term strictly, and in precisely the same sense, applicable to both, if warranted by the character of the images or thoughts which each in their respective languages conveyed.

Take, for instance, one of the most perfect poems or pictures (I use the words as synonymous) which modern times have seen:—the "Old Shepherd's Chief-mourner." Here the exquisite execution of the glossy and crisp hair of the dog, the bright sharp touching of the green bough beside it, the clear painting of the wood of the coffin and the folds of the blanket, are language—language clear and expressive in the highest degree. But the close pressure of the dog's breast against the wood, the convulsive clinging of the paws, which has dragged the blanket off the trestle, the total powerlessness of the head laid, close and motionless, upon its folds, the fixed and tearful fall of the eye in its utter hopelessness, the rigidity of repose which marks that there has been no motion nor change in the trance of agony since the last blow was struck on the coffin-lid, the quietness and gloom of the chamber, the spectacles marking the place where the Bible was last closed, indicating how lonely has been the life, how unwatched the departure, of him who is now laid solitary in his sleep;—these are all thoughts—thoughts by which the picture is separated at once from hundreds of equal merit, as far as mere painting goes, by which it ranks as a work of high art, and stamps its author, not as the neat imitator of the texture of a skin, or the fold of a drapery, but as the Man of Mind.

It is not, however, always easy, either in painting or literature, to determine where the influence of language stops, and where that of thought begins. Many thoughts are so dependent upon the language in which they are clothed, that they would lose half their beauty if otherwise expressed. But the highest thoughts are those which are least dependent on language, and the dignity of any composition, and praise to which it is entitled, are in exact proportion to its independency of language or expression. A composition is indeed usually most perfect, when to such intrinsic dignity is added all that expression can do to attract and adorn; but in every case of supreme excellence this all becomes as nothing. We are more gratified by the simplest lines or words which can suggest the idea in its own naked beauty, than by the robe and the gem which conceal while they decorate; we are better pleased to feel by their absence how little they could bestow, than by their presence how much they can destroy.

34

There is therefore a distinction to be made between what is ornamental in language and what is expressive. That part of it which is necessary to the embodying and conveying of the thought is worthy of respect and attention as necessary to excellence, though not the test of it. But that part of it which is decorative has little more to do with the intrinsic excellence of the picture than the frame or the varnishing of it. And this caution in distinguishing between the ornamental and the expressive is peculiarly necessary in painting; for in the language of words it is nearly impossible for that which is not expressive to be beautiful, except by mere rhythm or melody, any sacrifice to which is immediately stigmatized as error. But the beauty of mere language in painting is not only very attractive and entertaining to the spectator, but requires for its attainment no small exertion of mind and devotion of time by the artist. Hence, in art, men have frequently fancied that they were becoming rhetoricians and poets when they were only learning to speak melodiously, and the judge has over and over again advanced to the honour of authors those who were never more than ornamental writing-masters.

Most pictures of the Dutch school, for instance, excepting always those of Rubens, Vandyke, and Rembrandt, are ostentatious exhibitions of the artist's power of speech, the clear and vigorous elocution of useless and senseless words; while the early efforts of Cimabue and Giotto are the burning messages of prophecy, delivered by the stammering lips of infants. It is not by ranking the former as more than mechanics, or the latter as less than artists, that the taste of the multitude, always awake to the lowest pleasures which art can bestow, and blunt to the highest, is to be formed or elevated. It must be the part of the judicious critic carefully to distinguish what is language, and what is thought, and to rank and praise pictures chiefly for the latter, considering the former as a totally inferior excellence, and one which cannot be compared with nor weighed against thought in any way, or in any degree whatsoever. The picture which has the nobler and more numerous ideas, however awkwardly expressed, is a greater and a better picture than that which has the less noble and less numerous ideas, however beautifully expressed. No weight, nor mass nor beauty of execution, can outweigh one grain or fragment of thought. Three pen-strokes of Raffaelle are a greater and a better picture than the most finished work that ever Carlo Dolci polished into inanity. A finished work of a great artist is only better than its sketch, if the sources of pleasure belonging to colour and realization—valuable in themselves—are so employed as to increase the impressiveness of the thought. But if one atom of thought has vanished, all colour, all finish, all execution, all ornament, are too dearly bought. Nothing but thought can pay for thought, and the instant that the increasing refinement or finish of the picture begins to be paid for by the loss of the faintest shadow of an idea, that instant all refinement or finish is an excrescence and a deformity.

Yet although in all our speculations on art, language is thus to be distinguished from, and held subordinate to, that which it conveys, we must still remember that there are certain ideas inherent in language itself, and that, strictly speaking, every pleasure connected with art has in it some reference to the intellect. The mere sensual pleasure of the eye, received from the most brilliant piece of colouring, is as nothing to that which it receives from a crystal prism, except as it depends on our perception of a certain meaning and intended arrangement of colour, which has been the subject of intellect. Nay, the term idea, according to Locke's definition of it, will extend even to the sensual impressions themselves as far as they are "things which the mind occupies itself about in thinking;" that is, not as they are felt by the eye only, but as they are received by the mind through the eye. So that, if I say that the greatest picture is that which conveys to the mind of the spectator the greatest number of the greatest ideas, I have a definition which will include as subjects of comparison every pleasure which art is capable of conveying. If I were to say, on the contrary, that the best picture was that which most closely imitated nature, I should assume that art could only please by imitating nature; and I should cast out of the pale of criticism those parts of works of art which are not imitative, that is to say, intrinsic beauties of colour and form, and those works of art wholly, which, like the Arabesques of Raffaelle in the Loggias, are not imitative at all. Now, I want a definition of art wide enough to include all its varieties of aim. I do not say, therefore, that the art is greatest which gives most pleasure, because perhaps there is some art whose end is to teach, and not to please. I do not say that the art is greatest which teaches us most, because perhaps there is some art whose end is to please, and not to teach. I do not say that the art is greatest which imitates best, because perhaps there is some art whose end is to create and not to imitate. But I say that the art is greatest which conveys to the mind of the spectator, by any means whatsoever, the greatest number of the greatest ideas; and I call an idea great in proportion as it is received by a higher faculty of the mind, and as it more fully occupies, and in occupying, exercises and exalts, the faculty by which it is received.

If this, then, be the definition of great art, that of a great artist naturally follows. He is the greatest artist who has embodied, in the sum of his works, the greatest number of the greatest ideas.

Modern Painters, Vol. I, Sec. I, Ch. 1

The definition of art which I have just given requires me to determine what kinds of ideas can be received from works of art, and which of these are the greatest, before proceeding to any practical application of the test.

I think that all the sources of pleasure, or of any other good, to be derived from works of art, may be referred to five distinct heads.

I. Ideas of Power.—The perception or conception of the mental or bodily powers by which the work has been produced.

II. Ideas of Imitation.—The perception that the thing produced resembles something else.

III. Ideas of Truth.—The perception of faithfulness in a statement of facts by the thing produced.

IV. Ideas of Beauty.—The perception of beauty, either in the thing produced, or in what it suggests or resembles.

V. Ideas of Relation.—The perception of intellectual relations in the thing produced, or in what it suggests or resembles.

I shall briefly distinguish the nature and effects of each of these classes of ideas.

I. Ideas of Power.—These are the simple perception of the mental or bodily powers exerted in the production of any work of art. According to the dignity and degree of the power perceived is the dignity of the idea; but the whole class of ideas is received by the intellect, and they excite the best of the moral feelings, veneration, and the desire of exertion. As a species, therefore, they are one of the noblest connected with art; but the differences in degree of dignity among themselves are infinite, being correspondent with every order of power,—from that of the fingers to that of the most exalted intellect. Thus, when we see an Indian's paddle carved from the handle to the blade, we have a conception of prolonged manual labour, and are gratified in proportion to the supposed expenditure of time and exertion. These are, indeed, powers of a low order, yet the pleasure arising from the conception of them enters very largely into our admiration of all elaborate ornament, architectural decoration, etc. The delight with which we look on the fretted front of Rouen Cathedral depends in no small degree on the simple perception of time employed and labour expended in its production. But it is a right, that is, an ennobling pleasure, even in this its lowest phase; and even the pleasure felt by those persons who praise a drawing for its "finish" or its "work," which is one precisely of the same kind, would be right, if it did not imply a want of perception of the higher powers which render work unnecessary. If to the evidence of labour be added that of strength or dexterity, the sensation of power is yet increased; if to strength and dexterity be added that of ingenuity and judgment, it is multiplied tenfold; and so on, through all the subjects of action of body or mind, we receive the more exalted pleasure from the more exalted power.

So far the nature and effects of ideas of power cannot but be admitted by all. But the circumstance which I wish especially to insist upon, with respect to them, is one which may not, perhaps, be so readily allowed, namely, that they are independent of the nature or worthiness of the object from which they are received; and that whatever has been the subject of a great power, whether there be intrinsic and apparent worthiness in itself or not, bears with it the evidence of having been so, and is capable of giving the ideas of power, and the consequent pleasures in their full degree. For observe, that a thing is not properly said to have been the result of a great power, on which only some part of that power has been expended. A nut may be cracked by a steam-engine, but it has not, in being so, been the subject of the power of the engine. And thus it is falsely said of great men, that they waste their lofty powers on unworthy objects: the object may be dangerous or useless, but, as far as the phrase has reference to difficulty of performance, it cannot be unworthy of the power which it brings into exertion, because nothing can become a subject of action to a greater power which can be accomplished by a less, any more than bodily strength can be exerted where there is nothing to resist it.

So then, men may let their great powers lie dormant,

while they employ their mean and petty powers on mean and petty objects; but it is physically impossible to employ a great power, except on a great object. Consequently, wherever power of any kind or degree has been exerted, the marks and evidence of it are stamped upon its results: it is impossible that it should be lost or wasted, or without record, even in the "estimation of a hair;" and therefore, whatever has been the subject of a great power bears about with it the image of that which created it, and is what is commonly called "excellent." And this is the true meaning of the word Excellent, as distinguished from the terms, "beautiful," "useful," "good," etc.; and we shall always, in future, use the word excellent, as signifying that the thing to which it is applied required a great power for its production.

The faculty of perceiving what powers are required for the production of a thing, is the faculty of perceiving excellence. It is this faculty in which men, even of the most cultivated taste, must always be wanting, unless they have added practice to reflection; because none can estimate the power manifested in victory, unless they have personally measured the strength to be overcome. Though, therefore, it is possible, by the cultivation of sensibility and judgment, to become capable of distinguishing what is beautiful, it is totally impossible, without practice and knowledge, to distinguish or feel what is excellent. The beauty or the truth of Titian's flesh-tint may be appreciated by all; but it is only to the artist, whose multiplied hours of toil have not reached the slightest resemblance of one of its tones, that its *excellence* is manifest.

Wherever, then, difficulty has been overcome, there is excellence; and therefore, in order to prove a work excellent, we have only to prove the difficulty of its production; whether it be useful or beautiful is another question; its excellence depends on its difficulty alone. Nor is it a false or diseased taste which looks for the overcoming of difficulties, and has pleasure in it, even without any view to resultant good. It has been made part of our moral nature that we should have a pleasure in encountering and conquering opposition, for the sake of the struggle and the victory, not for the sake of any after result: and not only our own victory, but the perception of that of another, is in all cases the source of pure and ennobling pleasure. And if we often hear it said, and truly said, that an artist has erred by seeking rather to show his skill in overcoming technical difficulties, than to reach a great end, be it observed that he is only blamed because he has sought to conquer an inferior difficulty rather than a great one; for it is much easier to overcome technical difficulties than to reach a great end. Whenever the visible victory over difficulties is found painful or in false taste, it is owing to the preference of an inferior to a great difficulty, or to the false estimate of what is difficult and what is not. It is far more difficult to be simple than to be complicated; far more difficult to sacrifice skill and cease exertion in the proper place, than to expend both indiscriminately. We shall find, in the course of our investigation, that beauty and difficulty go together; and that they are only mean and paltry difficulties which it is wrong or contemptible to wrestle with. Be it remembered then—Power is never wasted. Whatever power has been employed, produces excellence in proportion to its own dignity and exertion; and the faculty of perceiving this exertion, and appreciating this dignity, is the faculty of perceiving excellence.

Modern Painters, Vol. I, Sec. I, Ch. 3

It is possible for all men, by care and attention, to form a just judgment of the fidelity of artists to nature. To do this no peculiar powers of mind are required, no sympathy with particular feelings, nothing which every man of ordinary intellect does not in some degree possess,—powers, namely, of observation and intelligence, which by cultivation may be brought to a high degree of perfection and acuteness. But until this cultivation has been bestowed, and until the instrument thereby perfected has been employed in a consistent series of careful observations, it is as absurd as it is audacious to pretend to form any judgment whatsoever respecting the truth of art: and my first business, before going a step farther, must be to combat the nearly universal error of belief among the thoughtless and unreflecting, that they know either what nature is, or what is like her; that they can discover truth by instinct, and that their minds are such pure Venice glass as to be shocked by all treachery. I have to prove to them that there are more things in heaven and earth than are dreamed of in their philosophy, and that the truth of nature is a part of the truth of God; to him who does not search it out, darkness, as it is to him who does, infinity.

The first great mistake that people make in the matter, is the supposition that they must *see* a thing if it be before their eyes. . . . And what is here said, which all must feel by their own experience to be true, is more remarkably and necessarily the case with sight than with any other of the senses, for this reason, that the ear is not accustomed to exercise constantly its functions of hearing; it is accustomed to stillness, and the occurrence of a sound of any kind whatsoever is apt to awake attention, and be followed with perception, in proportion to the degree of sound; but the eye during our waking hours, exercises constantly its function of seeing; it is its constant habit; we always, as far as the *bodily* organ is concerned, see something, and we always see in the same degree; so that the occurrence of sight, as such, to the eye, is only the continuance of its necessary state of action, and awakes no attention whatsoever, except by the particular nature and quality of the sight. And thus, unless the minds of men are particularly directed to the impressions of sight, objects pass perpetually before the eyes without conveying any impression to the brain at all; and so pass actually unseen, not merely unnoticed, but in the full clear sense of the word unseen. . . .

With this kind of bodily sensibility to colour and form is intimately connected that higher sensibility which we revere as one of the chief attributes of all noble minds, and as the chief spring of real poetry. I believe this kind of sensibility may be entirely resolved into the acuteness of bodily sense of which I have been speaking, associated with love, love I mean in its infinite and holy functions, as it embraces divine and human and brutal intelligences, and hallows the physical perception of external objects by association, gratitude, veneration, and other pure feelings of our moral nature. And although the discovery of truth is in itself altogether intellectual, and dependent merely on our powers of physical perception and abstract intellect, wholly independent of our moral nature, yet these instruments (perception and judgment) are so sharpened and brightened, and so far more swiftly and effectively used, when they have the energy and passion of our moral nature to bring them into action—perception is so quickened by love, and judgment so tempered by veneration, that, practically, a man of deadened moral sensation is always dull in his perception of truth.

Modern Painters, Vol. I, Part 2, Sec. I, Ch. 2

We have seen how indistinctness of individual distances becomes necessary in order to express the adaptation of the eye to one or other of them; we have now to examine that kind of indistinctness which is dependent on real retirement of the object, even when the focus of the eye is fully concentrated upon it. The first kind of indecision is that which belongs to all objects which the eye is not adapted to, whether near or far off: the second is that consequent upon the want of power in the eye to receive a clear image of objects at a great distance from it, however attentively it may regard them.

Draw on a piece of white paper a square and a circle, each about a twelfth or eighth of an inch in diameter, and blacken them so that their forms may be very distinct; place your paper against the wall at the end of the room, and retire from it a greater or less distance accordingly as you have drawn the figures larger or smaller. You will come to a point where, though you can see both the spots with perfect plainness, you cannot tell which is the square and which the circle.

Now this takes place of course with every object in a landscape, in proportion to its distance and size. The definite forms of the leaves of a tree, however sharply and separately they may appear to come against the sky, are quite indistinguishable at fifty yards off, and the form of everything becomes confused before we finally lose sight of it. Now if the character of an object, say the front of a house, be explained by a variety of forms in it, as the shadows in the tops of the windows, the lines of the architraves, the seams of the masonry, etc.; these lesser details, as the object falls into distance, become confused and undecided, each of them losing its definite form, but all being perfectly visible as something, a white or a dark spot or stroke, not lost sight of, observe, but yet so seen that we cannot tell what they are. As the distance increases, the confusion becomes greater, until at last the whole front of the house becomes merely a flat pale space, in which, however, there is still observable a kind of richness and chequering, caused by the details in it, which, though totally merged and lost in the mass, have still an influence on the texture of that mass; until at last the whole house itself becomes a mere light or dark spot which we can plainly see, but cannot tell what it is, nor distinguish it from a stone or any other object.

Now what I particularly wish to insist upon, is the state of vision in which all the details of an object are seen, and yet seen in such confusion and disorder that we cannot in the least tell what they are, or what they mean. It is not mist between us and the object, still less is it shade, still less is it want of character; it is a confusion, a mystery, an interfering of undecided lines with each other, not a diminution of their number; window and door, architrave and frieze, all are there: it is no cold and vacant mass, it is full and rich and abundant, and yet you cannot see a single form so as to know what it is. Observe your friend's face as he is coming up to you. First it is nothing more than a white spot; now it is a face, but you cannot see the two eyes, nor the mouth, even as spots; you see a confusion of lines, a something which you know from experience to be indicative of a face, and yet you cannot tell how it is so. Now he is nearer, and you can see the spots for the eyes and mouth, but they are not blank spots neither; there is detail in them; you cannot see the lips, nor the teeth, nor the brows, and yet you see more than mere spots; it is a mouth and an eye, and there is light and sparkle and expression in them, but nothing distinct. Now he is nearer still, and you can see that he is like your friend, but you cannot tell whether he is, or not; there is a vagueness and indecision of line still. Now you are sure, but even yet there are a thousand things in his face which have their effect in inducing the recognition, but which you cannot see so as to know what they are.

Changes like these, and states of vision corresponding to them, take place with each and all of the objects of nature, and two great principles of truth are deducible from their observation. First, place an object as close to the eye as you like, there is always something in it which you *cannot* see, except in the hinted and mysterious manner above described. You can see the texture of a piece of dress, but you cannot see the individual threads which compose it, though they are all felt, and have each of them influence on the eye. Secondly, place an object as far from the eye as you like, and until it becomes itself a mere spot, there is always something in it which you *can* see, though only in the hinted manner above described. Its shadows and lines and local colours are not lost sight of as it retires; they get mixed and indistinguishable, but they are still there, and there is a difference always perceivable between an object possessing such details and a flat or vacant space. The grass blades of a meadow a mile off, are so far discernible that there will be a marked difference between its appearance and that of a piece of wood painted green. And thus nature is never distinct and never vacant, she is always mysterious, but always abundant; you always see something, but you never see all.

And thus arise that exquisite finish and fulness which God has appointed to be the perpetual source of fresh pleasure to the cultivated and observant eye; a finish which no distance can render invisible, and no nearness comprehensible; which in every stone, every bough, every cloud, and every wave is multiplied around us, for ever presented, and for ever exhaustless. And hence in art, every space or touch in which we can see everything, or in which we can see nothing, is false. Nothing can be true which is either complete or vacant; every touch is false which does not suggest more than it represents, and every space is false which represents nothing.

Now, I would not wish for any more illustrative or marked examples of the total contradiction of these two great principles, than the landscape works of the old masters, taken as a body; the Dutch masters furnishing the cases of seeing everything, and the Italians of seeing nothing. The rule with both is indeed the same, differently applied—"You shall see the bricks in the wall, and be able to count them, or you shall see nothing but a dead flat:" but the Dutch give you the bricks, and the Italians the flat. Nature's rule being the precise reverse—"You shall never be able to count the bricks, but you shall never see a dead space."

Take, for instance, the street in the centre of the really great landscape of Poussin (great in feeling at least) marked 260 in the Dulwich Gallery. The houses are dead square masses with a light side and a dark side, and black touches for windows. There is no suggestion of anything in any of the spaces; the light wall is dead grey, the dark wall dead grey, and the windows dead black. How differently would nature have treated us! She would have let us see the Indian corn hanging on the walls, and the image of the Virgin at the angles, and the sharp, broken, broad shadows of the tiled eaves, and the deep-ribbed tiles with the doves upon them, and the carved Roman capital built into the wall, and the white and blue stripes of the mattresses stuffed out of the windows, and the flapping corners of the mat blinds. All would have been there; not as such, not like the corn, or blinds or tiles, not to be comprehended or understood, but a confusion of yellow and black spots and strokes, carried far too fine for the eye to follow, microscopic in its minuteness, and filling every atom and part of space with mystery, out of which

44

would have arranged itself the general impression of truth and life.

Again, take the distant city on the right bank of the river in Claude's Marriage of Isaac and Rebecca, in the National Gallery. I have seen many cities in my life, and drawn not a few; and I have seen many fortifications, fancy ones included, which frequently supply us with very few ideas indeed, especially in matters of proportion; but I do not remember ever having met with either a city or a fortress *entirely* composed of round towers of various heights and sizes, all facsimiles of each other, and absolutely agreeing in the number of battlements. I have, indeed, some faint recollection of having delineated such a one in the first page of a spelling book when I was four years old; but, somehow or other, the dignity and perfection of the ideal were not appreciated, and the volume was not considered to be increased in value by the frontispiece. Without, however, venturing to doubt the entire sublimity of the same ideal as it occurs in Claude, let us consider how nature, if she had been fortunate enough to originate so perfect a conception, would have managed it in its details. Claude has permitted us to see every battlement, and the first impulse we feel upon looking at the picture is to count how many there are. Nature would have given us a peculiar confused roughness of the upper lines, a multitude of intersections and spots, which we should have known from experience was indicative of battlements, but which we might as well have thought of creating as of counting. Claude has given you the walls below in one dead void of uniform grey. There is nothing to be seen, or felt, or guessed at in it; it is grey paint or grey shade, whichever you may choose to call it, but it is nothing more. Nature would have let you see, nay, would have compelled you to see, thousands of spots and lines, not one to be absolutely understood or accounted for, but yet all characteristic and different from each other; breaking lights on shattered stones, vague shadows from waving vegetation, irregular stains of time and weather, mouldering hollows, sparkling casements; all would have been there; none indeed, seen as such, none comprehensible or like themselves, but all visible; little shadows and sparkles, and scratches, making that whole space of colour a transparent, palpitating, various infinity....

Now it is, indeed, impossible for the painter to follow all this; he cannot come up to the same degree and order of infinity, but he can give us a lesser kind of infinity. He has not one thousandth part of the space to occupy which nature has; but he can, at least, leave no part of that space vacant and unprofitable. If nature carries out her minutiæ over miles, he has no excuse for generalizing in inches. And if he will only give us all he can, if he will give us a fulness as complete and as mysterious as nature's, we will pardon him for its being the fulness of a cup instead of an ocean. . . .

I am somewhat anticipating my subject here, because I can scarcely help answering the objections which I know must arise in the minds of most readers, especially of those who are *partially* artistical, respecting "generalization," "breadth," "effect," etc. It were to be wished that our writers on art would not dwell so frequently on the necessity of breadth, without explaining what it means; and that we had more constant reference made to the principle which I can only remember having seen once clearly explained and insisted on, that breadth is not vacancy. Generalization is unity, not destruction of parts; and composition is not annihilation, but arrangement of materials. The breadth which unites the truths of nature with her harmonies is meritorious and beautiful; but the breadth which annihilates those truths by the million is not painting nature, but painting over her. And so the masses which result from right concords and relations of details are sublime and impressive; but the masses which result from the eclipse of details are contemptible and painful. And we shall show . . . that distances like those of Poussin are mere meaningless tricks of clever execution, which, when once discovered, the artist may repeat over and over again, with mechanical contentment and perfect satisfaction, both to himself and to his superficial admirers, with no more exertion of intellect nor awakening of feeling than any tradesman has in multiplying some ornamental pattern of furniture. . . .

And now, take up one of Turner's distances, it matters not which or of what kind, drawing or painting, small or great, done thirty years ago or for last year's Academy, as you like; say that of the Mercury and Argus; and look if every fact which I have just been pointing out in nature be not carried out in it. Abundant beyond the power of the eye to embrace or follow, vast and various beyond the power of the mind to comprehend, there is yet not one atom in its whole extent and mass which does not suggest more than it represents; nor does it suggest vaguely, but in such a manner as to prove that the conception of each individual inch of that distance is absolutely clear and complete in the master's mind, a separate picture fully worked out: but yet, clearly and fully as the idea is formed, just so much of it is given, and no more, as nature would have allowed us to feel or see; just so much as would enable a spectator of experience and knowledge to understand almost every minute fragment of separate detail, but appears, to the unpractised and careless eye, just what a distance of nature's own would appear, an unintelligible mass. Not one line out of the millions there is without meaning, yet there is not one which is not affected and disguised by the dazzle and indecision of distance. No form is made out, and yet no form is unknown.

I believe it is a result of the experience of all artists, that it is the easiest thing in the world to give a certain degree of depth and transparency to water; but that it is next to impossible, to give a full impression of surface. If no reflection be given, a ripple being supposed, the water looks like lead: if reflection be given, it, in nine cases out of ten, looks *morbidly* clear and deep, so that we always go down *into* it, even when the artist most wishes us to glide *over* it. Now, this difficulty arises from the very same circumstance which occasions the frequent failure in effect of the best-drawn foregrounds . . . the change, namely, of focus necessary in the eye in order to receive rays of light coming from different distances. Go to the edge of a pond in a perfectly calm day, at some place where there is duckweed floating on the surface, not thick, but a leaf here and there. Now, you may either see in the water the reflection of the sky, or you may see the duckweed; but you cannot, by any effort, see both together. . . .

Hence it appears, that whenever we see plain reflections of comparatively distant objects, in near water, we cannot possibly see the surface, and *vice versâ;* so that when in a painting we give the reflections with the same clearness with which they are visible in nature, we presuppose the effort of the eye to look under the surface, and, of course, destroy the surface, and induce an effect of clearness which, perhaps, the artist has not particularly wished to attain, but which he has found himself forced into, by his reflections, in spite of himself. And the reason of this effect of clearness appearing preternatural is, that people are not in the habit of looking at water with the distant focus adapted to the reflections, unless by particular effort. We invariably, under ordinary circumstances, use the surface focus; and, in consequence, receive nothing more than a vague and confused impression of the reflected colours and lines. . . . If we take such a piece of water as that in the foreground of Turner's Château of Prince Albert, the first impression from it is, "What a wide *surface!*" We glide over it a quarter of a mile into the picture before we know where we are, and yet the water is as calm and crystalline as a mirror; but we are not allowed to tumble into it, and gasp for breath as we go down, we are kept upon the surface, though that surface is flashing and radiant with every hue of cloud, and sun, and sky, and foliage. But the secret is in the drawing of these reflections. We cannot tell, when we look *at* them and *for* them, what they mean. They have all character, and are evidently reflections of something definite and determined; but yet they are all uncertain and inexplicable; playing colour and palpitating shade, which, though we recognize them in an instant for images of something, and feel that the water is bright, and lovely, and calm, we cannot penetrate nor interpret; we are not allowed to go down to them, and we repose, as we should in nature, upon the lustre of the level surface. It is in this power of saying everything, and yet saying nothing too plainly, that the perfection of art here, as in all other cases, consists. . . .

Be it next observed, that the reflection of all near objects is not an exact copy of the parts of them which we see above the water, but a totally different view and arrangement of them, that which we should get if we were looking at them from beneath. Hence we see the dark sides of leaves hanging over a stream, in their reflection, though we see the light sides above; and all objects and groups of objects are thus seen in the reflection under different lights, and in different positions with respect to each other, from those which they assume above; some which we see on the bank being entirely lost in their reflection, and others which we cannot see on the bank brought into view. Hence nature contrives never to repeat herself, and the surface of water is not a mockery, but a new view of what is above it. And this difference in what is represented, as well as the obscurity of the representation, is one of the chief sources by which the sensation of surface is kept up in the reality. The reflection is not so remarkable, it does not attract the eye in the same degree when it is entirely different from the images above, as when it mocks them and repeats them, and we feel that the space and surface have colour and character of their own, and that the bank is one thing and the water another. It is by not making this change manifest, and giving

48

underneath a mere duplicate of what is seen above, that artists are apt to destroy the essence and substance of water, and to drop us through it.

Now one instance will be sufficient to show the exquisite care of Turner in this respect. On the left-hand side of his Nottingham, the water (a smooth canal) is terminated by a bank fenced up with wood, on which, just at the edge of the water, stands a white sign-post. A quarter of a mile back, the hill on which Nottingham Castle stands rises steeply nearly to the top of the picture. The upper part of this hill is in bright golden light, and the lower in very deep grey shadow, against which the white board of the sign-post is seen entirely in light relief, though, being turned from the light, it is itself in delicate middle tint, illumined only on the edge. But the image of all this in the canal is very different. First, we have the reflection of the piles of the bank sharp and clear, but under this we have not what we see above it, the dark *base* of the hill (for this being a quarter of a mile back, we could not see it over the fence if we were looking from below), but the golden summit of the hill, the shadow of the under part having no record nor place in the reflection. Now this summit, being very distant, cannot be seen clearly by the eye while its focus is adapted to the surface of the water, and accordingly its reflection is entirely vague and confused; you cannot tell what it is meant for, it is mere playing golden light. But the sign-post, being on the bank close to us, will be reflected clearly, and accordingly its distinct image is seen in the midst of this confusion; relieved, however, not now against the dark base, but against the illumined summit of the hill, and appearing therefore, instead of a white space thrown out from the blue shade, a dark grey space thrown out from golden light. I do not know that any more magnificent example could be given of concentrated knowledge, or of the daring statement of most difficult truth. For who but this consummate artist would have had courage, even if he had perceived the laws which required it, to undertake, in a single small space of water, the painting of an entirely new picture, with all its tones and arrangements altered,— what was made above bright by opposition to blue, being underneath made cool and dark by opposition to gold; or would have dared to contradict so boldly the ordinary expectation of the uncultivated eye, to find in the reflection a mockery of the reality? But the reward is immediate, for not only is the change most grateful to the eye, and most exquisite as composition, but the surface of the water in consequence of it is felt to be as spacious as it is clear, and the eye rests not on the inverted image of the material objects, but on the element which receives them. ...

It will be remembered that it was said above, that Turner was the only painter who had ever represented the surface of calm or the *force* of agitated water. He obtains this expression of force in falling or running water by fearless and full rendering of its forms. He never loses himself and his subject in the splash of the fall, his presence of mind never fails as he goes down; he does not blind us with the spray, or veil the countenance of his fall with its own drapery. A little crumbling white, or lightly rubbed paper, will soon give the effect of indiscriminate foam; but nature gives more than foam, she shows beneath it, and through it, a peculiar character of exquisitely studied form bestowed on every wave and line of fall; and it is this variety of definite character which Turner always aims at, rejecting, as much as possible, everything that conceals or overwhelms it. Thus, in the Upper Fall of the Tees, though the whole basin of the fall is blue and dim with the rising vapour, yet the attention of the spectator is chiefly directed to the concentric zones and delicate curves of the falling water itself; and it is impossible to express with what exquisite accuracy these are given. They are the characteristic of a powerful stream descending without impediment or break, but from a narrow channel, so as to expand as it falls. They are the constant form which such a stream assumes as it descends; and yet I think it would be difficult to point to another instance of their being rendered in art. You will find nothing in the waterfalls even of our best painters, but springing lines of parabolic descent, and splashing shapeless foam; and, in consequence, though they may make you understand the swiftness of the water, they never let you feel the weight of it; the stream in their hands looks *active,* not *supine,* as if it leaped, not as if it fell. Now water will leap a little way, it will leap down a weir or over a stone, but it *tumbles* over a high fall like this; and it is when we have lost the parabolic line, and arrived at the catenary, when we have lost the *spring* of the fall, and arrived at the *plunge* of it, that we begin really to feel its weight and wildness. Where water takes its first leap from the top, it is cool, and collected, and uninteresting, and mathematical; but it is when it finds that it has got into a scrape, and has farther to go than it thought, that its

50

character comes out; it is then that it begins to writhe, and twist, and sweep out, zone after zone, in wilder stretching as it falls; and to send down the rocket-like, lance-pointed, whizzing shafts at its sides, sounding for the bottom. And it is this prostration, this hopeless abandonment of its ponderous power to the air, which is always peculiarly expressed by Turner, and especially in the case before us; while our other artists, keeping to the parabolic line, where they do not lose themselves in smoke and foam, make their cataract look muscular and wiry, and may consider themselves fortunate if they can keep it from stopping. . . .

It is not, however, from the shore that Turner usually studies his sea. Seen from the land, the curl of the breakers, even in nature, is somewhat uniform and monotonous; the size of the waves out at sea is uncomprehended; and those nearer the eye seem to succeed and resemble each other, to move slowly to the beach, and to break in the same lines and forms.

Afloat even twenty yards from the shore, we receive a totally different impression. Every wave around us appears vast, every one different from all the rest; and the breakers present, now that we see them with their backs towards us, the grand, extended, and varied lines of long curvature which are peculiarly expressive both of velocity and power. Recklessness, before unfelt, is manifested in the mad, perpetual, changeful, undirected motion, not of wave after wave, as it appears from the shore, but of the very same water rising and falling. Of waves that successively approach and break, each appears to the mind a separate individual, whose part being performed, it perishes, and is succeeded by another; and there is nothing in this to impress us with the idea of restlessness, any more than in any successive and continuous functions of life and death. But it is when we perceive that it is no succession of wave, but the same water, constantly rising, and crashing, and recoiling, and rolling in again in new forms and with fresh fury, that we perceive the perturbed spirit, and feel the intensity of its unwearied rage. The sensation of power is also trebled; for not only is the vastness of apparent size much increased, but the whole action is different; it is not a passive wave, rolling sleepily forward until it tumbles heavily, prostrated upon the beach; but a sweeping exertion of tremendous and living strength, which does not now appear to *fall*, but to *burst* upon the shore; which never perishes but recoils and recovers.

Aiming at these grand characters of the sea, Turner almost always places the spectator, not on the shore, but twenty or thirty yards from it beyond the first range of the breakers, as in the Land's End, Fowey, Dunbar, and Laugharne. The latter . . . gives the surge and weight of the ocean in a gale, on a comparatively level shore; but the Land's End, the entire disorder of the surges when every one of them, divided and entangled among promontories as it rolls in, and beaten back part by part from walls of rock on this side and that side; recoils like the defeated division of a great army, throwing all behind it into disorder, breaking up the succeeding waves into vertical ridges, which in their turn, yet more totally shattered upon the shore, retire in more helpless confusion; until the whole surface of the sea becomes one dizzy whirl of rushing, writhing, tortured, undirected rage, bounding, and crashing, and coiling in an anarchy of enormous power; subdivided into myriads of waves, of which every one is not, be it remembered, a separate surge, but part and portion of a vast one, actuated by internal power, and giving in every direction the mighty undulation of impetuous line which glides over the rocks and writhes in the wind; overwhelming the one, and piercing the other with the form, fury, and swiftness of a sheet of lambent fire. And throughout the rendering of all this there is not one false curve given, not one which is not the perfect expression of visible motion; and the forms of the infinite sea are drawn throughout with that utmost mastery of art which, through the deepest study of every line, makes every line appear the wildest child of chance, while yet each is in itself a subject and a picture different from all else around. . . .

Few people, comparatively, have ever seen the effect on the sea of a powerful gale continued without intermission for three or four days and nights; and to those who have not, I believe it must be unimaginable, not from the mere force or size of surge, but from the complete annihilation of the limit between sea and air. The water from its prolonged agitation is beaten, not into mere creaming foam, but into masses of accumulated yeast, which hang in ropes and wreaths from wave to wave, and, where one curls over to break, form a festoon like a drapery from its edge; these are taken up by the wind, not in dissipating dust, but bodily, in writhing, hanging, coiling masses, which make the air white and thick as with snow, only the flakes are a foot or two long each: the surges themselves are full of foam in their very bodies, underneath, making them white all through, as the water is under a great cataract; and their masses, being thus half water and half air, are torn to pieces by the wind whenever they rise, and carried away in roaring smoke, which chokes and strangles like actual water. Add to this, that when the air has been exhausted of its moisture by long rain, the spray of the sea is caught by it . . . and covers its surface not merely with the smoke of finely divided water, but with boiling mist; imagine also the low rain-clouds brought down to the very level of the sea, as I have often seen them; whirling and flying in rags and fragments from wave to wave; and finally, conceive the surges themselves in their utmost pitch of power, velocity, vastness, and madness, lifting themselves in precipices and peaks, furrowed with their whirl of ascent, through all this chaos; and you will understand that there is indeed no distinction left between the sea and air; that no object, nor horizon, nor any landmark or natural evidence of position is left; that the heaven is all spray, and the ocean all cloud, and that you can see no farther in any direction than you could see through a cataract. Suppose the effect of the first sunbeam sent from above to show this annihilation to itself, and you have the sea picture of the Academy, 1842, the Snowstorm, one of the very grandest statements of sea-motion, mist, and light, that has ever been put on canvas, even by Turner. Of course it was not understood; his finest works never are: but there was some apology for the public's not comprehending this, for few people have had the opportunity of seeing the sea at such a time, and when they have, cannot face it. To hold by a mast or a rock, and watch it, is a prolonged endurance of drowning which few people have courage to go through. To those who have, it is one of the noblest lessons of nature.

But, I think, the noblest sea that Turner has ever painted, and, if so, the noblest certainly ever painted by man, is that of the Slave Ship, the chief Academy picture of the Exhibition of 1840. It is a sunset on the Atlantic, after prolonged storm; but the storm is partially lulled, and the torn and streaming rain-clouds are moving in scarlet lines to lose themselves in the hollow of the night. The whole surface of sea included in the picture is divided into two ridges of enormous swell, not high, nor local, but a low broad heaving of the whole ocean, like the lifting of its bosom by deep-drawn breath after the torture of the storm. Between these two ridges the fire of the sunset falls along the trough of the sea, dyeing it with an awful but glorious light, the intense and lurid splendour which burns

53

like gold, and bathes like blood. Along this fiery path and valley, the tossing waves by which the swell of the sea is restlessly divided, lift themselves in dark, indefinite, fantastic forms, each casting a faint and ghastly shadow behind it along the illumined foam. They do not rise everywhere, but three or four together in wild groups, fitfully and furiously, as the under strength of the swell compels or permits them; leaving between them treacherous spaces of level and whirling water, now lighted with green and lamp-like fire, now flashing back the gold of the declining sun, now fearfully dyed from above with the undistinguishable images of the burning clouds, which fall upon them in flakes of crimson and scarlet, and give to the reckless waves the added motion of their own fiery flying. Purple and blue, the lurid shadows of the hollow breakers are cast upon the mist of night, which gathers cold and low, advancing like the shadow of death upon the guilty ship as it labours amidst the lightning of the sea, its thin masts written upon the sky in lines of blood, girded with condemnation in that fearful hue which signs the sky with horror, and mixes its flaming flood with the sunlight, and, cast far along the desolate heave of the sepulchral waves, incarnadines the multitudinous sea.

I believe, if I were reduced to rest Turner's immortality upon any single work, I should choose this. Its daring conception, ideal in the highest sense of the word, is based on the purest truth, and wrought out with the concentrated knowledge of a life; its colour is absolutely perfect, not one false or morbid hue in any part or line, and so modulated that every square inch of canvas is a perfect composition; its drawing as accurate as fearless; the ship buoyant, bending, and full of motion; its tones as true as they are wonderful; and the whole picture dedicated to the most sublime of subjects and impressions (completing thus the perfect system of all truth, which we have shown to be formed by Turner's works)—the power, majesty, and deathfulness of the open, deep, illimitable sea.

Modern Painters, Vol. I, Part 2, Sec. V, Ch. 3

Modern Painters
(Volume II)
(1846)

Tintoretto

Knowing or feeling, that the expression of the human face was, in such circumstances, not to be rendered, and that the effort could only end in an ugly falsehood, he denies himself all aid from the features, he feels that if he is to place himself or us in the midst of that maddened multitude, there can be no time allowed for watching expression. Still less does he depend on details of murder or ghastliness of death; there is no blood, no stabbing or cutting, but there is an awful substitute for these in the chiaroscuro. The scene is the outer vestibule of a palace, the slippery marble floor is fearfully barred across by sanguine shadows, so that our eyes seem to become blood-shot and strained with strange horror and deadly vision; a lake of life before them, like the burning scene of the doomed Moabite on the water that came by the way of Edom; a huge flight of stairs, without parapet, descends on the left; down this rush a crowd of women mixed with the murderers; the child in the arms of one has been seized by the limbs, she hurls herself over the edge, and falls head downmost, dragging the child out of the grasp by her weight;—she will be dashed dead in a second; two others are farther in flight, they reach the edge of a deep river,—the water is beat into a hollow by the force of their plunge;—close to us is the great struggle; a heap of the mothers entangled in one mortal writhe with each other and the swords, one of the murderers dashed down and crushed beneath them, the sword of another caught by the blade and dragged at by a woman's naked hand; the youngest and fairest of the women, her child just torn away from a death grasp, and clasped to her breast with the grip of a steel vise, falls backwards, helplessly over the heap, right on the sword points; all knit together and hurled down in one hopeless, frenzied, furious abandonment of body and soul in the effort to save. Their shrieks ring in our ears till the marble seems rending around us, but far back, at the bottom of the stairs, there is something in the shadow like a heap of clothes. It is a woman, sitting quiet,—quite quiet,—still as any stone; she looks down steadfastly on her dead child, laid along on the floor before her, and her hand is pressed softly upon her brow.

I should exhaust the patience of the reader, if I were to dwell at length on the various stupendous developments of the imagination of Tintoret in the Scuola di San Rocco alone. I would fain join awhile in that solemn pause of the journey into Egypt, where the silver boughs of the shadowy trees lace with their tremulous lines the alternate folds of fair cloud, flushed by faint crimson light, and lie across the streams of blue between those rosy islands, like the white wakes of wandering ships; or watch beside the sleep of the disciples, among those massy leaves that lie so heavily on the dead of the night beneath the descent of the angel of the agony, and toss fearfully above the motion of the torches as the troop of the betrayer emerges out of the hollows of the olives; or wait through the hour of accusing beside the judgment seat of Pilate, where all is unseen, unfelt, except the one figure that stands with its head bowed down, pale, like a pillar of moonlight, half bathed in the glory of the Godhead, half wrapt in the whiteness of the shroud.

Modern Painters, Vol. II, Part 3, Sec. II, Ch. 3

I was lying by this fountain—on a dark evening of July, dark not with night, but with storm. The precipice above me lost itself in the air within fifty feet of my head—not in cloud—but in the dark, motionless atmosphere. The lower boughs of its pines shook like black plumes against the shade; their pointed tops faded into its body—faint as if woven of gossamer—spectral shadows of colossal strength. The valley lay for leagues on either side—roofed with the impenetrable gloom—walled with the steep bases of its hill—one boundless chamber—lighted only as it seemed, by the white foam of the forked Arve—cast like a stream of lightning along its floor. Through the veil of cloud, the presence of the great mountains was indicated only by the sound of their forests, by the sharp, sudden stroke—like a human cry,—the wail of the glacier upon its path of pain, and the gust—rising by fits and falling—of the wind, or the waves, the ear knew not which—among their chasms.

So it had been through the day—no rain—no motion—no light. One roof—one level veil, as of God's Holy Place, and the voices of the mountains from behind it and above.

I lay beside the fountain—watching the motion of its soundless domes, and the entangling within its depth of the green blades with their own shadows. From the rock above, a single oozy drop fell at intervals into the pool, with a sound like that of a passing bell far away. Among the thick herbage at its edge the grasshoppers, heavy and faint in the chill and darkness, climbed freely up the jointed stalks, staring about them with their black beaded eyes, and fell, rustling,—unable to lift their scarlet wings. It was as if the sun had been taken away from the world, and the life of the earth were ebbing away, groan by groan.

Suddenly, there came in the direction of Dome du Goûter a crash—of prolonged thunder; and when I looked up, I saw the cloud cloven, as it were by the avalanche itself, whose white stream came bounding down the eastern slope of the mountain, like slow lightning. The vapour parted before its fall, pierced by the whirlwind of its motion; the gap widened, the dark shade melted away on either side; and, like a risen spirit casting off its garment of corruption, and flushed with eternity of life, the Aiguilles of the south broke through the black foam of the storm clouds. One by one, pyramid above pyramid, the mighty range of its companions shot off their shrouds, and took to themselves their glory—all fire—no shade—no dimness. Spire of ice—dome of snow—wedge of rock—*all* fire in the light of the sunset, sank into the hollows of the crags—and pierced through the prisms of the glaciers, and dwelt within them—as it does in clouds. The ponderous storm writhed and moaned beneath them, the forests wailed and waved in the evening wind, the steep river flashed and leaped along the valley; but the mighty pyramids stood calmly—in the very heart of the high heaven—a celestial city with walls of amethyst and gates of gold—filled with the light and clothed with the Peace of God. And then I learned—what till then I had not known—

57

the real meaning of the word Beautiful. With all that I had ever seen before—there had come mingled the associations of humanity—the exertion of human power—the action of human mind. The image of self had not been effaced in that of God. It was then only beneath those glorious hills that I learned how thought itself may become ignoble and energy itself become base—when compared with the absorption of soul and spirit—the prostration of all power—and the cessation of all will—before, and in the Presence of, the manifested Deity. It was then only that I understood that to become nothing might be to become more than Man;—how without desire—without memory—without sense even of existence—the very sense of its own lost perception of a mightier—the immortal soul might be held for ever—impotent as a leaf—yet greater than tongue can tell—wrapt in the one contemplation of the Infinite God.

Appendix I

The draft of an introduction to *Modern Painters*, Vol. II

The Seven Lamps of
Architecture
(1849)

Architecture is the art which so disposes and adorns the
edifices raised by man, for whatsoever uses, that the sight
of them may contribute to his mental health, power, and
pleasure.

It is very necessary, in the outset of all inquiry, to
distinguish carefully between Architecture and Building.

To build,—literally, to confirm,—is by common understanding to put together and adjust the several pieces of
any edifice or receptacle of a considerable size. Thus we
have church building, house building, ship building, and
coach building. That one edifice stands, another floats, and
another is suspended on iron springs, makes no difference
in the nature of the art, if so it may be called, of building
or edification. The persons who profess that art, are severally builders, ecclesiastical, naval or whatever other name
their work may justify: but building does not become
architecture merely by the stability of what it erects; and
it is no more architecture which raises a church, or which
fits it to receive certain religious offices, than it is architecture which makes a carriage commodious, or a ship swift.
I do not, of course, mean that the word is not often, or
even may be not, legitimately applied in such a sense (as
we speak of naval architecture); but in that sense architecture ceases to be one of the fine arts, and it is
therefore better not to run the risk, by loose nomencla-
ture, of the confusion which would arise, and has often
arisen, from extending principles which belong altogether
to building, into the sphere of architecture proper.

Let us, therefore, at once confine the name to that art
which, taking up and admitting, as conditions of its working, the necessities and common uses of the building,
impresses on its form certain characters venerable or

beautiful, but otherwise unnecessary. Thus, I suppose, nō one would call the laws architectural which determine the height of a breastwork or the position of a bastion. But if to the stone facing of that bastion be added an unnecessary feature, as a cable moulding, *that* is Architecture. It would be similarly unreasonable to call battlements or machicolations architectural features, as long as they consist only of an advanced gallery supported on projecting masses, with open intervals beneath for offence. But if these projecting masses be carved into rounded courses, which are useless, and if the headings of the intervals be arched and trefoiled, which is useless, *that* is Architecture. It may not be always easy to draw the line so sharply, because there are few buildings which have not some pretence or colour of being architectural; neither can there be any architecture which is not based on building, nor any good architecture which is not based on good building; but it is perfectly easy, and very necessary, to keep the ideas distinct, and to understand fully that Architecture concerns itself only with those characters of an edifice which are above and beyond its common use. I say common; because a building raised to the honour of God, or in memory of men, has surely a use to which its architectural ornament fits it; but not a use which limits, by any inevitable necessities, its plan or details.

Architecture proper, then, naturally arranges itself under five heads:—

Devotional; including all buildings raised for God's service or honour.

Memorial; including both monuments and tombs.

Civil; including every edifice raised by nations or societies, for purposes of common business or pleasure.

Military; including all private and public architecture of defence.

Domestic; including every rank and kind of dwelling-place.

Now, of the principles which I would endeavour to develope, while all must be, as I have said, applicable to every stage and style of the art, some and especially those which are exciting rather than directing, have necessarily fuller reference to one kind of building than another; and among those I would place first that spirit which, having influence in all, has nevertheless such especial reference to devotional and memorial architecture—the spirit which offers for such work precious things, simply because they are precious; not as being necessary to the building, but as an offering, surrendering, and sacrifice of what is to ourselves desirable. It seems to me, not only that this feeling is in most cases wholly wanting in those who forward the devotional buildings of the present day; but that it would even be regarded as a dangerous, or perhaps criminal, principle by many among us. I have not space to enter into dispute of all the various objections which may be urged against it—they are many and specious; but I may, perhaps, ask the reader's patience while I set down those simple reasons which cause me to believe it a good and just feeling, and as well-pleasing to God and honourable in men, as it is beyond all dispute necessary to the production of any great work in the kind with which we are at present concerned.

Now, first, to define this Lamp, or Spirit, of Sacrifice, clearly. I have said that it prompts us to the offering of precious things, merely because they are precious, not because they are useful or necessary. It is a spirit, for instance, which of two marbles, equally beautiful, applicable, and durable, would choose the more costly, because it was so, and of two kinds of decoration, equally effective, would choose the more elaborate because it was so, in order that it might in the same compass present more cost and more thought. It is therefore most unreasoning and enthusiastic, and perhaps less negatively defined, as the opposite of the prevalent feelings of modern times, which desires to produce the largest results at the least cost. . . .

The question is not between God's house and His poor: it is not between God's house and His Gospel. It is between God's house and ours. Have we no tesselated colours on our floors? no frescoed fancies on our roofs? no niched statuary in our corridors? no gilded furniture in our chambers? no costly stones in our cabinets? Has even the tithe of these been offered? They are, or they ought to be, the signs that enough has been devoted to the great purposes of human stewardship, and that there remains to us what we can spend in luxury; but there is a greater and prouder luxury than this selfish one—that of bringing a portion of such things as these into sacred service, and presenting them for a memorial that our pleasure as well as our toil has been hallowed by the remembrance of Him who gave both the strength and the reward. And until this has been done, I do not see how such possessions can be retained in happiness. I do not understand the feeling which would arch our own gates and pave our own thresholds, and leave the church with its narrow door and foot-worn sill; the feeling which enriches our own chambers with all manner of costliness, and endures the bare wall and mean compass of the temple. There is seldom even so severe a choice to be made, seldom so much self-denial to be exercised. There are isolated cases, in which men's happiness and mental activity depend upon a certain degree of luxury in their houses; but then this is true luxury, felt and tasted, and profited by. In the plurality of instances nothing of the kind is attempted, nor can be enjoyed; men's average resources cannot reach it; and that which they *can* reach, gives them no pleasure, and might be spared. It will be seen, in the course of the following chapters, that I am no advocate for meanness of private habitation. I would fain introduce into it all magnificence, care, and beauty, where they are possible; but I would not have that useless expense in unnoticed fineries or formalities; cornicing of ceilings and graining of doors, and fringing of curtains, and thousands such; things which have become falsely and apathetically habitual—things on whose common appliance hang whole trades, to which there never yet belonged the blessing of giving one ray of real pleasure, or becoming of the remotest or most contemptible use—things which cause half the expense of life, and destroy more than half its comfort, manliness, respectability, freshness, and facility. I speak from experience: I know what is is to live in a cottage with a deal floor and roof, and a hearth of mica slate; and I know it to be in many respects healthier and happier than living between a Turkey carpet and gilded ceilings, beside a steel grate and polished fender. I do not say that such things have not their place and propriety; but I say this, emphatically, that the tenth part of the expense which is sacrificed in domestic vanities, if not absolutely and meaninglessly lost in domestic discomforts and incumbrances, would, if collectively offered and wisely employed, build a marble church for every town in England; such a church as it should be a joy and a blessing even to pass near in our daily ways and walks, and as it would bring the light into the eyes to see from afar, lifting its fair height above the purple crowd of humble roofs.

... All old work nearly has been hard work. It may be the hard work of children, of barbarians, of rustics; but it is always their utmost. Ours has as constantly the look of money's worth, of a stopping short wherever and whenever we can, of a lazy compliance with low conditions; never of a fair putting forth of our strength. Let us have done with this kind of work at once: cast off every temptation to it: do not let us degrade ourselves voluntarily, and then mutter and mourn over our shortcomings; let us confess our poverty or our parsimony, but not belie our human intellect. It is not even a question of how *much* we are to do, but of how it is to be done; it is not a question of doing more, but of doing better. Do not let us boss our roofs with wretched half-worked, blunt-edged rosettes; do not let us flank our gates with rigid imitations of mediæval statuary. Such things are mere insults to common sense, and only unfit us for feeling the nobility of their prototypes. We have so much, suppose, to be spent in decoration; let us go to the Flaxman of his time, whoever he may be; and bid him carve for us a single statue, frieze, or capital, or as many as we can afford, compelling upon him the one condition, that they shall be the best he can do; place them where they will be of the most value, and be content. Our other capitals may be mere blocks, and our other niches empty. No matter: better our work unfinished than all bad. It may be that we do not desire ornament of so high an order: choose, then, a less developed style, as also, if you will, rougher material; the law which we are enforcing requires only that what we pretend to do and to give, shall both be the best of their kind; choose, therefore, the Norman hatchet work, instead of the Flaxman frieze and statue, but let it be the best hatchet work; and if you cannot afford marble use Caen stone, but from the best bed; and if not stone, brick, but the best brick; preferring always what is good of a lower order of work or material, to what is bad of a higher; for this is not only the way to improve every form of work, and to put every kind of material to better use; but it is more honest and unpretending, and is in harmony with other just, upright, and manly principles. . . .

The other condition which we had to notice, was the value of the appearance of labour upon architecture. . . . It is, indeed, one of the most frequent sources of pleasure which belong to the art, always, however, within certain somewhat remarkable limits. For it does not at first appear easily to be explained why labour, as represented by materials of value, should, without sense of wrong or error, bear being wasted; while the waste of actual workmanship is always painful, so soon as it is apparent. But so it is, that, while precious materials may, with a certain profusion and negligence, be employed for the magnificence of what is seldom seen, the work of man cannot be carelessly and idly bestowed, without an immediate sense of wrong; as if the strength of the living creature were never intended by its Maker to be sacrificed in vain,

63

though it is well for us sometimes to part with what we esteem precious of substance, as showing that in such service it becomes but dross and dust. And in the nice balance between the straitening of effort or enthusiasm on the one hand, and vainly casting it away upon the other, there are more questions than can be met by any but very just and watchful feeling. In general it is less the mere loss of labour that offends us, than the lack of judgment implied by such loss; so that if men confessedly work for work's sake, and it does not appear that they are ignorant where or how to make their labour tell, we shall not be grossly offended. On the contrary, we shall be pleased if the work be lost in carrying out a principle, or in avoiding a deception. It, indeed, is a law properly belonging to another part of our subject, but it may be allowably stated here, that, whenever, by the construction of a building, some parts of it are hidden from the eye which are the continuation of others bearing some consistent ornament, it is not well that the ornament should cease in the parts concealed; credit is given for it, and it should not be deceptively withdrawn: as, for instance, in the sculpture of the backs of the statues of a temple pediment; never, perhaps, to be seen, but yet not lawfully to be left unfinished. And so in the working out of ornaments in dark or concealed places, in which it is best to err on the side of completion; and in the carrying round of string courses, and other such continuous work; not but that they may stop sometimes, on the point of going into some palpably impenetrable recess, but then let them stop boldly and markedly, on some distinct terminal ornament, and never be supposed to exist where they do not. The arches of the towers which flank the transepts of Rouen Cathedral have rosette ornaments on their spandrels, on the three visible sides; none on the side towards the roof. The right of this is rather a nice point for question.

Finally, work may be wasted by being too good for its material, or too fine to bear exposure; and this, generally a characteristic of late, especially of renaissance, work, is perhaps the worst fault of all. I do not know anything more painful or pitiful than the kind of ivory carving with which the Certosa of Pavia, and part of the Colleone sepulchral chapel at Bergamo, and other such buildings are incrusted, of which it is not possible so much as to think without exhaustion; and a heavy sense of the misery it would be, to be forced to look at it all. And this is not from the quantity of it, nor because it is bad work—much of it is inventive and able; but because it looks as if it were only fit to be put in inlaid cabinets and velveted caskets, and as if it could not bear one drifted shower or gnawing frost. We are afraid for it, anxious about it, and tormented by it; and we feel that a massy shaft and a bold shadow would be worth it all.

Nevertheless, even in cases like these, much depends on the accomplishment of the great ends of decoration. If the ornament does its duty—if it *is* ornament, and its points of shade and light tell in the general effect, we shall not be offended by finding that the sculptor in his fulness of fancy has chosen to give much more than these mere points of light, and has composed them of groups of figures. But if the ornament does not answer its purpose, if it have no distant, no truly decorative power; if, generally seen, it be a mere incrustation and meaningless roughness, we shall only be chagrined by finding when we look close, that the incrustation has cost years of labour, and has millions of figures and histories in it; and would be the better for being seen through a Stanhope lens. Hence the greatness of the northern Gothic as contrasted with the latest Italian. It reaches nearly the same extreme of detail; but it never loses sight of its architectural purpose, never fails in its decorative power; not a leaflet in it but speaks, and speaks far off too; and so long as this be the case, there is no limit to the luxuriance in which such work may legitimately and nobly be bestowed.

The Seven Lamps of Architecture, Ch. 1

. . . Architectural Deceits are broadly to be considered under three heads:

1st. The suggestion of a mode of structure or support, other than the true one; as in pendants of late Gothic roofs.

2nd. The painting of surfaces to represent some other material than that of which they actually consist (as in the marbling of wood), or the deceptive representation of sculptured ornament upon them.

3rd. The use of cast or machine-made ornaments of any kind.

Now, it may be broadly stated, that architecture will be noble exactly in the degree in which all these false expedients are avoided. Nevertheless, there are certain degrees of them, which, owing to their frequent usage, or to other causes, have so far lost the nature of deceit as to be admissible; as, for instance, gilding, which is in architecture no deceit, because it is therein not understood for gold; while in jewellery it is a deceit, because it is so understood, and therefore altogether to be reprehended. . . .

The architect is not *bound* to exhibit structure; nor are we to complain of him for concealing it, any more than we should regret that the outer surfaces of the human frame conceal much of its anatomy; nevertheless, that building will generally be the noblest, which to an intelligent eye discovers the great secrets of its structure, as an animal form does, although from a careless observer they may be concealed. In the vaulting of a Gothic roof it is no deceit to throw the strength into the ribs of it, and to make the intermediate vault a mere shell. Such a structure would be presumed by an intelligent observer, the first time he saw such a roof; and the beauty of its traceries would be enhanced to him if they confessed and followed the lines of its main strength. If, however, the intermediate shell were made of wood instead of stone, and whitewashed to look like the rest,—this would, of course, be direct deceit, and altogether unpardonable.

There is, however, a certain deception necessarily occurring in Gothic architecture, which relates not to the points, but to the manner of support. The resemblance in its shafts and ribs to the external relations of stems and branches, which has been the ground of so much foolish speculation, necessarily induces in the mind of the spectator a sense or belief of a correspondent internal structure; that is to say, of a fibrous and continuous strength from the root into the limbs, and an elasticity communicated *upwards,* sufficient for the support of the ramified portions. The idea of the real conditions, of a great weight of ceiling thrown upon certain narrow, jointed lines, which have a tendency partly to be crushed, and partly to separate and be pushed outwards, is with difficulty received; and the more so when the pillars would be, if unassisted, too slight for the weight, and are supported by external flying buttresses, as in the apse of Beauvais, and other such achievements of the bolder Gothic. Now, there is a nice question of conscience in this, which we shall hardly settle but by considering that, when the mind is informed beyond the possibility of mistake as to the true nature of things, the affecting it with a contrary impression, however distinct, is no dishonesty, but on the contrary, a legitimate appeal to the imagination. For instance, the greater part of the happiness which we have in contemplating clouds, results from the impression of their having massive, luminous, warm, and mountain-like surfaces; and our delight in the sky frequently depends upon our considering it as a blue vault. But, if we choose, we may know the contrary, in both instances; and easily ascertain the cloud to be a damp fog, or a drift of snowflakes; and the sky to be a lightless abyss. There is, therefore, no dishonesty, while there is much delight, in the irresistibly contrary impression. In the same way, so long as we see the stones and joints, and are not deceived as to the points of support in any piece of architecture, we may rather praise than regret the dexterous artifices which compel us to feel as if there were fibre in its shafts and life in its branches. Nor is even the concealment of the support of the external buttress reprehensible, so long as the pillars are not sensibly inadequate to their duty. For the weight of a roof is a circumstance of which the spectator generally has no idea, and the provisions for it, consequently, circumstances whose necessity or adaptation he could not understand. It is no deceit, therefore, when the weight to be borne is necessarily unknown, to conceal also the means of bearing it, leaving only to be perceived so much of the support as is indeed adequate to the weight supposed. For the shafts do, indeed, bear as much as they are ever imagined to bear, and the system of added support is no more, as a matter of conscience, to be exhibited, than, in the human or any other form, mechanical provisions for those functions which are themselves unperceived.

But the moment that the conditions of weight are apprehended, both truth and feeling require that the conditions of support should be also apprehended. Nothing can be worse, either as judged by the taste or the conscience, than affectedly inadequate supports—suspensions in air, and other such tricks and vanities. Mr. Hope wisely reprehends, for this reason, the arrangement of the main piers of St. Sophia at Constantinople. King's College Chapel, Cambridge, is a piece of architectural juggling, if possible still more to be condemned, because less sublime.

With deceptive concealments of structure are to be classed, though still more blameable, deceptive assumptions of it,—the introduction of members which should have, or profess to have, a duty, and have none. One of the most general instances of this will be found in the form of the flying buttress in late Gothic. The use of that member is, of course, to convey support from one pier to another when the plan of the building renders it necessary or desirable that the supporting masses should be divided into groups; the most frequent necessity of this kind arising from the intermediate range of chapels or aisles between the nave or choir walls and their supporting piers. The natural, healthy, and beautiful arrangement is that of a steeply sloping bar of stone, sustained by an arch with its spandrel carried farthest down on the lowest side, and dying into the vertical of the outer pier; that pier being, of course, not square, but rather a piece of wall set at right angles to the supported walls, and, if need be, crowned by a pinnacle to give it greater weight. The whole arrangement is exquisitely carried out in the choir of Beauvais. In later Gothic the pinnacle became gradually a decorative member, and was used in all places merely for the sake of its beauty. There is no objection to this; it is just as lawful to build a pinnacle for its beauty as a tower; but also the *buttress* became a decorative member; and was used, first, where it was not wanted, and, secondly, in forms in which it could be of no use, becoming a mere tie, not between the pier and wall, but between the wall and the top of the decorative pinnacle, thus attaching itself to the very point where its thrust, if it made any, could not be resisted. The most flagrant instance of this barbarism that I remember, (though it prevails partially in all the spires of the Netherlands,) is the lantern of St. Ouen at Rouen, where the pierced buttress, having an ogee curve, looks about as much calculated to bear a thrust as a switch of willow; and the pinnacles, huge and richly decorated, have evidently no work to do whatsoever, but stand round the central tower, like four idle servants, as they are—heraldic supporters, that central tower being merely a hollow crown, which needs no more buttressing than a basket does. In fact, I do not know anything more strange or unwise than the praise lavished upon this lantern; it is one of the basest pieces of Gothic in Europe; its flamboyant traceries being of the last and most degraded form, and its entire plan and decoration resembling, and deserving little more credit than, the burnt sugar ornaments of elaborate confectionery.

Perhaps the most fruitful source of these kinds of corruption which we have to guard against in recent times, is one which, nevertheless, comes in a 'questionable shape', and of which it is not easy to determine the proper laws and limits; I mean the use of iron. The definition of the art of architecture, given in the first Chapter, is independent of its materials. Nevertheless, that art having been, up to the beginning of the present century, practised for the most part in clay, stone, or wood, it has resulted that the sense of proportion and the laws of structure have been based, the one altogether, the other in great part, on the necessities consequent on the employment of those materials; and that the entire or principal employment of metallic framework would, therefore, be generally felt as a departure from the first principles of the art. Abstractedly there appears no reason why iron should not be used as well as wood; and the time is probably near when a new system of architectural laws will be developed, adapted entirely to metallic construction. But I believe that the tendency of all present sympathy and association is to limit the idea of architecture to non-metallic work; and that not without reason. For architecture being in its perfection the earliest, as in its elements it is necessarily the first, of arts, will always precede, in any barbarous nation, the possession of the science necessary either for the obtaining or the management of iron. Its first existence and its earliest laws must, therefore, depend upon the use of materials accessible in quantity, and on the surface of the earth; that is to say, clay, wood, or stone; and as I think it cannot but be generally felt that one of the chief dignities of architecture is its historical use, and since the latter is partly dependent on consistency of style, it will be felt right to retain as far as may be, even in periods of more advanced science, the materials and principles of earlier ages. . . .

The rule is, I think, that metals may be used as a *cement,* but not as a *support.* For as cements of other kinds are often so strong that the stones may easier be broken than separated, and the wall becomes a solid mass, without for that reason losing the character of architecture, there is no reason why, when a nation has obtained the knowledge and practice of iron work, metal rods or rivets should not be used in the place of cement, and establish the same or a greater strength and adherence, without in any wise inducing departure from the types and system of architecture before established; nor does it make any difference, except as to sightliness, whether the metal bands or rods so employed be in the body of the wall or on its exterior, or set as stays and cross-bands; so only that the use of them be always and distinctly one which might be superseded by mere strength of cement; as for instance if a pinnacle or mullion be propped or tied by an iron band, it is evident that the iron only prevents the separation of the stones by lateral force, which the cement would have done, had it been strong enough. But the moment that the iron in the least degree takes the place of the stone, and acts by its resistance to crushing, and bears super-incumbent weight, or if it acts by its own weight as a counterpoise, and so supersedes the use of pinnacles or buttresses in resisting a lateral thrust, or if, in the form of a rod or girder, it is used to do what wooden beams would have done as well, that instant the building ceases, so far as such applications of metal extend, to be true architecture.

The last form of fallacy which . . . we had to deprecate, was the substitution of cast or machine work for that of the hand, generally expressible as Operative Deceit.

There are two reasons, both weighty, against this practice; one, that all cast and machine work is bad, as work; the other, that it is dishonest. . . .

Ornament, as I have often before observed, has two entirely distinct sources of agreeableness, one, that of the abstract beauty of its forms, which, for the present, we will suppose to be the same whether they come from the hand or the machine; the other, the sense of human labour and care spent upon it. How great this latter influence we may perhaps judge, by considering that there is not a cluster of weeds growing in any cranny of ruin which has not a beauty in all respects *nearly* equal, and, in some, immeasurably superior, to that of the most elaborate sculpture of its stones: and that all our interest in the carved work, our sense of its richness, though it is tenfold less rich than the knots of grass beside it; of its delicacy, though it is a thousandfold less delicate; of its admirableness, though a millionfold less admirable; results from our consciousness of its being the work of poor, clumsy, toilsome man. Its true delightfulness depends on our discovering in it the record of thoughts, and intents, and trials, and heart-breakings—of recoveries and joyfulnesses of success: all this *can* be traced by a practised eye; but, granting it even obscure, it is presumed or understood; and in that is the worth of the thing, just as much as the worth of any thing else we call precious. The worth of a diamond is simply the understanding of the time it must take to look for it before it is found; and the worth of an ornament is the time it must take before it can be cut. It has an intrinsic value besides, which the diamond has not; (for a diamond has no more real beauty than a piece of glass;) but I do not speak of that at present; I place the two on the same ground; and I suppose that hand-wrought ornament can no more be generally known from machine work, than a diamond can be known from paste;

nay, that the latter may deceive for a moment, the mason's, as the other the jeweller's eye; and that it can be detected only by the closest examination. Yet exactly as a woman of feeling would not wear false jewels, so would a builder of honour disdain false ornaments. The using of them is just as downright and inexcusable a lie. . . .

Thus in the use of brick: since that is known to be originally moulded, there is no reason why it should not be moulded into diverse forms. It will never be supposed to have been cut, and, therefore, will cause no deception; it will have only the credit it deserves. In flat countries, far from any quarry of stone, cast brick may be legitimately, and most successfully, used in decoration, and that elaborate, and even refined. The brick mouldings of the Palazzo Pepoli at Bologna, and those which run round the market-place of Vercelli, are among the richest in Italy. So also, tile and porcelain work, of which the former is grotesquely, but successfully, employed in the domestic architecture of France, coloured tiles being inserted in the diamond spaces between the crossing timbers; and the latter admirably in Tuscany, in external bas-reliefs, by the Robbia family, in which works, while we cannot but sometimes regret the useless and ill-arranged colours, we would by no means blame the employment of a material which, whatever its defects, excels every other in permanence, and, perhaps, requires even greater skill in its management than marble. For it is not the material, but the absence of the human labour, which makes the thing worthless; and a piece of terra cotta, or of plaster of Paris, which has been wrought by the human hand, is worth all the stone in Carrara, cut by machinery. It is, indeed, possible, and even usual, for men to sink into machines themselves, so that even hand-work has all the characters of mechanism; of the difference between living and dead hand-work I shall speak presently; all that I ask at present is, what it is always in our power to secure—the confession of what we have done, and what we have given; so that when we use stone at all (since all stone is naturally supposed to be carved by hand,) we must not carve it by machinery; neither must we use any artificial stone cast into shape, nor any stucco ornaments of the colour of stone, or which might in any wise be mistaken for it, as the stucco-mouldings in the cortile of the Palazzo Vecchio at Florence, which cast a shame and suspicion over every part of the building.

The change of which I speak, is expressible in few words; but one more important, more radically influential, could not be. It was the substitution of the *line* for the *mass,* as the element of decoration.

We have seen the mode in which the openings or penetration of the window expanded, until what were, at first, awkward forms of intermediate stone, became delicate lines of tracery; and I have been careful in pointing out the peculiar attention bestowed on the proportion and decoration of the mouldings of the window at Rouen, ... as compared with earlier mouldings, because that beauty and care are singularly significant. They mark that the traceries had *caught the eye* of the architect. Up to that time, up to the very last instant in which the reduction and thinning of the intervening stone was consummated, his eye had been on the openings only, on the stars of light. He did not care about the stone; a rude border of moulding was all he needed, it was the penetrating shape which he was watching. But when that shape had received its last possible expansion, and when the stone-work became an arrangement of graceful and parallel lines, that arrangement, like some form in a picture, unseen and accidentally developed, struck suddenly, inevitably, on the sight. It had literally not been seen before. It flashed out in an instant, as an independent form. It became a feature of the work. The architect took it under his care, thought over it, and distributed its members as we see.

Now, the great pause was at the moment when the space and the dividing stone-work were both equally considered. It did not last fifty years. The forms of the tracery were seized with a childish delight in the novel source of beauty; and the intervening space was cast aside, as an element of decoration, for ever. ...

The reader will observe that, up to the last expansion of the penetrations, the stone-work was necessarily considered, as it actually is, *stiff,* and unyielding. It was so, also, during the pause of which I have spoken, when the forms of the tracery were still severe and pure; delicate indeed, but perfectly firm.

At the close of the period of pause, the first sign of serious change was like a low breeze, passing through the emaciated tracery, and making it tremble. It began to undulate like the threads of a cobweb lifted by the wind. It lost its essence as a structure of stone. Reduced to the slenderness of threads, it began to be considered as possessing also their flexibility. The architect was pleased with this his new fancy, and set himself to carry it out; and in a little time, the bars of tracery were caused to appear to the eye as if they had been woven together like a net. This

72

was a change which sacrificed a great principle of truth; it sacrificed the expression of the qualities of the material; and however delightful its results in their first developments, it was ultimately ruinous.

For, observe the difference between the supposition of ductility, and that of elastic structure noticed above in the resemblance to tree form. That resemblance was not sought, but necessary; it resulted from the natural conditions of strength in the pier or trunk, and slenderness in the ribs or branches, while many of the other suggested conditions of resemblance were perfectly true. A tree branch, though in a certain sense flexible, is not ductile; it is as firm in its own form as the rib of stone; both of them will yield up to certain limits, both of them breaking when those limits are exceeded; while the tree trunk will bend no more than the stone pillar. But when the tracery is assumed to be as yielding as a silken cord; when the whole fragility, elasticity, and weight of the material are to the eye, if not in terms, denied; when all the art of the architect is applied to disprove the first conditions of his working, and the first attributes of his materials; *this* is a deliberate treachery, only redeemed from the charge of direct falsehood by the visibility of the stone surface, and degrading all the traceries it affects exactly in the degree of its presence.

But the declining and morbid taste of the later architects was not satisfied with this much deception. They were delighted with the subtle charm they had created, and thought only of increasing its power. The next step was to consider and represent the tracery, as not only ductile, but penetrable; and when two mouldings met each other, to manage their intersection, so that one should appear to pass through the other, retaining its independence; or when two ran parallel to each other, to represent the one as partly contained within the other, and partly apparent above it. This form of falsity was that which crushed the art. The flexible traceries were often beautiful, though they were ignoble; but the penetrated traceries, rendered, as they finally were, merely the means of exhibiting the dexterity of the stone-cutter, annihilated both the beauty and dignity of the Gothic types.

The Seven Lamps of Architecture, Ch. 2

. . . Of the many broad divisions under which architecture may be considered, none appear to me more

73

significant than that into buildings, whose interest is in their walls and those whose interest is in the lines dividing their walls. In the Greek temple the wall is as nothing; the entire interest is in the detached columns and the frieze they bear; in French Flamboyant, and in our detestable Perpendicular, the object is to get rid of the wall surface, and keep the eye altogether on tracery of line: in Romanesque work and Egyptian, the wall is a confessed and honoured member, and the light is often allowed to fall on large areas of it, variously decorated. Now, both these principles are admitted by Nature, the one in her woods and thickets, the other in her plains, and cliffs, and waters; but the latter is pre-eminently the principle of power, and, in some sense, of beauty also. For, whatever infinity of fair form there may be in the maze of the forest, there is a fairer, as I think, in the surface of the quiet lake; and I hardly know that association of shaft or tracery, for which I would exchange the warm sleep of sunshine on some smooth, broad, human-like front of marble. Nevertheless, if breadth is to be beautiful, its substance must in some sort be beautiful; and we must not hastily condemn the exclusive resting of the northern architects in divided lines, until at least we have remembered the difference between a blank surface of Caen stone, and one mixed from Genoa and Carrara, of serpentine with snow; but as regards abstract power and awfulness, there is no question; without breadth of surface it is in vain to seek them, and it matters little, so that the surface be wide, bold, and unbroken, whether it be of brick or of jasper; the light of heaven upon it, and the weight of earth in it, are all we need: for it is singular how forgetful the mind may become both of material and workmanship, if only it have space enough over which to range, and to remind it, however feebly, of the joy that it has in contemplating the flatness and sweep of great plains and broad seas. And it is a noble thing for men to do this with their cut stone or moulded clay, and to make the face of a wall look infinite, and its edge against the sky like an horizon: or even if less than this be reached, it is still delightful to mark the play of passing light on its broad surface, and to see by how many artifices and gradations of tinting and shadow, time and storm will set their wild signatures upon it; and how in the rising or declining of the day the unbroken twilight rests long and luridly on its high lineless forehead, and fades away untraceably down its tiers of confused and countless stone.

Now, it does not seem to me sufficiently recollected, that a wall surface is to an architect simply what a white canvas is to a painter, with this only difference, that the wall was already a sublimity in its height, substance, and other characters . . . , on which it is more dangerous to break than to touch with shade the canvas surface, and, for my part, I think a smooth broad, freshly laid surface of gesso a fairer thing than most pictures I see painted on it; much more, a noble surface of stone than most architectural features which it is caused to assume. . . .

Positive shade is a more necessary and more sublime thing in an architect's hands than in a painter's. For the latter being able to temper his light with an undertone throughout, and to make it delightful with sweet colour, or awful with lurid colour, and to represent distance, and air, and sun, by the depth of it, and fill its whole space with expression, can deal with an enormous, nay, almost with an universal, extent of it, and the best painters most delight in such extent; but as light, with the architect, is nearly always liable to become full and untempered sunshine seen upon solid surface, his only rests, and his chief means of sublimity, are definite shades. So that, after size and weight, the Power of architecture may be said to depend on the quantity (whether measured in space or intenseness) of its shadow; and it seems to me, that the reality of its works, and the use and influence they have in the daily life of men, (as opposed to those works of art with which we have nothing to do but in times of rest or of pleasure,) require of it that it should express a kind of human sympathy, by a measure of darkness as great as there is in human life: and that as the great poem and great fiction generally affect us most by the majesty of their masses of shade, and cannot take hold upon us if they affect a continuance of lyric sprightliness, but must be often serious, and sometimes melancholy, else they do not express the truth of this wild world of ours; so there must be, in this magnificently human art of architecture, some equivalent expression for the trouble and wrath of life, for its sorrow and its mystery: and this it can only give by depth or diffusion of gloom, by the frown upon its front, and the shadow of its recess. So that Rembrandtism is a noble manner in architecture, though a false one in painting; and I do not believe that ever any building was truly great, unless it had mighty masses, vigorous and deep, of shadow mingled with its surface. And among the first habits that a young architect should learn, is that of thinking in shadow, not looking at a design in its miserably liny skeleton; but conceiving it as it will be when the dawn lights it, and the dusk leaves it; when its stones will be hot, and its crannies cool; when the lizards will bask on the one, and the birds build in the other. Let him design with the sense of cold and heat upon him; let him cut out the shadows, as men dig wells in unwatered plains; and lead along the lights, as a founder does his hot metal; let him keep the full command of both, and see that he knows how they fall, and where they fade. His paper lines and proportions are of no value: all that he has to do must be done by spaces of light and darkness; and his business is to see that the one is broad and bold enough not to be swallowed up by twilight, and the other deep enough not to be dried like a shallow pool by a noon-day sun.

... I know not how it is, unless that our English hearts have more oak than stone in them, and have more filial sympathy with acorns than Alps; but all that we do is small and mean, if not worse—thin, and wasted, and unsubstantial. It is not modern work only; we have built like frogs and mice since the thirteenth century (except only in our castles). What a contrast between the pitiful little pigeon-holes which stand for doors in the cast front of Salisbury, looking like the entrances to a beehive or a wasp's nest, and the soaring arches and kingly crowning of the gates of Abbeville, Rouen, and Rheims, or the rock-hewn piers of Chartres, or the dark and vaulted porches and writhed pillars of Verona! Of domestic architecture what need is there to speak? How small, how cramped, how poor, how miserable in its petty neatness is our best! how beneath the mark of attack, and the level of contempt, that which is common with us! What a strange sense of formalised deformity, of shrivelled precision, of starved accuracy, of minute misanthropy have we, as we leave even the rude streets of Picardy for the market towns of Kent! Until that street architecture of ours is bettered, until we give it some size and boldness, until we give our windows recess, and our walls thickness, I know not how we can blame our architects for their feebleness in more important work; their eyes are inured to narrowness and slightness: can we expect them at a word to conceive and deal with breadth and solidity? They ought not to live in our cities; there is that in their miserable walls which bricks up to death men's imaginations, as surely as ever perished forsworn nun. An architect should live as little in cities as a painter. Send him to our hills, and let him study there what nature understands by a buttress, and what by a dome. There was something in the old power of architecture, which it had from the recluse more than from the citizen. The buildings of which I have spoken with chief praise, rose, indeed, out of the war of the piazza, and above the fury of the populace: and Heaven forbid that for such cause we should ever have to lay a larger stone, or rivet a firmer bar, in our England! But we have other sources of power, in the imagery of our iron coasts and azure hills; of power more pure, nor less serene, than that of the hermit spirit which once lighted with white lines of cloisters the glades of the Alpine pine, and raised into ordered spires the wild rocks of the Norman sea; which gave to the temple gate the depth and darkness of Elijah's Horeb cave; and lifted, out of the populous city, grey cliffs of lonely stone, into the midst of sailing birds and silent air.

The Seven Lamps of Architecture, Ch. 3

Hence then a general law, of singular importance in the present day, a law of simple common sense,—not to decorate things belonging to purposes of active and occupied life. Wherever you can rest, there decorate; where rest is forbidden, so is beauty. You must not mix ornament with business any more than you may mix play. Work first, and then rest. Work first, and then gaze, but do not use golden ploughshares, nor bind ledgers in enamel. Do not thrash with sculptured flails: nor put bas-reliefs on millstones. What! it will be asked, are we in the habit of doing so? Even so; always and everywhere. The most familiar position of Greek mouldings is in these days on shop fronts. There is not a tradesman's sign nor shelf nor counter in all the streets of all our cities, which has not upon it ornaments which were invented to adorn temples and beautify kings' palaces. There is not the smallest advantage in them where they are. Absolutely valueless—utterly without the power of giving pleasure, they only satiate the eye, and vulgarize their own forms. Many of these are in themselves thoroughly good copies of fine things, which things themselves we shall never, in consequence, enjoy any more. Many a pretty beading and graceful bracket there is in wood, or stucco above our grocers' and cheesemongers' and hosiers' shops: how is it that the tradesmen cannot understand that custom is to be had only by selling good tea and cheese and cloth, and the people come to them for their honesty, and their readiness, and their right wares, and not because they have Greek cornices over their windows, or their names in large gilt letters on their house fronts? How pleasurable it would be to have the power of going through the streets of London, pulling down those brackets and friezes and large names, restoring to the tradesmen the capital they had spent in architecture, and putting them on honest and equal terms, each with his name in black letters over his door, not shouted down the street from the upper storeys, and each with a plain wooden shop casement, with small panes in it that people would not think of breaking in order to be sent to prison! How much better for them would it be—how much happier, how much wiser, to put their trust upon their own truth and industry, and not on the idiocy of their customers. It is curious, and it says little for our national probity on the one hand, or prudence on the other, to see the whole system of our street decorations based on the idea that people must be baited to a shop as moths are to a candle. . . .

Another of the strange and evil tendencies of the present day is to the decoration of the railroad station. Now, if there be any place in the world in which people are deprived of that portion of temper and discretion which is necessary to the contemplation of beauty, it is there. It is the very temple of discomfort, and the only charity that the builder can extend to us is to show us, plainly as may be, how soonest to escape from it. The whole system of railroad travelling is addressed to people who, being in a hurry, are therefore, for the time being, miserable. No one would travel in that manner who could help it—who had time to go leisurely over hills and between hedges, instead of through tunnels and between banks: at least, those who would, have no sense of beauty so acute as that we need consult it at the station. The railroad is in all its relations a matter of earnest business, to be got through as soon as possible. It transmutes a man from a traveller into a living parcel. For the time he has parted with the nobler characteristics of his humanity for the sake of a planetary power of locomotion. Do not ask him to admire anything. You might as well ask the wind. Carry him safely, dismiss him soon: he will thank you for nothing else. All attempts to please him in any other way are mere mockery, and insults to the things by which you endeavour to do so. There never was more flagrant nor impertinent folly than the smallest portion of ornament in anything concerned with railroads or near them. Keep

them out of the way, take them through the ugliest country you can find, confess them but the miserable things
they are, and spend nothing upon them but for safety and
speed. Give large salaries to efficient servants, large prices
to good manufacturers, large wages to able workmen; let
the iron be tough, and the brickwork solid, and the carriages strong. The time is perhaps not distant when these
first necessities may not be easily met: and to increase
expense in any other direction is madness. Better bury
gold in the embankments than put it in ornaments on the
stations. Will a single traveller be willing to pay an
increased fare on the South Western, because the columns
of the terminus are covered with patterns from Nineveh?—
he will only care less for the Ninevite ivories in the British
Museum: or on the North Western, because there are old
English-looking spandrels to the roof of the station at
Crewe? he will only have less pleasure in their prototypes
at Crewe House. Railroad architecture has, or would
have, a dignity of its own if it were only left to its work.
You would not put rings on the fingers of a smith at his
anvil.

The Seven Lamps of Architecture, Ch. 4

Frankness . . . is in itself no excuse for repetition, nor
Audacity for innovation, when the one is indolent, and the
other unwise. Nobler and surer signs of vitality must be
sought,—signs independent alike of the decorative or
original character of the style, and constant in every style
that is determinedly progressive.

Of these, one of the most important I believe to be a
certain neglect or contempt of refinement in execution, or,
at all events, a visible subordination of execution to conception commonly involuntary, but not unfrequently inten-
tional. . . . I would insist upon perfect and most delicate
finish in its right place as a characteristic of all the highest
schools of architecture, as much as it is of those of
painting. But on the other hand, as perfect finish belongs
to the perfected art, a progressive finish belongs to progressive art; and I do not think that any more fatal sign of
a stupor or numbness settling upon that undeveloped art
could possibly be detected, than that it had been *taken
aback* by its own execution, and that the workmanship
had gone ahead of the design; while, even in my admission
of absolute finish in the right place, as an attribute of the

perfected school, I must reserve tō myself the right of answering in my own way the two very important questions—what is finish? and what *is* its right place?

But in illustrating either of these points, we must remember that the correspondence of workmanship with thought is, in existent examples, interfered with by the adoption of the designs of an advanced period by the workmen of a rude one. All the beginnings of Christian architecture are of this kind, and the necessary consequence is of course an increase of the visible interval between the power of realization and the beauty of the idea. We have at first an intimation, almost savage in its rudeness, of a classical design; as the art advances, the design is modified by a mixture of Gothic grotesqueness, and the execution more complete, until a harmony is established between the two, in which balance they advance to new perfection. Now during the whole period in which the ground is being recovered, there will be found in the living architecture marks, not to be mistaken, of intense impatience; a struggle towards something unattained, which causes all minor points of handling to be neglected; and a restless disdain of all qualities which appear either to confess contentment, or to require a time and care which might be better spent. And, exactly as a good and earnest student of drawing will not lose time in ruling lines or finishing backgrounds about studies which, while they have answered his immediate purpose, he knows to be imperfect and inferior to what he will do hereafter,—so the vigour of a true school of early architecture, which is either working under the influence of high example or which is itself in a state of rapid development, is very curiously traceable, among other signs, in the contempt of exact symmetry and measurement, which in dead architecture are the most painful necessities.

. . . I think that impatience is a glorious character in an advancing school: and I love the Romanesque and early Gothic especially, because they afford so much room for it; accidental carelessness of measurement or of execution being mingled undistinguishably with the purposed departures from symmetrical regularity, and the luxuriousness of perpetually variable fancy, which are eminently characteristic of both styles. How great, how frequent they are, and how brightly the severity of architectural law is relieved by their grace and suddenness, has not, I think, been enough observed; still less, the unequal measurements of even important features professing to be absolutely symmetrical. I am not so familiar with modern practice as to speak with confidence respecting its ordinary precision; but I imagine that the following measures of the western front of the cathedral of Pisa, would be looked upon by present architects as very blundering approximations. That front is divided into seven arched compartments, of which the second, fourth or central, and sixth contain doors; the seven are in a most subtle alternating proportion; the central being the largest, next to it the second and sixth, then the first and seventh, lastly the third and fifth. By this arrangement, of course, these three pairs should be equal; and they are so to the eye, but I found their actual measures to be the following, taken from pillar to pillar; in Italian braccia, palmi (four inches each), and inches:

	Braccia	Palmi	Inches		Total in inches
1. Central door	8	0	0	=	192
2. Northern door ⎞	6	3	1½	=	157½
3. Southern door ⎠	6	4	3	=	163
4. Extreme northern space ⎞	5	5	3½	=	143½
5. Extreme southern space ⎠	6	1	0½	=	148½
6. Northern intervals between the doors ⎰	5	2	1	=	129
7. Southern intervals between the doors ⎱	5	2	1½	=	129½

There is thus a difference, severally, between 2, 3 and 4, 5 of five inches and a half in the one case, and five inches in the other. . . .

There is another very curious instance of distortion above the central door of the west front. All the intervals between the seven arches are filled with black marble, each containing in its centre a white parallelogram filled with animal mosaics, and the whole surmounted by a broad white band, which, generally, does not touch the parallelogram below. But the parallelogram on the north of the central arch has been forced into an oblique position, and touches the white band; and, as if the architect was determined to show that he did not care whether it did or not, the white band suddenly gets thicker at that place, and remains so over the next two arches. And these differences are the more curious because the workmanship of them all is most finished and masterly, and the distorted stones are fitted with as much neatness as if they tallied to a hair's breadth. There is no look of slurring or blundering about it; it is all coolly filled in, as if the builder had no

81

sense of anything being wrong or extraordinary; I only wish we had a little of his impudence.

Still, the reader will say that all these variations are probably dependent more on the bad foundation than on the architect's feelings. Not so the exquisite delicacies of change in the proportions and dimensions of the apparently symmetrical arcades of the west front. It will be remembered that I said the tower of Pisa was the only ugly tower in Italy, because its tiers were equal, or nearly so, in height, a fault this, so contrary to the spirit of the builders of the time, that it can be considered only as an unlucky caprice. Perhaps the general aspect of the west front of the cathedral may then have occurred to the reader's mind, as seemingly another contradiction of the rule I had advanced. It would not have been so, however, even had its four upper arcades been actually equal; as they are subordinated to the great seven-arched lower storey, in the manner before noticed respecting the spire of Salisbury, and as is actually the case in the Duomo of Lucca and Tower of Pistoja. But the Pisan front is far more subtly proportioned. Not one of its four arcades is of like height with another. The highest is the third, counting upwards; and they diminish in nearly arithmetical proportion alternately; in the order 3rd, 1st, 2nd, 4th. The inequalities in their arches are not less remarkable: they at first strike the eye as all equal; but there is a grace about them which equality never obtained: on closer observation, it is perceived that in the first row of nineteen arches, eighteen are equal, and the central one larger than the rest; in the second arcade, the nine central arches stand over the nine below, having, like them, the ninth central one largest. But on their flanks, where is the slope of the shoulder-like pediment, the arches vanish, and a wedge-shaped frieze takes their place, tapering outwards, in order to allow the columns to be carried to the extremity of the pediment; and here, where the heights of the shafts are so fast shortened, they are set thicker; five shafts, or rather four and a capital, above, to four of the arcade below, giving twenty-one intervals instead of nineteen. In the next or third arcade,—which, remember, is the highest, eight arches, all equal, are given in the space of the nine below, so that there is now a central shaft instead of a central arch and the span of the arches is increased in proportion to their increased height. Finally, in the uppermost arcade, which is the lowest of all, the arches, the same in number as those below, are narrower than any of the façade; and the whole eight going very nearly above the six below them, while the terminal arches of the lower arcade are surmounted by flanking masses of decorated wall with projecting figures.

Now I call *that* Living Architecture. There is sensation in every inch of it, and an accommodation to every architectural necessity, with a determined variation in arrangement, which is exactly like the related proportions and provisions in the structure of organic form. . . .

I believe the right question to ask, respecting all ornament, is simply this: Was it done with enjoyment—was the carver happy while he was about it? It may be the hardest work possible, and the harder because so much pleasure was taken in it; but it must have been happy too, or it will not be living. How much of the stone mason's toil this condition would exclude I hardly venture to consider, but the condition is absolute. There is a Gothic church lately built near Rouen, vile enough, indeed, in its general composition, but excessively rich in detail; many of the details are designed with taste, and all evidently by a man who has studied old work closely. But it is all as dead as leaves in December; there is not one tender touch, not one warm stroke on the whole façade. The men who did it hated it, and were thankful when it was done. And so long as they do so they are merely loading your walls with shapes of clay: the garlands of everlastings in Père la Chaise are more cheerful ornaments. You cannot get the feeling by paying for it—money will not buy life. I am not sure even that you can get it by watching or waiting for it. It is true that here and there a workman may be found who has it in him, but he does not rest contented in the inferior work—he struggles forward into an Academician; and from the mass of available handicraftsmen the power is gone—how recoverable I know not: this only I know, that all expense devoted to sculptural ornament, in the present condition of that power, comes literally under the head of Sacrifice for the sacrifice's sake, or worse, I believe the only manner of rich ornament that is open to us is the geometrical colour-mosaic, and that much might result from our strenuously taking up this mode of design. But, at all events, one thing we have in our power—the doing without machine ornament and cast-iron work. All the stamped metals, and artificial stones, and imitation woods and bronzes, over the invention of which we hear daily exultation—all the short, and cheap, and easy ways of doing that whose difficulty is its honour—are just so many new obstacles in our already encumbered road. They will not make one of us happier or wiser—they will extend neither the pride of judgment nor the privilege of enjoyment. They will only make us shallower in our understandings, colder in our hearts, and feebler in our wits. And most justly. For we are not sent into this world to do any thing into which we cannot put our hearts.

We have certain work to do for our bread, and that is to be done strenuously; other work to do for our delight, and that is to be done heartily: neither is to be done by halves and shifts, but with a will; and what is not worth this effort is not to be done at all. Perhaps all that we have to do is meant for nothing more than an exercise of the heart and of the will, and is useless in itself; but, at all events, the little use it has may well be spared if it is not worth putting our hands and our strength to. It does not become our immortality to take an ease inconsistent with its authority, nor to suffer any instruments with which it can dispense, to come between it and the things it rules; and he who would form the creations of his own mind by any other instrument than his own hand, would also, if he might, give grinding organs to Heaven's angels, to make their music easier. There is dreaming enough, and earthiness enough, and sensuality enough in human existence, without our burning the few glowing moments of it into mechanism; and since our life must at the best be but a vapour that appears for a little time and then vanishes away, let it at least appear as a cloud in the height of Heaven, not as the thick darkness that broods over the blast of the Furnace, and rolling of the Wheel.

The Seven Lamps of Architecture, Ch. 5

Among the hours of his life to which the writer looks back with peculiar gratitude, as having been marked by more than ordinary fulness of joy or clearness of teaching, is one passed, now some years ago, near time of sunset, among the broken masses of pine forest which skirt the course of the Ain, above the village of Champagnole, in the Jura. It is a spot which has all the solemnity, with none of the savageness, of the Alps; where there is a sense of a great power beginning to be manifested in the earth, and of a deep and majestic concord in the rise of the long low lines of piny hills; the first utterance of those mighty mountain symphonies, soon to be more loudly lifted and wildly broken along the battlements of the Alps. But their

strength is as yet restrained; and the far reaching ridges of
pastoral mountain succeed each other, like the long and
sighing swell which moves over quiet water from some far
off stormy sea. And there is a deep tenderness pervading
that vast monotony. The destructive forces and the stern
expression of the central ranges are alike withdrawn. No
frost-ploughed, dust-encumbered paths of ancient glacier
fret the soft Jura pastures; no splintered heaps of ruin
break the fair ranks of her forest; no pale, defiled, or
furious rivers send their rude and changeful ways among
her rocks. Patiently, eddy by eddy, the clear green streams
wind along their well-known beds; and under the dark
quietness of the undisturbed pines, there spring up, year
by year, such company of joyful flowers as I know not the
like of among all the blessings of the earth. It was
spring time, too; and all were coming forth in clusters
crowded for very love; there was room enough for all, but
they crushed their leaves into all manner of strange shapes
only to be nearer each other. There was the wood anem-
one, star after star, closing every now and then into
nebulae; and there was the oxalis, troop by troop, like
virginal processions of the Mois de Marie, the dark vertical clefts in the limestone choked with them as with heavy
snow, and touched with ivy on the edges—ivy as light and
lovely as the vine; and, ever and anon, a blue gush of
violets, and cowslip bells in sunny places; and in the more
open ground, the vetch, and comfrey, and mezereon, and
the small sapphire buds of the Polygala Alpina, and the
wild strawberry, just a blossom or two, all showered amidst
the golden softness of deep, warm, amber-coloured moss.
I came out presently on the edge of the ravine: the
solemn murmur of its waters rose suddenly from beneath,
mixed with the singing of the thrushes among the pine
boughs; and, on the opposite side of the valley, walled all
along as it was by grey cliffs of limestone, there was a hawk
sailing slowly off their brow, touching them nearly with his
wings, and with the shadows of the pines flickering upon
his plumage from above; but with the fall of a hundred
fathoms under his breast, and the curling pools of the
green river gliding and glittering dizzily beneath him, their
foam globes moving with him as he flew. It would be
difficult to conceive a scene less dependent upon any other
interest than that of its own secluded and serious beauty;
but the writer well remembers the sudden blankness and
chill which were cast upon it when he endeavoured, in
order more strictly to arrive at the sources of its impressiveness, to imagine it, for a moment, a scene in some

aboriginal forest of the New Continent. The flowers in an instant lost their light, the river its music; the hills became oppressively desolate; a heaviness in the boughs of the darkened forest showed how much of their former power had been dependent upon a life which was not theirs, how much of the glory of the imperishable, or continually renewed, creation is reflected from things more precious in their memories than it, in its renewing. Those ever springing flowers and ever flowing streams had been dyed by the deep colours of human endurance, valour and virtue; and the crests of the sable hills that rose against the evening sky received a deeper worship, because their far shadows fell eastward over the iron wall of Joux, and the four-square keep of Granson. . . .

. . . Neither by the public, nor by those who have the care of public monuments, is the true meaning of the ward *restoration* understood. It means the most total destruction which a building can suffer: a destruction out of which no remnants can be gathered: a destruction accompanied with false description of the thing destroyed. Do not let us deceive ourselves in this important matter; it is *impossible,* as impossible as to raise the dead, to restore anything that has ever been great or beautiful in architecture. That which I have above insisted upon as the life of the whole, that spirit which is given only by the hand and eye of the workman, can never be recalled. Another spirit may be given by another time, and it is then a new building; but the spirit of the dead workman cannot be summoned up, and commanded to direct other hands, and other thoughts. And as for direct and simple copying, it is palpably impossible. What copying can there be of surfaces that have been worn half an inch down? The whole finish of the work was in the half inch that is gone; if you attempt to restore that finish, you do it conjecturally; if you copy what is left, granting fidelity to be possible (and what care, or watchfulness, or cost can secure it,) how is the new work better than the old? There was yet in the old *some* life, some mysterious suggestion of what it had been, and of what it had lost, some sweetness in the gentle lines which rain and sun had wrought. There can be none in the brute hardness of the new carving. . . .

Do not let us talk then of restoration. The thing is a Lie from beginning to end. You may make a model of a building as you may of a corpse, and your model may have the shell of the old walls within it as your cast might have the skeleton, with what advantage I neither see nor care: but the old building is destroyed, and that more totally and mercilessly than if it had sunk into a heap of dust, or melted into a mass of clay: more has been gleaned out of desolated Nineveh than ever will be out of re-built Milan. But, it is said, there may come a necessity for restoration! Granted. Look the necessity full in the face, and understand it on its own terms. It is a necessity for destruction. Accept it as such, pull the building down, throw its stones into neglected corners, make ballast of them, or mortar, if you will; but do it honestly, and do not set up a Lie in their place. And look that necessity in the face before it comes, and you may prevent it. The principle of modern times (a principle which, I believe, at least in France, to be *systematically acted on by the masons,* in order to find themselves work, as the abbey of St. Ouen was pulled down by the magistrates of the town by way of giving work to some vagrants), is to neglect buildings first, and restore them afterwards. Take proper care of your monuments, and you will not need to restore them. A few sheets of lead put in time upon a roof, a few dead leaves and sticks swept in time out of a water-course, will save both roof and walls from ruin. Watch an old building with an anxious care; guard it as best you may, and at *any* cost, from every influence of dilapidation. Count its stones as you would jewels of a crown; set watches about it as if at the gates of a besieged city; bind it together with iron where it loosens; stay it with timber where it declines; do not care about the unsightliness of the aid: better a crutch than a lost limb; and do this tenderly, and reverently, and continually, and many a generation will still be born and pass away beneath its shadow. Its evil day must come at last; but let it come declaredly and openly and let no dishonouring and false substitute deprive it of the funeral offices of memory.

The Seven Lamps of Architecture, Ch. 6

The Architecture of a nation is great only when it is as universal and as established as its language; and when provincial differences of style are nothing more than so many dialects. Other necessities are matters of doubt: nations have been alike successful in their architecture in times of poverty and of wealth; in times of war and peace; in times of barbarism and of refinement; under governments the most liberal or the most arbitrary; but this one condition has been constant, this one requirement clear in all places and at all times, that the work shall be that of a *school*, that no individual caprice shall dispense with, or materially vary, accepted types and customary decorations; and that from the cottage to the palace, and from the chapel to the basilica, and from the garden fence to the fortress wall, every member and feature of the architecture of the nation shall be as commonly current, as frankly accepted, as its language or its coin. . . .

We want no new style of architecture. Who wants a new style of painting or sculpture? but we want *some* style. It is of marvellously little importance, if we have a code of laws and they be good laws, whether they be new or old, foreign or native, Roman or Saxon, or Norman, or English laws. But it is of considerable importance that we should have a code of laws of one kind or another, and that code accepted and enforced from one side of the island to another, and not one law made ground of judgment at York and another in Exeter. And in like manner it does not matter one marble splinter whether we have an old or new architecture, but it matters everything whether we have an architecture truly so called or not; that is, whether an architecture whose laws might be taught at our schools from Cornwall to Northumberland, as we teach English spelling and English grammar, or an architecture which is to be invented fresh every time we build a workhouse or a parish school. . . . Originality in expression does not depend on invention of new words; nor originality in poetry on invention of new measures; nor, in painting, on invention of new colours, or new modes of using them. . . . Originality depends on nothing of the kind. A man who has the gift, will take up any style that is going, the style of his day, and will work in that, and be great in that, and make everything that he does in it look as fresh as if every thought of it had just come down from heaven. I do not say that he will not take liberties with his materials, or with his rules: I do not say that strange changes will not sometimes be wrought by his efforts, or his fancies, in both. But those changes will be instructive, natural, facile, though sometimes marvellous; they will never be sought after as things necessary to his dignity or to his independence; and those liberties will be like the liberties that a great speaker takes with the language, not a defiance of its rules for the sake of singularity; but inevitable, uncalculated, and brilliant consequences of an effort to express what the language, without such infraction, could not.

The Seven Lamps of Architecture, Ch. 7

I found, after carefully investigating the character of the emotions which were generally felt by well-educated people respecting various forms of good architecture, that these emotions might be separated into four general heads:

1. Sentimental Admiration.—The kind of feeling which most travellers experience on first entering a cathedral by torchlight, and hearing a chant from concealed choristers; or in visiting a ruined abbey by moonlight, or any building with which interesting associations are connected, at any time when they can hardly see it.

2. Proud Admiration.—The delight which most worldly people take in showy, large or complete buildings, for the sake of the importance which such buildings confer on themselves, as their possessors, or admirers.

3. Workmanly Admiration.—The delight of seeing good and neat masonry, together with that belonging to incipient developments of taste; as, for instance, a perception of proportion in lines, masses, and mouldings.

4. Artistical and Rational Admiration.—The delight taken in reading the sculpture or painting on walls, capitals, friezes, etc. . . .

I found, finally, that this, the only admiration worth having, attached itself *wholly* to the meaning of the sculpture and colour on the building. That it was very regardless of general form and size; but intensely observant of the statuary, floral mouldings, mosaics, and other decorations. Upon which, little by little, it gradually became manifest to me that the sculpture and painting were, in fact, the all in all of the thing to be done; that these, which I had long been in the careless habit of thinking subordinate to the architecture, were in fact the entire masters of the architecture; and that the architect who was not a sculptor or a painter, was nothing better than a frame-maker on a large scale. Having once got this clue to the truth, every question about architecture immediately settled itself without further difficulty. I saw that the idea of an independent architectural profession was a mere modern fallacy, the thought of which had never so much as entered the heads of the great nations of earlier times; but that it had always, till lately, been understood, that in order to have a Parthenon, one had to get a preliminary Phidias; and to have a Cathedral of Florence, a preliminary Giotto; and to have even a Saint Peter's at Rome, a preliminary Michael Angelo. And as, with this new light, I examined the nobler examples of our Gothic cathedrals, it became apparent to me that the master workman must have been the person who carved the bas-reliefs in the porches; that to him all others must have been subordinate, and by him all the rest of the cathedral essentially arranged; but that in fact the whole company of builders, always large, were more or less divided into two great flocks of stone-layers, and sculptors; and that the number of sculptors was so great, and their average talent so considerable, that it would no more have been thought necessary to state respecting the master builder that he could carve a statue, than that he could measure an angle, or strike a curve.

If the reader will think over this statement carefully he will find that it is indeed true, and a key to many things. The fact is, there are only two fine arts possible to the human race, sculpture and painting. What we call architecture is only the association of these in noble masses, or the placing of them in fit places. All architecture other than this is, in fact, mere building; and though it may sometimes be graceful, as in the groinings of an abbey roof; or sublime, as in the battlement of a border tower; there is, in such examples of it, no more exertion of the powers of high art, than in the gracefulness of a well-ordered chamber, or the nobleness of a well-built ship of war.

All high art consists in the carving or painting natural objects, chiefly figures: it has always subject and meaning, never consisting solely in arrangement of lines, or even of colours. It always paints or carves something that it sees or believes in; nothing ideal or uncredited. For the most part, it paints and carves the men and things that are visible around it. And as soon as we possess a body of sculptors able, and willing, and having leave from the English public, to carve on the façades of our cathedrals portraits of the living bishops, deans, canons, and choristers, who are to minister in the said cathedrals; and on the façades of our public buildings, portraits of the men chiefly moving or acting in the same; and on our buildings, generally, the birds and flowers which are singing and budding in the fields around them, we shall have a school of English architecture. Not till then.

The Seven Lamps of Architecture, Preface to 2nd ed.

The Stones of Venice
(Volume II)
(1853)

In the olden days of travelling, now to return no more,
in which distance could not be vanquished without toil,
but in which that toil was rewarded, partly by the power
of deliberate survey of the countries through which the
journey lay, and partly by the happiness of the evening
hours, when from the top of the last hill he had surmounted, the traveller beheld the quiet village where he
was to rest, scattered among the meadows beside its valley
stream; or, from the long hoped for turn in the dusty
perspective of the causeway, saw, for the first time, the
towers of some famed city, faint in the rays of sunset—
hours of peaceful and thoughtful pleasure, for which the
rush of the arrival in the railway station is perhaps not
always, or to all men, an equivalent,—in those days, I say,
when there was something more to be anticipated and
remembered in the first aspect of each successive halting-
place, than a new arrangement of glass roofing and iron
girder, there were few moments of which the recollection
was more fondly cherished by the traveller, than that
which, as I endeavoured to describe in the close of the last
chapter, brought him within sight of Venice, as his gondola shot into the open lagoon from the canal of Mestre.
Not but that the aspect of the city itself was generally the
source of some slight disappointment, for, seen in this
direction, its buildings are far less characteristic than those
of the other great towns of Italy; but this inferiority was
partly disguised by distance, and more than atoned for by
the strange rising of its walls and towers out of the midst,
as it seemed, of the deep sea, for it was impossible that
the mind or the eye could at once comprehend the shal-
lowness of the vast sheet of water which stretched away in

leagues of rippling lustre to the north and south, or trace the narrow line of islets bounding it to the east. The salt breeze, the white moaning sea-birds, the masses of black weed separating and disappearing gradually, in knots of heaving shoal, under the advance of the steady tide, all proclaimed it to be indeed the ocean on whose bosom the great city rested so calmly; not such blue, soft, lake-like ocean as bathes the Neapolitan promontories, or sleeps beneath the marble rocks of Genoa, but a sea with the bleak power of our own northern waves, yet subdued into a strange spacious rest, and changed from its angry pallor into a field of burnished gold, as the sun declined behind the belfry tower of the lonely island church, fitly named "St. George of the Seaweed." As the boat drew nearer to the city, the coast which the traveller had just left sank behind him into one long, low, sad-coloured line, tufted irregularly with brushwood and willows: but, at what seemed its northern extremity, the hills of Arqua rose in a dark cluster of purple pyramids, balanced on the bright mirage of the lagoon; two or three smooth surges of inferior hill extended themselves about their roots, and beyond these, beginning with the craggy peaks above Vicenza, the chain of the Alps girded the whole horizon to the north—a wall of jagged blue, here and there showing through its clefts a wilderness of misty precipices, fading far back into the recesses of Cadore, and itself rising and breaking away eastward, where the sun struck opposite upon its snow, into mighty fragments of peaked light, standing up behind the barred clouds of evening, one after another, countless, the crown of the Adrian Sea, until the eye turned back from pursuing them, to rest upon the nearer burning of the campaniles of Murano, and on the great city, where it magnified itself along the waves, as the quick silent pacing of the gondola drew nearer and nearer. And at last, when its walls were reached, and the outmost of its untrodden streets was entered, not through towered gate or guarded rampart, but as a deep inlet between two rocks of coral in the Indian Sea; when first upon the traveller's sight opened the long ranges of columned palaces,—each with its black boat moored at the portal,—each with its image cast down, beneath its feet, upon that green pavement which every breeze broke into new fantasies of rich tessellation; when first, at the extremity of the bright vista, the shadowy Rialto threw its colossal curve slowly forth from behind the palace of the Camerlenghi; that strange curve, so delicate, so adamantine, strong as a mountain cavern,

92

graceful as a bow just bent; when first, before its moonlike circumference was all risen, the gondolier's cry, "Ah! Stalź," struck sharp upon the ear, and the prow turned aside under the mighty cornices that half met over the narrow canal, where the plash of the water followed close and loud, ringing along the marble by the boat's side; and when at last that boat darted forth upon the breadth of silver sea, across which the front of the Ducal Palace, flushed with its sanguine veins, looks to the snowy dome of Our Lady of Salvation, it was no marvel that the mind should be so deeply entranced by the visionary charm of a scene so beautiful and so strange, as to forget the darker truths of its history and its being. Well might it seem that such a city had owed her existence rather to the rod of the enchanter, than the fear of the fugitive; that the waters which encircled her had been chosen for the mirror of her state, rather than the shelter of her nakedness; and that all which in nature was wild or merciless,—Time and Decay, as well as the waves and tempests,—had been won to adorn her instead of to destroy, and might still spare, for ages to come, that beauty which seemed to have fixed for its throne the sands of the hour-glass as well as of the sea.

And although the last few eventful years, fraught with change to the face of the whole earth, have been more fatal in their influence on Venice than the five hundred that preceded them; though the noble landscape of approach to her can now be seen no more, or seen only by a glance, as the engine slackens its rushing on the iron line; and though many of her palaces are for ever defaced, and many in desecrated ruins, there is still so much of magic in her aspect, that the hurried traveller, who must leave her before the wonder of that first aspect has been worn away, may still be led to forget the humility of her origin, and to shut his eyes to the depth of her desolation. They, at least, are little to be envied, in whose hearts the great charities of the imagination lie dead, and for whom the fancy has no power to repress the importunity of painful impressions, or to raise what is ignoble, and disguise what is discordant, in a scene so rich in its remembrances, so surpassing in its beauty. But for this work of the imagination there must be no permission during the task which is before us. The impotent feelings of romance, so singularly characteristic of this century, may indeed gild, but never save, the remains of those mightier ages to which they are attached like climbing flowers; and they must be torn away from the magnificent fragments, if we would see them as they stood in their own strength. Those feelings, always as fruitless as they are fond, are in Venice not only incapable of protecting, but even of discerning, the objects to which they ought to have been attached. The Venice of modern fiction and drama is a thing of yesterday, a mere efflorescence of decay, a stage dream which the first ray of daylight must dissipate into dust. No prisoner, whose name is worth remembering, or whose sorrow deserved sympathy, ever crossed that "Bridge of Sighs," which is the centre of the Byronic ideal of Venice; no great merchant of Venice ever saw that Rialto under which the traveller now passes with breathless interest: the statue which Byron makes Faliero address as of one of his great ancestors was erected to a soldier of fortune a hundred and fifty years after Faliero's death; and the most conspicuous parts of the city have been so entirely altered in the course of the last three centuries, that if Henry Dandolo or Francis Foscari could be summoned from their tombs, and stood each on the deck of his galley at the entrance of the Grand Canal, that renowned entrance, the painter's favourite subject, the novelist's favourite scene, where the water first narrows by the steps of the Church of La Salute,—the mighty Doges would not know in what part of the world they stood, would literally not recognise one stone of the great city, for whose sake, and by whose ingratitude, their grey hairs had been brought down with bitterness to the grave. The remains of *their* Venice lie hidden behind the cumbrous masses which were the delight of the nation in its dotage; hidden in many a grass-grown court, and silent pathway, and lightless canal, where the slow waves have sapped their foundations for five hundred years, and must soon prevail over them for ever. It must be our task to glean and gather them forth, and restore out of them some faint image of the lost city; more gorgeous a thousandfold than that which now exists, yet not created in the day-dream of the prince, nor by the ostentation of the noble, but built by iron hands and patient hearts, contending against the adversity of nature and the fury of man, so that its wonderfulness cannot be grasped by the indolence of imagination, but only after frank inquiry into the true nature of that wild and solitary scene, whose restless tides and trembling sands did indeed shelter the birth of the city, but long denied her dominion.

When the eye falls casually on a map of Europe, there is no feature by which it is more likely to be arrested than the strange sweeping loop formed by the junction of the Alps and Apennines, and enclosing the great basin of

Lombardy. This return of the mountain chain upon itself causes a vast difference in the character of the distribution of its débris on its opposite sides. The rock fragments and sediments which the torrents on the north side of the Alps bear into the plains are distributed over a vast extent of country, and, though here and there lodged in beds of enormous thickness, soon permit the firm substrata to appear from underneath them; but all the torrents which descend from the southern side of the High Alps, and from the northern slope of the Apennines, meet concentrically in the recess or mountain bay which the two ridges enclose; every fragment which thunder breaks out of their battlements, and every grain of dust which the summer rain washes from their pastures, is at last laid at rest in the blue sweep of the Lombardic plain; and that plain must have risen within its rocky barriers as a cup fills with wine, but for two contrary influences which continually depress, or disperse from its surface, the accumulation of the ruins of ages.

I will not tax the reader's faith in modern science by insisting on the singular depression of the surface of Lombardy, which appears for many centuries to have taken place steadily and continually; the main fact with which we have to do is the gradual transport, by the Po and its great collateral rivers, of vast masses of the finer sediment to the sea. The character of the Lombardic plains is most strikingly expressed by the ancient walls of its cities, composed for the most part of large rounded Alpine pebbles alternating with narrow courses of brick; and was curiously illustrated in 1848, by the ramparts of these same pebbles thrown up four or five feet high round every field, to check the Austrian cavalry in the battle under the walls of Verona. The finer dust among which these pebbles are dispersed is taken up by the rivers, fed into continual strength by the Alpine snow, so that, however pure their waters may be when they issue from the lakes at the foot of the great chain, they become of the colour and opacity of clay before they reach the Adriatic; the sediment which they bear is at once thrown down as they enter the sea, forming a vast belt of low land along the eastern coast of Italy. The powerful stream of the Po of course builds forward the fastest; on each side of it, north and south, there is a tract of marsh, fed by more feeble streams, and less liable to rapid change than the delta of the central river. In one of these tracts is built RAVENNA, and in the other VENICE.

What circumstances directed the peculiar arrangement

of this great belt of sediment in the earliest times, it is not
here the place to inquire. It is enough for us to know that
from the mouths of the Adige to those of the Piave there
stretches, at a variable distance of from three to five miles
from the actual shore, a bank of sand, divided into long
islands by narrow channels of sea. The space between this
bank and the true shore consists of the sedimentary de-
posits from these and other rivers, a great plain of cal-
careous mud, covered, in the neighbourhood of Venice, by
the sea at high water, to the depth in most places of a
foot or a foot and a half, and nearly everywhere exposed
at low tide, but divided by an intricate network of narrow
and winding channels, from which the sea never retires. In
some places, according to the run of the currents, the land
has risen into marshy islets, consolidated, some by art, and
some by time, into ground firm enough to be built upon,
or fruitful enough to be cultivated: in others, on the
contrary, it has not reached the sea level; so that, at the
average low water, shallow lakelets glitter among its irregularly exposed fields of sea-weed. In the midst of the
largest of these, increased in importance by the confluence
of several large river channels towards one of the openings in the sea bank, the city of Venice itself is built, on a
crowded cluster of islands; the various plots of higher
ground which appear to the north and south of this
central cluster, have at different periods been also thickly
inhabited, and now bear, according to their size, the remains of cities, villages, or isolated convents and churches,
scattered among spaces of open ground, partly waste and
encumbered by ruins, partly under cultivation for the
supply of the metropolis.

The average rise and fall of the tide is about three feet
(varying considerably with the seasons); but this fall, on
so flat a shore, is enough to cause continual movement in
the waters, and in the main canals to produce a reflux
which frequently runs like a mill stream. At high water no
land is visible for many miles to the north or south of
Venice, except in the form of small islands crowned with
towers or gleaming with villages: there is a channel, some
three miles wide, between the city and the mainland, and
some mile and a half wide between it and the sandy
breakwater called the Lido, which divides the lagoon from
the Adriatic, but which is so low as hardly to disturb the
impression of the city's having been built in the midst of
the ocean, although the secret of its true position is partly,
yet not painfully, betrayed by the clusters of piles set to
mark the deep-water channels, which undulate far away in

spotty chains like the studded backs of huge sea-snakes, and by the quick glittering of the crisped and crowded waves that flicker and dance before the strong winds upon the uplifted level of the shallow sea. But the scene is widely different at low tide. A fall of eighteen or twenty inches is enough to show ground over the greater part of the lagoon; and at the complete ebb the city is seen standing in the midst of a dark plain of sea-weed, of gloomy green, except only where the larger branches of the Brenta and its associated streams converge towards the port of the Lido. Through this salt and sombre plain the gondola and the fishing-boat advance by tortuous channels, seldom more than four or five feet deep, and often so choked with slime that the heavier keels furrow the bottom till their crossing tracts are seen through the clear sea water like the ruts upon a wintry road, and the oar leaves blue gashes upon the ground at every stroke, or is entangled among the thick weed that fringes the banks with the weight of its sullen waves, leaning to and fro upon the uncertain sway of the exhausted tide. The scene is often profoundly oppressive, even at this day, when every plot of higher ground bears some fragment of fair building: but, in order to know what it was once, let the traveller follow in his boat at evening the windings of some unfrequented channel far into the midst of the melancholy plain; let him remove, in his imagination, the brightness of the great city that still extends itself in the distance, and the walls and towers from the islands that are near; and so wait, until the bright investiture and sweet warmth of the sunset are withdrawn from the waters, and the black desert of their shore lies in its nakedness beneath the night, pathless, comfortless, infirm, lost in dark languor and fearful silence, except where the salt runlets plash into the tideless pools, or the sea-birds flit from their margins with a questioning cry; and he will be enabled to enter in some sort into the horror of heart with which this solitude was anciently chosen by man for his habitation. They little thought, who first drove the stakes into the sand, and strewed the ocean reeds for their rest, that their children were to be the princes of that ocean, and their palaces its pride; and yet, in the great natural laws that rule that sorrowful wilderness, let it be remembered what strange preparation had been made for the things which no human imagination could have foretold, and how the whole existence and fortune of the Venetian nation were anticipated or compelled, by the setting of those bars and doors to the rivers and the sea.

Had deeper currents divided their islands, hostile navies would again and again have reduced the rising city into servitude: had stronger surges beaten their shores, all the richness and refinement of the Venetian architecture must have been exchanged for the walls and bulwarks of an ordinary sea-port. Had there been no tide, as in other parts of the Mediterranean, the narrow canals of the city would have become noisome, and the marsh in which it was built pestiferous. Had the tide been only a foot or eighteen inches higher in its rise, the water-access to the doors of the palaces would have been impossible: even as it is, there is sometimes a little difficulty, at the ebb, in landing without setting foot upon the lower and slippery steps; and the highest tides sometimes enter the courtyards, and overflow the entrance halls. Eighteen inches more of difference between the level of the flood and ebb would have rendered the doorsteps of every palace, at low water, a treacherous mass of weeds and limpets, and the entire system of water-carriage for the higher classes, in their easy and daily intercourse, must have been done away with. The streets of the city would have been widened, its network of canals filled up, and all the peculiar character of the place and the people destroyed.

The reader may perhaps have felt some pain in the contrast between this faithful view of the site of the Venetian Throne, and the romantic conception of it which we ordinarily form: but this pain, if he have felt it, ought to be more than counterbalanced by the value of the instance thus afforded to us at once of the inscrutableness and the wisdom of the ways of God. If, two thousand years ago, we had been permitted to watch the slow settling of the slime of those turbid rivers into the polluted sea, and the gaining upon its deep and fresh waters of the lifeless, impassable, unvoyageable plain, how little could we have understood the purpose with which those islands were shaped out of the void, and the torpid waters enclosed with their desolate walls of sand! How little could we have known, any more than of what now seems to us most distressful, dark, and objectless, the glorious aim which was then in the mind of Him in whose hands are all the corners of the earth! how little imagined that in the laws which were stretching forth the gloomy margins of those fruitless banks, and feeding the bitter grass among their shallows, there was indeed a preparation, and *the only preparation possible,* for the founding of a city which was to be set like a golden clasp on the girdle of the earth, to write her history on the white scrolls of the

sea-surges, and to word it in their thunder, and to gather
and give forth, in world-wide pulsation, the glory of the
West and of the East, from the burning heart of her
Fortitude and Splendour!

The Stones of Venice, Vol. II, Ch. 1

Torcello

Seven miles to the north of Venice, the banks of sand,
which near the city rise little above low-water mark,
attain by degrees a higher level, and knit themselves at
last into fields of salt morass, raised here and there into
shapeless mounds, and intercepted by narrow creeks of sea.
One of the feeblest of these inlets, after winding for some
time among buried fragments of masonry, and knots of
sunburnt weeds whitened with webs of fucus, stays itself in
an utterly stagnant pool beside a plot of greener grass
covered with ground ivy and violets. On this mound is
built a rude brick campanile, of the commonest Lombardic type, which if we ascend towards evening (and
there are none to hinder us, the door of its ruinous
staircase swinging idly on its hinges), we may command
from it one of the most notable scenes in this wide world
of ours. Far as the eye can reach, a waste of wild sea
moor, of a lurid ashen grey; not like our northern moors
with their jet-black pools and purple heath, but lifeless, the
colour of sackcloth, with the corrupted sea-water soaking
through the roots of its acrid weeds, and gleaming hither
and thither through its snaky channels. No gathering of
fantastic mists, nor coursing of clouds across it; but
melancholy clearness of space in the warm sunset, oppressive, reaching to the horizon of its level gloom. To the
very horizon, on the north-east; but, to the north and
west, there is a blue line of higher land along the border
of it, and above this, but farther back, a misty band of
mountains, touched with snow. To the east, the paleness
and roar of the Adriatic, louder at momentary intervals as
the surf breaks on the bars of sand; to the south, the
widening branches of the calm lagoon, alternately purple
and pale green, as they reflect the evening clouds or
twilight sky; and almost beneath our feet, on the same
field which sustains the tower we gaze from, a group of
four buildings, two of them little larger than cottages

(though built of stone, and one adorned by a quaint belfry), the third an octagonal chapel, of which we can see but little more than the flat red roof with its rayed tiling, the fourth, a considerable church with nave and aisles, but of which, in like manner, we can see little but the long central ridge and lateral slopes of roof, which the sunlight separates in one glowing mass from the green field beneath and grey moor beyond. There are no living creatures near the buildings, nor any vestige of village or city round about them. They lie like a little company of ships becalmed on a far-away sea.

Then look farther to the south. Beyond the widening branches of the lagoon, and rising out of the bright lake into which they gather, there are a multitude of towers, dark, and scattered among square-set shapes of clustered palaces, a long and irregular line fretting the southern sky.

Mother and daughter, you behold them both in their widowhood,—TORCELLO, and VENICE.

Thirteen hundred years ago, the grey moorland looked as it does this day, and the purple mountains stood as radiantly in the deep distances of evening; but on the line of the horizon, there were strange fires mixed with the light of sunset, and the lament of many human voices mixed with the fretting of the waves on their ridges of sand. The flames rose from the ruins of Altinum; the lament from the multitude of its people, seeking, like Israel of old, a refuge from the sword in the paths of the sea.

The cattle are feeding and resting upon the site of the city that they left; the mower's scythe swept this day at dawn over the chief street of the city that they built, and the swathes of soft grass are now sending up their scent into the night air, the only incense that fills the temple of their ancient worship. Let us go down into that little space of meadow land.

The inlet which runs nearest to the base of the campanile is not that by which Torcello is commonly approached. Another, somewhat broader, and overhung by alder copse, winds out of the main channel of the lagoon up to the very edge of the little meadow which was once the Piazza of the city, and there, stayed by a few grey stones which present some semblance of a quay, forms its boundary at one extremity. Hardly larger than an ordinary English farmyard, and roughly enclosed on each side by broken palings and hedges of honeysuckle and briar, the narrow field retires from the water's edge, traversed by a scarcely traceable footpath, for some forty or fifty

100

paces, and then expanding into the form of a small square, with buildings on three sides of it, the fourth that which opens to the water. Two of these, that on our left and that in front of us as we approach from the canal, are so small that they might well be taken for the outhouses of the farm, though the first is a conventual building, and the other aspires to the title of the "Palazzo publico," both dating as far back as the beginning of the fourteenth century; the third, the octagonal church of Santa Fosca, is far more ancient than either, yet hardly on a larger scale. Though the pillars of the portico which surrounds it are of pure Greek marble, and their capitals are enriched with delicate sculpture, they, and the arches they sustain, together only raise the roof to the height of a cattle-shed; and the first strong impression which the spectator receives from the whole scene is, that whatever sin it may have been which has on this spot been visited with so utter a desolation, it could not at least have been ambition. Nor will this impression be diminished as we approach, or enter, the larger church, to which the whole group of buildings is subordinate. It has evidently been built by men in flight and distress, who sought in the hurried erection of their island church such a shelter for their earnest and sorrowful worship as, on the one hand, could not attract the eyes of their enemies by its splendour, and yet, on the other, might not awaken too bitter feelings by its contrast with the churches which they had seen destroyed. There is visible everywhere a simple and tender effort to recover some of the form of the temples which they had loved, and to do honour to God by that which they were erecting, while distress and humiliation prevented the desire, and prudence precluded the admission, either of luxury of ornament or magnificence of plan. The exterior is absolutely devoid of decoration, with the exception only of the western entrance and the lateral door, of which the former has carved sideposts and architrave, and the latter, crosses of rich sculpture; while the massy stone shutters of the windows, turning on huge rings of stone, which answer the double purpose of stanchions and brackets, cause the whole building rather to resemble a refuge from Alpine storm than the cathedral of a populous city; and, internally, the two solemn mosaics of the eastern and western extremities,—one representing the Last Judgment, the other the Madonna, her tears falling as her hands are raised to bless,—and the noble range of pillars which enclose the space between, terminated by the high throne for the pastor and the semicircular raised seats for the superior clergy, are expressive at once of the deep sorrow and the sacred courage of men who had no home left them upon earth, but who looked for one to come, of men "persecuted but not forsaken, cast down but not destroyed."

The Stones of Venice, Vol. II, Ch. 2

And now I wish that the reader, before I bring him into St. Mark's Place, would imagine himself for a little time in a quiet English cathedral town, and walk with me to the west front of its cathedral. Let us go together up the more retired street, at the end of which we can see the pinnacles of one of the towers, and then through the low grey gateway, with its battlemented top and small latticed window in the centre, into the inner private-looking road or close, where nothing goes in but the carts of the tradesmen who supply the bishop and the chapter, and where there are little shaven grass-plots, fenced in by neat rails, before old-fashioned groups of somewhat diminutive and excessively trim houses, with little oriel and bay windows jutting out here and there, and deep wooden cornices and eaves painted cream colour and white, and small porches to their doors in the shape of cockle-shells, or little, crooked, thick, indescribable wooden gables warped a little on one side; and so forward till we come to larger houses, also old-fashioned, but of red brick, and with garden behind them, and fruit walls, which show here and there, among the nectarines, the vestiges of an old cloister arch or shaft, and looking in front on the cathedral square itself, laid out in rigid divisions of smooth grass and gravel walk, yet not uncheerful, especially on the sunny side, where the canon's children are walking with their nursery-maids. And so, taking care not to tread on the grass, we will go along the straight walk to the west front, and there stand for a time, looking up at its deep-pointed porches and the dark places between their pillars where there were statues once, and where the fragments, here and there, of a stately figure are still left, which has in it the likeness of a king, perhaps indeed a king on earth, perhaps a saintly king long ago in heaven; and so higher and higher up to the great mouldering wall of rugged sculpture and confused arcades, shattered, and grey, and grisly with heads of dragons and mocking fiends, worn by the rain and swirling winds into yet unseemlier shape, and coloured on their stony scales by the deep russet-orange lichen, melancholy gold; and so, higher still, to the bleak towers, so far above that the eye loses itself among the bosses of their traceries, though they are rude and strong, and only sees like a drift of eddying black points, now closing, now scattering, and now settling suddenly into invisible places among the bosses and flowers, the crowd of restless birds that fill the whole square with that strange clangour of theirs, so harsh and yet so soothing, like the cries of birds on a solitary coast between the cliffs and sea.

Think for a little while of that scene, and the meaning of all its small formalisms, mixed with its serene sublimity. Estimate its secluded, continuous, drowsy felicities, and its evidence of the sense and steady performance of such kind of duties as can be regulated by the cathedral clock; and weigh the influence of those dark towers on all who have passed through the lonely square at their feet for centuries, and on all who have seen them rising far away over the wooden plain, or catching on their square masses the last rays of the sunset, when the city at their feet was indicated only by the mist at the bend of the river. And then let us quickly recollect that we are in Venice, and land at the extremity of the Calle Lunga San Moisè, which may be considered as there answering to the secluded street that led us to our English cathedral gateway.

We find ourselves in a paved alley, some seven feet wide where it is widest, full of people, and resonant with cries of itinerant salesmen,—a shriek in their beginning, and dying away into a kind of brazen ringing, all the worse for its confinement between the high houses of the passage along which we have to make our way. Overhead, an inextricable confusion of rugged shutters, and iron balconies and chimney flues, pushed out on brackets to save room, and arched windows with projecting sills of Istrian stone, and gleams of green leaves here and there where a fig-tree branch escapes over a lower wall from some inner cortile, leading the eye up to the narrow stream of blue sky high over all. On each side, a row of shops, as densely set as may be, occupying, in fact, intervals between the square stone shafts, about eight feet high, which carry the first floors: intervals of which one is narrow and serves as a door; the other is, in the more respectable shops, wainscotted to the height of the counter and glazed above, but in those of the poorer tradesmen left open to the ground, and the wares laid on benches and tables in the open air, the light in all cases entering at the front only, and fading away in a few feet from the threshold into a gloom which the eye from without cannot penetrate, but which is generally broken by a ray or two from a feeble lamp at the back of the shop, suspended before a print of the Virgin. The less pious shopkeeper sometimes leaves his lamp unlighted, and is contented with a penny print; the more religious one has his print coloured and set in a little shrine with a gilded or figured fringe, with perhaps a faded flower or two on each side, and his lamp burning brilliantly. Here at the fruiterer's, where the dark-green water-melons are heaped upon the counter like cannon balls, the Madonna has a tabernacle of fresh laurel leaves; but the pewterer next door has let his lamp out, and there is nothing to be seen in his shop but the dull gleam of the studded patterns on the copper pans, hanging from his roof in the darkness. Next comes a "Vendita Frittole e Liquori," where the Virgin, enthroned in a very humble manner beside a tallow candle on a back shelf, presides over certain ambrosial morsels of a nature too ambiguous to be defined or enumerated. But a few steps farther on, at the regular wine-shop of the calle, where we are offered "Vino Nostrani a Soldi 28.32," the Madonna is in great glory, enthroned above ten or a dozen large red casks of three-year-old vintage, and flanked by goodly ranks of bottles of Maraschino, and two crimson lamps; and for the evening, when the gondoliers will come to drink out, under her auspices, the money they have gained during the day, she will have a whole chandelier.

A yard or two farther, we pass the hostelry of the Black Eagle, and glancing as we pass through the square door of marble, deeply moulded, in the outer wall, we see the shadows of its pergola of vines resting on an ancient well, with a pointed shield carved on its side; and so presently emerge on the bridge and Campo San Moisè, whence to the entrance into St. Mark's Place, called the Bocca di Piazza (mouth of the square), the Venetian character is nearly destroyed, first by the frightful façade of San Moisè, which we will pause at another time to examine, and then by the modernizing of the shops as they near the piazza, and the mingling with the lower Venetian populace of lounging groups of English and Austrians. We will push fast through them into the shadow of the pillars at the end of the 'Bocca di Piazza,' and then we forget them all; for between those pillars there opens a great light, and, in the midst of it, as we advance slowly, the vast tower of St. Mark seems to lift itself visibly forth from the level field of chequered stones;

and, on each side, the countless arches prolong themselves into ranged symmetry, as if the rugged and irregular houses that pressed together above us in the dark alley had been struck back into sudden obedience and lovely order, and all their rude casements and broken walls had been transformed into arches charged with goodly sculpture, and fluted shafts of delicate stone.

And well may they fall back, for beyond those troops of ordered arches there rises a vision out of the earth, and all the great square seems to have opened from it in a kind of awe, that we may see it far away;—a multitude of pillars and white domes, clustered into a long low pyramid of coloured light; a treasure-heap, it seems, partly of gold, and partly of opal and mother-of-pearl, hollowed beneath into five great vaulted porches, ceiled with fair mosaic, and beset with sculpture of alabaster, clear as amber and delicate as ivory,—sculpture fantastic and involved, of palm leaves and lilies, and grapes and pomegranates, and birds clinging and fluttering among the branches, all twined together into an endless network of buds and plumes; and in the midst of it, the solemn forms of angels, sceptred, and robed to the feet, and leaning to each other across the gates, their figures indistinct among the gleaming of the golden ground through the leaves beside them, interrupted and dim, like the morning light as it faded back among the branches of Eden, when first its gates were angel-guarded long ago. And round the walls of the porches there are set pillars of variegated stones, jasper and porphyry, and deep-green serpentine spotted with flakes of snow, and marbles, that half refuse and half yield to the sunshine, Cleopatra-like, "their bluest veins to kiss" —the shadow, as it steals back from them, revealing line after line of azure undulations, as a receding tide leaves the waved sand; their capitals rich with interwoven tracery, rooted knots of herbage, and drifting leaves of acanthus and vine, and mystical signs, all beginning and ending in the Cross; and above them, in the broad archivolts, a continuous chain of language and of life— angels, and the signs of heaven, and the labours of men, each in its appointed season upon the earth; and above these, another range of glittering pinnacles, mixed with white arches edged with scarlet flowers,—a confusion of delight, amidst which the breasts of the Greek horses are seen blazing in their breadth of golden strength, and the St. Mark's lion, lifted on a blue field covered with stars, until at last, as if in ecstasy, the crests of the arches break into a marble foam, and toss themselves far into the blue sky in flashes and wreaths of sculptured spray, as if the breakers on the Lido shore had been frost-bound before they fell, and the sea-nymphs had inlaid them with coral and amethyst.

Between that grim cathedral of England and this, what an interval! There is a type of it in the very birds that haunt them; for, instead of the restless crowd, hoarse-voiced and sable-winged, drifting on the bleak upper air, the St. Mark's porches are full of doves, that nestle among the marble foliage, and mingle the soft iridescence of their living plumes, changing at every motion, with the tints, hardly less lovely, that have stood unchanged for seven hundred years.

And what effect has this splendour on those who pass beneath it? You may walk from sunrise to sunset, to and fro, before the gateway of St. Mark's, and you will not see an eye lifted to it, nor a countenance brightened by it. Priest and layman, soldier and civilian, rich and poor, pass by it alike regardlessly. Up to the very recesses of the porches, the meanest tradesmen of the city push their counters; nay, the foundations of its pillars are themselves the seats—not "of them that sell doves" for sacrifice, but of the vendors of toys and caricatures. Round the whole square in front of the church there is almost a continuous line of cafés, where the idle Venetians of the middle classes lounge, and read empty journals; in its centre the Austrian bands play during the time of vespers, their martial music jarring with the organ notes,—the march drowning the miserere, and the sullen crowd thickening round them,—a crowd, which, if it had its will, would stiletto every soldier that pipes to it. And in the recesses of the porches, all day long, knots of men of the lowest classes, unemployed and listless, lie basking in the sun like lizards; and unregarded children,—every heavy glance of their young eyes full of desperation and stony depravity, and their throats hoarse with cursing,—gamble and fight, and snarl, and sleep, hour after hour, clashing their bruised centesimi upon the marble ledges of the church porch. And the images of Christ and His angels look down upon it continually.

The Stones of Venice, Vol. II, Ch. 4

If the reader will look back to the division of our subject which was made in the first chapter of the first volume, he will find that we are now about to enter upon the examination of that school of Venetian architecture which forms an intermediate step between the Byzantine and Gothic forms; but which I find may be conveniently considered in its connexion with the latter style. In order that we may discern the tendency of each step of this change, it will be wise in the outset to endeavour to form some general idea of its final result. We know already what the Byzantine architecture is from which the transition was made, but we ought to know something of the Gothic architecture into which it led. I shall endeavour therefore to give the reader in this chapter an idea, at once broad and definite, of the true nature of *Gothic* architecture, properly so called; not of that of Venice only, but of universal Gothic: for it will be one of the most interesting parts of our subsequent inquiry to find out how far Venetian architecture reached the universal or perfect type of Gothic, and how far it either fell short of it, or assumed foreign and independent forms.

The principal difficulty in doing this arises from the fact that every building of the Gothic period differs in some important respect from every other; and many include features which, if they occurred in other buildings, would not be considered Gothic at all; so that all we have to reason upon is merely, if I may be allowed so to express it, a greater or less degree of *Gothicness* in each building we examine. And it is this Gothicness,—the character which, according as it is found more or less in a building, makes it more or less Gothic,—of which I want to define the nature; and I feel the same kind of difficulty in doing so which would be encountered by any one who undertook to explain, for instance, the nature of Redness, without any actually red thing to point to, but only orange and purple things. Suppose he had only a piece of heather and a dead oak-leaf to do it with. He might say, the colour which is mixed with the yellow in this oak-leaf, and with the blue in this heather, would be red, if you had it separate; but it would be difficult, nevertheless, to make the abstraction perfectly intelligible: and it is so in a far greater degree to make the abstraction of the Gothic character intelligible, because that character itself is made up of many mingled ideas, and can consist only in their union. That is to say, pointed arches do not constitute Gothic, nor vaulted roofs, nor flying buttresses, nor grotesque sculptures; but all or some of these things, and many other things with them, when they come together so as to have life.

Observe also, that, in the definition proposed, I shall only endeavour to analyze the idea which I suppose already to exist in the reader's mind. We all have some notion, most of us a very determined one, of the meaning of the term Gothic, but I know that many persons have this idea in their minds without being able to define it: that is to say, understanding generally that Westminster Abbey is Gothic, and St. Paul's is not, that Strasburg Cathedral is Gothic, and St. Peter's is not, they have, nevertheless, no clear notion of what it is that they recognize in the one or miss in the other, such as would enable them to say how far the work at Westminster or Strasburg is good and pure of its kind; still less to say of any nondescript building, like St. James's Palace or Windsor Castle, how much right Gothic element there is in it, and how much wanting. And I believe this inquiry to be a pleasant and profitable one; and that there will be found something more than usually interesting in tracing out this grey, shadowy, many-pinnacled image of the Gothic spirit within us; and discerning what fellowship there is between it and our Northern hearts. And if, at any point of the inquiry, I should interfere with any of the reader's previously formed conceptions, and use the term Gothic in any sense which he would not willingly attach to it, I do not ask him to accept, but only to examine and understand, my interpretation, as necessary to the intelligibility of what follows in the rest of the work.

We have, then, the Gothic character submitted to our analysis, just as the rough mineral is submitted to that of the chemist, entangled with many other foreign substances, itself perhaps in no place pure, or ever to be obtained or seen in purity for more than an instant; but nevertheless a thing of definite and separate nature, however inextricable or confused in appearance. Now observe: the chemist defines his mineral by two separate kinds of character; one external, its crystalline form, hardness, lustre, &c.; the other internal, the proportions and nature of its constituent atoms. Exactly in the same manner, we shall find that Gothic architecture has external forms, and internal elements. Its elements are certain mental tendencies of the builders, legibly expressed in it; as fancifulness, love of variety, love of richness, and such others. Its external forms are pointed arches, vaulted roofs, &c. And unless both the elements and the forms are there, we have no right to call the style Gothic. It is not enough that it has the Form, if it have not also the power and life. It is not enough that it has the Power, if it have not the form. We must therefore inquire into each of these characters successively; and determine first, what is the Mental Expression, and secondly, what the Material Form, of Gothic architecture, properly so called.

1st. Mental Power or Expression. What characters, we have to discover, did the Gothic builders love, or instinctively express in their work, as distinguished from all other builders?

Let us go back for a moment to our chemistry, and note that, in defining a mineral by its constituent parts, it is not one nor another of them, that can make up the mineral, but the union of all: for instance, it is neither in charcoal, nor in oxygen, nor in lime, that there is the making of chalk; but in the combination of all three in certain measures; they are all found in very different things from chalk, and there is nothing like chalk either in charcoal or in oxygen, but they are nevertheless necessary to its existence.

So in the various mental characters which make up the soul of Gothic. It is not one nor another that produces it; but their union in certain measures. Each one of them is found in many other architectures besides Gothic; but Gothic cannot exist where they are not found, or, at least, where their place is not in some way supplied. Only there is this great difference between the composition of the mineral, and of the architectural style, that if we withdraw one of its elements from the stone, its form is utterly changed, and its existence as such and such a mineral is destroyed; but if we withdraw one of its mental elements from the Gothic style, it is only a little less Gothic than it was before, and the union of two or three of its elements is enough already to bestow a certain Gothicness of character, which gains in intensity as we add the others, and loses as we again withdraw them.

I believe, then, that the characteristic or moral elements of Gothic are the following, placed in the order of their importance:

1. Savageness.	4. Grotesqueness.
2. Changefulness.	5. Rigidity.
3. Naturalism.	6. Redundance.

These characters are here expressed as belonging to the building; as belonging to the builder, they would be expressed thus:—1. Savageness, or Rudeness. 2. Love of Change. 3. Love of Nature. 4. Disturbed Imagination. 5. Obstinacy. 6. Generosity. And I repeat, that the withdrawal of any one, or any two, will not at once destroy the Gothic character of a building, but the removal of a majority of them will. I shall proceed to examine them in their order.

1. SAVAGENESS. I am not sure when the word "Gothic" was first generally applied to the architecture of the North; but I presume that, whatever the date of its original usage, it was intended to imply reproach, and express the barbaric character of the nations among whom that architecture arose. It never implied that they were literally of Gothic lineage, far less that their architecture had been originally invented by the Goths themselves; but it did imply that they and their buildings together exhibited a degree of sternness and rudeness, which, in contradistinction to the character of Southern and Eastern nations, appeared like a perpetual reflection of the contrast between the Goth and the Roman in their first encounter. And when that fallen Roman, in the utmost impotence of his luxury, and insolence of his guilt, became the model for the imitation of civilised Europe, at the close of the so-called Dark ages, the word Gothic became a term of unmitigated contempt, not unmixed with aversion. From that contempt, by the exertion of the antiquaries and architects of this century, Gothic architecture has been sufficiently vindicated; and perhaps some among us, in our admiration of the magnificent science of its structure, and sacredness of its expression, might desire that the term of ancient reproach should be withdrawn, and some other, of more apparent honourableness, adopted in its place. There is no chance, as there is no need, of such a substitution. As far as the epithet was used scornfully, it was used falsely; but there is no reproach in the word, rightly understood; on the contrary, there is a profound truth, which the instinct of mankind almost unconsciously recognises. It is true, greatly and deeply true, that the architecture of the North is rude and wild; but it is not true, that, for this reason, we are to condemn it, or despise. Far

otherwise: I believe it is in this very character that it deserves our profoundest reverence.

The charts of the world which have been drawn up by modern science have thrown into a narrow space the expression of a vast amount of knowledge, but I have never yet seen any one pictorial enough to enable the spectator to imagine the kind of contrast in physical character which exists between Northern and Southern countries. We know the differences in detail, but we have not that broad glance and grasp which would enable us to feel them in their fulness. We know that gentians grow on the Alps, and olives on the Apennines; but we do not enough conceive for ourselves that variegated mosaic of the world's surface which a bird sees in its migration, that difference between the district of the gentian and of the olive which the stork and the swallow see far off, as they lean upon the sirocco wind. Let us, for a moment, try to raise ourselves even above the level of their flight, and imagine the Mediterranean lying beneath us like an irregular lake, and all its ancient promontories sleeping in the sun: here and there an angry spot of thunder, a grey stain of storm, moving upon the burning field; and here and there a fixed wreath of white volcano smoke, surrounded by its circle of ashes; but for the most part a great peacefulness of light, Syria and Greece, Italy and Spain, laid like pieces of a golden pavement into the sea-blue, chased, as we stoop nearer to them, with bossy beaten work of mountain chains, and glowing softly with terraced gardens, and flowers heavy with frankincense, mixed among masses of laurel, and orange, and plumy palm, that abate with their grey-green shadows the burning of the marble rocks, and of the ledges of porphyry sloping under lucent sand. Then let us pass farther towards the north, until we see the orient colours change gradually into a vast belt of rainy green, where the pastures of Switzerland, and poplar valleys of France, and dark forests of the Danube and Carpathians stretch from the mouths of the Loire to those of the Volga, seen through clefts in grey swirls of rain-cloud and flaky veils of the mist of the brooks, spreading low along the pasture lands: and then, farther north still, to see the earth heave into mighty masses of leaden rock and healthy moor, bordering with a broad waste of gloomy purple that belt of field and wood, and splintering into irregular and grisly islands amidst the northern seas, beaten by storm, and chilled by ice-drift, and tormented by furious pulses of contending tide, until the roots of the last forests fail from among the hill ravines, and the hunger of the north wind bites their peaks into barrenness; and, at last, the wall of ice, durable like iron, sets, deathlike, its white teeth against us out of the polar twilight. And, having once traversed in thought this gradation of the zoned iris of the earth in all its material vastness, let us go down nearer to it, and watch the parallel change in the belt of animal life: the multitudes of swift and brilliant creatures that glance in the air and sea, or tread the sands of the southern zone; striped zebras and spotted leopards, glistening serpents, and birds arrayed in purple and scarlet. Let us contrast their delicacy and brilliancy of colour, and swiftness of motion, with the frost-cramped strength, and shaggy covering, and dusky plumage of the northern tribes, contrast the Arabian horse with the Shetland, the tiger and leopard with the wolf and bear, the antelope with the elk, the bird of paradise with the osprey: and then, submissively acknowledging the great laws by which the earth and all that it bears are ruled throughout their being, let us not condemn, but rejoice in the expression by man of his own rest in the statutes of the lands that gave him birth. Let us watch him with reverence as he sets side by side the burning gems, and smooths with soft sculpture the jasper pillars, that are to reflect a ceaseless sunshine, and rise into a cloudless sky: but not with less reverence let us stand by him, when, with rough strength and hurried stroke, he smites an uncouth animation out of the rocks which he has torn from among the moss of the moorland, and heaves into the darkened air the pile of iron buttress and rugged wall, instinct with work of an imagination as wild and wayward as the northern sea; creations of ungainly shape and rigid limb, but full of wolfish life; fierce as the winds that beat, and changeful as the clouds that shade them.

There is, I repeat, no degradation, no reproach in this, but all dignity and honourableness: and we should err grievously in refusing either to recognise as an essential character of the existing architecture of the North, or to admit as a desirable character in that which it yet may be, this wildness of thought, and roughness of work; this look of mountain brotherhood between the cathedral and the Alp; this magnificence of sturdy power, put forth only the more energetically because the fine finger-touch was chilled away by the frosty wind, and the eye dimmed by the moor-mist, or blinded by the hail; this outspeaking of the strong spirit of men who may not gather redundant fruitage from the earth, nor bask in dreamy benignity of sunshine, but must break the rock for bread, and cleave the forest for fire, and show, even in what they did for their delight, some of the hard habits of the arm and heart that grew on them as they swung the axe or pressed the plough.

If, however, the savageness of Gothic architecture, merely as an expression of its origin among Northern nations, may be considered, in some sort, a noble character, it possesses a higher nobility still, when considered as an index, not of climate, but of religious principle.

In the 13th and 14th paragraphs of Chapter XXI, of the first volume of this work, it was noticed that the systems of architectural ornament, properly so called, might be divided into three:—1. Servile ornament, in which the execution or power of the inferior workman is entirely subjected to the intellect of the higher;—2. Constitutional ornament, in which the executive inferior power is, to a certain point, emancipated and independent, having a will of its own, yet confessing its inferiority and rendering obedience to higher powers;—and 3. Revolutionary ornament, in which no executive inferiority is admitted at all. I must here explain the nature of these divisions at somewhat greater length.

Of Servile ornament, the principal schools are the Greek, Ninevite, and Egyptian; but their servility is of different kinds. The Greek master-workman was far advanced in knowledge and power above the Assyrian or Egyptian. Neither he nor those for whom he worked could endure the appearance of imperfection in anything; and, therefore, what ornament he appointed to be done by those beneath him was composed of mere geometrical forms,—balls, ridges, and perfectly symmetrical foliage,—which could be executed with absolute precision by line and rule, and were as perfect in their way, when completed, as his own figure sculpture. The Assyrian and Egyptian, on the contrary, less cognisant of accurate form in anything, were content to allow their figure sculpture to be executed by inferior workmen, but lowered the method of its treatment to a standard which every workman could reach, and then trained him by discipline so rigid, that there was no chance of his falling beneath the standard appointed. The Greek gave to the lower workman no subject which he could not perfectly execute. The Assyrian gave him subjects which he could only execute imperfect-

113

ly, but fixed a legal standard for his imperfection. The workman was, in both systems, a slave.*

But in the mediæval, or especially Christian, system of ornament, this slavery is done away with altogether; Christianity having recognised, in small things as well as great, the individual value of every soul. But it not only recognises its value; it confesses its imperfection, in only bestowing dignity upon the acknowledgment of unworthiness. That admission of lost power and fallen nature, which the Greek or Ninevite felt to be intensely painful, and, as far as might be, altogether refused, the Christian makes daily and hourly, contemplating the fact of it without fear, as tending, in the end, to God's great glory. Therefore, to every spirit which Christianity summons to her service, her exhortation is: Do what you can, and confess frankly what you are unable to do; neither let your effort be shortened for fear of failure, nor your confession silenced for fear of shame. And it is, perhaps, the principal admirableness of the Gothic schools of architecture, that they thus receive the results of the labour of inferior minds; and out of fragments full of imperfection, and betraying that imperfection in every touch, indulgently raise up a stately and unaccusable whole.

But the modern English mind has this much in common with that of the Greek, that it intensely desires, in all things, the utmost completion or perfection compatible with their nature. This is a noble character in the abstract, but becomes ignoble when it causes us to forget the relative dignities of that nature itself, and to prefer the perfectness of the lower nature to the imperfection of the higher; not considering that as, judged by such a rule, all the brute animals would be preferable to man, because more perfect in their functions and kind, and yet are always held inferior to him, so also in the works of man, those which are more perfect in their kind are always inferior to those which are, in their nature, liable to more faults and shortcomings. For the finer the nature, the more flaws it will show through the clearness of it; and it

* The third kind of ornament, the Renaissance, is that in which the inferior detail becomes principal, the executor of every minor portion being required to exhibit skill and possess knowledge as great as that which is processed by the master of the design; and in the endeavour to endow him with this skill and knowledge, his own original power is overwhelmed, and the whole building becomes a wearisome exhibition of well-educated imbecility. We must fully inquire into the nature of this form of error, when we arrive at the examination of the Renaissance schools.

is a law of this universe, that the best things shall be seldomest seen in their best form. The wild grass grows well and strongly, one year with another; but the wheat is, according to the greater nobleness of its nature, liable to the bitterer blight. And therefore, while in all things that we see, or do, we are to desire perfection, and strive for it, we are nevertheless not to set the meaner thing, in its narrow accomplishment, above the nobler thing, in its mighty progress; not to esteem smooth minuteness above shattered majesty; not to prefer mean victory to honourable defeat; not to lower the level of our aim, that we may the more surely enjoy the complacency of success. But, above all, in our dealings with the souls of other men, we are to take care how we check, by severe requirement or narrow caution, efforts which might otherwise lead to a noble issue; and, still more, how we withhold our admiration from great excellencies, because they are mingled with rough faults. Now, in the make and nature of every man, however rude or simple, whom we employ in manual labour, there are some powers for better things: some tardy imagination, torpid capacity of emotion, tottering steps of thought, there are, even at the worst; and in most cases it is all our own fault that they *are* tardy or torpid. But they cannot be strengthened, unless we are content to take them in their feebleness, and unless we prize and honour them in their imperfection above the best and most perfect manual skill. And this is what we have to do with all our labourers; to look for the *thoughtful* part of them, and get that out of them, whatever we lose for it, whatever faults and errors we are obliged to take with it. For the best that is in them cannot manifest itself, but in company with much error. Understand this clearly: You can teach a man to draw a straight line; and to cut one; to strike a curved line, and to carve it; and to copy and carve any number of given lines or forms, with admirable speed and perfect precision; and you find his work perfect of its kind: but if you ask him to think about any of those forms, to consider if he cannot find any better in his own head, he stops; his execution becomes hesitating; he thinks, and ten to one he thinks wrong; ten to one he makes a mistake in the first touch he gives to his work as a thinking being. But you have made a man of him for all that. He was only a machine before, an animated tool.

And observe, you are put to stern choice in this matter. You must either make a tool of the creature, or a man of him. You cannot make both. Men were not intended to work with the accuracy of tools, to be precise and perfect in all their actions. If you will have that precision out of them, and make their fingers measure degrees like cogwheels, and their arms strike curves like compasses, you must unhumanise them. All the energy of their spirits must be given to make cogs and compasses of themselves. All their attention and strength must go to the accomplishment of the mean act. The eye of the soul must be bent upon the finger-point, and the soul's force must fill all the invisible nerves that guide it, ten hours a day, that it may not err from its steely precision, and so soul and sight be worn away, and the whole human being be lost at last—a heap of sawdust, so far as its intellectual work in this world is concerned; saved only by its Heart, which cannot go into the form of cogs and compasses, but expands, after the ten hours are over, into fireside humanity. On the other hand, if you will make a man of the working creature, you cannot make a tool. Let him but begin to imagine, to think, to try to do anything worth doing; and the engine-turned precision is lost at once. Out come all his roughness, all his dulness, all his incapability; shame upon shame, failure upon failure, pause after pause: but out comes the whole majesty of him also; and we know the height of it only, when we see the clouds settling upon him. And, whether the clouds be bright or dark, there will be transfiguration behind and within them.

And now, reader, look round this English room of yours, about which you have been proud so often, because the work of it was so good and strong, and the ornaments of it so finished. Examine again all those accurate mouldings, and perfect polishings, and unerring adjustments of the seasoned wood and tempered steel. Many a time you have exulted over them, and thought how great England was, because her slightest work was done so thoroughly. Alas! if read rightly, these perfectnesses are signs of a slavery in our England a thousand times more bitter and more degrading than that of the scourged African, or helot Greek. Men may be beaten, chained, tormented, yoked like cattle, slaughtered like summer flies, and yet remain in one sense, and the best sense, free. But to smother their souls within them, to blight and hew into rotting pollards the suckling branches of their human intelligence, to make the flesh and skin which, after the worm's work on it, is to see God, into leathern thongs to yoke machinery with,—that it is to be slave-masters indeed; and there might be more freedom in England, though her feudal lords' lightest words were worth men's lives, and though the blood of the vexed husbandman dropped in the furrows of her fields, than there is while the animation of her multitudes is sent like fuel to feed the factory smoke, and the strength of them is given daily to be wasted into the fineness of a web, or racked into the exactness of a line.

And, on the other hand, go forth again to gaze upon the old cathedral front, where you have smiled so often at the fantastic ignorance of the old sculptors: examine once more those ugly goblins, and formless monsters, and stern statues, anatomiless and rigid; but do not mock at them, for they are signs of the life and liberty of every workman who struck the stone; a freedom of thought, and rank in scale of being, such as no laws, no charters, no charities can secure; but which it must be the first aim of all Europe at this day to regain for her children.

Let me not be thought to speak wildly or extravagantly. It is verily this degradation of the operative into a machine, which, more than any other evil of the times, is leading the mass of the nations everywhere into vain, incoherent, destructive struggling for a freedom of which they cannot explain the nature to themselves. Their universal outcry against wealth, and against nobility, is not forced from them either by the pressure of famine, or the sting of mortified pride. These do much, and have done much in all ages; but the foundations of society were never yet shaken as they are at this day. It is not that men are ill fed, but that they have no pleasure in the work by which they make their bread, and therefore look to wealth as the only means of pleasure. It is not that men are pained by the scorn of the upper classes, but they cannot endure their own; for they feel that the kind of labour to which they are condemned is verily a degrading one, and makes them less than men. Never had the upper classes so much sympathy with the lower, or charity for them, as they have at this day, and yet never were they so much hated by them: for, of old, the separation between the noble and the poor was merely a wall built by law; now it is a veritable difference in level of standing, a precipice between upper and lower grounds in the field of humanity, and there is pestilential air at the bottom of it. I know not if a day is ever to come when the nature of right freedom will be understood, and when men will see that to obey another man, to labour for him, yield reverence to him or to his place, is not slavery. It is often the best kind

117

of liberty,—liberty from care. The man who says to one, Go, and he goeth, and to another, Come, and he cometh, has, in most cases, more sense of restraint and difficulty than the man who obeys him. The movements of the one are hindered by the burden on his shoulder; of the other, by the bridle on his lips: there is no way by which the burden may be lightened; but we need not suffer from the bridle if we do not champ at it. To yield reverence to another, to hold ourselves and our lives at his disposal, is not slavery; often, it is the noblest state in which a man can live in this world. There is, indeed, a reverence which is servile, that is to say irrational or selfish: but there is also noble reverence, that is to say, reasonable and loving; and a man is never so noble as when he is reverent in this kind; nay, even if the feeling pass the bounds of mere reason, so that it be loving, a man is raised by it. Which had, in reality, most of the serf nature in him,—the Irish peasant who was lying in wait yesterday for his landlord, with his musket muzzle thrust through the ragged hedge; or that old mountain servant, who, 200 years ago, at Inverkeithing, gave up his own life and the lives of his seven sons for his chief*?—as each fell, calling forth his brother to the death, "Another for Hector!" And therefore, in all ages and all countries, reverence has been paid and sacrifice made by men to each other, not only without complaint, but rejoicingly; and famine, and peril, and sword, and all evil, and all shame, have been borne willingly in the causes of masters and kings; for all these gifts of the heart ennobled the men who gave, not less than the men who received them, and nature prompted, and God rewarded the sacrifice. But to feel their souls withering within them, unthanked, to find their whole being sunk into an unrecognised abyss, to be counted off into a heap of mechanism, numbered with its wheels, and weighed with its hammer strokes;—this nature bade not,—this God blesses not,—this humanity for no long time is able to endure.

We have much studied and much perfected, of late, the great civilised invention of the division of labour; only we give it a false name. It is not, truly speaking, the labour that is divided; but the men:—Divided into mere segments of men—broken into small fragments and crumbs of life; so that all the little piece of intelligence that is left in a man is not enough to make a pin, or a nail, but exhausts

* Vide Preface to "Fair Maid of Perth."

itself in making the point of a pin, or the head of a nail. Now it is a good and desirable thing, truly, to make many pins in a day; but if we could only see with what crystal sand their points were polished,—sand of human soul, much to be magnified before it can be discerned for what it is,—we should think there might be some loss in it also. And the great cry that rises from all our manufacturing cities, louder than their furnace blast, is all in very deed for this,—that we manufacture everything there except men; we blanch cotton, and strengthen steel, and refine sugar, and shape pottery; but to brighten, to strengthen, to refine, or to form a single living spirit, never enters into our estimate of advantages. And all the evil to which that cry is urging our myriads can be met only in one way: not by teaching nor preaching, for to teach them is but to show them their misery, and to preach to them, if we do nothing more than preach, is to mock at it. It can be met only by a right understanding, on the part of all classes, of what kinds of labour are good for men, raising them, and making them happy; by a determined sacrifice of such convenience, or beauty, or cheapness as is to be got only by the degradation of the workman; and by equally determined demand for the products and results of healthy and ennobling labour.

And how, it will be asked, are these products to be recognised, and this demand to be regulated? Easily: by the observance of three broad and simple rules:

1. Never encourage the manufacture of any article not absolutely necessary, in the production of which *Invention* has no share.

2. Never demand an exact finish for its own sake, but only for some practical or noble end.

3. Never encourage imitation or copying of any kind, except for the sake of preserving record of great works.

The second of these principles is the only one which directly rises out of the consideration of our immediate subject; but I shall briefly explain the meaning and extent of the first also, reserving the enforcement of the third for another place.

1. Never encourage the manufacture of anything not necessary, in the production of which invention has no share.

For instance. Glass beads are utterly unnecessary, and there is no design or thought employed in their manufacture. They are formed by first drawing out the glass into rods; these rods are chopped up into fragments of the size of beads by the human hand, and the fragments are then rounded in the furnace. The men who chop up the rods sit at their work all day, their hands vibrating with a perpetual and exquisitely timed palsy, and the beads dropping beneath their vibration like hail. Neither they, nor the men who draw out the rods or fuse the fragments, have the smallest occasion for the use of any single human faculty; and every young lady, therefore, who buys glass beads is engaged in the slave-trade, and in a much more cruel one than that which we have so long been endeavouring to put down.

But glass cups and vessels may become the subjects of exquisite invention; and if in buying these we pay for the invention, that is to say for the beautiful form, or colour, or engraving, and not for mere finish of execution, we are doing good to humanity.

So, again, the cutting of precious stones, in all ordinary cases, requires little exertion of any mental faculty; some tact and judgment in avoiding flaws, and so on, but nothing to bring out the whole mind. Every person who wears cut jewels merely for the sake of their value is, therefore, a slave-driver.

But the working of the goldsmith, and the various designing of grouped jewellery and enamel-work, may become the subject of the most noble human intelligence. Therefore, money spent in the purchase of well-designed plate, of precious engraved vases, cameos, or enamels, does good to humanity; and, in work of this kind, jewels may be employed to heighten its splendour; and their cutting is then a price paid for the attainment of a noble end, and thus perfectly allowable.

I shall perhaps press this law farther elsewhere, but our immediate concern is chiefly with the second, namely, never to demand an exact finish, when it does not lead to a noble end. For observe, I have only dwelt upon the rudeness of Gothic, or any other kind of imperfectness, as admirable, where it was impossible to get design or thought without it. If you are to have the thought of a rough and untaught man, you must have it in a rough and untaught way; but from an educated man, who can without effort express his thoughts in an educated way, take the graceful expression, and be thankful. Only *get* the thought, and do not silence the peasant because he cannot speak good grammar, or until you have taught him his grammar. Grammar and refinement are good things, both, only be sure of the better thing first. And thus in art, delicate finish is desirable from the greatest masters, and is always given by them. In some places Michael Angelo, Leonardo, Phidias, Perugino, Turner, all finished with the most exquisite care; and the finish they give always leads to the fuller accomplishment of their noble purposes. But lower men than these cannot finish, for it requires consummate knowledge to finish consummately, and then we must take their thoughts as they are able to give them. So the rule is simple: Always look for invention first, and after that, for such execution as will help the invention, and as the inventor is capable of without painful effort, and *no more*. Above all, demand no refinement of execution where there is no thought, for that is slaves' work, unredeemed. Rather choose rough work than smooth work, so only that the practical purpose be answered, and never imagine there is reason to be proud of anything that may be accomplished by patience and sand-paper.

I shall only give one example, which however will show the reader what I mean, from the manufacture already alluded to, that of glass. Our modern glass is exquisitely clear in its substance, true in its form, accurate in its cutting. We are proud of this. We ought to be ashamed of it. The old Venice glass was muddy, inaccurate in all its forms, and clumsily cut, if at all. And the old Venetian was justly proud of it. For there is this difference between the English and Venetian workman, that the former thinks only of accurately matching his patterns, and getting his curves perfectly true and his edges perfectly sharp, and becomes a mere machine for rounding curves and sharpening edges, while the old Venetian cared not a whit whether his edges were sharp or not, but he invented a new design for every glass that he made, and never moulded a handle or a lip without a new fancy in it. And therefore, though some Venetian glass is ugly and clumsy enough, when made by clumsy and uninventive workmen, other Venetian glass is so lovely in its forms that no price is too great for it; and we never see the same form in it twice. Now you cannot have the finish and the varied form too. If the workman is thinking about his edges, he cannot be thinking of his design; if of his design, he cannot think of his edges. Choose whether you will pay for the lovely form or the perfect finish, and choose at the same moment whether you will make the worker a man or a grindstone.

Nay, but the reader interrupts me,—"If the workman can design beautifully, I would not have him kept at the furnace. Let him be taken away and made a gentleman, and have a studio, and design his glass there, and I will have it blown and cut for him by common workmen, and so I will have my design and my finish too."

All ideas of this kind are founded upon two mistaken suppositions: the first, that one man's thoughts can be, or ought to be, executed by another man's hands; the second, that manual labour is a degradation, when it is governed by intellect.

On a large scale, and in work determinable by line and rule, it is indeed both possible and necessary that the thoughts of one man should be carried out by the labour of others; in this sense I have already defined the best architecture to be the expression of the mind of manhood by the hands of childhood. But on a smaller scale, and in a design which cannot be mathematically defined, one man's thoughts can never be expressed by another: and the difference between the spirit of touch of the man who is inventing, and of the man who is obeying directions, is often all the difference between a great and a common work of art. How wide the separation is between original and second-hand execution, I shall endeavour to show elsewhere; it is not so much to our purpose here as to mark the other and more fatal error of despising manual labour when governed by intellect; for it is no less fatal an error to despise it when thus regulated by intellect, than to value it for its own sake. We are always in these days endeavouring to separate the two; we want one man to be always thinking, and another to be always working, and we call one a gentleman, and the other an operative; whereas the workman ought often to be thinking, and the thinker often to be working, and both should be gentlemen, in the best sense. As it is, we make both ungentle, the one envying, the other despising, his brother; and the mass of society is made up of morbid thinkers, and miserable workers. Now it is only by labour that thought can be made healthy, and only by thought that labour can be made happy, and the two cannot be separated with impunity. It would be well if all of us were good handicraftsmen in some kind, and the dishonour of manual labour done away with altogether; so that though there should still be a trenchant distinction of race between nobles and commoners, there should not, among the latter, be a trenchant distinction of employment, as between idle and working men, or between men of liberal and illiberal professions. All professions should be liberal, and there should be less pride felt in peculiarity of employment, and more in excellence of achievement. And yet more, in each several profession, no master should be too proud to do its hardest work. The painter should grind his own colours; the architect work in the mason's yard with his men; the master-manufacturer be himself a more skilful operative than any man in his mills; and the distinction between one man and another be only in experience and skill, and the authority and wealth which these must naturally and justly obtain.

I should be led far from the matter in hand, if I were to pursue this interesting subject. Enough, I trust, has been said to show the reader that the rudeness or imperfection which at first rendered the term "Gothic" one of reproach is indeed, when rightly understood, one of the most noble characters of Christian architecture, and not only a noble but an *essential* one. It seems a fantastic paradox, but it is nevertheless a most important truth, that no architecture can be truly noble which is *not* imperfect. And this is easily demonstrable. For since the architect, whom we will suppose capable of doing all in perfection, cannot execute the whole with his own hands, he must either make slaves of his workmen in the old Greek, and present English fashion, and level his work to a slave's capacities, which is to degrade it; or else he must take his workmen as he finds them, and let them show their weaknesses together with their strength, which will involve the Gothic imperfection, but render the whole work as noble as the intellect of the age can make it.

But the principle may be stated more broadly still. I have confined the illustration of it to architecture, but I must not leave it as if true of architecture only. Hitherto I have used the words imperfect and perfect merely to distinguish between work grossly unskilful, and work executed with average precision and science; and I have been pleading that any degree of unskilfulness should be admitted, so only that the labourer's mind had room for expression. But, accurately speaking, no good work whatever can be perfect, and *the demand for perfection is always a sign of a misunderstanding of the ends of art*.

This for two reasons, both based on everlasting laws. The first, that no great man ever stops working till he has reached his point of failure; that is to say, his mind is always far in advance of his powers of execution, and the latter will now and then give way in trying to follow it; besides that he will always give to the inferior portions of

123

his work only such inferior attention as they require; and according to his greatness he becomes so accustomed to the feeling of dissatisfaction with the best he can do, that in moments of lassitude or anger with himself he will not care though the beholder be dissatisfied also. I believe there has only been one man who would not acknowledge this necessity, and strove always to reach perfection, Leonardo; the end of his vain effort being merely that he would take ten years to a picture, and leave it unfinished. And therefore, if we are to have great men working at all, or less men doing their best, the work will be imperfect, however beautiful. Of human work none but what is bad can be perfect, in its own bad way.*

The second reason is, that imperfection is in some sort essential to all that we know of life. It is the sign of life in a mortal body, that is to say, of a state of progress and change. Nothing that lives is, or can be, rigidly perfect; part of it is decaying, part nascent. The foxglove blossom,—a third part bud, a third part past, a third part in full bloom,—is a type of the life of this world. And in all things that live there are certain irregularities and deficiencies which are not only signs of life, but sources of beauty. No human face is exactly the same in its lines on each side, no leaf perfect in its lobes, no branch in its symmetry. All admit irregularity as they imply change; and to banish imperfection is to destroy expression, to check exertion, to paralyse vitality. All things are literally better, lovelier, and more beloved for the imperfections which have been divinely appointed, that the law of human life may be Effort, and the law of human judgment, Mercy.

Accept this then for a universal law, that neither architecture nor any other noble work of man can be good unless it be imperfect; and let us be prepared for the otherwise strange fact, which we shall discern clearly as we approach the period of the Renaissance, that the first cause of the fall of the arts of Europe was a relentless requirement of perfection, incapable alike either of being silenced by veneration for greatness, or softened into forgiveness of simplicity.

Thus far then of the Rudeness or Savageness, which is

* The Elgin marbles are supposed by many persons to be "perfect." In the most important portions they indeed approach perfection, but only there. The draperies are unfinished, the hair and wool of the animals are unfinished, and the entire bas-reliefs of the frieze are roughly cut.

the first mental element of Gothic architecture. It is an element in many other healthy architectures also, as in Byzantine and Romanesque; but true Gothic cannot exist without it.

The second mental element above named was CHANGE-FULNESS, or Variety.

I have already enforced the allowing independent operation to the inferior workman, simply as a duty *to him,* and as ennobling the architecture by rendering it more Christian. We have now to consider what reward we obtain for the performance of this duty, namely, the perpetual variety of every feature of the building.

Wherever the workman is utterly enslaved, the parts of the building must of course be absolutely like each other; for the perfection of his execution can only be reached by exercising him in doing one thing, and giving him nothing else to do. The degree in which the workman is degraded may be thus known at a glance, by observing whether the several parts of the building are similar or not; and if, as in Greek work, all the capitals are alike, and all the mouldings unvaried, then the degradation is complete; if, as in Egyptian or Ninevite work, though the manner of executing certain figures is always the same, the order of design is perpetually varied, the degradation is less total; if, as in Gothic work, there is perpetual change both in design and execution, the workman must have been altogether set free.

How much the beholder gains from the liberty of the labourer may perhaps be questioned in England, where one of the strongest instincts in nearly every mind is that Love of Order which makes us desire that our house windows should pair like our carriage horses, and allows us to yield our faith unhesitatingly to architectural theories which fix a form for everything, and forbid variation from it. I would not impeach love of order: it is one of the most useful elements of the English mind; it helps us in our commerce and in all purely practical matters; and it is in many cases one of the foundation stones of morality. Only do not let us suppose that love of order is love of art. It is true that order, in its highest sense, is one of the necessities of art, just as time is a necessity of music; but love of order has no more to do with our right enjoyment of architecture or painting, than love of punctuality with the appreciation of an opera. Experience, I fear, teaches us that accurate and methodical habits in daily life are seldom characteristic of those who either quickly perceive, or richly possess, the creative powers of art; there is, however, nothing inconsistent between the two instincts, and nothing to hinder us from retaining our business habits, and yet fully allowing and enjoying the noblest gifts of Invention. We already do so, in every other branch of art except architecture, and we only do *not* so there because we have been taught that it would be wrong. Our architects gravely inform us that, as there are four rules of arithmetic, there are five orders of architecture; we, in our simplicity, think that this sounds consistent, and believe them. They inform us also that there is one proper form for Corinthian capitals, another for Doric, and another for Ionic. We, considering that there is also a proper form for the letters A, B, and C, think that this also sounds consistent, and accept the proposition. Understanding, therefore, that one form of the said capitals is proper, and no other, and having a conscientious horror of all impropriety, we allow the architect to provide us with the said capitals, of the proper form, in such and such a quantity, and in all other points to take care that the legal forms are observed; which having done, we rest in forced confidence that we are well housed.

But our higher instincts are not deceived. We take no pleasure in the building provided for us, resembling that which we take in a new book or a new picture. We may be proud of its size, complacent in its correctness, and happy in its convenience. We may take the same pleasure in its symmetry and workmanship as in a well-ordered room, or a skilful piece of manufacture. And this we suppose to be all the pleasure that architecture was ever intended to give us. The idea of reading a building as we would read Milton or Dante, and getting the same kind of delight out of the stones as out of the stanzas, never enters our minds for a moment. And for good reason;—There is indeed rhythm in the verses, quite as strict as the symmetries or rhythm of the architecture, and a thousand times more beautiful, but there is something else than rhythm. The verses were neither made to order, nor to match, as the capitals were; and we have therefore a kind of pleasure in them other than a sense of propriety. But it requires a strong effort of common sense to shake ourselves quit of all that we have been taught for the last two centuries, and wake to the perception of a truth just as simple and certain as it is new: that great art, whether expressing itself in words, colours, or stones, does *not* say the same thing over and over again; that the merit of architectural, as of every other art, consists in its saying new and different things; that to repeat itself is no more a characteristic of genius in marble than it is of genius in print; and that we may, without offending any laws of good taste, require of an architect, as we do of a novelist, that he should be not only correct, but entertaining.

Yet all this is true, and self-evident; only hidden from us, as many other self-evident things are, by false teaching. Nothing is a great work of art, for the production of which either rules or models can be given. Exactly so far as architecture works on known rules, and from given models, it is not an art, but a manufacture; and it is, of the two procedures, rather less rational (because more easy) to copy capitals or mouldings from Phidias, and call ourselves architects, than to copy heads and hands from Titian, and call ourselves painters.

Let us then understand at once, that change or variety is as much a necessity to the human heart and brain in buildings as in books; that there is no merit, though there is some occasional use, in monotony; and that we must no more expect to derive either pleasure or profit from an architecture whose ornaments are of one pattern, and whose pillars are of one proportion, than we should out of a universe in which the clouds were all of one shape, and the trees all of one size.

And this we confess in deeds, though not in words. All the pleasure which the people of the nineteenth century take in art, is in pictures, sculpture, minor objects of virtù, or mediæval architecture, which we enjoy under the term picturesque: no pleasure is taken anywhere in modern buildings, and we find all men of true feeling delighting to escape out of modern cities into natural scenery: hence, as I shall hereafter show, that peculiar love of landscape which is characteristic of the age. It would be well if in all other matters, we were as ready to put up with what we dislike, for the sake of compliance with established law, as we are in architecture.

How so debased a law ever came to be established, we shall see when we come to describe the Renaissance schools; here we have only to note, as a second most essential element of the Gothic spirit, that it broke through that law wherever it found it in existence; it not only dared, but delighted in, the infringement of every servile principle; and invented a series of forms of which the merit was, not merely that they were new, but that they were *capable of perpetual novelty*. The pointed arch was not merely a bold variation from the round, but it admitted of millions of variations in itself; for the proportions of a pointed arch are changeable to infinity, while a circular arch is always the same. The grouped shaft was not merely a bold variation from the single one, but it admitted of millions of variations in its grouping, and in the proportions resultant from its grouping. The introduction of tracery was not only a startling change in the treatment of window lights, but admitted endless changes in the interlacement of the tracery bars themselves. So that, while in all living Christian architecture the love of variety exists, the Gothic schools exhibited that love in culminating energy; and their influence, wherever it extended itself, may be sooner and farther traced by this character than by any other; the tendency to the adoption of Gothic types being always first shown by greater irregularity, and richer variation in the forms of architecture it is about to supersede, long before the appearance of the pointed arch or of any other recognizable *outward* sign of the Gothic mind.

We must, however, herein note carefully what distinction there is between a healthy and a diseased love of change; for as it was in healthy love of change that the Gothic architecture rose, it was partly in consequence of diseased love of change that it was destroyed. In order to understand this clearly, it will be necessary to consider the different ways in which change and monotony are presented to us in nature; both having their use, like darkness and light, and the one incapable of being enjoyed without the other: change being most delightful after some prolongation of monotony, as light appears most brilliant after the eyes have been for some time closed.

I believe that the true relations of monotony and change may be most simply understood by observing them in music. We may therein notice first, that there is a sublimity and majesty in monotony, which there is not in rapid or frequent variation. This is true throughout all nature. The greater part of the sublimity of the sea depends on its monotony; so also that of desolate moor and mountain scenery; and especially the sublimity of motion, as in the quiet, unchanged fall and rise of an engine beam. So also there is sublimity in darkness which there is not in light.

Again, monotony after a certain time, or beyond a certain degree, becomes either uninteresting or intolerable, and the musician is obliged to break it in one of two ways: either while the air or passage is perpetually repeated, its notes are variously enriched and harmonized; or else, after a certain number of repeated passages, an entirely new passage is introduced, which is more or less delightful according to the length of the previous monotony. Nature, of course, uses both these kinds of variation perpetually. The sea-waves, resembling each other in general mass, but none like its brother in minor divisions and curves, are a monotony of the first kind; the great plain, broken by an emergent rock or clump of trees, is a monotony of the second.

Farther: in order to the enjoyment of the change in either case, a certain degree of patience is required from the hearer or observer. In the first case, he must be satisfied to endure with patience the recurrence of the great masses of sound or form, and to seek for entertainment in a careful watchfulness of the minor details. In the second case, he must bear patiently the infliction of the monotony for some moments, in order to feel the full refreshment of the change. This is true even of the shortest musical passage in which the element of monotony is employed. In cases of more majestic monotony, the patience required is so considerable that it becomes a kind of pain,—a price paid for the future pleasure.

Again: the talent of the composer is not in the monotony, but in the changes: he may show feeling and taste by his use of monotony in certain places or degrees; that is to say, by his *various* employment of it; but it is always in the new arrangement or invention that his intellect is shown, and not in the monotony which relieves it.

Lastly: if the pleasure of change be too often repeated, it ceases to be delightful, for then change itself becomes monotonous, and we are driven to seek delight in extreme and fantastic degrees of it. This is the diseased love of change of which we have above spoken.

From these facts we may gather generally that monotony is, and ought to be, in itself painful to us, just as darkness is; that an architecture which is altogether monotonous is a dark or dead architecture; and of those who love it, it may be truly said, "they love darkness rather than light." But monotony in certain measure, used in order to give value to change, and above all, that *transparent* monotony, which, like the shadows of a great painter, suffers all manner of dimly suggested form to be seen through the body of it, is an essential in architectural as in all other composition; and the endurance of monotony has about the same place in a healthy mind that the endurance of darkness has: that is to say, as a strong intellect will have pleasure in the solemnities of storm and twilight, and in the broken and mysterious lights that gleam among them, rather than in mere brilliancy and glare, while a frivolous mind will dread the shadow and the storm; and as a great man will be ready to endure much darkness of fortune in order to reach greater eminence of power or felicity, while an inferior man will not pay the price; exactly in like manner a great mind will accept, or even delight in, monotony which would be wearisome to an inferior intellect, because it has more patience and power of expectation, and is ready to pay the full price for the great future pleasure of change. But in all cases it is not that the noble nature loves monotony, any more than it loves darkness or pain. But it can bear with it, and receive a high pleasure in the endurance or patience, a pleasure necessary to the well-being of this world; while those who will not submit to the temporary sameness, but rush from one change to another, gradually dull the edge of change itself, and bring a shadow and weariness over the whole world from which there is no more escape.

From these general uses of variety in the economy of the world, we may at once understand its use and abuse in architecture. The variety of the Gothic schools is the more healthy and beautiful, because in many cases it is entirely unstudied, and results, not from mere love of change, but from practical necessities. For in one point of view Gothic is not only the best, but the *only rational* architecture, as being that which can fit itself most easily to all services, vulgar or noble. Undefined in its slope of roof, height of shaft, breadth of arch, or disposition of ground plan, it can shrink into a turret, expand into a hall, coil into a staircase, or spring into a spire, with undegraded grace and unexhausted energy; and whenever it finds occasion for change in its form or purpose, it submits to it without the slightest sense of loss either to its unity or majesty,— subtle and flexible like a fiery serpent, but ever attractive to the voice of the charmer. And it is one of the chief virtues of the Gothic builders, that they never suffered ideas of outside symmetries and consistencies to interfere with the real use and value of what they did. If they wanted a window, they opened one; a room, they added one; a buttress, they built one; utterly regardless of any established conventionalities of external appearance, knowing (as indeed it always happened) that such daring interruptions of the formal plan would rather give additional interest to its symmetry than injure it. So that, in the best times of Gothic, a useless window would rather have been opened in an unexpected place for the sake of the surprise, than a useful one forbidden for the sake of symmetry. Every successive architect, employed upon a great work, built the pieces he added in his own way, utterly regardless of the style adopted by his predecessors; and if two towers were raised in nominal correspondence at the sides of a cathedral front, one was nearly sure to be different from the other, and in each the style at the top to be different from the style at the bottom.

These marked variations were, however, only permitted as part of the great system of perpetual change which ran through every member of Gothic design, and rendered it as endless a field for the beholder's inquiry as for the builder's imagination: change, which in the best schools is subtle and delicate, and rendered more delightful by intermingling of a noble monotony; in the more barbaric schools is somewhat fantastic and redundant; but, in all, a necessary and constant condition of the life of the school. Sometimes the variety is in one feature, sometimes in another; it may be in the capitals or crockets, in the niches or the traceries, or in all together, but in some one or other of the features it will be found always. If the mouldings are constant, the surface sculpture will change; if the capitals are of a fixed design, the traceries will change; if the traceries are monotonous, the capitals will change; and if even, as in some fine schools, the early English for example, there is the slightest approximation to an unvarying type of mouldings, capitals, and floral decoration, the variety is found in the disposition of the masses, and in the figure sculpture.

I must now refer for a moment, before we quit the consideration of this, the second mental element of Gothic, to the opening of the third chapter of the *Seven Lamps of Architecture,* in which the distinction was drawn between man gathering and man governing; between his acceptance of the sources of delight from nature, and his development of authoritative or imaginative power in their arrangement; for the two mental elements, not only of Gothic, but of all good architecture, which we have just been examining, belong to it, and are admirable in it, chiefly as it is, more than any other subject of art, the work of man, and the expression of the average power of

131

man. A picture or poem is often little more than a feeble utterance of man's admiration of something out of himself; but architecture approaches more to a creation of his own, born of his necessities, and expressive of his nature. It is also, in some sort, the work of the whole race, while the picture or statue is the work of one only, in most cases more highly gifted than his fellows. And therefore we may expect that the first two elements of good architecture should be expressive of some great truths commonly belonging to the whole race, and necessary to be understood or felt by them in all their work that they do under the sun. And observe what they are: the confession of Imperfection, and the confession of Desire of Change. The building of the bird and the bee needs not express anything like this. It is perfect and unchanging. But just because we are something better than birds or bees, our building must confess that we have not reached the perfection we can imagine, and cannot rest in the condition we have attained. If we pretend to have reached either perfection or satisfaction, we have degraded ourselves and our work. God's work only may express that; but ours may never have that sentence written upon it,—"And behold, it was very good." And, observe again, it is not merely as it renders the edifice a book of various knowledge, or a mine of precious thought, that variety is essential to its nobleness. The vital principle is not the love of *Knowledge,* but the love of *Change.* It is that strange *disquietude* of the Gothic spirit that is its greatness; that restlessness of the dreaming mind, that wanders hither and thither among the niches, and flickers feverishly around the pinnacles, and frets and fades in labyrinthine knots and shadows along wall and roof, and yet is not satisfied, nor shall be satisfied. The Greek could stay in his triglyph furrow, and be at peace; but the work of the Gothic heart is fretwork still, and it can neither rest in, nor from, its labour, but must pass on, sleeplessly, until its love of change shall be pacified for ever in the change that must come alike on them that wake and them that sleep.

The third constituent element of the Gothic mind was stated to be NATURALISM; that is to say, the love of natural objects for their own sake, and the effect to represent them frankly, unconstrained by artistical laws.

This characteristic of the style partly follows in necessary connection with those named above. For, so soon as the workman is left free to represent what subjects he chooses, he must look to the nature that is round him for material, and will endeavour to represent it as he sees it, with more or less accuracy according to the skill he possesses, and with much play of fancy, but with small respect for law. There is, however, a marked distinction between the imaginations of the Western and Eastern races, even when both are left free; the Western, or Gothic, delighting most in the representation of facts, and the Eastern (Arabian, Persian, and Chinese) in the harmony of colours and forms. Each of these intellectual dispositions has its particular forms of error and abuse, which, though I have often before stated, I must here again briefly explain; and this the rather, because the word Naturalism is, in one of its senses, justly used as a term of reproach, and the questions respecting the real relations of art and nature are so many and so confused throughout all the schools of Europe at this day, that I cannot clearly enunciate any single truth without appearing to admit, in fellowship with it, some kind of error, unless the reader will bear with me in entering into such an analysis of the subject as will serve us for general guidance.

We are to remember, in the first place, that the arrangement of colours and lines is an art analogous to the composition* of music, and entirely independent of the representation of facts. Good colouring does not necessarily convey the image of anything but itself. It consists in certain proportions and arrangements of rays of light, but not in likenesses to anything. A few touches of certain greys and purples laid by a master's hand on white paper will be good colouring; as more touches are added beside them, we may find out that they were intended to represent a dove's neck, and we may praise, as the drawing advances, the perfect imitation of the dove's neck. But the good colouring does not consist in that imitation, but in the abstract qualities and relations of the grey and purple.

In like manner, as soon as a great sculptor begins to

* I am always afraid to use the word "Composition;" it is so utterly misused in the general parlance respecting art. Nothing is more common than to hear divisions of art into "form, composition, and colour," or "light and shade and composition," or "sentiment and composition," or it matters not what else and composition; the speakers in each case attaching a perfectly different meaning to the word, generally an indistinct one, and always a wrong one. Composition is, in plain English, "putting together," and it means the putting together of lines, of forms, of colours, of shades, or of ideas. Painters compose in colour, compose in thought, compose in form, and compose in effect; the word being of use merely in order to express a scientific, disciplined, and inventive arrangement of any of these, instead of a merely natural or accidental one.

133

shape his work out of the block, we shall see that its lines are nobly arranged, and of noble character. We may not have the slightest idea for what the forms are intended, whether they are of man or beast, of vegetation or drapery. Their likeness to anything does not affect their nobleness. They are magnificent forms, and that is all we need care to know of them, in order to say whether the workman is a good or bad sculptor.

Now the noblest art is an exact unison of the abstract value, with the imitative power, of forms and colours. It is the noblest composition, used to express the noblest facts. But the human mind cannot in general unite the two perfections: it either pursues the fact to the neglect of the composition, or pursues the composition to the neglect of the fact.

And it is intended by the Deity that it *should* do this: the best art is not always wanted. Facts are often wanted without art, as in a geological diagram; and art often without facts, as in a Turkey carpet. And most men have been made capable of giving either one or the other, but not both; only one or two, the very highest, can give both.

Observe then. Men are universally divided, as respects their artistical qualifications, into three great classes; a right, a left, and a centre. On the right side are the men of facts, on the left the men of design, in the centre the men of both.

The three classes of course pass into each other by imperceptible gradations. The men of facts are hardly ever altogether without powers of design; the men of design are always in some measure cognizant of facts; and as each class possesses more or less of the powers of the opposite one, it approaches to the character of the central class. Few men, even in that central rank, are so exactly throned on the summit of the crest that they cannot be perceived to incline in the least one way or the other, embracing both horizons with their glance. Now each of these classes has, as I above said, a healthy function in the world, and correlative diseases or unhealthy functions; and, when the work of either of them is seen in its morbid condition, we are apt to find fault with the class of workmen, instead of finding fault only with the particular abuse which has perverted their action.

Let us first take an instance of the healthy action of the three classes on a simple subject, so as fully to understand the distinction between them, and then we shall more easily examine the corruptions to which they are liable. A spray of vine with a bough of cherry-tree, which I have outlined from nature as accurately as I could, without in the least endeavouring to compose or arrange the form, is a simple piece of fact-work, healthy and good, as such, and useful to any one who wanted to know plain truths about tendrils of vines, but there is no attempt at design in it. A branch of vine used to decorate the angle of the Ducal Palace is faithful as a representation of vine, and yet so designed that every leaf serves an architectural purpose, and could not be spared from its place without harm. This is central work; fact and design together. A spandril from St. Mark's, in which the forms of the vine are dimly suggested, the object of the design is merely to obtain graceful lines, and well-proportioned masses upon the gold ground. There is not the least attempt to inform the spectator of any facts about the growth of the vine; there are no stalks or tendrils,—merely running bands with leaves emergent from them, of which nothing but the outline is taken from the vine, and even that imperfectly. This is design, unregardful of facts.

Now the work is, in all these three cases, perfectly healthy. Example 1 is not bad work because it has not design, nor Example 2 bad work because it has not facts. The object of the one is to give pleasure through truth, and of the other to give pleasure through composition. And both are right.

What, then, are the diseased operations to which the three classes of workmen are liable?

Primarily, two; affecting the two inferior classes;

1st, When either of those two classes Despises the other;

2nd, When either of the two classes Envies the other; producing, therefore, four forms of dangerous error.

First, when the men of facts despise design. This is the error of the common Dutch painters, of merely imitative painters of still life, flowers, etc., and other men who, having either the gift of accurate imitation or strong sympathies with nature, suppose that all is done when the imitation is perfected or sympathy expressed. A large body of English landscapists come into this class, including most clever sketchers from nature, who fancy that to get a sky of true tone, and a gleam of sunshine or sweep of shower faithfully expressed, is all that can be required of art. These men are generally themselves answerable for much of their deadness of feeling to the higher qualities of composition. They probably have not originally the high gifts of design, but they lose such powers as they originally possessed by despising, and refusing to study, the results of great power of design in others. Their knowledge, as far as it goes, being accurate, they are usually presumptuous and self-conceited, and gradually become incapable of admiring anything but what is like their own works. They see nothing in the works of great designers but the faults, and do harm almost incalculable in the European society of the present day by sneering at the compositions of the greatest men of the earlier ages,* because they do not absolutely tally with their own ideas of "Nature."

The second form of error is when the men of design despise facts. All noble design must deal with facts to a certain extent, for there is no food for it but in nature. The best colourist invents best by taking hints from natural colours; from birds, skies, or groups of figures. And if, in the delight of inventing fantastic colour and form, the truths of nature are wilfully neglected, the intellect becomes comparatively decrepit, and that state of art results which we find among the Chinese. The Greek designers delighted in the facts of the human form, and became great in consequence; but the facts of lower nature were disregarded by them, and their inferior ornament became, therefore, dead and valueless.

The third form of error is when the men of facts envy design; that is to say, when, having only imitative powers, they refuse to employ those powers upon the visible world around them; but, having been taught that composition is the end of art, strive to obtain the inventive powers which nature has denied them, study nothing but the works of reputed designers, and perish in a fungous growth of plagiarism and laws of art.

Here was the great error of the beginning of this century; it is the error of the meanest kind of men that employ themselves in painting, and it is the most fatal of all, rendering those who fall into it utterly useless, incapable of helping the world with either truth or fancy, while in all probability, they deceive it by base resemblances of both, until it hardly recognizes truth or fancy when they really exist.

The fourth form of error is when the men of design envy facts; that is to say, when the temptation of closely imitating nature leads them to forget their own proper

---

* "Earlier," that is to say, pre-Raphaelite ages. Men of this stamp will praise Claude, and such other comparatively debased artists; but they cannot taste the work of the thirteenth century.

136

ornamental function, and when they lose the power of the composition for the sake of graphic truth; as, for instance, in the hawthorn moulding so often spoken of round the porch of Bourges Cathedral, which, though very lovely, might perhaps, as we saw above, have been better, if the old builder, in his excessive desire to make it look like hawthorn, had not painted it green.

It is, however, carefully to be noted, that the two morbid conditions to which the men of facts are liable are much more dangerous and harmful than those to which the men of design are liable. The morbid state of men of design injures themselves only; that of the men of facts injures the whole world. The Chinese porcelain-painter is, indeed, not so great a man as he might be, but he does not want to break everything that is not porcelain: but the modern English fact-hunter, despising design, wants to destroy everything that does not agree with his own notions of truth, and becomes the most dangerous and despicable of iconoclasts, excited by egotism instead of religion. Again: the Bourges sculptor, painting his hawthorns green, did indeed somewhat hurt the effect of his own beautiful design, but did not prevent any one from loving hawthorn: but Sir George Beaumont, trying to make Constable paint grass brown *instead* of green, was setting himself between Constable and nature, blinding the painter, and blaspheming the work of God.

So much, then, of the diseases of the inferior classes, caused by their envying or despising each other. It is evident that the men of the central class cannot be liable to any morbid operation of this kind, they possessing the powers of both.

But there is another order of diseases which affect all the three classes, considered with respect to their pursuit of facts. For observe, all the three classes are in some degree pursuers of facts; even the men of design not being in any case altogether independent of external truth. Now, considering them *all* as more or less searchers after truth, there is another triple division to be made of them. Everything presented to them in nature has good and evil mingled in it: and artists, considered as searchers after truth, are again to be divided into three great classes, a right, a left, and a centre. Those on the right perceive, and pursue, the good, and leave the evil: those in the centre, the greatest, perceive and pursue the good and evil together, the whole thing as it verily is: those on the left perceive and pursue the evil, and leave the good.

The first class, I say, take the good and leave the evil. Out of whatever is presented to them, they gather what it has of grace, and life, and light, and holiness, and leave all, or at least as much as possible, of the rest undrawn. The faces of their figures express no evil passions; the skies of their landscapes are without storm; the prevalent character of their colour is brightness, and of their chiaroscuro fulness of light. The early Italian and Flemish painters Angelico and Memling, Perugino, Francia, Raffaelle in his best time, John Bellini, and our own Stothard, belong eminently to this class.

The second, or greatest class, render all that they see in nature unhesitatingly, with a kind of divine grasp and government of the whole, sympathizing with all the good, and yet confessing, permitting, and bringing good out of the evil also. Their subject is infinite as nature, their colour equally balanced between splendour and sadness, reaching occasionally the highest degrees of both, and their chiaroscuro equally balanced between light and shade.

The principal men of this class are Michael Angelo, Leonardo, Giotto, Tintoret, and Turner. Raffaelle in his second time, Titian, and Rubens are transitional; the first inclining to the eclectic, and the last two to the impure class, Raffaelle rarely giving all the evil, Titian and Rubens rarely all the good.

The last class perceive and imitate evil only. They cannot draw the trunk of a tree without blasting and shattering it, nor a sky except covered with stormy clouds; they delight in the beggary and brutality of the human race; their colour is for the most part subdued or lurid, and the greatest spaces of their pictures are occupied by darkness.

Happily the examples of this class are seldom seen in perfection. Salvator Rosa and Caravaggio are the most characteristic: the other men belonging to it approach towards the central rank by imperceptible gradations, as they perceive and represent more and more of good. But Murillo, Zurbaran, Camillo Procaccini, Rembrandt, and Teniers, all belong naturally to this lower class.

Now, observe: the three classes into which artists were previously divided, of men of fact, men of design, and men of both, are all of Divine institution; but of these latter three, the last is in nowise of Divine institution. It is entirely human, and the men who belong to it have sunk into it by their own faults. They are, so far forth, either useless or harmful men. It is indeed good that evil should be occasionally represented, even in its worst forms, but never that it should be taken delight in: and the mighty men of the central class will always give us all that is needful of it; sometimes, as Hogarth did, dwelling upon it bitterly as satirists,—but this with the more effect, because they will neither exaggerate it, nor represent it mercilessly, and without the atoning points that all evil shows to a Divinely guided glance, even at its deepest. So then, though the third class will always, I fear, in some measure exist, the two necessary classes are only the first two: and this is so far acknowledged by the general sense of men, that the basest class has been confounded with the second; and painters have been divided commonly only into two ranks, now known, I believe, throughout Europe by the names which they first received in Italy, "Puristi and Naturalisti." Since, however, in the existing state of things, the degraded or evil-loving class, though less defined than that of the Puristi, is just as vast as it is indistinct, this division has done infinite dishonour to the great faithful painters of nature: and it has long been one of the objects I have had most at heart to show that, in reality, the Purists, in their sanctity, are less separated from these natural painters than the Sensualists in their foulness; and that the difference, though less discernible, is in reality greater, between the man who pursues evil for its own sake, and him who bears with it for the sake of truth, than between this latter and the man who will not endure it at all.

Let us, then, endeavour briefly to mark the real relations of these three vast ranks of men, whom I shall call, for convenience in speaking of them, Purists, Naturalists, and Sensualists; not that these terms express their real characters, but I know no word, and cannot coin a convenient one, which would accurately express the opposite of Purist; and I keep the terms Purist and Naturalist in order to comply, as far as possible, with the established usage of language on the Continent. Now, observe: in saying that nearly everything presented to us in nature has mingling in it of good and evil, I do not mean that nature is conceivably improvable, or that anything that God has made could be called evil, if we could see far enough into its uses, but that, with respect to immediate effects or appearances, it may be so, just as the hard rind or bitter kernel of a fruit may be an evil to the eater, though in the one is the protection of the fruit, and in the other its continuance. The Purist, therefore, does not mend nature, but receives from nature and from God that which is good for him;

while the Sensualist fills himself "with the husks that the swine did eat" (Luke xv. 16).

The three classes may, therefore, be likened to men reaping wheat, of which the Purists take the fine flour, and the Sensualists the chaff and straw, but the Naturalists take all home, and make their cake of the one, and their couch of the other.

For instance. We know more certainly every day that whatever appears to us harmful in the universe has some beneficent or necessary operation; that the storm which destroys a harvest brightens the sunbeams for harvests yet unsown, and that the volcano which buries a city preserves a thousand from destruction. But the evil is not for the time less fearful, because we have learned it to be necessary; and we easily understand the timidity or the tenderness of the spirit which would withdraw itself from the presence of destruction, and create in its imagination a world of which the peace should be unbroken, in which the sky should not darken nor the sea rage, in which the leaf should not change nor the blossom wither. That man is greater, however, who contemplates with an equal mind the alternations of terror and of beauty; who, not rejoicing less beneath the sunny sky, can bear also to watch the bars of twilight narrowing on the horizon; and, not less sensible to the blessing of the peace of nature, can rejoice in the magnificence of the ordinances by which that peace is protected and secured. But separated from both by an immeasurable distance would be the man who delighted in convulsion and disease for their own sake; who found his daily food in the disorder of nature mingled with the suffering of humanity; and watched joyfully at the right hand of the Angel whose appointed work is to destroy as well as to accuse, while the corners of the house of feasting were struck by the wind from the wilderness.

And far more is this true, when the subject of contemplation is humanity itself. The passions of mankind are partly protective, partly beneficent, like the chaff and grain of the corn; but none without their use, none without nobleness when seen in balanced unity with the rest of the spirit which they are charged to defend. The passions of which the end is the continuance of the race: the indignation which is to arm it against injustice, or strengthen it to resist wanton injury; and the fear which lies at the root of prudence, reverence, and awe, are all honourable and beautiful, so long as man is regarded in his relations to the existing world. The religious Purist, striving to conceive him withdrawn from those relations, effaces from the countenance the traces of all transitory passion, illumines it with holy hope and love, and seals it with the serenity of heavenly peace; he conceals the forms of the body by the deep-folded garment, or else represents them under severely chastened types, and would rather paint them emaciated by the fact, or pale from the torture, than strengthened by exertion, or flushed by emotion. But the great Naturalist takes the human being in its wholeness, in its mortal as well as its spiritual strength. Capable of sounding and sympathizing with the whole range of its passions, he brings one majestic harmony out of them all; he represents it fearlessly in all its acts and thoughts, in its haste, its anger, its sensuality, and its pride, as well as in its fortitude or faith, but makes it noble in them all; he casts aside the veil from the body, and beholds the mysteries of its form like an angel looking down on an inferior creature: there is nothing which he is reluctant to behold, nothing that he is ashamed to confess; with all that lives, triumphing, falling, or suffering, he claims kindred, either in majesty or in mercy, yet standing, in a sort, afar off, unmoved even in the deepness of his sympathy; for the spirit within him is too thoughtful to be grieved, too brave to be applied, and too pure to be polluted.

How far beneath these two ranks of men shall we place, in the scale of being, those whose pleasure is only in sin or in suffering; who habitually contemplate humanity in poverty or decrepitude, fury or sensuality; whose works are either temptations to its weakness, or triumphs over its ruin, and recognize no other subjects for thought or admiration than the subtlety of the robber, the rage of the soldier, or the joy of the Sybarite? It seems strange, when thus definitely stated, that such a school should exist. Yet consider a little what gaps and blanks would disfigure our gallery and chamber walls, in places that we have long approached with reverence, if every picture, every statue, were removed from them, of which the subject was either the vice or the misery of mankind, portrayed without any moral purpose; consider the innumerable groups having reference merely to various forms of passion, low or high: drunken revels and brawls among peasants, gambling or fighting scenes among soldiers, amours and intrigues among every class, brutal battle pieces, banditti subjects, gluts of torture and death in famine, wreck, or slaughter, for the sake merely of the excitement,—that quickening

141

and suppling of the dull spirit that cannot be gained for it but by bathing it in blood, afterward to wither back into stained and stiffened apathy; and then that whole vast false heaven of sensual passion, full of nymphs, satyrs, graces, goddesses, and I know not what, from its high seventh circle in Correggio's Antiope, down to the Grecized ballet-dancers and smirking Cupids of the Parisian upholsterer. Sweep away all this, remorselessly, and see how much art we should have left.

And yet these are only the grossest manifestations of the tendency of the school. There are subtler, yet not less certain, signs of it in the works of men who stand high in the world's list of sacred painters. I doubt not that the reader was surprised when I named Murillo among the men of this third rank. Yet, go into the Dulwich Gallery, and meditate for a little over that much celebrated picture of the two beggar boys, one eating, lying on the ground, the other standing beside him. We have among our own painters one who cannot indeed be set beside Murillo as a painter of Madonnas, for he is a pure Naturalist, and, never having seen a Madonna, does not paint any; but who, as a painter of beggar or peasant boys, may be set beside Murillo, or any one else,—W. Hunt. He loves peasant boys, because he finds them more roughly and picturesquely dressed, and more healthily coloured, than others. And he paints all that he sees in them fearlessly; all the health and humour, and freshness and vitality, together with such awkwardness and stupidity, and what else of negative or positive harm there may be in the creature; but yet so that on the whole we love it, and find it perhaps even beautiful, or if not, at least we see that there is capability of good in it, rather than of evil; and all is lighted up by a sunshine and sweet colour that makes the smock frock as precious as cloth of gold. But look at those two ragged and vicious vagrants that Murillo has gathered out of the street. You smile at first, because they are eating so naturally, and their roguery is so complete. But is there anything else than roguery there, or was it well for the painter to give his time to the painting of those repulsive and wicked children? Do you feel moved with any charity towards children as you look at them? Are we the least more likely to take any interest in ragged schools, or to help the next pauper child that comes in our way, because the painter has shown us a cunning beggar feeding greedily? Mark the choice of the act. He might have shown hunger in other ways, and given interest to

142

even this act of eating, by making the face wasted, or the eye wistful. But he did not care to do this. He delighted merely in the disgusting manner of eating, the food filling the cheek; the boy is not hungry, else he would not turn round to talk and grin as he eats.

But observe another point in the lower figure. It lies so that the sole of the foot is turned towards the spectator; not because it would have lain less easily in another attitude, but that the painter may draw, and exhibit, the grey dust engrained in the foot. Do not call this the painting of nature: it is mere delight in foulness. The lesson, if there be any, in the picture, is not one whit the stronger. We all know that a begger's bare foot cannot be clean; there is no need to thrust its degradation into the light, as if no human imagination were vigorous enough for its conception.

The position of the Sensualists, in treatment of landscape, is less distinctly marked than in that of the figure, because even the wildest passions of nature are noble: but the inclination is manifested by carelessness in marking generic form in trees and flowers: by their preferring confused and irregular arrangements of foliage or foreground to symmetrical and simple grouping; by their general choice of such picturesqueness as results from decay, disorder, and disease, rather than of that which is consistent with the perfection of the things in which it is found; and by their imperfect rendering of the elements of strength and beauty in all things. I propose to work out this subject fully in the last volume of *Modern Painters;* but I trust that enough has been here said to enable the reader to understand the relations of the three great classes of artists, and therefore also the kinds of morbid condition into which the two higher (for the last has no other than a morbid condition) are liable to fall. For since the function of the Naturalists is to represent, as far as may be, the whole of nature, and of the Purists to represent what is absolutely good for some special purpose or time, it is evident that both are liable to err from shortness of sight, and the last also from weakness of judgment. I say, in the first place, both may err from shortness of sight, from not seeing all that there is in nature; seeing only the outside of things, or those points of them which bear least on the matter in hand. For instance, a modern continental Naturalist sees the anatomy of a limb thoroughly, but does not see its colour against the sky, which latter fact is to a painter far the more important of

143

the two. And because it is always easier to see the surface than the depth of things, the full sight of them requiring the highest powers of penetration, sympathy, and imagination, the world is full of vulgar Naturalists: not Sensualists, observe, not men who delight in evil; but men who never see the deepest good, and who bring discredit on all painting of Nature by the little that they discover in her. And the Purist, besides being liable to this same shortsightedness, is liable also to fatal errors of judgment; for he may think that good which is not so, and that the highest good which is the least. And thus the world is full of vulgar Purists,* who bring discredit on all selection by the silliness of their choice; and this the more, because the very becoming a Purist is commonly indicative of some slight degree of weakness, readiness to be offered, or narrowness of understanding of the ends of things: the greatest men being, in all times of art, Naturalists, without any exception; and the greatest Purists being those who approach nearest to the Naturalists, as Benozzo Gozzoli and Perugino. Hence there is a tendency in the Naturalists to despise the Purists, and in the Purists to be offended with the Naturalists (not understanding them, and confounding them with the Sensualists); and this is grievously harmful to both.

Of the various forms of resultant mischief it is not here the place to speak; the reader may already be somewhat wearied with a statement which has led us apparently so far from our immediate subject. But the digression was necessary, in order that I might clearly define the sense in which I use the word Naturalism when I state it

* I reserve for another place the full discussion of this interesting subject, which here would have led me too far; but it must be noted, in passing, that this vulgar Purism, which rejects truth, not because it is vicious, but because it is humble, and consists not in choosing what is good, but in disguising what is rough, extends itself into every species of art. The most definite instance of it is the dressing of characters of peasantry in an opera or ballet scene; and the walls of our exhibitions are full of works of art which "exalt nature" in the same way, not by revealing what is great in the heart, but by smoothing what is coarse in the complexion. There is nothing, I believe, so vulgar, so hopeless, so indicative of an irretrievably base mind, as this species of Purism. Of healthy Purism carried to the utmost endurable length in this direction, exalting the heart first, and the features with it, perhaps the most characteristic instance I can give is Stothard's vignette to "Jorasse," in Rogers's *Italy;* at least it would be so if it could be seen beside a real group of Swiss girls. The poems of Rogers, compared with those of Crabbe, are admirable instances of the healthiest Purism and healthiest Naturalism in poetry. The first great Naturalists of Christian art were Orcagna and Giotto.

to be the third most essential characteristic of Gothic architecture. I mean that the Gothic builders belong to the central or greatest rank in *both* the classifications of artists which we have just made; that considering all artists as either men of design, men of facts, or men of both, the Gothic builders were men of both; and that again, considering all artists as either Purists, Naturalists, or Sensualists, the Gothic builders were Naturalists.

I say first, that the Gothic builders were of that central class which unites fact with design; but that the part of the work which was more especially their own was the truthfulness. Their power of artistical invention or arrangement was not greater than that of Romanesque and Byzantine workmen: by those workmen they were taught the principles, and from them received their models, of design; but to the ornamental feeling and rich fancy of the Byzantine the Gothic builder added a love of *fact* which is never found in the South. Both Greek and Roman used conventional foliage in their ornament, passing into something that was not foliage at all, knotting itself into strange cup-like buds or clusters, and growing out of lifeless rods instead of stems; the Gothic sculptor received these types at first, as things that ought to be, just as we have a second time received them; but he could not rest in them. He saw there was no veracity in them, no knowledge, no vitality. Do what he would, he could not help liking the true leaves better; and cautiously, a little at a time, he put more of nature into his work, until at last it was all true, retaining, nevertheless, every valuable character of the original well-disciplined and designed arrangement.

Nor is it only in external and visible subject that the Gothic workman wrought for truth: he is as firm in his rendering of imaginative as of actual truth; that is to say, when an idea would have been by a Roman, or Byzantine, symbolically represented, the Gothic mind realizes it to the utmost. For instance, the purgatorial fire is represented in the mosaic of Torcello (Romanesque) as a red stream, longitudinally striped like a riband, descending out of the throne of Christ, and gradually extending itself to envelope the wicked. When we are once informed what this means, it is enough for its purpose; but the Gothic inventor does not leave the sign in need of interpretation. He makes the fire as like real fire as he can; and in the porch of St. Maclou at Rouen the sculptured flames burst out of the Hades gate, and flicker up, in writhing tongues of stone, through the interstices of the niches, as if the church itself were on fire. This is an extreme instance, but it is all the more illustrative of the entire difference in temper and thought between the two schools of art, and of the intense love of veracity which influenced the Gothic design.

I do not say that this love of veracity is always healthy in its operation. I have above noticed the errors into which it falls from despising design; and there is another kind of error noticeable in the instance just given, in which the true love of truth is too hasty, and seizes on a surface truth instead of an inner one. For in representing the Hades fire, it is not the mere *form* of the flame which needs most to be told, but its unquenchableness, its Divine ordainment and limitation, and its inner fierceness, not physical and material, but in being the expression of the wrath of God. And these things are not to be told by imitating the fire that flashes out of a bundle of sticks. If we think over his symbol a little, we shall perhaps find that the Romanesque builder told more truth in that likeness of a blood-red stream, flowing between definite shores, and out of God's throne, and expanding, as if fed by a perpetual current, into the lake wherein the wicked are cast, than the Gothic builder in those torch flickerings about his niches. But this is not to our immediate purpose; I am not at present to insist upon the faults into which the love of truth was led in the later Gothic times, but on the feeling itself, as a glorious and peculiar characteristic of the Northern builders. For, observe, it is not, even in the above instance, love of truth, but want of thought, which *causes* the fault. The love of truth, as such, is good, but when it is misdirected by thoughtlessness or over-excited by vanity, and either seizes on facts of small value, or gathers them chiefly that it may boast of its grasp and apprehension, its work may well become dull or offensive. Yet let us not, therefore, blame the inherent love of facts, but the incautiousness of their selection, and impertinence of their statement.

I said, in the second place, that Gothic work, when referred to the arrangement of all art, as purist, naturalist, or sensualist, was naturalist. This character follows necessarily on its extreme love of truth, prevailing over the sense of beauty, and causing it to take delight in portraiture of every kind, and to express the various characters of the human countenance and form, as it did the varieties of leaves and the ruggedness of branches. And this tendency is both increased and ennobled by the same Christian humility which we saw expressed in the first character of Gothic work, its rudeness. For as that resulted from a humility which confessed the imperfection of the *workman,* so this naturalist portraiture is rendered more faithful by the humility which confesses the imperfection of the *subject.* The Greek sculptor could neither bear to confess his own feebleness, nor to tell the faults of the forms that he portrayed. But the Christian workman, believing that all is finally to work together for good, freely confesses both, and neither seeks to disguise his own roughness of work, nor his subject's roughness of make. Yet this frankness being joined, for the most part, with depth of religious feeling in other directions, and especially with charity, there is sometimes a tendency to Purism in the best Gothic sculpture; so that it frequently reaches great dignity of form and tenderness of expression, yet never so as to lose the veracity of portraiture wherever portraiture is possible: not exalting its kings into demi-gods, nor its saints into archangels, but giving what kingliness and sanctity was in them, to the full, mixed with due record of their faults; and this in the most part with a great indifference like that of Scripture history, which sets down, with unmoved and unexcusing resoluteness, the virtues and errors of all men of whom it speaks, often leaving the reader to form his own estimate of them, without an indication of the judgment of the historian. And this veracity is carried out by the Gothic sculptors in the minuteness and generality, as well as the equity, of their delineation: for they do not limit their art to the portraiture of saints and kings, but introduce the most familiar scenes and most simple subjects: filling up the backgrounds of Scripture histories with vivid and curious representations of the commonest incidents of daily life, and availing themselves of every occasion in which, either as a symbol, or an explanation of a scene or time, the things familiar to the eye of the workman could be introduced and made of account. Hence Gothic sculpture and painting are not only full of valuable portraiture of the greatest men, but copious records of all the domestic customs and inferior arts of the ages in which it flourished.*

There is, however, one direction in which the Naturalism of the Gothic workmen is peculiarly manifested; and this direction is even more characteristic of the school than

* The best art either represents the facts of its own day, or, if facts of the past, expresses them with accessories of the time in

147

the Naturalism itself; I mean their peculiar fondness for the forms of Vegetation. In rendering the various circumstances of daily life, Egyptian and Ninevite sculpture is as frank and as diffuse as the Gothic. From the highest pomps of state or triumphs of battle, to the most trivial domestic arts and amusements, all is taken advantage of to fill the field of granite with the perpetual interest of a crowded drama; and the early Lombardic and Romanesque sculpture is equally copious in its description of the familiar circumstances of war and the chase. But in all the scenes portrayed by the workmen of these nations, vegetation occurs only as an explanatory accessory; the reed is introduced to mark the course of the river, or the tree to mark the covert of the wild beast, or the ambush of the enemy, but there is no especial interest in the forms of the vegetation strong enough to induce them to make it a subject of separate and accurate study. Again, among the nations who followed the arts of design exclusively, the forms of foliage introduced were meagre and general, and their real intricacy and life were neither admired nor expressed. But to the Gothic workman the living foliage became a subject of intense affection, and he struggled to render all its characters with as much accuracy as was compatible with the laws of his design and the nature of his material, not unfrequently tempted in his enthusiasm to transgress the one and disguise the other.

There is a peculiar significance in this, indicative both of higher civilization and gentler temperament, than had before been manifested in architecture. Rudeness, and the love of change, which we have insisted upon as the first elements of Gothic, are also elements common to all healthy schools. But here is a softer element mingled with them, peculiar to the Gothic itself. The rudeness or ignorance which would have been painfully exposed in the treatment of the human form, are still not so great as to prevent the successful rendering of the wayside herbage; and the love of change, which becomes morbid and feverish in following the haste of the hunter and the rage of the combatant, is at once soothed and satisfied as it watches the wandering of the tendril, and the budding of the

---

which the work was done. All good art, representing past events, is therefore full of the most frank anachronism, and always *ought* to be. No painter has any business to be an antiquarian. We do not want his impressions or suppositions respecting things that are past. We want his clear assertions respecting things present.

flower. Nor is this all: the new direction of mental interest marks an infinite change in the means and the habits of life. The nations whose chief support was in the chase, whose chief interest was in the battle, whose chief pleasure was in the banquet, would take small care respecting the shapes of leaves and flowers; and notice little in the forms of the forest trees which sheltered them, except the signs indicative of the wood which would make the toughest lance, the closest roof, or the clearest fire. The affectionate observation of the grace and outward character of vegetation is the sure sign of a more tranquil and gentle existence, sustained by the gifts, and gladdened by the splendour, of the earth. In that careful distinction of species, and richness of delicate and undisturbed organization, which characterize the Gothic design, there is the history of rural and thoughtful life, influenced by habitual tenderness, and devoted to subtle inquiry; and every discriminating and delicate touch of the chisel, as it rounds the petal or guides the branch, is a prophecy of the development of the entire body of the natural sciences, beginning with that of medicine, of the recovery of literature, and the establishment of the most necessary principles of domestic wisdom and national peace.

I have before alluded to the strange and vain supposition, that the original conception of Gothic architecture had been derived from vegetation,—from the symmetry of avenues, and the interlacing of branches. It is a supposition which never could have existed for a moment in the mind of any person acquainted with early Gothic; but, however idle as a theory, it is most valuable as a testimony to the character of the perfected style. It is precisely because the reverse of this theory is the fact, because the Gothic did not arise out of, but develop itself into, a resemblance to vegetation, that this resemblance is so instructive as an indication of the temper of the builders. It was no chance suggestion of the form of an arch from the bending of a bough, but a gradual and continual discovery of a beauty in natural forms which could be more and more perfectly transferred into those of stone, that influenced at once the heart of the people, and the form of the edifice. The Gothic architecture arose in massy and mountainous strength, axe-hewn, and iron-bound, block heaved upon block by the monk's enthusiasm and the soldier's force; and cramped and stanchioned into such weight of grisly wall, as might bury the anchoret in darkness, and beat back the utmost storm of battle, suffering but by the same narrow crosslet the passing of the sunbeam, or of the arrow. Gradually, as that monkish enthusiasm became more thoughtful, and as the sound of war became more and more intermittent beyond the gates of the convent or the keep, the stony pillar grew slender and the vaulted roof grew light, till they had wreathed themselves into the semblance of the summer woods at their fairest, and of the dead field-flowers, long trodden down in blood, sweet monumental statues were set to bloom for ever, beneath the porch of the temple, or the canopy of the tomb.

Nor is it only as a sign of greater gentleness or refinement of mind, but as a proof of the best possible direction of this refinement, that the tendency of the Gothic to the expression of vegetative life is to be admired. That sentence of Genesis, "I have given thee every green herb for meat," like all the rest of the book, has a profound symbolical as well as a literal meaning. It is not merely the nourishment of the body, but the food of the soul, that is intended. The green herb is, of all nature, that which is most essential to the healthy spiritual life of man. Most of us do not need fine scenery; the precipice and the mountain peak are not intended to be seen by all men,—perhaps their power is greatest over those who are unaccustomed to them. But trees and fields and flowers were made for all, and are necessary for all. God has connected the labour which is essential to the bodily sustenance with the pleasures which are healthiest for the heart; and while He made the ground stubborn, He made its herbage fragrant, and its blossoms fair. The proudest architecture that man can build has no higher honour than to bear the image and recall the memory of that grass of the field which is, at once, the type and the support of his existence; the goodly building is then most glorious when it is sculptured into the likeness of the leaves of Paradise; and the great Gothic spirit, as we showed it to be noble in its disquietude, is also noble in its hold of nature; it is, indeed, like the dove of Noah, in that she found no rest upon the face of the waters,—but like her in this also, "Lo, IN HER MOUTH WAS AN OLIVE BRANCH, PLUCKED OFF."

The fourth essential element of the Gothic mind was above stated to be the sense of the GROTESQUE; but I shall defer the endeavour to define this most curious and subtle character until we have occasion to examine one of the divisions of the Renaissance schools, which was morbidly influenced by it. It is the less necessary to insist upon it here, because every reader familiar with Gothic architecture must understand what I mean, and will, I believe, have no hesitation in admitting, that the tendency to delight in fantastic and ludicrous, as well as in sublime, images, is a universal instinct of the Gothic imagination.

The fifth element above named was RIGIDITY, and this character I must endeavour carefully to define, for neither the word I have used, nor any other that I can think of, will express it accurately. For I mean, not merely stable, but *active* rigidity; the peculiar energy which gives tension to movement, and stiffness to resistance, which makes the fiercest lightning forked rather than curved, and the stoutest oak-branch angular rather than bending, and is as much seen in the quivering of the lance as in the glittering of the icicle.

I have before had occasion to note some manifestations of this energy or fixedness; but it must be still more attentively considered here, as it shows itself throughout the whole structure and decoration of Gothic work. Egyptian and Greek buildings stand, for the most part, by their own weight and mass, one stone passively incumbent on another; but in the Gothic vaults and traceries there is a stiffness analogous to that of the bones of a limb, or fibres of a tree; an elastic tension and communication of force from part to part, and also a studious expression of this throughout every visible line of the building. And, in like manner, the Greek and Egyptian ornament is either mere surface engraving, as if the face of the wall had been stamped with a seal, or its lines are flowing, lithe, and luxuriant; in either case, there is no expression of energy in the framework of the ornament itself. But the Gothic ornament stands out in prickly independence, and frosty fortitude, jutting into crockets, and freezing into pinnacles; here starting up into a monster, there germinating into a blossom, anon knitting itself into a branch, alternately thorny, bossy, and bristly, or writhed into every form of nervous entanglement; but, even when most graceful, never for an instant languid, always quickset: erring, if at all, ever on the side of brusquerie.

The feelings or habits in the workman which give rise to this character in the work, are more complicated and various than those indicated by any other sculptural expression hitherto named. There is, first, the habit of hard and rapid working; the industry of the tribes of the North, quickened by the coldness of the climate, and giving an expression of sharp energy to all they do, as opposed to the languor of the Southern tribes, however much of fire there may be in the heart of that languor, for lava itself may flow languidly. There is also the habit of finding enjoyment in the signs of cold, which is never found, I believe, in the inhabitants of countries south of the Alps. Cold is to them an unredeemed evil, to be suffered and forgotten as soon as may be; but the long winter of the North forces the Goth (I mean the Englishman, Frenchman, Dane, or German), if he would lead a happy life at all, to find sources of happiness in foul weather as well as fair, and to rejoice in the leafless as well as in the shady forest. And this we do with all our hearts; finding perhaps nearly as much contentment by the Christmas fire as in the summer sunshine, and gaining health and strength on the ice-fields of winter, as well as among the meadows of spring. So that there is nothing adverse or painful to our feelings in the cramped and stiffened structure of vegetation checked by cold; and instead of seeking, like the Southern sculpture, to express only the softness of leafage nourished in all tenderness, and tempted into all luxuriance by warm winds and glowing rays, we find pleasure in dwelling upon the crabbed, perverse, and morose animation of plants that have known little kindness from earth or heaven, but, season after season, have had their best efforts palsied by frost, their brightest buds buried under snow, and their goodliest limbs lopped by tempest.

There are many subtle sympathies and affections which join to confirm the Gothic mind in this peculiar choice of subject; and when we add to the influence of these, the necessities consequent upon the employment of a rougher material, compelling the workman to seek for vigour of effect, rather than refinement of texture or accuracy of form, we have direct and manifest causes for much of the difference between the Northern and Southern cast of conception: but there are indirect causes holding a far more important place in the Gothic heart, though less immediate in their influence on design. Strength of will, independence of character, resoluteness of purpose, impatience of undue control, and that general tendency to set the individual reason against authority, and the individual deed against destiny, which, in the Northern tribes, has opposed itself throughout all ages to the languid submission, in the Southern, of thought to tradition, and purpose to fatality, are all more or less traceable in the rigid lines, vigorous and various masses, and daringly projecting and independent structure of the Northern Gothic ornament:

while the opposite feelings are in like manner legible in the graceful and softly guided waves and wreathed bands, in which Southern decoration is constantly disposed; in its tendency to lose its independence, and fuse itself into the surface of the masses upon which it is traced; and in the expression seen so often, in the arrangement of those masses themselves, of an abandonment of their strength to an inevitable necessity, or a listless repose.

There is virtue in the measure, and error in the excess, of both these characters of mind, and in both of the styles which they have created; the best architecture, and the best temper, are those which unite them both; and this fifth impulse of the Gothic heart is therefore that which needs most caution in its indulgence. It is more definitely Gothic than any other, but the best Gothic building is not that which is *most* Gothic: it can hardly be too frank in its confession of rudeness, hardly too rich in its changefulness, hardly too faithful in its naturalism; but it may go too far in its rigidity, and, like the great Puritan spirit in its extreme, lose itself either in frivolity of division, or perversity of purpose.* It actually did so in its later times; but it is gladdening to remember that in its utmost nobleness, the very temper which has been thought most adverse to it, the Protestant spirit of self-dependence and inquiry, was expressed in its every line. Faith and aspiration there were, in every Christian ecclesiastical building, from the first century to the fifteenth; but the moral habits to which England in this age owes the kind of greatness that she has,—the habits of philosophical investigation, or accurate thought, of domestic seclusion and independence, of stern self-reliance and sincere upright searching into religious truth,—were only traceable in the features which were the distinctive creation of the Gothic schools, in the veined foliage, and thorny fretwork, and shadowy niche, and buttressed pier, and fearless height of subtle pinnacle and crested tower, sent like an "unperplexed question up to Heaven."†

Last, because the least essential, of the constituent ele-

---

* See the account of the meeting at Talla Linns, in 1682, given in the fourth chapter of the *Heart of Midlothian*. At length they arrived at the conclusion that "they who owned (or allowed) such names as Monday, Tuesday, January, February, and so forth, served themselves heirs to the same if not greater punishment than had been denounced against the idolaters of old."

† See the beautiful description of Florence in Elizabeth Browning's *Casa Guidi Windows*, which is not only a noble poem, but the

ments of this noble school, was placed that of REDUN-
DANCE,—the uncalculating bestowal of the wealth of its
labour. There is, indeed, much Gothic, and that of the
best period, in which this element is hardly traceable, and
which depends for its effect almost exclusively on loveliness of simple design and grace of uninvolved proportion; still, in the most characteristic buildings, a certain
portion of their effect depends upon accumulation of ornament; and many of those which have most influence on
the minds of men, have attained it by means of this
attribute alone. And although, by careful study of the
school, it is possible to arrive at a condition of taste which
shall be better contented by a few perfect lines than by a
whole façade covered with fretwork, the building which
only satisfies such a taste is not to be considered the best.
For the very first requirement of Gothic architecture being, as we saw above, that it shall both admit the aid, and
appeal to the admiration, of the rudest as well as the most
refined minds, the richness of the work is, paradoxical as
the statement may appear, a part of its humility. No architecture is so haughty as that which is simple; which refuses
to address the eye, except in a few clear and forceful
lines; which implies, in offering so little to our regards, that
all it has offered is perfect; and disdains, either by the
complexity or the attractiveness of its features, to em-
barrass our investigation, or betray us into delight. That
humility, which is the very life of the Gothic school, is
shown not only in the imperfection, but in the accumulation, of ornament. The inferior rank of the workman is
often shown as much in the richness, as the roughness, of
his work; and if the co-operation of every hand, and the
sympathy of every heart, are to be received, we must be
content to allow the redundance which disguises the failure of the feeble, and wins the regard of the inattentive.
There are, however, far nobler interests mingling, in the
Gothic heart, with the rude love of decorative accumulation: a magnificent enthusiasm, which feels as if it never
could do enough to reach the fulness of its ideal; an
unselfishness of sacrifice, which would rather cast fruitless
labour before the altar than stand idle in the market; and,
finally, a profound sympathy with the fulness and wealth
of the material universe, rising out of that Naturalism
whose operation we have already endeavoured to define.

only book I have seen which, favouring the Liberal cause in Italy,
gives a just account of the incapacities of the modern Italian.

The sculptor who sought for his models among the forest leaves, could not but quickly and deeply feel that complexity need not involve the loss of grace, nor richness that of repose; and every hour which he spent in the study of the minute and various work of Nature, made him feel more forcibly the barrenness of what was best in that of man: nor is it to be wondered at, that, seeing her perfect and exquisite creations poured forth in a profusion which conception could not grasp nor calculation sum, he should think that it ill became him to be niggardly of his own rude craftsmanship; and where he saw throughout the universe a faultless beauty lavished on measureless spaces of broidered field and blooming mountain, to grudge his poor and imperfect labour to the few stones that he had raised one upon another, for habitation or memorial. The years of his life passed away before his task was accomplished; but generation succeeded generation with unwearied enthusiasm, and the cathedral front was at last lost in the tapestry of its traceries, like a rock among the thickets and herbage of spring.

We have now, I believe, obtained a view approaching to completeness of the various moral or imaginative elements which composed the inner spirit of Gothic architecture. We have, in the second place, to define its outward form.

We have now, I believe, obtained a sufficiently accurate knowledge both of the spirit and form of Gothic architecture; but it may, perhaps, be useful to the general reader, if, in conclusion, I set down a few plain and practical rules for determining, in every instance, whether a given building be good Gothic or not, and, if not Gothic, whether its architecture is of a kind which will probably reward the pains of careful examination.

First, Look if the roof rises in a steep gable, high above the walls. If it does not do this, there is something wrong: the building is not quite pure Gothic, or has been altered.

Secondly, Look if the principal windows and doors have pointed arches with gables over them. If not pointed arches, the building is not Gothic; if they have not any gables over them, it is either not pure, or not first-rate.

If, however, it has the steep roof, the pointed arch, and gable all united, it is nearly certain to be a Gothic building of a very fine time.

Thirdly, Look if the arches are cusped, or apertures foliated. If the building has met the first two conditions, it is sure to be foliated somewhere; but, if not everywhere, the parts which are unfoliated are imperfect, unless they are large bearing arches, or small and sharp arches in groups, forming a kind of foliation by their own multiplicity, and relieved by sculpture and rich mouldings. The upper windows, for instance, in the east end of Westminster Abbey are imperfect for want of foliation. If there be no foliation anywhere, the building is assuredly imperfect Gothic.

Fourthly, If the building meets all the first three conditions, look if its arches in general, whether of windows and doors, or of minor ornamentation, are carried on *true shafts with bases and capitals*. If they are, then the building is assuredly of the finest Gothic style. It may still, perhaps, be an imitation, a feeble copy, or a bad example, of a noble style; but the manner of it, having met all these four conditions, is assuredly first-rate.

If its apertures have not shafts and capitals, look if they are plain openings in the walls, studiously simple, and unmoulded at the sides. If so, the building may still be of the finest Gothic adapted to some domestic or military service. But if the sides of the window be moulded, and yet there are no capitals at the spring of the arch, it is assuredly of an inferior school.

This is all that is necessary to determine whether the building be of a fine Gothic style. The next tests to be applied are in order to discover whether it be good architecture or not; for it may be very impure Gothic, and yet very noble architecture; or it may be very pure Gothic, and yet if a copy, or originally raised by an ungifted builder, very bad architecture.

If it belong to any of the great schools of colour, its criticism becomes as complicated, and needs as much care, as that of a piece of music, and no general rules for it can be given; but if not—

First, See if it looks as if it had been built by strong men; if it has the sort of roughness, and largeness, and nonchalance, mixed in places with the exquisite tenderness which seems always to be the sign-manual of the broad vision, and massy power of men, who can see *past* the work they are doing, and betray here and there something like disdain for it. If the building has this character, it is much already in its favour; it will go hard but it proves a noble one. If it has not this, but is altogether accurate, minute, and scrupulous, in its workmanship, it must belong to either the very best or the very worst of schools: the very best, in which exquisite design is wrought out with untiring and conscientious care, as in the Giottesque Gothic; or the very worst, in which mechanism has taken the place of design. It is more likely, in general, that it should belong to the worst than the best: so that, on the whole, very accurate workmanship is to be esteemed a bad sign; and if there is nothing remarkable about the building but its precision, it may be passed at once with contempt.

Secondly, Observe if it be irregular, its different parts fitting themselves to different purposes, no one caring what becomes of them, so that they do their work. If one part always answers accurately to another part, it is sure to be a bad building; and the greater and more conspicuous the irregularities, the greater the chances are that it is a good one. For instance, in the Ducal Palace, the general idea is sternly symmetrical; but two windows are lower than the rest of the six; and if the reader will count the arches of the small arcade as far as to the great balcony, he will find it is not in the centre, but set to the right-hand side by the whole width of one of those arches. We may be pretty sure that the building is a good one; none but a master of his craft would have ventured to do this.

Thirdly, Observe if all the traceries, capitals, and other ornaments are of perpetually varied design. If not, the work is assuredly bad.

Lastly, *Read* the sculpture. Preparatory to reading it, you will have to discover whether it is legible (and, if legible, it is nearly certain to be worth reading). On a good building, the sculpture is *always* so set, and on such a scale, that at the ordinary distance from which the edifice is seen, the sculpture shall be thoroughly intelligible and interesting. In order to accomplish this, the uppermost statues will be ten or twelve feet high, and the upper ornamentation will be colossal, increasing in fineness as it descends, till on the foundation it will often be wrought as if for a precious cabinet in a king's chamber; but the spectator will not notice that the upper sculptures are colossal. He will merely feel that he can see them plainly, and make them all out at his ease.

And having ascertained this, let him set himself to read them. Thenceforward the criticism of the building is to be conducted precisely on the same principles as that of a book; and it must depend on the knowledge, feeling, and not a little on the industry and perseverance of the reader, whether, even in the case of the best works, he either perceive them to be great, or feel them to be entertaining.

Modern Painters
(Volumes III and IV)
(1856)

Of the Received Opinions Touching the "Grand Style"

In taking up the clue of an inquiry, now intermitted for nearly ten years, it may be well to do as a traveller would, who had to recommence an interrupted journey in a guideless country; and, ascending, as it were, some little hill beside our road, note how far we have already advanced, and what pleasantest ways we may choose for farther progress.

I endeavoured, in the beginning of the first volume, to divide the sources of pleasure open to us in Art into certain groups, which might conveniently be studied in succession. After some preliminary discussion, it was concluded that these groups were, in the main, three; consisting, first, of the pleasures taken in perceiving simple resemblance to Nature (Ideas of Truth); secondly, of the pleasures taken in the beauty of the things chosen to be painted (Ideas of Beauty); and, lastly, of pleasures taken in the meanings and relations of these things (Ideas of Relation).

The first volume, treating of the Ideas of Truth, was chiefly occupied with an inquiry into the various success with which different artists had represented the facts of Nature,—an inquiry necessarily conducted very imperfectly, owing to the want of pictorial illustration.

The second volume merely opened the inquiry into the nature of ideas of Beauty and Relation, by analysing (as far as I was able to do so) the two faculties of the human mind which mainly seized such ideas; namely, the contemplative and imaginative faculties.

It remains for us to examine the various success of artists, especially of the great landscape-painter whose works have been throughout our principal subject, in addressing these faculties of the human mind, and to consider who among them has conveyed the noblest ideas of beauty, and touched the deepest sources of thought. . . .

I have said that the art is greatest which includes the greatest ideas; but I have not endeavoured to define the nature of this greatness in the ideas themselves. We speak of great truths, of great beauties, great thoughts. What is it which makes one truth greater than another, one thought greater than another? This question is, I repeat, of peculiar importance at the present time; for, during a period now of some hundred and fifty years, all writers on Art who have pretended to eminence, have insisted much on a supposed distinction between what they call the Great and the Low Schools; using the terms "High Art," "Great or Ideal Style," and other such, as descriptive of a certain noble manner of painting, which it was desirable that all students of Art should be early led to reverence and adopt; and characterising as "vulgar," or "low," or "realist," another manner of painting and conceiving, which it was equally necessary that all students should be taught to avoid.

But lately this established teaching, never very intelligible, has been gravely called in question. The advocates and self-supposed practisers of "High Art" are beginning to be looked upon with doubt, and their peculiar phraseology to be treated with even a certain degree of ridicule. And other forms of Art are partly developed among us, which do not pretend to be high, but rather to be strong, healthy, and humble. This matter of "highness" in Art, therefore, deserves our most careful consideration. Has it been, or is it, a true highness, a true princeliness, or only a show of it, consisting in courtly manners and robes of state? Is it rocky height or cloudy height, adamant or vapour, on which the sun of praise so long has risen and set? It will be well at once to consider this.

And first, let us get, as quickly as may be, at the exact meaning with which the advocates of "High Art" use that somewhat obscure and figurative term.

I do not know that the principles in question are anywhere more distinctly expressed than in two papers in the *Idler*, written by Sir Joshua Reynolds, of course under the immediate sanction of Johnson; and which may thus be considered as the utterance of the views then held upon the subject by the artists of chief skill, and critics of most sense, arranged in a form so brief and clear, as to admit of their being brought before the public for a morning's entertainment. I cannot, therefore, it seems to me, do better than quote these two letters, or at least the important parts of them, examining the exact meaning of each passage as it occurs. There are, in all, in the *Idler* three letters on painting, Nos. 76, 79, and 82; of these, the first is directed only against the impertinences of pretended connoisseurs, and is as notable for its faithfulness, as for its wit, in the description of the several modes of criticism in an artificial and ignorant state of society: it is only, therefore, in the two last papers that we find the expression of the doctrines which it is our business to examine.

No. 79 (Saturday, Oct. 20th, 1759) begins, after a short preamble, with the following passage:—

"Amongst the Painters, and the writers on Painting, there is one maxim universally admitted and continually inculcated. *Imitate nature* is the invariable rule; but I know none who have explained in what manner this rule is to be understood; the consequence of which is, that every one takes it in the most obvious sense—that objects are represented naturally, when they have such relief that they seem real. It may appear strange, perhaps, to hear this sense of the rule disputed; but it must be considered, that, if the excellency of a Painter consisted only in this kind of imitation, Painting must lose its rank, and be no longer considered as a liberal art, and sister to Poetry: this imitation being merely mechanical, in which the slowest intellect is always sure to succeed best; for the Painter of genius cannot stoop to drudgery, in which the understanding has no part; and what pretence has the Art to claim kindred with Poetry, but by its power over the imagination? To this power the Painter of genius directs him; in this sense he studies Nature, and often arrives at his end, even by being unnatural in the confined sense of the word.

"The grand style of Painting requires this minute attention to be carefully avoided, and must be kept as separate from it as the style of Poetry from that of History. (Poetical ornaments destroy that air of truth and plainness which ought to characterise History; but the very being of Poetry consists in departing from this plain narrative, and adopting every ornament that will warm the imagination.) To desire to see the excellences of each style united—to mingle the Dutch with the Italian school, is to join contrarieties which cannot subsist together, and which destroy the efficacy of each other."

We find, first, from this interesting passage, that the writer considers the Dutch and Italian masters as severally representative of the low and high schools; next, that he considers the Dutch painters as excelling in a mechanical imitation, "in which the slowest intellect is always sure to succeed best;" and, thirdly, that he considers the Italian painters as excelling in a style which corresponds to that of imaginative poetry in literature, and which has an exclusive right to be called the grand style. . . .

We observe, however, farther, that the imitation which Reynolds supposes to be characteristic of the Dutch School is that which gives to objects such relief that they seem real, and that he then speaks of this art of realistic imitation as corresponding to *history* in literature.

Reynolds, therefore, seems to class these dull works of the Dutch School under a general head, to which they are not commonly referred—that of *Historical* painting; while he speaks of the works of the Italian School not as historical, but as *poetical* painting. His next sentence will farther manifest his meaning.

"The Italian attends only to the invariable, the great and general ideas which are fixed and inherent in universal Nature; the Dutch, on the contrary, to literal truth, and a minute exactness in the detail, as I may say, of Nature modified by accident. The attention to these petty peculiarities is the very cause of this naturalness so much admired in the Dutch pictures, which, if we suppose it to be a beauty, is certainly of a lower order, which ought to give place to a beauty of a superior kind, since one cannot be obtained but by departing from the other.

"If my opinion were asked concerning the works of Michael Angelo, whether they would receive any advantage from possessing this mechanical merit, I should not scruple to say, they would not only receive no advantage, but would lose, in a great measure, the effect which they now have on every mind susceptible of great and noble ideas. His works may be said to be all genius and soul; and why should they be loaded with heavy matter, which can only counteract his purpose by retarding the progress of the imagination?"

Examining carefully this and the preceding passage, we find the author's unmistakable meaning to be, that Dutch painting is *history;* attending to literal truth and "minute

161

exactness in the details of nature modified by accident."
That Italian painting is *poetry*, attending only to the
invariable; and that works which attend only to the invariable are full of genius and soul; but that literal truth and
exact detail are "heavy matter which retards the progress
of the imagination."

This being then indisputably what Reynolds means to
tell us, let us think a little whether he is in all respects
right. And first, as he compares his two kinds of painting
to history and poetry, let us see how poetry and history
themselves differ, in their use of *variable* and *invariable*
details. I am writing at a window which commands a view
of the head of the Lake of Geneva; and as I look up from
my paper, to consider this point, I see, beyond it, a blue
breadth of softly moving water, and the outline of the
mountains above Chillon, bathed in morning mist. The
first verses which naturally come into my mind are—

> *"A thousand feet in depth below*
> *The massy waters meet and flow;*
> *So far the fathom line was sent*
> *From Chillon's snow-white battlement."*

Let us see in what manner this poetical statement is
distinguished from a historical one.

It is distinguished from a truly historical statement,
first, in being simply false. The water under the Castle of
Chillon is not a thousand feet deep, nor anything like it.
Herein, certainly, these lines fulfil Reynolds's first requirement in poetry, "that it should be inattentive to literal
truth and minute exactness in detail." In order, however,
to make our comparison more closely in other points, let
us assume that what is stated is indeed a fact, and that it
was to be recorded, first historically, and then poetically.

Historically stating it, then, we should say: "The lake
was sounded from the walls of the Castle of Chillon, and
found to be a thousand feet deep."

Now, if Reynolds be right in his idea of the difference
between history and poetry, we shall find that Byron
leaves out of this statement certain *un*necessary details,
and retains only the invariable,—that is to say, the points
which the Lake of Geneva and Castle of Chillon have in
common with all other lakes and castles.

Let us hear, therefore.

> *"A thousand feet in depth below."*

"Below?" Here is, at all events, a word added (instead of anything being taken away); invariable, certainly in the case of lakes, but not absolutely necessary.

"The massy waters meet and flow."

"Massy!" why massy? Because deep water is heavy. The word is a good word, but it is assuredly an added detail, and expresses a character, not which the Lake of Geneva has in common with all other lakes, but which it has in distinction from those which are narrow, or shallow.

"Meet and flow." Why meet and flow? Partly to make up a rhyme; partly to tell us that the waters are forceful as well as massy, and changeful as well as deep. Observe, a farther addition of details, and of details more or less peculiar to the spot, or, according to Reynolds's definition, of "heavy matter, retarding the progress of the imagination."

"So far the fathom line was sent."

Why fathom line? All lines for sounding are not fathom lines. If the lake was ever sounded from Chillon, it was probably sounded in mètres, not fathoms. This is an addition of another particular detail, in which the only compliance with Reynolds's requirement is, that there is some chance of its being an inaccurate one.

"From Chillon's snow-white battlement."

Why snow-white? Because castle battlements are not usually snow-white. This is another added detail, and a detail quite peculiar to Chillon, and therefore exactly the most striking word in the whole passage.

"Battlement!" Why battlement? Because all walls have not battlements, and the addition of the term marks the castle to be not merely a prison, but a fortress.

This is a curious result. Instead of finding, as we expected, the poetry distinguished from the history by the omission of details, we find it consists entirely in the *addition* of details; and instead of being characterised by regard only of the invariable, we find its whole power to consist in the clear expression of what is singular and particular!

The reader may pursue the investigation for himself in other instances. He will find in every case that a poetical is distinguished from a merely historical statement, not by

163

being more vague, but more specific; and it might, there-fore, at first appear that our author's comparison should be simply reversed, and that the Dutch School should be called poetical, and the Italian historical. But the term poetical does not appear very applicable to the generality of Dutch painting; and a little reflection will show us, that if the Italians represent only the invariable, they cannot be properly compared even to historians. For that which is incapable of change has no history, and records which state only the invariable need not be written, and could not be read.

It is evident, therefore, that our author has entangled himself in some grave fallacy, by introducing this idea of invariableness as forming a distinction between poetical and historical art. What the fallacy is, we shall discover as we proceed; but as an invading army should not leave an untaken fortress in its rear, we must not go on with our inquiry into the views of Reynolds until we have settled satisfactorily the question already suggested to us, in what the essence of poetical treatment really consists. For though, as we have seen, it certainly involves the addition of specific details, it cannot be simply that addition which turns the history into poetry. For it is perfectly possible to add any number of details to a historical statement, and to make it more prosaic with every added word. As, for instance, "The lake was sounded out of a flat-bottomed boat, near the crab-tree at the corner of the kitchen-garden, and was found to be a thousand feet nine inches deep, with a muddy bottom." It thus appears that it is not the multiplication of details which constitutes poetry; nor their subtraction which constitutes history, but details themselves, or the method of using them, which invests them with poetical power or historical propriety.

It seems to me, and may seem to the reader, strange that we should need to ask the question, "What is poetry?" Here is a word we have been using all our lives, and, I suppose, with a very distinct idea attached to it; and when I am now called upon to give a definition of this idea, I find myself at a pause. What is more singular, I do not at present recollect hearing the question often asked, though surely it is a very natural one; and I never recollect hearing it answered, or even attempted to be answered. In general, people shelter themselves under metaphors, and while we hear poetry described as an utterance of the soul, an effusion of Divinity, or voice of nature, or in other terms equally elevated and obscure, we never attain anything like a definite explanation of the character which actually distinguishes it from prose.

I come, after some embarrassment, to the conclusion, that poetry is "the suggestion, by the imagination, of noble grounds for the noble emotions." I mean, by the noble emotions, those four principal sacred passions—Love, Veneration, Admiration, and Joy (this latter especially, if unselfish); and their opposites—Hatred, Indignation (or Scorn), Horror, and Grief,—this last, when unselfish, becoming Compassion. These passions in their various combinations constitute what is called "poetical feeling," when they are felt on noble grounds, that is, on great and true grounds. Indignation, for instance, is a poetical feeling, if excited by serious injury; but it is not a poetical feeling if entertained on being cheated out of a small sum of money. It is very possible the manner of the cheat may have been such as to justify considerable indignation; but the feeling is nevertheless not poetical unless the grounds of it be large as well as just. In like manner, energetic admiration may be excited in certain minds by a display of fireworks, or a street of handsome shops; but the feeling is not poetical, because the grounds of it are false, and therefore ignoble. There is in reality nothing to deserve admiration either in the firing of packets of gunpowder, or in the display of the stocks of warehouses. But admiration excited by the budding of a flower is a poetical feeling, because it is impossible that this manifestation of spiritual power and vital beauty can ever be enough admired.

Farther, it is necessary to the existence of poetry that the grounds of these feelings should be *furnished by the imagination.* Poetical feeling, that is to say, mere noble emotion, is not poetry. It is happily inherent in all human nature deserving the name, and is found often to be purest in the least sophisticated. But the power of assembling, by *the help of the imagination,* such images as will excite these feelings, is the power of the poet or literally of the "Maker."

Now this power of exciting the emotions depends of course on the richness of the imagination, and on its choice of those images which, in combination, will be most effective, or, for the particular work to be done, most fit. And it is altogether impossible for a writer not endowed with invention to conceive what tools a true poet will make use of, or in what way he will apply them, or what unexpected results he will bring out by them; so that it is vain to say that the details of poetry ought to possess, or ever do possess, any *definite* character. Generally speaking, poetry runs into finer and more delicate details than prose; but the details are not poetical because they are more delicate, but because they are employed so as to bring out an affecting result. For instance, no one but a true poet would have thought of exciting our pity for a bereaved father by describing his way of locking the door of his house:

> "*Perhaps to himself at that moment he said,*
> '*The key I must take, for my Ellen is dead.*'
> *But of this in my ears not a word did he speak;*
> *And he went to the chase with a tear on his cheek.*"

In like manner, in painting, it is altogether impossible to say beforehand what details a great painter may make poetical by his use of them to excite noble emotions: and we shall, therefore, find presently that a painting is to be classed in the great or inferior schools, not according to the kind of details which it represents, but according to the uses for which it employs them.

It is only farther to be noticed, that infinite confusion has been introduced into this subject by the careless and illogical custom of opposing painting to poetry, instead of regarding poetry as consisting in a noble use, whether of colours or words. Painting is properly to be opposed to *speaking* or *writing,* but not to *poetry.* Both painting and speaking are methods of expression. Poetry is the employment of either for the noblest purposes.

This question being thus far determined, we may proceed with our paper in the *Idler.*

"It is very difficult to determine the exact degree of enthusiasm that the arts of Painting and Poetry may admit. There may, perhaps, be too great an indulgence as well as too great a restraint of imagination; if the one produces incoherent monsters, the other produces what is full as bad, lifeless insipidity. An intimate knowledge of the passions, and good sense, but no common sense, must at least determine its limits. It has been thought, and I believe with reason, that Michael Angelo sometimes transgressed those limits; and, I think, I have seen figures of him of which it was very difficult to determine whether they were in the highest degree sublime or extremely ridiculous. Such faults may be said to be the ebullitions of genius; but at least he had this merit, that he never was insipid; and whatever passion his works may excite, they will always escape contempt.

"What I have had under consideration is the sublimest style, particularly that of Michael Angelo, the Homer of painting. Other kinds may admit of this naturalness, which of the lowest kind is the chief merit; but in painting, as in poetry, the highest style has the least of common nature."

From this passage we gather three important indications of the supposed nature of the Great Style. That it is the work of men in a state of enthusiasm. That it is like the writing of Homer; and that it has as little as possible of "common nature" in it.

First, it is produced by men in a state of enthusiasm. That is, by men who feel *strongly* and *nobly;* for we do not call a strong feeling of envy, jealousy, or ambition, enthusiasm. That is, therefore, by men who feel poetically. This much we may admit, I think, with perfect safety. Great art is produced by men who feel acutely and nobly; and it is in some sort an expression of the personal feeling. We can easily conceive that there may be a sufficiently marked distinction between such art, and that which is produced by men who do not feel at all, but who reproduce, though ever so accurately, yet coldly, like human mirrors, the scenes which pass before their eyes.

Secondly, Great Art is like the writing of Homer, and this chiefly because it has little of "common nature" in it. We are not clearly informed what is meant by common nature in this passage. Homer seems to describe a great deal of what is common:—cookery, for instance, very carefully in all its processes. I suppose the passage in the *Iliad* which, on the whole, has excited most admiration, is that which describes a wife's sorrow at parting from her husband, and a child's fright at its father's helmet; and I hope, at least, the former feeling may be considered "common nature." But the true greatness of Homer's style is, doubtless, held by our author to consist in his imaginations of things not only uncommon but impossible (such as spirits in brazen armour, or monsters with heads of men and bodies of beasts), and in his occasional delineations of the human character and form in their utmost, or heroic, strength and beauty. We gather then on the whole, that a painter in the Great Style must be enthusiastic, or full of emotion, and must paint the human form in its utmost strength and beauty, and perhaps certain impossible forms besides, liable by persons not in an equally enthusiastic state of mind to be looked upon as in some degree absurd. This I presume to be Reynolds's meaning, and to be all that he intends us to gather from his comparison of the Great Style with the writings of Homer. But if that comparison be a just one in all respects, surely two other corollaries ought to be drawn from it, namely,—first, that these Heroic or Impossible images are to be mingled with others very unheroic and very possible; and, secondly, that in the representation of the Heroic or Impossible forms, the greatest care must be taken in *finishing the details,* so that a painter must not be satisfied with painting well the countenance and the body of his hero, but ought to spend the greatest part of his time (as Homer the greatest number of verses) in elaborating the sculptured pattern on his shield.

Let us, however, proceed with our paper.

"One may very safely recommend a little more enthusiasm to the modern painters; too much is certainly not the vice of the present age. The Italians seem to have been continually declining in this respect from the time of Michael Angelo to that of Carlo Maratti, and from thence to the very bathos of insipidity to which they are now sunk; so that there is no need of remarking, that where I mentioned the Italian painters in opposition to the Dutch, I mean not the moderns, but the heads of the old Roman and Bolognian Schools; nor did I mean to include, in my idea of an Italian painter, the Venetian school, *which may be said to be the Dutch part of the Italian genius.* I have only to add a word of advice to the painters,—that, however excellent they may be in painting naturally, they would not flatter themselves very much upon it; and to the connoisseurs, that when they see a cat or a fiddle painted so finely, that, as the phrase is, it looks as if you could take it up, they would not for that reason immediately compare the painter to Raffaelle and Michael Angelo."

In this passage there are four points chiefly to be remarked. The first, that in the year 1759 the Italian painters were, in our author's opinion, sunk in the very bathos of insipidity. The second, that the Venetian painters, *i.e.,* Titian, Tintoret, and Veronese, are, in our author's opinion, to be classed with the Dutch; that is to say, are painters in a style "in which the slowest intellect is always sure to succeed best." Thirdly, that painting naturally is not a difficult thing, nor one on which a painter should pride himself. And finally, that connoisseurs, seeing a cat or a fiddle successfully painted, ought not therefore immediately to compare the painter to Raphael or Michael Angelo.

Yet Raphael painted fiddles very carefully in the foreground of his St. Cecilia,—so carefully, that they quite look as if they might be taken up. So carefully, that I never yet looked at the picture without wishing that somebody *would* take them up, and out of the way. And I am under a very strong persuasion that Raphael did not think painting "naturally" an easy thing.

Modern Painters, Vol. III, Part 4, Ch. 1

Of the Naturalist Ideal

We now enter on the consideration of that central and highest branch of ideal art which concerns itself simply with things as they ARE, and accepts, in all of them, alike the evil and the good. The question is, therefore, how the art which represents things simply as they are, can be called ideal at all. . . .

In Tintoret's Adoration of the Magi, the Madonna is not an enthroned queen, but a fair girl, full of simplicity and almost childish sweetness. To her are opposed (as Magi) two of the noblest and most thoughtful of the Venetian senators in extreme old age,—the utmost manly dignity, in its decline, being set beside the utmost feminine simplicity, in its dawn. The steep foreheads and refined features of the nobles are, again, opposed to the head of a negro servant, and of an Indian; both, however, noble of their kind. On the other side of the picture, the delicacy of the Madonna is farther enhanced by contrast with a largely made farm-servant, leaning on a basket. All these figures are in repose; outside, the troop of the attendants of the Magi is seen coming up at the gallop.

I bring forward this picture, observe, not as an example of the ideal in conception of religious subject, but of the general ideal treatment of the human form; in which the peculiarity is, that the beauty of each figure is displayed to the utmost, while yet, taken separately, the Madonna is an unaltered portrait of a Venetian girl, the Magi are unaltered Venetian senators, and the figure with the basket, an unaltered market-woman of Mestre.

And the greater the master of the ideal, the more perfectly true in *portraiture* will his individual figures be always found, the more subtle and bold his arts of harmony and contrast. This is a universal principle, common to all great art. Consider, in Shakspere, how Prince Henry is opposed to Falstaff, Falstaff to Shallow, Titania to Bottom, Cordelia to Regan, Imogen to Cloten, and so on; while all the meaner idealists disdain the naturalism, and are shocked at the contrasts. The fact is, a man who can see truth at all, sees it wholly, and neither desires nor dares to mutilate it.

It is evident that *within* this faithful idealism, and as one branch of it only, will arrange itself the representation of the human form and mind in perfection, when this perfection is rationally to be supposed or introduced,—that is to say, in the highest personages of the story. The careless habit of confining the term "ideal" to such representations, and not understanding the imperfect ones to be *equally* ideal in their place, has greatly added to the embarrassment and multiplied the errors of artists. Thersites is just as ideal as Achilles, and Alecto as Helen; and, what is more, all the nobleness of the beautiful ideal depends upon its being just as probable and natural as the ugly one, and having in itself, occasionally or partially, both faults and familiarities. If the next painter who desires to illustrate the character of Homer's Achilles, would represent him cutting pork chops for Ulysses, he would enable the public to understand the Homeric ideal better than they have done for several centuries. For it is to be kept in mind that the *naturalist ideal* has always in it, to the full, the power expressed by those two words. It is naturalist, because studied from nature, and ideal, because it is mentally arranged in a certain manner. Achilles must be represented cutting pork chops, because that was one of the things which the nature of Achilles involved his doing: he could not be shown wholly as Achilles, if he were not shown doing that. But he shall do it at such time and place as Homer chooses.

Now, therefore, observe the main conclusions which follow from these two conditions, attached always to art of this kind. First, it is to be taken straight from nature: it is to be the plain narration of something the painter or writer saw. Herein is the chief practical difference between the higher and lower artists; a difference which I feel more and more every day that I give to the study of art. All the great men *see* what they paint before they paint it,—see it in a perfectly passive manner,—cannot help seeing it if they would; whether in their mind's eye, or in bodily fact, does not matter; very often the mental vision is, I believe, in men of imagination, clearer than the bodily one; but vision it is, of one kind or another,—the whole scene, character, or incident passing before them as in second sight, whether they will or no, and requiring them to paint it as they see it; they not daring, under the might of its presence, to alter one jot or tittle of it as they write it down or paint it down; it being to them in its own kind and degree always a true vision or Apocalypse, and invariably accompanied in their hearts by a feeling correspondent to the words,—"Write the things *which thou hast seen*, and the things which *are*."

And the whole power, whether of painter or poet, to describe rightly what we call an ideal thing, depends upon its being thus, to him, not an idea, but a *real* thing. No man ever did or ever will work well, but either from actual sight or sight of faith; and all that we call ideal in Greek or any other art, because to us it is false and visionary, was, to the makers of it, true and existent. The heroes of Phidias are simply representations of such noble human persons as he every day saw, and the gods of Phidias simply representations of such noble divine persons as he thoroughly believed to exist, and did in mental vision truly behold. Hence I said in the second preface to *The Seven Lamps of Architecture:* "All great art represents something that it sees or believes in;—nothing unseen or uncredited."

And just because it is always something that it sees or believes in, there is the peculiar character above noted, almost unmistakable, in all high and true ideals, of having been as it were studied from the life, and involving pieces of sudden familiarity, and close *specific* painting which never would have been admitted or even thought of, had not the painter drawn either from the bodily life or from the life of faith. For instance, Dante's centaur, Chiron, dividing his beard with his arrow before he can speak, is a thing that no mortal would ever have thought of, if he had not actually seen the centaur do it. They might have composed handsome bodies of men and horses in all possible ways, through a whole life of pseudo-idealism, and yet never dreamed of any such thing. But the real living centaur actually trotted across Dante's brain, and he saw him do it.

And on account of this reality it is, that the great idealists venture into all kinds of what, to the pseudo-idealists, are "vulgarities." Nay, *venturing* is the wrong word; the great men have no choice in the matter; they do not know or care whether the things they describe are

171

vulgarities or not. They *saw* them; they are the facts of the case. If they had merely composed what they describe, they would have had it at their will to refuse this circumstance or add that. But they did not compose it. It came to them ready fashioned; they were too much impressed by it to think what was vulgar or not vulgar in it. It might be a very wrong thing in a centaur to have so much beard; but so it was. And therefore, among the various ready tests of true greatness there is not any more certain than this daring reference to, or use of, mean and little things—mean and little, that is, to mean and little minds; but, when used by the great men, evidently part of the noble whole which is authoritatively present before them. . . . Thus, in the highest poetry there is no word so familiar but a great man will bring good out of it, or rather, it will bring good to him, and answer some end for which no other word would have done equally well.

A common person, for instance, would be mightily puzzled to apply the word "whelp" to any one, with a view of flattering him. There is a certain freshness and energy in the term, which gives it agreeableness; but it seems difficult, at first hearing, to use it complimentarily. If the person spoken of be a prince, the difficulty seems increased; and when, farther, he is at one and the same moment to be called a "whelp" and contemplated as a hero, it seems that a common idealist might well be brought to a pause. But hear Shakspere do it:—

> *"Awake his warlike spirit,*
> *And your great uncle's, Edward the Black Prince,*
> *Who on the French ground play'd a tragedy,*
> *Making defeat on the full power of France,*
> *While his most mighty father on a hill*
> *Stood smiling, to behold his lion's whelp*
> *Forage in blood of French nobility."*

So a common idealist would have been rather alarmed at the thought of introducing the name of a street in Paris—Straw Street—Rue de Fouarre—into the midst of a description of the highest heavens. Not so Dante. . . .

We may dismiss this matter of vulgarity in plain and few words, at least as far as regards art. There is never vulgarity in a *whole* truth, however commonplace. It may be unimportant or painful. It cannot be vulgar. Vulgarity is only in concealment of truth, or in affectation.

"Well, but," (at this point the reader asks doubtfully,) "if then your great central idealist is to show all truth, low as well as lovely, receiving it in this passive way, what becomes of all your principles of selection, and of setting in the right place, which you were talking about up to the end of your fifth paragraph? How is Homer to enforce upon Achilles the cutting of the pork chops 'only at such time as Homer chooses,' if Homer is to have *no* choice, but merely to see the thing done, and sing it as he sees it?" Why, the choice, as well as the vision, is *manifested* to Homer. The vision comes to him in its chosen order. Chosen *for* him, not *by* him, but yet full of visible and exquisite choice, just as a sweet and perfect dream will come to a sweet and perfect person, so that, in some sense, they may be said to have chosen their dream, or composed it; and yet they could not help dreaming it so, and in no otherwise. Thus, exactly thus, in all results of true inventive power, the whole harmony of the thing done seems as if it had been wrought by the most exquisite rules. But to him who did it, it presented itself so, and his will, and knowledge, and personality, for the moment went for nothing; he became simply a scribe, and wrote what he heard and saw. . . .

Finally, as far as I can observe, it is a constant law that the greatest men, whether poets or historians, live entirely in their own age, and that the greatest fruits of their work are gathered out of their own age. Dante paints Italy in the thirteenth century; Chaucer, England in the fourteenth; Masaccio, Florence in the fifteenth; Tintoret, Venice in the sixteenth; all of them utterly regardless of anachronism and minor error of every kind, but getting always vital truth out of the vital present.

If it be said that Shakspere wrote perfect historical plays on subjects belonging to the preceding centuries, I answer that they *are* perfect plays just because there is no care about centuries in them, but a life which all men recognize for the human life of all time; and this it is, not because Shakspere sought to give universal truth, but because, painting honestly and completely from the men about him, he painted that human nature which is indeed constant enough,—a rogue in the fifteenth century being, *at heart,* what a rogue is in the nineteenth and was in the twelfth; and an honest or a knightly man being, in like manner, very similar to other such at any other time. And the work of these great idealists is, therefore, always universal; not because it is *not portrait,* but because it is *complete* portrait down to the heart, which is the same in all ages; and the work of the mean idealists is *not* universal, not because it is portrait, but because it is *half* portrait,—of the outside, the manners and the dress, not of the heart. Thus Tintoret and Shakspere paint, both of them, simply Venetian and English nature as they saw it in their time, down to the root; and it does for *all* time; but as for any care to cast themselves into the particular ways and tones of thought, or custom, of past time in their historical work, you will find it in neither of them, nor in any other perfectly great man that I know of.

Modern Painters, Vol. III, Part 4, Ch. 7

It [the imagination] is eminently a *wearable* faculty, eminently delicate, and incapable of bearing fatigue; so that if we give it too many objects at a time to employ itself upon, or very grand ones for a long time together, it fails under the effort, becomes jaded, exactly as the limbs do by bodily fatigue, and incapable of answering any farther appeal till it has had rest. . . .

I well recollect the walk on which I first found out this; it was on the winding road from Sallenches, sloping up the hills towards St. Gervais, one cloudless Sunday afternoon. The road circles softly between bits of rocky bank and mounded pasture; little cottages and chapels gleaming out from among the trees at every turn. Behind me, some leagues in length, rose the jagged range of the mountains of the Réposoir; on the other side of the valley, the mass of the Aiguille de Varens, heaving its seven thousand feet of cliff into the air at a single effort, its gentle gift of waterfall, the Nant d'Arpenaz, like a pillar of cloud at its feet; Mount Blanc and all its aiguilles, one silver flame, in front of me; marvellous blocks of mossy granite and dark glades of pine around me; but I could enjoy nothing, and could not for a long while make out what was the matter with me, until at last I discovered that if I confined myself to one thing,—and that a little thing,—a tuft of moss, or a single crag at the top of the Varens, or a wreath or two of foam at the bottom of the Nant d'Arpenaz, I began to enjoy it directly, because then I had mind enough to put into the thing, and the enjoyment arose from the quantity of the imaginative energy I could bring to bear upon it but when I looked at or thought of all together, moss, stones, Varens, Nant d'Arpenaz, and Mont Blanc, I had not mind enough to give to all, and none were of any value. The conclusion which would have been formed, upon this, by a German philosopher, would have been that the Mont Blanc *was* of no value; that he and his imagination only were of value; that the Mont Blanc, in fact, except so far as he was able to look at it, could not be considered as having any existence. But the only conclusion which occurred to me as reasonable under the circumstances (I have seen no ground for altering it since) was, that I was an exceedingly small creature, much tired, and, at the moment, not a little stupid, for whom a blade of grass, or a wreath of foam, was quite food enough and to spare, and that if I tried to take any more, I should make myself ill. Whereupon, associating myself fraternally with some ants, who were deeply interested in the conveyance of some small sticks over the road, and rather, as I think they generally are, in too great a hurry about it, I returned home in a little while with great contentment; thinking how well it was ordered that, as Mont Blanc and his pine forests could not be everywhere, nor all the world come to see them, the human mind, on the whole, should enjoy itself most surely, in an antlike manner, and be happy and busy with the bits of sticks and grains of crystal that fall in its way to be handled, in daily duty.

Modern Painters, Vol. III, Part 4, Ch. 10

Consider a little what a depth there is in this great instinct of the human race. Gather a single blade of grass, and examine for a minute, quietly, its narrow sword-shaped strip of fluted green. Nothing, as it seems here, of notable goodness or beauty. A very little strength, and a very little tallness, and a few delicate long lines meeting in a point,—not a perfect point neither, but blunt and unfinished, by no means a creditable or apparently much cared-for example of Nature's workmanship; made, as it seems, only to be trodden on to-day, and to-morrow to be cast into the oven; and a little pale and hollow stalk, feeble and flaccid, leading down to the dull brown fibres of roots. And yet, think of it well, and judge whether of all the gorgeous flowers that beam in summer air, and of all strong and goodly trees, pleasant to the eyes or good for food,—stately palm and pine, strong ash and oak, scented citron, burdened vine,—there be any by man so deeply loved, by God so highly graced, as that narrow point of feeble green. . . . And well does it fulfil its mission. Consider what we owe merely to the meadow grass, to the covering of the dark ground by that glorious enamel, by the companies of these soft, and countless, and peaceful spears. The fields! Follow but forth for a little time the thoughts of all that we ought to recognize in those words. All spring and summer is in them,—the walks by silent, scented paths,—the rest in noonday heat, —the joy of herds and flocks,—the power of all shepherd life and meditation,—the life of sunlight upon the world, falling in emerald streaks, and failing in soft blue shadows, where else it would have struck upon the dark mould, or scorching dust,—pastures beside the pacing brooks,—soft banks and knolls of lowly hills,—thymy slopes of down overlooked by the blue line of lifted sea,—crisp lawns all dim with early dew, or smooth in evening warmth of barred sunshine, dinted by happy feet, and softening in their fall and sound of loving voices: all these are summed in those simple words; and these are not all. We may not measure to the full the depth of this heavenly gift in our own land; though still, as we think of it longer, the infinite of that meadow sweetness, Shakspere's peculiar joy, would open on us more and more, yet we have it but in part. Go out, in the spring-time, among the meadows that slope from the shores of the Swiss lakes to the roots of their lower mountains. There, mingled with the taller gentians and the white narcissus, the grass grows deep and free; and as you follow the winding mountain paths, beneath arching boughs all veiled and dim with blossom,— paths that for ever droop and rise over the green banks and mounds sweeping down in scented undulation, steep to the blue water, studded here and there with new-mown heaps, filling all the air with fainter sweetness,—look up towards the higher hills, where the waves of everlasting green roll silently into their long inlets among the shadows of the pines; and we may, perhaps, at last know the meaning of those quiet words of the 147th Psalm, 'He maketh grass to grow upon the mountains.'

Modern Painters, Vol. III, Part 4, Ch. 14

Of Classical Landscape

My reason for asking the reader to give so much of his time to the examination of the pathetic fallacy was, that, whether in literature or in art, he will find it eminently characteristic of the modern mind. . . . For instance, Keats, describing a wave breaking out at sea, says of it—

"Down whose green back the short-lived foam, all hoar,
Bursts gradual, with a wayward indolence."

That is quite perfect, as an example of the modern manner. The idea of the peculiar action with which foam rolls down a long, large wave could not have been given by any other words so well as by this "wayward indolence." But Homer would never have written, never thought of, such words. He could not by any possibility have lost sight of the great fact that the wave, from the beginning to the end of it, do what it might, was still nothing else than salt water; and that salt water could not be either wayward or indolent. He will call the waves "over-roofed," "full-charged," "monstrous," "compact-black," "dark-clear," "violet-coloured," "wine-coloured," and so on. But every one of these epithets is descriptive of pure physical nature. "Over-roofed" is the term he invariably uses of anything—rock, house, or wave—that nods over at the brow; the other terms need no explanation; they are as accurate and intense in truth as words can be, but they never show the slightest feeling of anything animated in the ocean. Black or clear, monstrous or violet-coloured, cold salt water it is always, and nothing but that.

"Well, but the modern writer, by his admission of the tinge of fallacy, has given an idea of something in the action of the wave which Homer could not, and surely, therefore, has made a step in advance? Also there appears to be a degree of sympathy and feeling in the one writer, which there is not in the other; and as it has been received for a first principle that writers are great in proportion to the intensity of their feelings, and Homer seems to have no feelings about the sea but that it is black and deep, surely in this respect also the modern writer is the greater?"

Stay a moment. Homer *had* some feeling about the sea; a faith in the animation of it much stronger than Keats's. But all this sense of something living in it, he separates in his mind into a great abstract image of a Sea Power. He never says the waves rage, or the waves are idle. But he says there is somewhat in, and greater than, the waves, which rages, and is idle, and *that* he calls a god.

I do not think we ever enough endeavour to enter into what a Greek's real notion of a god was. We are so accustomed to the modern mockeries of the classical religion, so accustomed to hear and see the Greek gods introduced as living personages, or invoked for help, by men who believe neither in them nor in any other gods, that we seem to have infected the Greek ages themselves with the breath, and dimmed them with the shade, of our hypocrisy; and are apt to think that Homer, as we know that Pope, was merely an ingenious fabulist; nay, more than this, that all the nations of past time were ingenious fabulists also, to whom the universe was a lyrical drama, and by whom whatsoever was said about it was merely a witty allegory, or a grateful lie, of which the entire upshot and consummation was a pretty statue in the middle of the court, or at the end of the garden. ...

What, then, was actually the Greek god? In what way were these two ideas of human form, and divine power, credibly associated in the ancient heart, so as to become a subject of true faith irrespective equally of fable, allegory, superstitious trust in stone, and demoniacal influence?

It seems to me that the Greek had exactly the same instinctive feeling about the elements that we have ourselves; that to Homer, as much as to Casimir de la Vigne, fire seemed ravenous and pitiless; to Homer, as much as to Keats, the sea-wave appeared wayward or idle, or whatever else it may be to the poetical passion. But then the Greek reasoned upon this sensation, saying to himself: "I can light the fire, and put it out; I can dry this water up, or drink it. It cannot be the fire or the water that rages, or that is wayward. But it must be something *in* this fire and *in* the water, which I cannot destroy by extinguishing the one, or evaporating the other, any more than I destroy myself by cutting off my finger; *I* was *in* my finger—something of me at least was; I had a power over it and felt pain in it, though I am still as much myself when it is gone. So there may be a power in the water which is not water, but to which the water is as a body;—which can strike with it, move in it, suffer in it, yet not be destroyed with it. This something, this Great Water Spirit, I must not confuse with the waves, which are only its body. *They* may flow hither and thither, increase or diminish. *That* must be indivisible—imperishable—a god. So of fire also; those rays which I can stop, and in the midst of which I cast a shadow, cannot be divine, nor greater than I. They cannot feel, but there may be something in them that feels,—a glorious intelligence, as much nobler and more swift than mine, as these rays, which are its body, are nobler and swifter than my flesh;—the spirit of all light, and truth, and melody, and revolving hours."

It was easy to conceive, farther, that such spirits should be able to assume at will a human form, in order to hold intercourse with men, or to perform any act for which

178

their proper body, whether of fire, earth, or air, was unfitted. And it would have been to place them beneath, instead of above, humanity, if, assuming the form of man, they could not also have tasted his pleasures. Hence the easy step to the more or less material ideas of deities, which are apt at first to shock us, but which are indeed only dishonourable so far as they represent the gods as false and unholy. It is not the materialism, but the vice, which degrades the conception; for the materialism itself is never positive, or complete. There is always some sense of exaltation in the spiritual and immortal body; and of a power proceeding from the visible form through all the infinity of the element ruled by the particular god. The precise nature of the idea is well seen in the passage of the *Iliad* which describes the river Scamander defending the Trojans against Achilles. In order to remonstrate with the hero, the god assumes a human form, which nevertheless is in some way or other instantly recognized by Achilles as that of the river-god: it is addressed at once as a river, not as a man; and its voice is the voice of a river "out of the deep whirlpools." Achilles refuses to obey its commands; and from the human form it returns instantly into its natural or divine one, and endeavours to overwhelm him with waves. Vulcan defends Achilles, and sends fire against the river, which suffers in its water-body, till it is able to bear no more. At last even the "nerve of the river," or "strength of the river" (note the expression), feels the fire, and this "strength of the river" addresses Vulcan in supplications for respite. There is in this precisely the idea of a vital part of the river-body, which acted and felt, to which, if the fire reached, it was death, just as would be the case if it touched a vital part of the human body. Throughout the passage the manner of conception is perfectly clear and consistent; and if, in other places, the exact connection between the ruling spirit and the thing ruled is not so manifest, it is only because it is almost impossible for the human mind to dwell long upon such subjects without falling into inconsistencies, and gradually slackening its effort to grasp the entire truth; until the more spiritual part of it slips from its hold, and only the human form of the god is left, to be conceived and described as subject to all the errors of humanity. But I do not believe that the idea ever weakens itself down to mere allegory. When Pallas is said to attack and strike down Mars, it does not mean merely that Wisdom at that moment prevailed against wrath. It means that there are, indeed, two great spirits, one entrusted to guide the human soul to wisdom and chastity, the other to kindle wrath and prompt to battle. It means that these two spirits, on the spot where, and at the moment when, a great contest was to be decided between all that they each governed in man, then and there (assumed) human form, and human weapons, and did verily and materially strike at each other, until the Spirit of Wrath was crushed. And when Diana is said to hunt with her nymphs in the woods, it does not mean merely, as Wordsworth puts it, that the poet or shepherd saw the moon and stars glancing between the branches of the trees, and wished to say so figuratively. It means that there is a living spirit, to which the light of the moon is a body; which takes delight in glancing between the clouds and following the wild beasts as they wander through the night; and that this spirit sometimes assumes a perfect human form, and in this form, with real arrows, pursues and slays the wild beasts, which with its mere arrows of moonlight it could not slay; retaining, nevertheless, all the while, its power and being in the moonlight, and in all else that it rules.

There is not the smallest inconsistency or unspirituality in this conception. If there were, it would attach equally to the appearance of the angels to Jacob, Abraham, Joshua, or Manoah. In all those instances the highest authority which governs our own faith requires us to conceive divine power clothed with a human form (a form so real that it is recognized for superhuman only by its "doing wondrously"), and retaining, nevertheless, sovereignty and omnipresence in all the world. This is precisely, as I understand it, the heathen idea of God; and it is impossible to comprehend any single part of the Greek mind until we grasp this faithfully, not endeavouring to explain it away in any wise, but accepting, with frank decision and definition, the tangible existence of its deities: —blue-eyed—white-fleshed—human-hearted,—capable at their choice of meeting man absolutely in his own nature —feasting with him—talking with him—fighting with him, eye to eye, or breast to breast, as Mars with Diomed; or else, dealing with him in a more retired spirituality as Apollo sending the plague upon the Greeks, when his quiver rattles at his shoulders as he moves, and yet the darts sent forth of it strike not as arrows, but as plague; or, finally, retiring completely into the material universe which they properly inhabit, and dealing with man through that, as Scamander with Achilles, through his waves.

Nor is there anything whatever in the various actions

180

recorded of the gods, however apparently ignoble, to indicate weakness of belief in them. Very frequently things which appear to us ignoble are merely the simplicities of a pure and truthful age. When Juno beats Diana about the ears with her own quiver, for instance, we start at first, as if Homer could not have believed that they were both real goddesses. But what should Juno have done? Killed Diana with a look? Nay, she neither wished to do so, nor could she have done so, by the very faith of Diana's goddess-ship. Diana is as immortal as herself. Frowned Diana into submission? But Diana has come expressly to try conclusions with her, and will by no means be frowned into submission. Wounded her with a celestial lance? That sounds more poetical, but it is in reality partly more savage and partly more absurd, than Homer. More savage, for it makes Juno more cruel, therefore less divine; and more absurd, for it only seems elevated in tone, because we use the word "celestial," which means nothing. What sort of a thing is a "celestial" lance? Not a wooden one. Of what then? Of moonbeams, or clouds, or mist. Well, therefore, Diana's arrows were of mist too; and her quiver, and herself, and Juno, with her lance, and all, vanish into mist. Why not have said at once, if that is all you mean, that two mists met, and one drove the other back? That would have been rational and intelligible, but not to talk of celestial lances. Homer had no such misty fancy; he believed the two goddesses were there in true bodies, with true weapons, on the true earth; and still I ask, what should Juno have done? Not beaten Diana? No; for it is unlady-like. Un-English-lady-like, yes; but by no means un-Greek-lady-like, nor even un-natural-lady-like. If a modern lady does *not* beat her servant or her rival about the ears, it is oftener because she is too weak, or too proud, than because she is of purer mind than Homer's Juno. She will not strike them; but she will overwork the one or slander the other without pity; and Homer would not have thought that one whit more goddess-like than striking them with her open hand.

If, however, the reader likes to suppose that while the two goddesses in personal presence thus fought with arrow and quiver, there was also a broader and vaster contest supposed by Homer between the elements they ruled; and that the goddess of the heavens, as she struck the goddess of the moon on the flushing cheek, was at the same instant exercising omnipresent power in the heavens themselves, and gathering clouds, with which, filled with the moon's own arrows or beams, she was encumbering and concealing the moon; he is welcome to this outcarrying of the idea, provided that he does not pretend to make it an interpretation instead of a mere extension, nor think to explain away my real, running, beautiful beaten Diana, into a moon behind clouds. . . .

Such being their general idea of the gods, we can now easily understand the habitual tone of their feelings towards what was beautiful in nature. With us, observe, the idea of the Divinity is apt to get separated from the life of nature; and imagining our God upon a cloudy throne, far above the earth, and not in the flowers or waters, we approach these visible things with a theory that they are dead; governed by physical laws, and so forth. But coming to them, we find the theory fail; that they are not dead; that, say what we choose about them, the instinctive sense of their being alive is too strong for us; and in scorn of all physical law, the wilful fountain sings, and the kindly flowers rejoice. And then, puzzled, and yet happy; pleased, and yet ashamed of being so; accepting sympathy from nature, which we do not believe it gives, and giving sympathy to nature, which we do not believe it receives,—mixing, besides, all manner of purposeful play and conceit with these involuntary fellowships,—we fall necessarily into the curious web of hesitating sentiment, pathetic fallacy, and wandering fancy, which form a great part of our modern view of nature. But the Greek never removed his god out of nature at all; never attempted for a moment to contradict his instinctive sense that God was everywhere. "The tree *is* glad," said he, "I know it is; I can cut it down: no matter, there was a nymph in it. The water *does* sing," said he; "I can dry it up; but no matter, there was a naiad in it." But in thus clearly defining his belief, observe, he threw it entirely into a human form, and gave his faith to nothing but the image of his own humanity. What sympathy and fellowship he had, were always for the spirit *in* the stream, not for the stream; always for the dryad *in* the wood, not for the wood. Content with this human sympathy, he approached the actual waves and woody fibres with no sympathy at all. The spirit that ruled them, he received as a plain fact. Them, also, ruled and material, he received as plain facts; they, without their spirit, were dead enough. A rose was good for scent, and a stream for sound and coolness; for the rest, one was no more than leaves, the other no more than water; he could not make anything else of them; and the divine power, which was involved in their existence, having been all distilled away by him into an independent

182

Flora or Thetis, the poor leaves or waves were left, in mere cold corporealness, to make the most of their being discernibly red and soft, clear and wet, and unacknowledged in any other power whatsoever.

Then, observe farther, the Greeks lived in the midst of the most beautiful nature, and were as familiar with blue sea, clear air, and sweet outlines of mountain, as we are with brick walls, black smoke, and level fields. This perfect familiarity rendered all such scenes of natural beauty unexciting, if not indifferent to them, by lulling and overwearying the imagination as far as it was concerned with such things; but there was another kind of beauty which they found it required effort to obtain, and which, when thoroughly obtained, seemed more glorious than any of this wild loveliness—the beauty of the human countenance and form. This, they perceived, could only be reached by continual exercise of virtue; and it was in Heaven's sight, and theirs, all the more beautiful because it needed this self-denial to obtain it. . . .

Farther, the human beauty, which, whether in its bodily being or in imagined divinity, had become, for the reasons we have seen, the principal object of culture and sympathy to these Greeks, was, in its perfection, eminently orderly, symmetrical, and tender. Hence, contemplating it constantly in this state, they could not but feel a proportionate fear of all that was disorderly, unbalanced, and rugged. Having trained their stoutest soldiers into a strength so delicate and lovely, that their white flesh, with their blood upon it, should look like ivory stained with purple; and having always around them, in the motion and majesty of this beauty, enough for the full employment of their imagination, they shrank with dread or hatred from all the ruggedness of lower nature,—from the wrinkled forest bark, the jagged hill-crest, and irregular, inorganic storm of sky; looking to these for the most part as adverse powers, and taking pleasure only in such portions of the lower world as were at once conducive to the rest and health of the human frame, and in harmony with the laws of its gentler beauty.

Thus, as far as I recollect, without a single exception, every Homeric landscape, intended to be beautiful, is composed of a fountain, a meadow, and a shady grove. This ideal is very interestingly marked, as intended for a perfect one, in the fifth book of the *Odyssey;* when Mercury himself stops for a moment, though on a message, to look at a landscape "which even an immortal might be gladdened to behold." This landscape consists of a cave covered with a running vine, all blooming into grapes, and surrounded by a grove of alder, poplar, and sweet-smelling cypress. Four fountains of white (foaming) water, springing *in succession* (mark the orderliness), and close to one another, flow away in different directions, through a meadow full of violets and parsley (parsley, to mark its moisture, being elsewhere called "marsh-nourished," and associated with the lotus); the air is perfumed not only by these violets, and by the sweet cypress, but by Calypso's fire of finely chopped cedar-wood, which sends a smoke, as of incense, through the island; Calypso herself is singing; and finally, upon the trees are resting, or roosting, owls, hawks, and "long-tongued sea-crows." Whether these last are considered as a part of the ideal landscape, as marine singing birds, I know not; but the approval of Mercury appears to be elicited chiefly by the fountains and violet meadow.

Now the notable things in this description are, first, the evident subservience of the whole landscape to human comfort, to the foot, the taste, or the smell; and, secondly, that throughout the passage there is not a single figurative word expressive of the things being in any wise other than plain grass, fruit, or flower. I have used the term "spring" of the fountains, because, without doubt, Homer means that they sprang forth brightly, having their source at the foot of the rocks (as copious fountains nearly always have); but Homer does not say "spring," he says simply flow, and uses only one word for "growing softly," or "richly," of the tall trees, the vine, and the violets. There is, however, some expression of sympathy with the sea-birds; he speaks of them in precisely the same terms, as in other places of naval nations, saying they "have care of the works of the sea."

If we glance through the references to pleasant land-scape which occur in other parts of the *Odyssey,* we shall always be struck by this quiet subjection of their every feature to human service, and by the excessive similarity in the scenes. . . . In all this I cannot too strongly mark the utter absence of any trace of the feeling for what we call the picturesque, and the constant dwelling of the writer's mind on what was available, pleasant, or useful; his ideas respecting all landscape being not uncharacteris-tically summed, finally, by Pallas herself; when, meeting Ulysses, who after his long wandering does not recognize his own country, and meaning to describe it as politely and soothingly as possible, she says:—"This Ithaca of ours is, indeed, a rough country enough, and not good for driving in; but, still, things might be worse: it has plenty of corn, and good wine, and *always rain*, and soft nourishing dew, and it has good feeding for goats and oxen, and all manner of wood, and springs fit to drink at all the year round."

We shall see presently how the blundering, pseudo-picturesque pseudo-classical minds of Claude and the Renaissance landscape-painters, wholly missing Homer's practical common sense, and equally incapable of feeling the quiet natural grace and sweetness of his asphodel meadows, tender aspen poplars, or running vines,—fastened on his *ports* and *caves*, as the only available features of his scenery; and appointed the type of "classical landscape" thenceforward to consist in a bay of insipid sea, and a rock with a hole through it. . . .

We think of the Greeks as poetical, ideal, imaginative, in a way that a modern poet or novelist is; supposing that their thoughts about their mythology and world were as visionary and artificial as ours are: but I think the passages I have quoted show that it was not so, although it may be difficult for us to apprehend the strange minglings in them of the elements of faith, which, in our days, have been blended wtih other parts of human nature in a totally different guise. Perhaps the Greek mind may be best imagined by taking, as its groundwork, that of a good, conscientious, but illiterate Scotch Presbyterian Border farmer of a century or two back, having perfect faith in the bodily appearances of Satan and his imps; and in all kelpies, brownies, and fairies. Substitute for the indignant terrors in this man's mind, a general persuasion of the *Divinity*, more or less beneficent, yet faultful, of all these beings; that is to say, take away his belief in the demoniacal malignity of the fallen spiritual world, and lower, in the same degree, his conceptions of the angelical, retaining for him the same firm faith in both; keep his ideas about flowers and beautiful scenery much as they are,—his delight in regular ploughed land and meadows, and a neat garden (only with rows of gooseberry bushes instead of vines), being, in all probability, about accurately representative of the feelings of Ulysses; then, let the military spirit that is in him, glowing against the Border forager, or the foe of old Flodden and Chevy-Chase, be made more principal, with a higher sense of nobleness in soldiership, not as a careless excitement, but a knightly duty; and increased by high cultivation of every personal quality, not of mere shaggy strength, but graceful strength, aided by a

softer climate, and educated in all proper harmony of
sight and sound; finally, instead of an informed Christian,
suppose him to have only the patriarchal Jewish knowledge of the Deity, and even this obscured by tradition, but
still thoroughly solemn and faithful, requiring his continual
service as a priest of burnt sacrifice and meat offering;
and I think we shall get a pretty close approximation to
the vital being of a true old Greek.

Modern Painters, Vol. III, Part 4, Ch. 13

Of Modern Landscape

We turn our eyes, therefore, as boldly and as quickly as
may be, from these serene fields and skies of mediæval art,
to the most characteristic examples of modern landscape.
And, I believe, the first thing that will strike us, or that
ought to strike us, is their *cloudiness*.

Out of perfect light and motionless air, we find ourselves on a sudden brought under sombre skies, and into
drifting wind: and, with fickle sunbeams flashing in our
face, or utterly drenched with sweep of rain, we are
reduced to track the changes of the shadows on the grass,
or watch the rents of twilight through angry cloud. And
we find that whereas all the pleasure of the mediæval was
in *stability, definiteness,* and *luminousness,* we are expected to rejoice in darkness, and triumph in mutability; to lay
the foundation of happiness in things which momentarily
change or fade; and to expect the utmost satisfaction and
instruction from what it is impossible to arrest, and difficult to comprehend.

We find, however, together with this general delight in
breeze and darkness, much attention to the real form of
clouds, and careful drawing of effects of mist; so that the
appearance of objects, as seen through it, becomes a
subject of science with us; and the faithful representation
of that appearance is made of primal importance, under
the name of aerial perspective. The aspects of sunset and
sunrise, with all their attendant phenomena of cloud and
mist, are watchfully delineated; and in ordinary daylight
landscape, the sky is considered of so much importance,
that a principal mass of foliage, or a whole foreground, is
unhesitatingly thrown into shade merely to bring out the
form of a white cloud. So that, if a general and character-

istic name were needed for modern landscape art, none better could be invented than "the service of clouds."

And this name would, unfortunately, be characteristic of our art in more ways than one. . . . I said that all the Greeks spoke kindly about the clouds, except Aristophanes; and he, I am sorry to say (since his report is so unfavourable), is the only Greek who had studied them attentively. He tells us, first, that they are "great goddesses to idle men"; then, that they are "mistresses of disputings, and logic, and monstrosities, and noisy chattering"; declares that whoso believes in their divinity must first disbelieve in Jupiter, and place supreme power in the hands of an unknown god "Whirlwind"; and, finally, he displays their influence over the mind of one of their disciples, in his sudden desire "to speak ingeniously concerning smoke."

There is, I fear, an infinite truth in this Aristophanic judgment applied to our modern cloud-worship. Assuredly, much of the love of mystery in our romances, our poetry, our art, and, above all, in our metaphysics, must come under that definition so long ago given by the great Greek, "speaking ingeniously concerning smoke." And much of the instinct, which, partially developed in painting, may be now seen throughout every mode of exertion of mind,—the easily encouraged doubt, easily excited curiosity, habitual agitation, and delight in the changing and the marvellous, as opposed to the old quiet serenity of social custom and religious faith,—is again deeply defined in those few words, the "dethroning of Jupiter," the "coronation of the whirlwind." . . .

The next thing that will strike us, after this love of the clouds, is the love of liberty. Whereas the mediæval was always shutting himself into castles, and behind fosses, and drawing brickwork neatly, and beds of flowers primly, our painters delight in getting to the open fields and moors, abhor all hedges and moats; never paint anything but free-growing trees, and rivers gliding "at their own sweet will"; eschew formality down to the smallest detail; break and displace the brickwork which the mediæval would have carefully cemented; leave unpruned the thickets he would have delicately trimmed; and, carrying the love of liberty even to license, and the love of wildness even to ruin, take pleasure at last in every aspect of age and desolation which emancipates the objects of nature from the government of men;—on the castle wall displacing its tapestry with ivy, and spreading, through the garden, the bramble for the rose.

Connected with this love of liberty we find a singular

manifestation of love of mountains, and see our painters traversing the wildest places of the globe in order to obtain subjects with craggy foregrounds and purple distances. Some few of them remain content with pollards and flat land; but these are always men of third-rate order; and the leading masters, while they do not reject the beauty of the low grounds, reserve their highest powers to paint Alpine peaks or Italian promontories. And it is eminently noticeable, also, that this pleasure in the mountains is never mingled with fear, or tempered by a spirit of meditation, as with the mediæval; but is always free and fearless, brightly exhilarating, and wholly unreflective; so that the painter feels that his mountain foreground may be more consistently animated by a sportsman than a hermit; and our modern society in general goes to the mountains, not to fast, but to feast, and leaves their glaciers covered with chicken-bones and egg-shells.

Connected with this want of any sense of solemnity in mountain scenery, is a general profanity of temper in regarding all the rest of nature; that is to say, a total absence of faith in the presence of any deity therein. Whereas the mediæval never painted a cloud, but with the purpose of placing an angel in it; and a Greek never entered a wood without expecting to meet a god in it; *we* should think the appearance of an angel in the cloud wholly unnatural, and should be seriously surprised by meeting a god anywhere. Our chief ideas about the wood are connected with poaching. We have no belief that the clouds contain more than so many inches of rain or hail, and from our ponds and ditches expect nothing more divine than ducks and watercresses.

Finally: connected with this profanity of temper is a strong tendency to deny the sacred element of colour, and make our boast in blackness. For though occasionally glaring or violent, modern colour is on the whole eminently sombre, tending continually to grey or brown, and by many of our best painters consistently falsified, with a confessed pride in what they call chaste or subdued tints; so that, whereas a mediæval paints his sky bright blue and his foreground bright green, gilds the towers of his castles, and clothes his figures with purple and white, we paint our sky grey, our foreground black, and our foliage brown, and think that enough is sacrificed to the sun in admitting the dangerous brightness of a scarlet cloak or a blue jacket.

These, I believe, are the principal points which would

strike us instantly, if we were to be brought suddenly into an exhibition of modern landscapes out of a room filled with mediæval work. It is evident that there are both evil and good in this change; but how much evil, or how much good, we can only estimate by considering, as in the former divisions of our inquiry, what are the real roots of the habits of mind which have caused them.

At first, it is evident that the title "Dark Ages," given to the mediæval centuries, is, respecting art, wholly inapplicable. They were, on the contrary, the bright ages; ours are the dark ones. I do not mean metaphysically, but literally. They were the ages of gold; ours are the ages of umber.

This is partly mere mistake in us; we build brown brick walls, and wear brown coats, because we have been blunderingly taught to do so, and go on doing so mechanically. There is, however, also some cause for the change in our own tempers. On the whole, these are much *sadder* ages than the early ones; not sadder in a noble and deep way, but in a dim wearied way,—the way of ennui, and jaded intellect, and uncomfortableness of soul and body. The Middle Ages had their wars and agonies, but also intense delights. Their gold was dashed with blood; but ours is sprinkled with dust. Their life was inwoven with white and purple: ours is one seamless stuff of brown. Not that we are without apparent festivity, but festivity more or less forced, mistaken, embittered, incomplete—not of the heart. How wonderfully, since Shakspere's time, have we lost the power of laughing at bad jests! The very finish of our wit belies our gaiety.

The profoundest reason of this darkness of heart is, I believe, our want of faith. There never yet was a generation of men (savage or civilized) who, taken as a body, so wofully fulfilled the words "having no hope, and without God in the world," as the present civilized European race. A Red Indian or Otaheitan savage has more sense of a divine existence round him, or government over him, than the plurality of refined Londoners and Parisians: and those among us who may in some sense be said to believe, are divided almost without exception into two broad classes, Romanist and Puritan; who, but for the interference of the unbelieving portions of society, would, either of them, reduce the other sect as speedily as possible to ashes. . . . Nearly all our powerful men in this age of the world are unbelievers; the best of them in doubt and misery; the worst in reckless defiance; the plurality, in plodding hesitation, doing, as well as they can, what practical work lies ready to their hands. Most of our scientific men are in the last class: our popular authors either set themselves definitely against all religious form, pleading for simple truth and benevolence, (Thackeray, Dickens,) or give themselves up to bitter and fruitless statement of facts, (De Balzac,) or surface-painting, (Scott,) or careless blasphemy, sad or smiling, (Byron, Beranger). Our earnest poets and deepest thinkers are doubtful and indignant, (Tennyson, Carlyle); one or two, anchored, indeed, but anxious or weeping, (Wordsworth, Mrs. Browning); and of these two, the first is not so sure of his anchor, but that now and then it drags with him, even to make him cry out,—

"Great God, I had rather be
A Pagan suckled in some creed outworn;
So might I, standing on this pleasant lea,
Have glimpses that would make me less forlorn."

In politics, religion is now a name; in art, a hypocrisy or affectation. Over German religious pictures the inscription, "See how Pious I am," can be read at a glance by any clear-sighted person. Over French and English religious pictures the inscription, "See how Impious I am," is equally legible. All sincere and modest art is, among us, profane.

This faithlessness operates among us according to our tempers, producing either sadness or levity, and being the ultimate root alike of our discontents and of our wantonnesses. It is marvellous how full of contradiction it makes us: we are first dull, and seek for wild and lonely places because we have no heart for the garden; presently we recover our spirits, and build an assembly-room among the mountains, because we have no reverence for the desert. I do not know if there be game on Sinai, but I am always expecting to hear of some one's shooting over it.

There is, however, another, and a more innocent root of our delight in wild scenery.

All the Renaissance principles of art tended, as I have before often explained, to the setting Beauty above Truth, and seeking for it always at the expense of truth. And the proper punishment of such pursuit—the punishment which all the laws of the universe rendered inevitable—was, that those who thus pursued beauty should wholly lose sight of beauty. All the thinkers of the age, as we saw previously, declared that it did not exist. The age seconded their efforts, and banished beauty, so far as human effort could succeed in doing so, from the face of the earth, and the form of man. To powder the hair, to patch the cheek, to hoop the body, to buckle the foot, were all part and parcel of the same system which reduced streets to brick walls, and pictures to brown stains. One desert of Ugliness was extended before the eyes of mankind; and their pursuit of the beautiful, so recklessly continued, received unexpected consummation in high-heeled shoes and periwigs—Gower Street, and Gaspar Poussin.

Reaction from this state was inevitable, if any true life was left in the races of mankind; and, accordingly, though still forced, by rule and fashion, to the producing and wearing all that is ugly, men steal out, half-ashamed of themselves for doing so, to the fields and mountains; and, finding among these the colour, and liberty, and variety, and power, which are for ever grateful to them, delight in these to an extent never before known; rejoice in all the wildest shattering of the mountain side, as an opposition to Gower Street, gaze in a rapt manner at sunsets and sunrises, to see there the blue, and gold, and purple, which glow for them no longer on knight's armour or temple porch; and gather with care out of the fields, into their blotted herbaria, the flowers which the five orders of architecture have banished from their doors and casements. . . .

It is not, however, only to existing inanimate nature that our want of beauty in person and dress has driven us. The imagination of it, as it was seen in our ancestors, haunts us continually; and while we yield to the present fashions, or act in accordance with the dullest modern principles of economy and utility, we look fondly back to the manners of the ages of chivalry, and delight in painting, to the fancy, the fashions we pretend to despise, and the splendours we think it wise to abandon. The furniture and personages of our romance are sought, when the writer desires to please most easily, in the centuries which we profess to have surpassed in everything; the art which takes us into the present times is considered as both daring and degraded, and while the weakest words please us, and are regarded as poetry, which recall the manners of our forefathers, or of strangers, it is only as familiar and vulgar that we accept the description of our own.

In this we are wholly different from all the races that preceded us. All other nations have regarded their ancestors with reverence as saints or heroes; but have nevertheless thought their own deeds and ways of life the fitting

191

subjects for their arts of painting or of verse. We, on the contrary, regard our ancestors as foolish and wicked, but yet find our chief artistic pleasure in descriptions of their ways of life.

The Greeks and mediævals honoured, but did not imitate their forefathers; we imitate, but do not honour. . . .

Farther: as the admiration of mankind is found, in our times, to have in great part passed from men to mountains, and from human emotion to natural phenomena, we may anticipate that the great strength of art will also be warped in this direction; with this notable result for us, that whereas the greatest painters or painter of classical and mediæval periods, being wholly devoted to the representation of humanity, furnished us with but little to examine in landscape, the greatest painters or painter of modern times will in all probability be devoted to landscape principally; and farther, because in representing human emotion words surpass painting, but in representing natural scenery painting surpasses words, we may anticipate also that the painter and poet (for convenience sake I here use the words in opposition) will somewhat change their relations of rank in illustrating the mind of the age; that the painter will become of more importance, the poet of less; and that the relations between the men who are the types and first-fruits of the age in word and work,—namely, Scott and Turner,—will be, in many curious respects, different from those between Homer and Phidias, or Dante and Giotto. . . .

Then, as touching the kind of work done by these two men, the more I think of it I find this conclusion more impressed upon me,—that the greatest thing a human soul ever does in this world is to *see* something, and tell what it *saw* in a plain way. Hundreds of people can talk for one who can think, but thousands can think for one who can see. To see clearly is poetry, prophecy, and religion,—all in one.

Modern Painters, Vol. III, Part 4, Ch. 16

But not only is there a *partial* and variable mystery thus caused by clouds and vapours throughout great spaces of landscape; there is a continual mystery caused throughout *all* spaces, caused by the absolute infinity of things. WE NEVER SEE ANYTHING CLEARLY. I stated this fact partly in the chapter on Truth of Space, in the first volume, but not with sufficient illustration, so that the reader might by that chapter have been led to infer that the mystery spoken of belonged to some special distance of the landscape, whereas the fact is, that everything we look at, be it large or small, near or distant, has an equal quantity of mystery in it; and the only question is, not how much mystery there is, but at what part of the object mystification begins. We suppose we see the ground under our feet clearly, but if we try to number its grains of dust, we shall find that it is as full of confusion and doubtful form, as anything else; so that there is literally *no* point of clear sight, and there never can be. What we call seeing a thing clearly, is only seeing enough of it to *make out what it is;* this point of intelligibility varying in distance for different magnitudes and kinds of things, while the appointed quantity of mystery remains nearly the same for all. Thus: throwing an open book and an embroidered handkerchief on a lawn, at a distance of a quarter of a mile we cannot tell which is which; that is the point of mystery for the whole of those things. They are then merely white spots of indistinct shape. We approach them, and perceive that one is a book, the other a handkerchief, but cannot read the one, nor trace the embroidery of the other. The mystery has ceased to be in the whole things, and has gone into their details. We go nearer, and can now read the text and trace the embroidery, but cannot see the fibres of the paper, nor the threads of the stuff. The mystery has gone into a third place. We take both up and look closely at them; we see the watermark and the threads, but not the hills and dales in the paper's surface, nor the fine fibres which shoot off from every thread. The mystery has gone into a fourth place, where it must stay, till we take a microscope, which will send it into a fifth, sixth, hundredth, or thousandth place, according to the power we use. When, therefore, we say, we see the book *clearly,* we mean only that we know it is a book. When we say that we see the letters clearly, we mean that we know what letters they are; and artists feel that they are drawing objects at a convenient distance when they are so near them as to know, and to be able in painting to show that they know, what the objects are, in a tolerably complete manner: but this power does not depend on any definite distance of the object, but on its size, kind, and distance, together; so that a small thing in the foreground may be precisely in the same *phase* or place of mystery as a large thing far away.

The other day, as I was lying down to rest on the side

of the hill round which the Rhone sweeps in its main angle, opposite Martigny, and looking carefully across the valley to the ridge of the hill which rises above Martigny itself, then distant about four miles, a plantain seed-vessel about an inch long, and a withered head of a scabious half an inch broad, happened to be seen rising up, out of the grass near me, across the outline of the distant hill, so as seemingly to set themselves closely beside the large pines and chestnuts which fringed that distant ridge. The plantain was eight yards from me, and the scabious seven; and to my sight, at these distances, the plantain and the far-away pines were equally clear (it being a clear day, and the sun stooping to the west). The pines, four miles off, showed their branches, but I could not count them: and two or three young and old Spanish chestnuts beside them showed their broken masses distinctly; but I could not count those masses, only I knew the trees to be chestnuts by their general look. The plantain and scabious in like manner I knew to be plantain and scabious by their general look. I saw the plantain seed-vessel to be, somehow, rough, and that there were two little projections at the bottom of the scabious head which I knew to mean the leaves of the calyx; but I could no more count distinctly the seeds of the plantain, or the group of leaves forming the calyx of the scabious, than I could count the branches of the far-away pines.

Under these circumstances, it is quite evident that neither the pine nor plantain could have been rightly represented by a single dot or stroke of colour. Still less could they be represented by a definite drawing, on a small scale, of a pine with all its branches clear, or of a plantain with all its seeds clear. The round dot or long stroke would represent nothing, and the clear delineation too much. They were not mere dots of colour which I saw on the hill, but something full of essence of pine; out of which I could gather which were young and which were old, and discern the distorted and crabbed pines from the symmetrical and healthy pines; and feel how the evening sun was sending its searching threads among their dark leaves;—assuredly they were more than dots of colour. And yet not one of their boughs or outlines could be distinctly made out, or distinctly drawn. Therefore, if I had drawn either a definite pine, or a dot, I should have been equally wrong, the right lying in an inexplicable, almost inimitable, confusion between the two.

Of the Materials of Mountains:—
Secondly, Slaty Chrystallines

It is to be remembered that these are the rocks which, on the average, will be oftenest observed, and with the greatest interest, by the human race. The central granites are too far removed, the lower rocks too common, to be carefully studied; these slaty crystallines form the noblest hills that are easily accessible, and seem to be thus calculated especially to attract observation, and reward it. Well, we begin to examine them; and, first, we find a notable hardness in them, and a thorough boldness of general character, which make us regard them as very types of perfect rocks. They have nothing of the look of dried earth about them, nothing petty or limited in the display of their bulk. Where they are, they seem to form the world; no mere bank of a river here, or of a lane there, peeping out among the hedges or forests: but from the lowest valley to the highest clouds, all is theirs—one adamantine dominion and rigid authority of rock. We yield ourselves to the impression of their eternal, unconquerable stubbornness of strength, their mass seems the least yielding, least to be softened, or in anywise dealt with by external force, of all earthly substance. And, behold, as we look farther into it, it is all touched and troubled, like waves by a summer breeze; rippled, far more delicately than seas or lakes are rippled: they only undulate along their surfaces—this rock trembles through its every fibre, like the chords of an Eolian harp—like the stillest air of spring with the echoes of a child's voice. Into the heart of all those great mountains, through every tossing of their boundless crests, and deep beneath all their unfathomable defiles, flows that strange quivering of their substance. Other and weaker things seem to express their subjection to an Infinite power only by momentary terrors: as the weeds bow down before the feverish wind, and the sound of the going in the tops of the taller trees passes on before the clouds, and the fitful opening of pale spaces on the dark water, as if some invisible hand were casting dust abroad upon it, gives warning of the anger that is to come, we may well imagine that there is indeed a fear passing upon the grass, and leaves, and waters, at the presence of some great spirit commissioned to let the tempest loose; but the terror passes, and their sweet rest is perpetually restored to the pastures and the waves. Not so to the mountains. They, which at first seemed strengthened beyond the dread of any violence or change, are yet also ordained to bear upon them the symbol of a perpetual Fear: the tremor which fades from the soft lake and gliding river is sealed, to all eternity, upon the rock; and while things that pass visibly from birth to death may sometimes forget their feebleness, the mountains are made to possess a perpetual memorial of their infancy,—that infancy which the prophet saw in his vision: 'I beheld the earth, and lo, it was without form and void, and the heavens and they had no light. I beheld the mountains, and lo, they *trembled;* and all the hills *moved lightly.*'

Modern Painters, Vol. IV, Part 5, Ch. 9

I do not know any district possessing a more pure or uninterrupted fulness of mountain character (and that of the highest order), or which appears to have been less disturbed by foreign agencies, than that which borders the course of the Trient between Valorcine and Martigny. The paths which lead to it out of the valley of the Rhone, rising at first in steep circles among the walnut trees, like winding stairs among the pillars of a Gothic tower, retire over the shoulders of the hills into a valley almost unknown, but thickly inhabited by an industrious and patient population. . . .

Green field, and glowing rock, and glancing streamlet, all slope together in the sunshine towards the brows of ravines, where the pines take up their own dominion of saddened shade; and with everlasting roar in the twilight, the stronger torrents thunder down, pale from the glaciers, filling all their chasms with enchanted cold, beating themselves to pieces against the great rocks that they have themselves cast down, and forcing fierce way beneath their ghastly poise.

The mountain paths stoop to these glens in forky zigzags, leading to some grey and narrow arch, all fringed under its shuddering curve with the ferns that fear the light; a cross of rough-hewn pine, iron-bound to its parapet, standing dark against the lurid fury of the foam. Far up the glen, as we pause beside the cross, the sky is seen through the openings in the pines, thin with excess of light; and, in its clear, consuming flame of white space, the summits of the rocky mountains are gathered into solemn crowns and circlets, all flushed in that strange, faint silence of possession by the sunshine which has in it so deep a melancholy; full of power, yet as frail as shadows: lifeless, like the walls of a sepulchre, yet beautiful in tender fall of crimson folds, like the veil of some sea spirit, that lives and dies as the foam flashes; fixed on a perpetual throne, stern against all strength, lifted above all sorrows, and yet effaced and melted utterly into the air by that last sunbeam that has crossed to them from between the two golden clouds.

High above all sorrow: yes; but not unwitnessing to it. The traveller on his happy journey, as his foot springs from the deep turf and strikes the pebbles gaily over the edge of the mountain road, sees with a glance of delight the clusters of nutbrown cottages that nestle among those sloping orchards, and glow beneath the boughs of the pines. Here it may well seem to him, if there be sometimes hardship, there must be at least innocence and peace, and fellowship of the human soul with nature. It is not so. The wild goats that leap along those rocks have as much passion of joy in all that fair work of God as the men that toil among them. Perhaps more. Enter the street of one of those villages, and you will find it foul with that gloomy foulness that is suffered only by torpor, or by anguish of soul. Here, it is torpor—not absolute suffering —not starvation or disease, but darkness of calm enduring; the spring known only as the time of the scythe, and the autumn as the time of the sickle, and the sun only as a warmth, the wind as a chill, and the mountains as a danger. They do not understand so much as the name of beauty, or of knowledge. They understand dimly that of virtue. Love, patience, hospitality, faith,—these things they know. To glean their meadows side by side, so happier; to bear the burden up the breathless mountain flank, unmurmuringly; to bid the stranger drink from their vessel of milk; to see at the foot of their low death-beds a pale figure upon a cross, dying, also patiently;—in this they are different from the cattle and from the stones, but in all this unrewarded as far as concerns the present life. For them, there is neither hope nor passion of spirit; for them neither advance nor exultation. Black bread, rude roof, dark night, laborious day, weary arm at sunset; and life ebbs away. No books, no thoughts, no attainments, no rest; except only sometimes a little sitting in the sun under the church wall, as the bell tolls thin and far in the mountain air; a pattering of a few prayers, not understood, by the altar rails of the dimly gilded chapel, and so back to the sombre home, with the cloud upon them still unbroken—that cloud of rocky gloom, born out of the wild torrents and ruinous stones, and unlightened, even in their religion, except by the vague promise of some better thing unknown, mingled with threatening, and obscured by an unspeakable horror,—a smoke, as it were, of martyrdom, coiling up with the incense, and, amidst the images of tortured bodies and lamenting spirits in hurtling flames, the very cross, for them, dashed more deeply than for others, with gouts of blood.

Do not let this be thought a darkened picture of the life of these mountaineers. It is literal fact. . . . As we penetrate farther among the hills we shall find it becoming very painful. We are walking, perhaps, in a summer afternoon, up the valley of Zermatt (a German valley), the sun shining brightly on grassy knolls and through fringes of pines, the goat leaping happily, and the cattle bells ringing sweetly, and the snowy mountains shining like heavenly castles far above. We see, a little way off, a small white chapel, sheltered behind one of the flowery hillocks of mountain turf; and we approach its little window, thinking to look through it into some quiet home of prayer; but the window is grated with iron, and open to the winds, and when we look through it, behold—a heap of white human bones mouldering into whiter dust!

So also in that same sweet valley, of which I have just been speaking, between Chamouni and the Valais, at every turn of the pleasant pathway, where the scent of the thyme lies richest upon its rock, we shall see a little cross and shrine set under one of them; and go up to it, hoping to receive some happy thought of the Redeemer, by whom all these lovely things were made, and still consist. But when we come near—behold, beneath the cross, a rude picture of souls tormented in red tongues of hell fire, and pierced by demons.

As we pass towards Italy the appearance of this gloom deepens; and when we descend the southern slope of the Alps we shall find this bringing forward of the image of Death associated with an endurance of the most painful aspects of disease; so that conditions of human suffering, which in any other country would be confined in hospitals, are permitted to be openly exhibited by the wayside; and with this exposure of the degraded human form is farther connected an insensibility to ugliness and imperfection in other things; so that the ruined wall, neglected garden, and uncleansed chamber, seem to unite in expressing a gloom of spirit possessing the inhabitants of the whole land. It does not appear to arise from poverty, nor careless contentment with little: there is here nothing of Irish recklessness or humour; but there seems a settled obscurity in the soul,—a chill and plague, as if risen out of a sepulchre, which partly deadens, partly darkens, the eyes and hearts of men, and breathes a leprosy of decay through every breeze, and every stone. "Instead of well-set hair, baldness, and burning instead of beauty." ...

Of places subjected to such evil influence, none are quite so characteristic as the town of Sion in the Valais. ... It consists of little more than one main street, winding round the roots of two ridges of crag, and branching, on the side towards the rocks, into a few narrow lanes, on the other, into spaces of waste ground, of which part serve for military exercises, part are enclosed in an uncertain and vague way; a ditch half-filled up, or wall half-broken down, seeming to indicate their belonging, or having been intended to belong, to some of the unfinished houses which are springing up amidst their weeds. But it is difficult to say, in any part of the town, what is garden ground and what is waste; still more, what is new building and what old. The houses have been for the most part built roughly of the coarse limestone of the neighbouring hills, then coated with plaster, and painted, in imitation of Palladian palaces, with grey architraves and pilasters, having draperies from capital to capital. With this false decoration is curiously contrasted a great deal of graceful, honest, and original ironwork, in bulging balconies, and floreted gratings of huge windows, and branching sprays, for any and every purpose of support or guard. The plaster, with its fresco, has in most instances dropped away, leaving the houses peeled and scarred; daubed into uncertain restoration with new mortar, and in the best cases thus left; but commonly fallen also, more or less, into ruin, and either roofed over at the first story when the second has fallen, or hopelessly abandoned;—not pulled down, but left in white and ghastly shells to crumble into heaps of limestone and dust, a pauper or two still inhabiting where inhabitation is possible. The lanes wind among these ruins; the blue sky and mountain grass are seen through the windows of their rooms and over their partitions, on which old gaudy papers flaunt in rags: the weeds gather, and the dogs scratch about their foundations; yet there are no luxuriant weeds, for their ragged leaves are blanched with lime, crushed under perpetually falling fragments, and worn away by listless standing of idle feet. There is always mason's work doing, always some fresh patching and whitening; a dull smell of mortar, mixed with that of stale foulness of every kind, rises with the dust, and defiles every current of air; the corners are filled with accumulations of stones, partly broken, with crusts of cement sticking to them, and blotches of nitre oozing out of their pores. The lichenous rocks and sunburnt slopes of grass stretch themselves hither and thither among the wreck; . . . the grass, in strange sympathy with the inhabitants, will not grow *as* grass, but chokes itself with a network of grey weeds, quite wonderful in their various expression of thorny discontent and savageness; the blue flower of the borage, which mingles with them in quantities, hardly interrupting their character, for the violent black spot in the centre of its blue takes away the tenderness of the flower, and it seems to have grown there in some supernatural mockery of its old renown of being good against melancholy. The rest of the herbage is chiefly composed of the dwarf mallow, the wild succory, the wall-rocket, goose-foot, and milfoil; plants, nearly all of them, jagged in the leaf, broken and dimly clustered in flower, haunters of waste ground and places of outcast refuse. . . .

I know not how far this universal grasp of the sorrowful spirit might be relaxed if sincere energy were directed to amend the ways of life of the Valaisan. But it has always appeared to me that there was, even in more healthy mountain districts, a certain degree of inevitable melancholy; nor could I ever escape from the feeling that here, where chiefly the beauty of God's working was manifested to men, warning was also given, and that to the full, of the enduring of His indignation against sin.

It seems one of the most cunning and frequent of self-deceptions to turn the heart away from this warning, and refuse to acknowledge anything in the fair scenes of the natural creation but beneficence. . . . And in this mountain gloom, which weighs so strongly upon the human heart that in all time hitherto, as we have seen, the hill defiles have been either avoided in terror or inhabited in penance, there is but the fulfilment of the universal law, that where the beauty and wisdom of the Divine working are most manifested, there also are manifested most clearly the terror of God's wrath, and inevitableness of His power.

Modern Painters, Vol. IV, Part 5, Ch. 19

A Joy for Ever:
The Political Economy of Art
(1857)

... To begin, then, with one of these necessary truisms:
all economy, whether of states, households, or individuals,
may be defined to be the art of managing labour. The
world is so regulated by the laws of Providence, that a
man's labour, well applied, is always amply sufficient to
provide him during his life with all things needful to him,
and not only with those, but with many pleasant objects of
luxury; and yet farther, to procure him large intervals of
healthful rest and serviceable leisure. And a nation's
labour well applied, is, in like manner, amply sufficient to
provide its whole population with good food and comfortable habitation; and not with those only, but with good
education besides, and objects of luxury, art treasures,
such as these you have around you now. But by those same
laws of Nature and Providence, if the labour of the nation
or of the individual be misapplied, and much more if it be
insufficient,—if the nation or man be indolent and unwise,—suffering and want result, exactly in proportion to
the indolence and improvidence—to the refusal of labour,
or to the misapplication of it. Wherever you see want, or
misery, or degradation, in this world about you, there, be
sure, either industry has been wanting, or industry has
been in error. It is not accident, it is not Heaven-
commanded calamity, it is not the original and inevitable
evil of man's nature, which fill your streets with lamenta-
tion, and your graves with prey. It is only that, when there
should have been providence, there has been waste; when
there should have been labour, there has been lascivious-
ness and wilfulness, when there should have been subordination. ...

Now, we have warped the word "economy" in our
English language into a meaning which it has no business
whatever to bear. In our use of it, it constantly signifies
merely sparing or saving; economy of money means saving money—economy of time, sparing time, and so on. But
that is a wholly barbarous use of the word—barbarous in
a double sense, for it is not English, and it is bad Greek;

barbarous in a treble sense, for it is not English, it is bad Greek, and it is worse sense. Economy no more means saving money than it means spending money. It means the administration of a house, its stewardship; spending or saving, that is whether money or time, or anything else, to the best possible advantage. In the simplest and clearest definition of it, economy whether public or private, means the wise management of labour; and it means this mainly in three senses: namely, first, *applying* your labour rationally, and secondly *preserving* its produce carefully; lastly, *distributing* its produce seasonably.

I say first, applying your labour rationally; that is, so as to obtain the most precious things you can, and the most lasting things, by it: not growing oats in land where you can grow wheat, nor putting fine embroidery on a stuff that will not wear. Secondly, preserving its produce carefully; that is to say, laying up your wheat wisely in store-houses for the time of famine, and keeping your embroidery watchfully from the moth: and lastly, distributing its produce seasonably; that is to say, being able to carry your corn at once to the place where the people are hungry, and your embroideries to the places where they are gay; so fulfilling in all ways the Wise Man's description, whether of the queenly housewife or queenly nation: 'She riseth while it is yet night, and giveth meat to her household, and a portion to her maidens. She maketh herself coverings of tapestry, her clothing is silk and purple. Strength and honour are in her clothing, and she shall rejoice in time to come.' . . .

I. Discovery.—How are we to get our men of genius: that is to say, by what means may we produce among us, at any given time, the greatest quantity of effective art-intellect? A wide question, you say, involving an account of all the best means of art education. Yes, but I do not mean to go into the consideration of those; I want only to state the few principles which lie at the foundation of the matter. Of these, the first is that you have always to find your artist, not to make him; you can't manufacture him, any more than you can manufacture gold. You can find him, and refine him; you dig him out as he lies nugget-fashion in the mountain-stream; you bring him home; and you make him into current coin, or household plate, but not one grain of him can you originally produce. A certain quantity of art-intellect is born annually in every nation, greater or less according to the nature and cultivation of the nation, or race of men; but a perfectly fixed quantity annually, not increasable by one grain. You may lose it, or you may gather it; you may let it lie loose in the ravine, and buried in the sands, or you may make king's thrones of it, and overlay temple gates with it, as you choose: but the best you can do with it is always merely sifting, melting, hammering, purifying—never creating.

And there is another thing notable about this artistical gold; not only is it limited in quantity, but in use. You need not make thrones or golden gates with it unless you like, but assuredly you can't do anything else with it. You can't make knives of it, nor armour, nor railroads. The gold won't cut you, and it won't carry you: put it to a mechanical use, and you destroy it at once. It is quite true that, in the greatest artists, their proper artistical faculty is united with every other; and you may make use of the other faculties, and let the artistical one lie dormant. For aught I know, there may be two or three Leonardo da Vincis employed at this moment in your harbours and railroads: but you are not employing their Leonardesque or golden faculty there,—you are only oppressing and destroying it. And the artistical gift in average men is not joined with others: your born painter, if you don't make a painter of him, won't be a first-rate merchant, or lawyer; at all events, whatever he turns out, his own special gift is unemployed by you; and in no wise helps him in that other business. So here you have a certain quantity of a particular sort of intelligence, produced for you annually by providential laws, which you can only make use of by setting it to its own proper work, and which any attempt to use otherwise involves the dead loss of so much human energy.

Well then, supposing we wish to employ it, how is it to be best discovered and refined? It is easily enough discovered. To wish to employ it is to discover it. All that you need is, a school of trial in every important town, in which those idle farmers' lads whom their masters never can keep out of mischief, and those stupid tailors' 'prentices who are always stitching the sleeves in wrong way upwards, may have a try at this other trade; only this school of trial must not be entirely regulated by formal laws of art education, but must ultimately be the workshop of a good master painter, who will try the lads with one kind of art and another, till he finds out what they are fit for.

Next, after your trial school, you want your easy and secure employment, which is the matter of chief importance. For, even on the present system, the boys who have really intense art capacity, generally make painters of themselves; but then, the best half of their early energy is lost in the battle of life. Before a good painter can get employment, his mind has always been embittered, and his genius distorted. A common mind usually stoops, in plastic chill, to whatever is asked of it, and scrapes or daubs its way complacently into public favour. But your great men quarrel with you, and you revenge yourselves by starving them for the first half of their lives. Precisely in the degree in which any painter possesses original genius, is at present the increase of moral certainty that during his early years he will have a hard battle to fight; and that just at the time when his conceptions ought to be full and happy, his temper gentle, and his hopes enthusiastic—just at the most critical period, his heart is full of anxieties and household cares; he is chilled by disappointments, and vexed by injustice; he becomes obstinate in his errors, no less than in his virtues, and the arrows of his aims are blunted, as the reeds of his trust are broken.

What we mainly want, therefore, is a means of sufficient and unagitated employment: not holding out great prizes for which young painters are to scramble; but furnishing all with adequate support, and opportunity to display such power as they possess without rejection or mortification. I need not say that the best field of labour of this kind would be presented by the constant progress of public works involving various decoration; and we will presently examine what kind of public works may thus, advantageously for the nation, be in constant progress. But a more important matter even than this of steady employment, is the kind of criticism with which you, the public, receive the works of the young men submitted to you. You may do much harm by indiscreet praise and by indiscreet blame; but remember the chief harm is always done by blame. It stands to reason that a young man's work cannot be perfect. It *must* be more or less ignorant; it must be more or less feeble; it is likely that it may be more or less experimental, and if experimental, here and there mistaken. If, therefore, you allow yourself to launch out into sudden barking at the first faults you see, the probability is that you are abusing the youth for some defect naturally and inevitably belonging to that stage of his progress; and that you might just as rationally find fault with a child for not being as prudent as a privy councillor, or with a kitten for not being as grave as a cat.

But there is one fault which you may be quite sure is unnecessary, and therefore a real and blamable fault: that is haste, involving negligence. Whenever you see that a young man's work is either bold or slovenly, then you may attack it firmly; sure of being right. If his work is bold, it is insolent; repress his insolence: if it is slovenly, it is indolent; spur his indolence. So long as he works in that dashing or impetuous way, the best hope for him is in your contempt: and it is only by the fact of his seeming not to seek your approbation that you may conjecture he deserves it.

But if he does deserve it, be sure that you give it him, else you not only run a chance of driving him from the right road by want of encouragement, but you deprive yourselves of the happiest privilege you will ever have of rewarding his labour. For it is only the young who can receive much reward from men's praise: the old, when they are great, get too far beyond and above you to care what you think of them. You may urge them then with sympathy, and surround them then with acclamation; but they will doubt your pleasure, and despise your praise. You might have cheered them in their race through the asphodel meadows of their youth; you might have brought the proud, bright scarlet into their faces, if you had but cried once to them 'Well done', as they dashed up to the first goal of their early ambition. But now, their pleasure is in memory, and their ambition is in heaven. They can be kind to you, but you nevermore can be kind to them. You may be fed with the fruit and fulness of their old age, but you were as the nipping blight to them in their blossoming, and your praise is only as the warm winds of autumn to the dying branches.

There is one thought still, the saddest of all, bearing on this withholding of early help. It is possible, in some noble natures, that the warmth and the affections of childhood may remain unchilled, though unanswered; and that the old man's heart may still be capable of gladness, when the long-withheld sympathy is given at last. But in these noble natures it nearly always happens that the chief motive of earthly ambition has not been to give delight to themselves, but to their parents. Every noble youth looks back, as to the chiefest joy which this world's honour ever gave him, to the moment when first he saw his father's eyes flash with pride, and his mother turn away her head, lest he should take her tears for tears of sorrow. Even the lover's joy, when some worthiness of his is acknowledged before his mistress, is not so great as that, for it is not so pure—the desire to exalt himself in her eyes mixes with that of giving her delight; but he does not need to exalt

206

himself in his parents' eyes: it is with the pure hope of giving them pleasure that he comes to tell them what he has done, or what has been said of him; and therefore he has a purer pleasure of his own. And this purest and best of rewards you keep from him if you can: you feed him in his tender youth with ashes and dishonour; and then you come to him, obsequious, but too late, with your sharp laurel crown, the dew all dried from off its leaves; and you thrust it into his languid hand, and he looks at you wistfully. What shall he do with it? What can he do, but go and lay it on his mother's grave?

Thus, then, you see that you have to provide for your young men: first, the searching or discovering school; then the calm employment; then the justice of praise: one thing more you have to do for them in preparing them for full service—namely, to make, in the noble sense of the word, gentlemen of them; that is to say, to take care that their minds receive such training, that in all they paint they shall see and feel the noblest things. I am sorry to say that, of all parts of an artist's education, this is the most neglected among us; and that even where the natural taste and feeling of the youth have been pure and true, where there was the right stuff in him to make a gentleman of, you may too frequently discern some jarring rents in his mind, and elements of degradation in his treatment of subject, owing to want of gentle training, and of the liberal influence of literature. This is quite visible in our greatest artists, even in men like Turner and Gainsborough; while in the common grade of our second-rate painters the evil attains a pitch which is far too sadly manifest to need my dwelling upon it. Now, no branch of art economy is more important than that of making the intellect at your disposal pure as well as powerful; so that it may always gather for you the sweetest and fairest things. The same quantity of labour from the same man's hand, will, according as you have trained him, produce a lovely and useful work, or a base and hurtful one; and depend upon it, whatever value it may possess, by reason of the painter's skill, its chief and final value, to any nation, depends upon its being able to exalt and refine, as well as to please; and that the picture which most truly deserves the name of an art-treasure is that which has been painted by a good man.

You cannot but see how far this would lead, if I were to enlarge upon it. I must take it up as a separate subject some other time: only noticing at present that no money could be better spent by a nation than in providing a liberal and disciplined education for its painters; as they advance into the critical period of their youth; and that, also, a large part of their power during life depends upon the kind of subjects which you, the public, ask them for, and therefore the kind of thoughts with which you require them to be habitually familiar. I shall have more to say on this head when we come to consider what employment they should have in public buildings. . . .

II. Application.—There are three main points the economist has to attend to in this.

> First, To set his men to various work.
> Secondly, To easy work
> Thirdly, To lasting work.

I shall briefly touch on the first two, for I want to arrest your attention on the last.

I say first to various work. Supposing you have two men of equal power as landscape painters—and both of them have an hour at your disposal. You would not set them both to paint the same piece of landscape. You would, of course, rather have two subjects than a repetition of one.

Well, supposing them sculptors, will not the same rule hold? You naturally conclude at once that it will; but you will have hard work to convince your modern architects of that. They will put twenty men to work, to carve twenty capitals; and all shall be the same. If I could show you the architects' yards in England just now, all open at once, perhaps you might see a thousand clever men, all employed in carving the same design. Of the degradation and deathfulness to the art-intellect of the country involved in such a habit, I have more or less been led to speak before now; but I have not hitherto marked its definite tendency to increase the price of *work*, as such. When men are employed continually in carving the same ornaments, they get into a monotonous and methodical habit of labour—precisely correspondent to that in which they would break stones, or paint house-walls. Of course, what they do so constantly, they do easily; and if you excite them temporarily by an increase of wages, you may get much work done by them in a little time. But, unless so stimulated, men condemned to a monotonous exertion, work—and always, by the laws of human nature, *must* work—only at a tranquil rate, not producing by any means a maximum result in a given time. But if you allow them to vary their designs, and thus interest their heads and hearts in what they are doing, you will find them become eager first, to get their ideas expressed, and then to finish the expression of them; and the moral energy thus brought to bear on the matter quickens, and therefore cheapens, the production in a most important degree. Sir Thomas Deane, the architect of the new Museum at Oxford, told me, as I passed through Oxford on my way here, that he found that, owing to this cause alone, capitals of various design could be executed cheaper than capitals of similar design (the amount of hand labour in each being the same) by about 30 per cent.

Well, that is the first way, then, in which you will employ your intellect well; and the simple observance of this plain rule of political economy will effect a noble revolution in your architecture, such as you cannot at present so much as conceive. Then the second way in which we are to guard against waste is by setting our men to the easiest, and therefore the quickest, work which will answer the purpose. Marble, for instance, lasts quite as long as granite, and is much softer to work; therefore, when you get hold of a good sculptor, give him marble to carve—not granite.

That, you say, is obvious enough. Yes; but it is not so obvious how much of your workmen's time you waste annually in making them cut glass, after it has got hard, when you ought to make them mould it while it is soft. It is not so obvious how much expense you waste in cutting diamonds and rubies, which are the hardest things you can find, into shapes that mean nothing, when the same men might be cutting sandstone and freestone into shapes that mean something. It is not so obvious how much of the artists' time in Italy you waste, by forcing them to make wretched little pictures for you out of crumbs of stone glued together at enormous cost, when the tenth of the time would make good and noble pictures for you out of water-colour.

I could go on giving you almost numberless instances of this great commercial mistake; but I should only weary and confuse you. I therefore commend also this head of our subject to your own meditation, and proceed to the last I named—the last I shall task your patience with to-night. You know we are now considering how to apply our genius; and we were to do it as economists, in three ways:

To *various* work;
To *easy* work;
To *lasting* work.

This lasting of the work, then, is our final question.

Many of you may perhaps remember that Michael Angelo was once commanded by Pietro di Medici to mould a statue out of snow, and that he obeyed the command. I am glad, and we have all reason to be glad, that such a fancy ever came into the mind of the unworthy prince, and for this cause: that Pietro di Medici then gave, at the period of one great epoch of consummate power in the arts, the perfect, accurate, and intensest possible type of the greatest error which nations and princes can commit, respecting the power of genius entrusted to their guidance. You had there, observe, the strongest genius in the most perfect obedience; capable of iron independence, yet wholly submissive to the patron's will; at once the most highly accomplished and the most original, capable of doing as much as man could do, in any direction that man could ask. And its governor, and guide, and patron sets it to build a statue in snow—to put itself into the service of annihilation—to make a cloud of itself, and pass away from the earth.

Now this, so precisely and completely done by Pietro di Medici, is what we are all doing, exactly in the degree in which we direct the genius under our patronage to work in more or less perishable materials. So far as we induce painters to work in fading colours, or architects to build with imperfect structure, or in any other way consult only immediate ease and cheapness in the production of what we want, to the exclusion of provident thought as to its permanence and serviceableness in after ages; so far we are forcing our Michael Angelos to carve in snow. The first duty of the economist in art is, to see that no intellect shall thus glitter merely in the manner of hoar-frost; but that it shall be well vitrified, like a painted window, and shall be set so between shafts of stone and bands of iron, that it shall bear the sunshine upon it, and send the sunshine through it, from generation to generation.

I can conceive, however, some political economist to interrupt me here, and say, 'If you make your art wear too well, you will soon have too much of it; you will throw your artists quite out of work. Better allow for a little wholesome evanescence—beneficent destruction: let each age provide art for itself, or we shall soon have so many good pictures that we shall not know what to do with them.'

Remember, my dear hearers, who are thus thinking, that political economy, like every other subject, cannot be dealt with effectively if we try to solve two questions at a

210

time instead of one. It is one question, how to get plenty of a thing; and another, whether plenty of it will be good for us. Consider these two matters separately; never confuse yourself by interweaving one with the other. It is one question, how to treat your fields so as to get a good harvest; another, whether you wish to have a good harvest, or would rather like to keep up the price of corn. It is one question how to graft your trees so as to grow most apples; and quite another, whether having such a heap of apples in the storeroom will not make them all rot.

Now, therefore, that we are talking only about grafting and growing, pray do not vex yourselves with thinking what you are to do with the pippins. It may be desirable for us to have much art, or little—we will examine that by-and-bye; but just now, let us keep to the simple consideration how to get plenty of good art if we want it. Perhaps it might be just as well that a man of moderate income should be able to possess a good picture, as that any work of real merit should cost £500 or £1,000; at all events, it is certainly one of the branches of political economy to ascertain how, if we like, we can get things in quantities—plenty of corn, plenty of wine, plenty of gold, or plenty of pictures.

It has just been said, that the first great secret is to produce work that will last. Now, the conditions of work lasting are twofold: it must not only be in materials that will last, but it must be itself of a quality that will last—it must be good enough to bear the test of time. If it is not good, we shall tire of it quickly, and throw it aside—we shall have no pleasure in the accumulation of it. So that the first question of a good art-economist respecting any work is, Will it lose its flavour by keeping? It may be very amusing now, and look much like a work of genius; but what will be its value a hundred years hence?

You cannot always ascertain this. You may get what you fancy to be work of the best quality, and yet find to your astonishment that it won't keep. But of one thing you may be sure, that art which is produced hastily will also perish hastily; and that what is cheapest to you now, is likely to be dearest in the end.

I am sorry to say, the great tendency of this age is to expend its genius in perishable art of this kind, as if it were a triumph to burn its thoughts away in bonfires. There is a vast quantity of intellect and of labour consumed annually in our cheap illustrated publications; you triumph in them; and you think it so grand a thing to get so many woodcuts for a penny. Why, woodcuts, penny and

211

all, are as much lost to you as if you had invested your money in gossamer. More lost, for the gossamer could only tickle your face, and glitter in your eyes; it could not catch your feet and trip you up: but the bad art can, and does; for you can't like good woodcuts as long as you look at the bad ones. If we were at this moment to come across a Titian woodcut, or a Dürer woodcut, we should not like it—those of us at least who are accustomed to the cheap work of the day. We don't like, and can't like, *that* long; but when we are tired of one bad cheap thing, we throw it aside and buy another bad cheap thing; and so keep looking at the bad things all our lives. Now, the very men who do all that quick bad work for us are capable of doing perfect work. Only, perfect work can't be hurried, and therefore it can't be cheap beyond a certain point. But suppose you pay twelve times as much as you do now, and you have one woodcut for a shilling instead of twelve; and the one woodcut for a shilling is as good as art can be, so that you will never tire of looking at it; and struck on good paper with good ink, so that you will never wear it out by handling it; while you are sick of your penny-each cuts by the end of the week, and have torn them mostly in half too. Isn't your shilling's worth the best bargain?

It is not, however, only in getting prints or woodcuts of the best kind that you will practise economy. There is a certain quality about an original drawing which you cannot get in a woodcut, and the best part of the genius of many men is only expressible in original work, whether with pen or ink—pencil or colours. This is not always the case; but in general, the best men are those who can only express themselves on paper or canvas; and you will therefore, in the long run, get most for your money by buying original work; proceeding on the principle already laid down, that the best is likely to be the cheapest in the end. Of course, original work cannot be produced under a certain cost. If you want a man to make you a drawing which takes him six days, you must, at all events, keep him for six days in bread and water, fire and lodging; that is the lowest price at which he can do it for you, but that is not very dear: and the best bargain which can possibly be made honestly in art—the very ideal of a cheap purchase to the purchaser—is the original work of a great man fed for as many days as are necessary on bread and water, or perhaps we may say with as many onions as will keep him in good humour. That is the way by which you will always get most of your money; no mechanical multiplication or ingenuity of commercial arrangements will ever get you a better penny's worth of art than that.

Without, however, pushing our calculations quite to this prison-discipline extreme, we may lay it down as a rule in art-economy, that original work is, on the whole, cheapest and best worth having. But precisely in proportion to the value of it as a production, becomes the importance of having it executed in permanent materials. And here we come to note the second main error of the day, that we not only ask our workmen for bad art, but we make them put it into bad substance. We have, for example, put a great quantity of genius, within the last twenty years, into water-colour drawing, and we have done this with the most reckless disregard whether either the colours or the paper will stand. In most instances, neither will. By accident, it may happen that the colours in a given drawing have been of good quality, and its paper uninjured by chemical processes. But you take not the least care to ensure these being so; I have myself seen the most destructive changes take place in water-colour drawings within twenty years after they were painted; and from all I can gather respecting the recklessness of modern paper manufacture, my belief is, that though you may still handle an Albert Dürer engraving, two hundred years old, fearlessly, not one-half of that time will have passed over your modern water-colours, before most of them will be reduced to mere white or brown rags; and your descendants, twitching them contemptuously into fragments between finger and thumb, will mutter against you, half in scorn and half in anger, 'Those wretched nineteenth century people! they kept vapouring and fuming about the world, doing what they called business, and they couldn't make a sheet of paper that wasn't rotten.' . . .

But I cannot pass without some brief notice our habit—continually, as it seems to me, gaining strength—of putting a large quantity of thought and work, annually, into things which are either in their nature necessarily perishable, as dress; or else into compliances with the fashion of the day, in things not necessarily perishable, as plate. I am afraid almost the first idea of a young rich couple setting up house in London, is, that they must have new plate. Their father's plate may be very handsome, but the fashion is changed. They will have a new service from the leading manufacturer, and the old plate, except a few apostle spoons and a cup which Charles the Second drank a health in to their pretty ancestress, is sent to be melted down, and made up with new flourishes and fresh lustre. Now, so long as this is the case—so long, observe, as

213

fashion has influence on the manufacture of plate—so long *you cannot have a goldsmith's art in this country.* Do you suppose any workman worthy the name will put his brains into a cup, or an urn, which he knows is to go to the melting-pot in half a score years? He will not; you don't ask or expect it of him. You ask of him nothing but a little quick handicraft—a clever twist of a handle here, and a foot there, a convolvulus from the newest school of design, a pheasant from Landseer's game cards; a couple of sentimental figures for supporters, in the style of the signs of insurance offices, then a clever touch with the burnisher, and there's your epergne, the admiration of all the footmen at the wedding-breakfast, and the torment of some unfortunate youth who cannot see the pretty girl opposite to him, through its tyrannous branches.

But you don't suppose that *that's* goldsmith's work? Goldsmith's work is made to last, and made with the men's whole heart and soul in it; true goldsmith's work, when it exists, is generally the means of education of the greatest painters and sculptors of the day. Francia was a goldsmith; Francia was not his own name, but that of his master the jeweller; and he signed his pictures almost always, 'Francia, the goldsmith', for love of his master; Ghirlandajo was a goldsmith, and was the master of Michael Angelo; Verrocchio was a goldsmith, and was the master of Leonardo da Vinci. Ghiberti was a goldsmith, and beat out the bronze gates which Michael Angelo said might serve for gates of Paradise.* But if ever you want work like theirs again, you must keep it, though it should have the misfortune to become old-fashioned. You must not break it up, nor melt it any more. There is no economy in that; you could not easily waste intellect more grievously. Nature may melt her goldsmith's work at every sunset if she chooses; and beat it out into chased bars again at every sunrise; but you must not. The way to have a truly noble service of plate, is to keep adding to it, not melting it. At every marriage, and at every birth, get a new piece of gold or silver if you will, but with noble workmanship on it, done for all time, and put it among

* Several reasons may account for the fact that goldsmith's work is so wholesome for young artists: first, that it gives great firmness of hand to deal for some time with a solid substance; again, that it induces caution and steadiness—a boy trusted with chalk and paper suffers an immediate temptation to scrawl upon it and play with it, but he dares not scrawl on gold, and he cannot play with it; and, lastly, that it gives great delicacy and precision of touch to work upon minute forms, and to aim at producing richness and finish of design correspondent to the preciousness of the material.

your treasures; that is one of the chief things which gold was made for, and made incorruptible for. When we know a little more of political economy, we shall find that none but partially savage nations need, imperatively, gold for their currency; but gold has been given us, among other things, that we might put beautiful work into its imperishable splendour, and that the artists who have the most wilful fancies may have a material which will drag out, and beat out, as their dreams require, and will hold itself together with fantastic tenacity, whatever rare and delicate service they set it upon.

So here is one branch of decorative art in which rich people may indulge themselves unselfishly; if they ask for good art in it, they may be sure in buying gold and silver plate that they are enforcing useful education on young artists. But there is another branch of decorative art in which I am sorry to say we cannot, at least under existing circumstances, indulge ourselves, with the hope of doing good to anybody: I mean the great and subtle art of dress.

And here I must interrupt the pursuit of our subject for a moment or two, in order to state one of the principles of political economy, which, though it is, I believe, now sufficiently understood and asserted by the leading masters of the science, is not yet, I grieve to say, acted upon by the plurality of those who have the management of riches. Whenever we spend money, we of course set people to work: that is the meaning of spending money; we may, indeed, lose it without employing anybody; but, whenever we spend it, we set a number of people to work, greater or less, of course, according to the rate of wages, but, in the long run, proportioned to the sum we spend. Well, your shallow people, because they see that however they spend money they are always employing somebody, and, therefore, doing some good, think and say to themselves, that it is all one *how* they spend it—that all their apparently selfish luxury is, in reality, unselfish, and is doing just as much good as if they gave all their money away, or perhaps more good; and I have heard foolish people even declare it as a principle of political economy, that whoever invented a new want conferred a good on the community. I have not words strong enough—at least, I could not, without shocking you, use the words which would be strong enough—to express my estimate of the absurdity and the mischievousness of this popular fallacy. So, putting a great restraint upon myself, and using no hard words, I will simply try to state the nature of it, and the extent of its influence.

Granted, that whenever we spend money for whatever purpose, we set people to work; and passing by, for the moment, the question whether the work we set them to is all equally healthy and good for them, we will assume that whenever we spend a guinea we provide an equal number of people with healthy maintenance for a given time. But, by the way in which we spend it, we entirely direct the labour of these people during that given time. We become their masters or mistresses, and we compel them to produce, within a certain period, a certain article. Now, that article may be a useful and lasting one, or it may be a useless and perishable one—it may be one useful to the whole community, or useful only to ourselves. And our selfishness and folly, or our virtue and prudence, are shown, not by our spending money; but by our spending it for the wrong or right thing; and we are wise and kind, not in maintaining a certain number of people for a given period, but only in requiring them to produce during that period, the kind of things which shall be useful to society, instead of those which are only useful to ourselves.

Thus, for instance: if you are a young lady, and employ a certain number of sempstresses for a given time, in making a given number of simple and serviceable dresses— suppose, seven; of which you can wear one yourself for half the winter, and give six away to poor girls who have none, you are spending your money unselfishly. But if you employ the same number of sempstresses for the same number of days, in making four, or five, or six beautiful flounces for your own ball-dress—flounces which will clothe no one but yourself, and which you will yourself be unable to wear at more than one ball—you are employing your money selfishly. You have maintained, indeed, in each case, the same number of people; but in the one case you have directed their labour to the service of the community; in the other case you have consumed it wholly upon yourself. I don't say you are never to do so; I don't say you ought not sometimes to think of yourselves only, and to make yourselves as pretty as you can; only do not confuse coquettishness with benevolence, nor cheat yourselves into thinking that all the finery you can wear is so much put into the hungry mouths of those beneath you: it is not so; it is what you yourselves, whether you will or no, must sometimes instinctively feel it to be—it is what those who stand shivering in the streets, forming a line to watch you as you step out of your carriages, *know* it to be; those fine dresses do not mean that so much has been put into their mouths, but that so much has been taken out of their mouths.

The real politico-economical signification of every one of those beautiful toilettes, is just this: that you have had a certain number of people put for a certain number of days wholly under your authority, by the sternest of slave-masters—hunger and cold; and you have said to them, 'I will feed you, indeed, and clothe you, and give you fuel for so many days; but during those days you shall work for me only: your little brothers need clothes, but you shall make none for them: your sick friend needs clothes, but you shall make none for her: you yourself will soon need another and a warmer dress, but you shall make none for yourself. You shall make nothing but lace and roses for me; for this fortnight to come, you shall work at the patterns and petals, and then I will crush and consume them away in an hour.' You will perhaps answer—'It may not be particularly benevolent to do this, and we won't call it so; but at any rate we do no wrong in taking their labour when we pay them their wages; if we pay for their work, we have a right to it.'

No;—a thousand times no. The labour which you have paid for, does indeed become, by the act of purchase, your own labour: you have bought the hands and the time of those workers; they are, by right and justice, your own hands, your own time. But have you a right to spend your own time, to work with your own hands, only for your own advantage?—much more, when, by purchase, you have invested your own person with the strength of others; and added to your own life, a part of the life of others? You may, indeed, to a certain extent, use their labour for your delight: remember, I am making no general assertions against splendour of dress, or pomp of accessories of life; on the contrary, there are many reasons for thinking that we do not at present attach enough importance to beautiful dress, as one of the means of influencing general taste and character. But I *do* say, that you must weigh the value of what you ask these workers to produce for you in its own distinct balance; that on its own worthiness or desirableness rests the question of your kindness, and not merely on the fact of your having employed people in producing it; and I say further, that as long as there are cold and nakedness in the land around you, so long there can be no question at all but that splendour of dress is a crime. In due time, when we have nothing better to set people to work at, it may be right to let them make lace and cut jewels; but as long as there are any who have no blankets for their beds, and no rags for their bodies, so long it is blanket-making and tailoring we must set people to work at—not lace. . . .

III. Accumulation.—And now, in the outset, it will be well to face that objection which we put aside a little while ago; namely, that perhaps it is not well to have a great deal of good art; and that it should not be made too cheap.

'Nay', I can imagine some of the more generous among you exclaiming, 'we will not trouble you to disprove that objection; of course it is a selfish and base one; good art, as well as other good things, ought to be made as cheap as possible, and put as far as we can within the reach of everybody'.

Pardon me, I am not prepared to admit that. I rather side with the selfish objectors, and believe that art ought not to be made cheap, beyond a certain point; for the amount of pleasure that you can receive from any great work, depends wholly on the quantity of attention and energy of mind you can bring to bear upon it. Now, that attention and energy depend much more on the freshness of the thing than you would at all suppose; unless you very carefully studied the movements of your own minds. If you see things of the same kind and of equal value very frequently, your reverence for them is infallibly diminished, your powers of attention get gradually wearied, and your interest and enthusiasm worn out; and you cannot in that state bring to any given work the energy necessary to enjoy it. If, indeed, the question were only between enjoying a great many pictures each a little, or one picture very much, the sum of enjoyment being in each case the same, you might rationally desire to possess rather the large quantity than the small; both because one work of art always in some sort illustrates another, and because quantity diminishes the chances of destruction.

But the question is not a merely arithmetical one of this kind. Your fragments of broken admirations will not, when they are put together, make up one whole admiration; two and two, in this case, do not make four, nor anything like four. Your good picture, or book, or work of art of any kind, is always in some degree fenced and closed about with difficulty. You may think of it as of a kind of cocoanut, with very often rather an unseemly shell, but good milk and kernel inside. Now, if you possess twenty cocoanuts, and being thirsty, go impatiently from one to the other, giving only a single scratch with the point of your knife to the shell of each, you will get no milk from all the twenty. But if you leave nineteen of them alone, and give twenty cuts to the shell of one, you will get through it, and at the milk of it. And the tendency of the human mind is always to get tired before it has made its twenty cuts; and to try another nut: and moreover, even if it has perseverance enough to crack its nuts, it is sure to try to eat too many, and to choke itself. Hence, it is wisely appointed for us that few of the things we desire can be had without considerable labour, and at considerable intervals of time. We cannot generally get our dinner without working for it, and that gives us appetite for it; we cannot get our holiday without waiting for it, and that gives us zest for it; and we ought not to get our picture without paying for it, and that gives us a mind to look at it. . . .

Meantime, returning to our immediate subject, I say to my generous hearers, who want to shower Titians and Turners upon us, like falling leaves, 'Pictures ought not to be too cheap'; but in much stronger tone I would say to those who want to keep up the prices of pictorial property, that pictures ought not to be too dear—that is to say, not as dear as they are. For, as matters at present stand, it is wholly impossible for any man in the ordinary circumstances of English life to possess himself of a piece of great art. A modern drawing of average merit, or a first-class engraving, may, perhaps, not without some self-reproach, be purchased out of his savings by a man of narrow income; but a satisfactory example of first-rate art—masterhands' work—is wholly out of his reach. And we are so accustomed to look upon this as the natural course and necessity of things, that we never set ourselves in any wise to diminish the evil; and yet it is an evil perfectly capable of diminution.

It is an evil precisely similar in kind to that which existed in the Middle Ages, respecting good books, and which everybody then, I suppose, thought as natural as we do now our small supply of good pictures. You could not then study the work of a great historian, or great poet, any more than you can now study that of a great painter, but at heavy cost. If you wanted a book, you had to get it written out for you, or to write it out for yourself. But printing came, and the poor man may read his Dante and his Homer; and Dante and Homer are none the worse for that. But it is only in literature that private persons of moderate fortune can possess and study greatness: they can study at home no greatness in art; and the object of that accumulation which we are at present aiming at, as our third object in political economy, is to bring great art in some degree within the reach of the multitude; and, both in larger and more numerous galleries than we now possess, and by distribution, according to his wealth and wish, in each man's home, to render the influence of art somewhat correspondent in extent to that of literature. Here, then, is the subtle balance which your economist has to strike: to accumulate so much art as to be able to give the whole nation a supply of it, according to its need, and yet to regulate its distribution so that there shall be no glut of it, nor contempt.

A difficult balance, indeed, for us to hold, if it were left merely to our skill to poise; but the just point between poverty and profusion has been fixed for us accurately by the wise laws of Providence. If you carefully watch for all the genius you can detect, apply it to good service, and then reverently preserve what it produces, you will never have too little art; and if, on the other hand, you never force an artist to work hurriedly, for daily bread, nor imperfectly, because you would rather have showy works than complete ones, you will never have too much. Do not force the multiplication of art, and you will not have it too cheap; do not wantonly destroy it, and you will not have it too dear.

'But who wantonly destroys it?' you will ask. Why, we all do. Perhaps you thought, when I came to this part of our subject, corresponding to that set forth in our housewife's economy by the 'keeping her embroidery from the moth,' that I was going to tell you only how to take better care of pictures, how to clean them, and varnish them, and where to put them away safely when you went out of town. Ah, not at all. The utmost I have to ask of you is, that you will not pull them to pieces, and trample them under your feet. 'What!' you will say, 'when do we do such things? Haven't we built a perfectly beautiful gallery for all the pictures we have to take care of?' Yes, you have, for the pictures which are definitely sent to Manchester to be taken care of. But there are quantities of pictures out of Manchester which it is your business, and mine too, to take care of no less than of these, and which we are at this moment employing ourselves in pulling to pieces by deputy. . . .

. . . Consider, then, this similitude of ourselves. Suppose you saw (as I doubt not you often do see) a prudent and kind young lady sitting at work, in the corner of a quiet room, knitting comforters for her cousins, and that just outside, in the hall, you saw a cat and her kittens at play among the family pictures; amusing themselves especially with the best Vandykes, by getting on the tops of the frames, and then scrambling down the canvases by their claws; and on some one's informing the young lady of these proceedings of the cat and kittens, suppose she answered that it wasn't her cat, but her sister's, and the pictures weren't hers, but her uncle's, and she couldn't leave her work, for she had to make so many pairs of comforters before dinner. Would you not say that the prudent and kind young lady was, on the whole, answerable for the additional touches of claw on the Vandykes?

Now, that is precisely what we prudent and kind English are doing, only on a larger scale. Here we sit in Manchester, hard at work, very properly, making comforters for our cousins all over the world. Just outside there in the hall—that beautiful marble hall of Italy—the cats and kittens and monkeys are at play among the pictures; I assure you, in the course of the fifteen years in which I have been working in those places in which the most precious remnants of European art exist, a sensation, whether I would or no, was gradually made distinct and deep in my mind, that I was living and working in the midst of a den of monkeys;—sometimes amiable and affectionate monkeys, with all manner of winning ways and kind intentions,—more frequently selfish and malicious monkeys; but, whatever their disposition, squabbling continually about nuts, and the best place on the barren sticks of trees; and that all this monkeys' den was filled, by mischance, with precious pictures, and the witty and wilful beasts were always wrapping themselves up and going to sleep in pictures, or tearing holes in them to grin through; or tasting them and spitting them out again, or twisting them up into ropes and making swings of them; and that sometimes only, by watching one's opportunity, and bearing a scratch or a bite, one could rescue the corner of a Tintoret, or Paul Veronese, and push it through the bars into a place of safety.

Literally, I assure you, this was, and this is, the fixed impression on my mind of the state of matters in Italy. And see how. The professors of art in Italy, having long followed a method of study peculiar to themselves, have at last arrived at a form of art peculiar to themselves; very different from that which was arrived at by Correggio and Titian. Naturally, the professors like their own form best; and, as the old pictures are generally not so startling to the eye as the modern ones, the dukes and counts who possess them, and who like to see their galleries look new and fine (and are persuaded also that a celebrated chef-d'œuvre ought always to catch the eye at a quarter of a mile off), believe the professors who tell them their sober pictures are quite faded, and good for nothing, and should all be brought bright again; and, accordingly, give the sober pictures to the professors, to be put right by rules of art. Then, the professors repaint the old pictures in all the principal places, leaving perhaps only a bit of background to set off their own work. And thus the professors come to be generally figured, in my mind, as the monkeys who tear holes in the pictures, to grin through. Then the picture-dealers, who live by the pictures, cannot sell them to the English in their old and pure state; all the good work must be covered with new paint, and varnished so as to look like one of the professorial pictures in the great gallery, before it is saleable. And thus the dealers come to be imaged, in my mind, as the monkeys who make ropes of the pictures, to swing by. Then, every now and then at some old stable, or wine-cellar, or timber-shed, behind some forgotten vats or faggots, somebody finds a fresco of Perugino's or Giotto's, but doesn't think much of it, and has no idea of having people coming into his cellar, or being obliged to move his faggots; and so he whitewashes the fresco, and puts the faggots back again; and these kind of persons, therefore, come generally to be imaged, in my mind, as the monkeys who taste the pictures, and spit them out, not finding them nice. While, finally, the squabbling for nuts and apples (called in Italy 'bella libertà') goes on all day long.

Now, all this might soon be put an end to, if we English who are so fond of travelling in the body, would also travel a little in soul! We think it a great triumph to get our packages and our persons carried at a fast pace, but we never take the slightest trouble to put any pace into our perceptions; we stay usually at home in thought, or if we ever mentally see the world, it is at the old stage-coach or waggon rate. Do but consider what an odd sight it would be, if it were only quite clear to you how things are really going on—how, here in England, we are making enormous and expensive efforts to produce new art of all kinds, knowing and confessing all the while that the greater part of it is bad, but struggling still to produce new patterns of wall-papers, and new shapes of teapots, and new pictures, and statues, and architecture; and pluming and cackling if ever a teapot or a picture has the least good in it;—all the while

222

taking no thought whatever of the best possible pictures, and statues, and wall-patterns already in existence, which require nothing but to be taken common care of, and kept from damp and dust: but we let the walls fall that Giotto patterned, and the canvases rot that Tintoret painted, and the architecture be dashed to pieces that St. Louis built, while we are furnishing our drawing-rooms with prize upholstery, and writing accounts for our handsome warehouses to the country papers. Don't think I use my words vaguely or generally: I speak of literal facts. Giotto's frescoes at Assisi are perishing at this moment for want of decent care; Tintoret's pictures in San Sebastian, at Venice, are at this instant rotting piecemeal into grey rags; St. Louis's chapel, at Carcassonne, is at this moment lying in shattered fragments in the market-place. And here we are all cawing and crowing, poor little half-fledged daws as we are, about the pretty sticks and wool in our own nests. There's hardly a day passes, when I am at home, but I get a letter from some well-meaning country clergyman, deeply anxious about the state of his parish church, and breaking his heart to get money together that he may hold up some wretched remnant of Tudor tracery, with one niche in the corner and no statue—when all the while the mightiest piles of religious architecture and sculpture that ever the world saw are being blasted and withered away, without one glance of pity or regret. The country clergyman does not care for *them*—he has a sea-sick imagination that cannot cross channel. What is it to him, if the angels of Assisi fade from its vaults, or the queens and kings of Chartres fall from their pedestals? They are not in his parish.

'What!' you will say, 'are we not to produce any new art, nor take care of our parish churches?' No, certainly not, until you have taken proper care of the art you have got already, and of the best churches out of the parish. Your first and proper standing is not as churchwardens and parish overseers, in an English county, but as members of the great Christian community of Europe. And as members of that community (in which alone, observe, pure and precious ancient art exists, for there is none in America, none in Asia, none in Africa), you conduct yourself precisely as a manufacturer would, who attended to his looms, but left his warehouse without a roof. The rain floods your warehouse, the rats frolic in it, the spiders spin in it, the choughs build in it, the wall-plague frets and festers in it; and still you keep weave, weave, weaving at your wretched webs, and thinking you

223

are growing rich, while more is gnawed out of your warehouse in an hour than you can weave in a twelve-month.

Even this similitude is not absurd enough to set us rightly forth. The weaver would, or might, at least, hope that his new woof was as stout as the old ones, and that, therefore, in spite of rain and ravage, he would have something to wrap himself in when he needed it. But *our* webs rot as we spin. The very fact that we despise the great art of the past shows that we cannot produce great art now. If we could do it, we should love it when we saw it done—if we really cared for it, we should recognize it and keep it; but we don't care for it. It is not art that we want; it is amusement, gratification of pride, present gain—anything in the world but art: let it rot, we shall always have enough to talk about and hang over our sideboards.

You will (I hope) finally ask me what is the outcome of all this, practicable to-morrow morning by us who are sitting here? These are the main practical outcomes of it: In the first place, don't grumble when you hear of a new picture being bought by Government at a large price. There are many pictures in Europe now in danger of destruction which are, in the true sense of the word, priceless; the proper price is simply that which it is necessary to give to get and to save them. If you can get them for fifty pounds, do; if not for less than a hundred, do; if not for less than five thousand, do; if not for less than twenty thousand, do; never mind being imposed upon: there is nothing disgraceful in being imposed upon; the only disgrace is in imposing; and you can't in general get anything much worth having, in the way of Continental art, but it must be with the help or connivance of numbers of people who, indeed, ought to have nothing to do with the matter, but who practically have, and always will have, everything to do with it; and if you don't choose to submit to be cheated by them out of a ducat here and a zecchin there, you will be cheated by them out of your picture; and whether you are most imposed upon in losing that, or the zecchins, I think I may leave you to judge; though I know there are many political economists, who would rather leave a bag of gold on a garret-table, than give a porter sixpence extra to carry it downstairs.

That, then, is the first practical outcome of the matter. Never grumble, but be glad when you hear of a new picture being bought at a large price. In the long run, the dearest pictures are always the best bargains; and, I repeat, (for else you might think I said it in mere hurry of

224

talk, and not deliberately,) there are some pictures which are without price. You should stand, nationally, at the edge of Dover Cliffs—Shakespere's—and wave blank cheques in the eyes of the nations on the other side of the sea, freely offered, for such and such canvases of theirs.

Then, the next practical outcome of it is—Never buy a copy of a picture, under any circumstances whatever. All copies are bad; because no painter who is worth a straw ever *will* copy. He will make a study of a picture he likes, for his own use, in his own way; but he won't and can't copy. Whenever you buy a copy, you buy so much misunderstanding of the original, and encourage a dull person in following a business he is not fit for, besides increasing ultimately chances of mistake and imposture, and farthering, as directly as money *can* farther, the cause of ignorance in all directions. You may, in fact, consider yourself as having purchased a certain quantity of mistakes; and, according to your power, being engaged in disseminating them.

I do not mean, however, that copies should never be made. A certain number of dull persons should always be employed by a Government in making the most accurate copies possible of all good pictures; these copies, though artistically valueless, would be historically and documentarily valuable, in the event of the destruction of the original picture. The studies also made by great artists for their own use, should be sought after with the greatest eagerness; they are often to be bought cheap; and in connection with the mechanical copies, would become very precious: tracings from frescoes and other large works are also of great value; for though a tracing is liable to just as many mistakes as a copy, the mistakes in a tracing are of one kind only, which may be allowed for, but the mistakes of a common copyist are of all conceivable kinds: finally, engravings, in so far as they convey certain facts about the pictures, without pretending adequately to represent or give an idea of the pictures, are often serviceable and valuable. I can't, of course, enter into details in these matters just now; only this main piece of advice I can safely give you—never to buy copies of pictures (for your private possession) which pretend to give a facsimile that shall be in any wise representative of, or equal to, the original. Whenever you do so, you are only lowering your taste, and wasting your money. And if you are generous and wise, you will be ready rather to subscribe as much as you would have given for a copy of a great picture towards its purchase, or the purchase of some other like it, by the nation. There ought to be a great National Society instituted for the purchase of pictures; presenting them to the various galleries in our great cities, and watching there over their safety: but in the meantime, you can always act safely and beneficially by merely allowing your artist friends to buy pictures for you, when they see good ones. Never buy for yourselves, nor go to the foreign dealers; but let any painter whom you know be entrusted, when he finds a neglected old picture in an old house, to try if he cannot get it for you; then, if you like it, keep it; if not, send it to the hammer, and you will find that you do not lose money on pictures so purchased.

And the third and chief practical outcome of the matter is this general one: Wherever you go, whatever you do, act more for *preservation* and less for *production*. I assure you, the world is, generally speaking, in calamitous disorder, and just because you have managed to thrust some of the lumber aside, and get an available corner for yourselves, you think you should do nothing but sit spinning in it all day long—while, as householders and economists, your first thought and effort should be, to set things more square all about you. Try to set the ground floors in order, and get the rottenness out of your granaries. *Then* sit and spin, but not till then.

IV. Distribution.—And now, lastly, we come to the fourth great head of our inquiry, the question of the wise distribution of the art we have gathered and preserved. It must be evident to us, at a moment's thought, that the way in which works of art are on the whole most useful to the nation to which they belong, must be by their collection in public galleries, supposing those galleries properly managed. But there is one disadvantage attached necessarily to gallery exhibition—namely, the extent of mischief which may be done by one foolish curator. As long as the pictures which form the national wealth are disposed in private collections, the chance is always that the people who buy them will be just the people who are fond of them; and that the sense of exchangeable value in the commodity they possess, will induce them, even if they do not esteem it themselves, to take such care of it as will preserve its value undiminished. At all events, so long as works of art are scattered through the nation, no universal destruction of them is possible; a certain average only are lost by accidents from time to time. But when they are once collected in a large public gallery, if the appointment of curator becomes in any way a matter of formality, or the post is so lucrative as to be disputed by place-hunters, let but one foolish or careless person get possession of it, and perhaps you may have all your fine pictures repainted, and the national property destroyed, in a month. That is actually the case at this moment, in several great foreign galleries. They are the places of execution of pictures: over their doors you only want the Dantesque inscription, 'Lasciate ogni speranza, voi che entrate'.

Supposing, however, this danger properly guarded against, as it would be always by a nation which either knew the value, or understood the meaning, of painting, arrangement in a public gallery is the safest, as well as the most serviceable, method of exhibiting pictures; and it is the only mode in which their historical value can be brought out, and their historical meaning made clear. But great good is also to be done by encouraging the private possession of pictures; partly as a means of study, (much more being always discovered in any work of art by a person who has it perpetually near him than by one who only sees it from time to time), and also as a means of refining the habits and touching the hearts of the masses of the nation in their domestic life.

For these last purposes, the most serviceable art is the living art of the time; the particular tastes of the people will be best met, and their particular ignorances best corrected, by painters labouring in the midst of them, more or less guided to the knowledge of what is wanted by the degree of sympathy with which their work is received. So then, generally, it should be the object of government, and of all patrons of art, to collect, as far as may be, the works of dead masters in public galleries, arranging them so as to illustrate the history of nations, and the progress and influence of their arts; and to encourage the private possession of the works of *living* masters. And the first and best way in which to encourage such private possession is, of course, to keep down the prices of them as far as you can. . . .

I know how many objections must arise in your minds at this moment to what I say; but you must be aware that it is not possible for me in an hour to explain all the moral and commercial bearings of such a principle as this. Only, believe me, I do not speak lightly; I think I have considered all the objections which could be rationally brought forward, though I have time at present only to glance at the main one—namely, the idea that the high prices paid for modern pictures are either honourable, or serviceable, to the painter. So far from this being so, I believe one of

227

the principal obstacles to the progress of modern art to be the high prices given for good modern pictures. For observe first the action of this high remuneration on the artist's mind. If he 'gets on', as it is called, catches the eye of the public, and especially of the public of the upper classes, there is hardly any limit to the fortune he may acquire; so that, in his early years, his mind is naturally led to dwell on this worldly and wealthy eminence as the main thing to be reached by his art; if he finds that he is not gradually rising towards it, he thinks there is something wrong in his work; or, if he is too proud to think that, still the bribe of wealth and honour warps him from his honest labour into efforts to attract attention; and he gradually loses both his power of mind and his rectitude of purpose. This, according to the degree of avarice or ambition which exists in any painter's mind, is the necessary influence upon him of the hope of great wealth and reputation. But the harm is still greater, in so far as the possibility of attaining fortune of this kind tempts people continually to become painters who have no real gift for the work; and on whom these motives of mere worldly interest have exclusive influence;—men who torment and abuse the patient workers, eclipse or thrust aside all delicate and good pictures by their own gaudy and coarse ones, corrupt the taste of the public, and do the greatest amount of mischief to the schools of art in their day which it is possible for their capacities to effect; and it is quite wonderful how much mischief may be done even by small capacity. If you could by any means succeed in keeping the prices of pictures down, you would throw all these disturbers out of the way at once. . . .

But, observe, it is not only the painter himself whom you injure, by giving him too high prices; you injure all the inferior painters of the day. If they are modest, they will be discouraged and depressed by the feeling that their doings are worth so little, comparatively, in your eyes; —if proud, all their worst passions will be aroused, and the insult or opprobrium which they will try to cast on their successful rival will not only afflict and wound him, but at last sour and harden him: he cannot pass through such a trial without grievous harm. . . .

For remember always, that the price of a picture by a living artist never represents, never *can* represent, the quantity of labour or value in it. Its price represents, for the most part, the degree of desire which the rich people of the country have to possess it. Once get the wealthy classes to imagine that the possession of pictures by a given artist adds to their 'gentility,' and there is no price which his work may not immediately reach, and for years maintain; and in buying at that price, you are not getting value for your money, but merely disputing for victory in a contest of ostentation. And it is hardly possible to spend your money in a worse or more wasteful way; for though you may not be doing it for ostentation yourself, you are, by your pertinacity, nourishing the ostentation of others; you meet them in their game of wealth, and continue it for them; if they had not found an opposite player, the game would have been done; for a proud man can find no enjoyment in possessing himself of what nobody disputes with him. So that by every farthing you give for a picture beyond its fair price—that is to say, the price which will pay the painter for his time—you are not only cheating yourself and buying vanity, but you are stimulating the vanity of others; paying, literally, for the cultivation of pride. You may consider every pound that you spend above the just price of a work of art, as an investment in a cargo of a mental quick-lime or guano, which, being laid on the fields of human nature, is to grow a harvest of pride. You are in fact ploughing and harrowing, in a most valuable part of your land, in order to reap the whirlwind; you are setting your hand stoutly to Job's agriculture—'Let thistles grow instead of wheat, and cockle instead of barley.' . . .

So far then of the motives which should induce us to keep down the prices of modern art, and thus render it, as a private possession, attainable by greater numbers of people than at present. But we should strive to render it accessible to them in other ways also—chiefly by the permanent decoration of public buildings. . . .

The first and most important kind of public buildings which we are always sure to want, are schools: and I would ask you to consider very carefully, whether we may not wisely introduce some great changes in the way of school decoration. Hitherto, as far as I know, it has either been so difficult to give all the education we wanted to our lads, that we have been obliged to do it, if at all, with cheap furniture and bare walls; or else we have considered that cheap furniture and bare walls are a proper part of the means of education; and supposed that boys learned best when they sat on hard forms, and had nothing but blank plaster about and above them whereupon to employ their spare attention; also, that it was as well they should be accustomed to rough and ugly conditions of things, partly by way of preparing them for the hardships of life, and partly that there might be the least possible damage done to floors and forms, in the event of their becoming, during the master's absence, the fields or instruments of battle. All this is so far well and necessary, as it relates to the training of country lads, and the first training of boys in general. But there certainly comes a period in the life of a well-educated youth, in which one of the principal elements of his education is, or ought to be, to give him refinement of habits; and not only to teach him the strong exercises of which his frame is capable, but also to increase his bodily sensibility and refinement, and show him such small matters as the way of handling things properly, and treating them considerately.

Not only so; but I believe the notion of fixing the attention by keeping the room empty, is a wholly mistaken one: I think it is just in the emptiest room that the mind wanders most; for it gets restless, like a bird, for want of a perch, and casts about for any possible means of getting out and away. And even if it be fixed, by an effort, on the business in hand, that business becomes itself repulsive, more than it need be, by the vileness of its associations; and many a study appears dull or painful to a boy, when it is pursued on a blotted deal desk, under a wall with nothing on it but scratches and pegs, which would have been pursued pleasantly enough in a curtained corner of his father's library, or at the lattice window of his cottage. Now, my own belief is, that the best study of all is the most beautiful; and that a quiet glade of forest, or the nook of a lake shore, are worth all the schoolrooms in Christendom, when once you are past the multiplication table; but be that as it may, there is no question at all but that a time ought to come in the life of a well-trained youth, when he can sit at a writing-table without wanting to throw the inkstand at his neighbour; and when also he will feel more capable of certain efforts of mind with beautiful and refined forms about him than with ugly ones. When that time comes, he ought to be advanced into the decorated schools; and this advance ought to be one of the important and honourable epochs of his life. . . .

For you who have [the responsibility of guiding labour] in your hands are in reality the pilots of the power and effort of the State. It is entrusted to you as an authority to be used for good or evil, just as completely as kingly authority was ever given to a prince, or military command to a captain. And, according to the quantity of it that you have in your hands, you are the arbiters of the will and work of England; and the whole issue, whether the work of the State shall suffice for the State or not, depends upon you. You may stretch out your sceptre over the heads of the English labourers, and say to them, as they stoop to its waving, 'Subdue this obstacle that has baffled our fathers, put away this plague that consumes our children; water these dry places, plough these desert ones, carry this food to those who are in hunger; carry this light to those who are in darkness; carry this life to those who are in death'; or on the other side you may say to her labourers: 'Here am I; this power is in my hand; come, build a mound here for me to be throned upon, high and wide; come, make crowns for my head, that men may see them shine from far away; come, weave tapestries for my feet, that I may tread softly on the silk and purple; come, dance before me, that I may be gay; and sing sweetly to me, that I may slumber; so shall I live in joy, and die in honour.' And better than such an honourable death it were that the day had perished wherein we were born, and the night in which it was said there is a child conceived.

I trust that in a little while there will be few of our rich men who, through carelessness or covetousness, thus forfeit the glorious office which is intended for their hands. I said, just now, that wealth ill-used was as the net of the spider, entangling and destroying: but wealth well used is as the net of the sacred fisher who gathers souls of men out of the sleep. A time will come—I do not think even now it is far from us—when this golden net of the world's wealth will be spread abroad as the flaming meshes of morning cloud are over the sky; bearing with them the joy of light and the dew of the morning, as well as the summons to honourable and peaceful toil. What less can we hope from your wealth than this, rich men of England, when once you feel fully how, by the strength of your possessions—not, observe, by the exhaustion, but by the administration of them and the power,—you can direct the acts—command the energies—inform the ignorance—prolong the existence, of the whole human race; and how, even of worldly wisdom, which man employs faithfully, it is true, not only that her ways are pleasantness, but that her paths are peace; and that, for all the children of men, as well as for those to whom she is given, Length of days is in her right hand, as in her left hand Riches and Honour?

A Joy for Ever: The Political Economy of Art

The Two Paths

(1859)

---

*An Address delivered to the Members of the
Architectural Association ...*

If we were to be asked abruptly, and required to
answer briefly, what qualities chiefly distinguish great artists from feeble artists, we should answer, I suppose, first,
their sensibility and tenderness; secondly, their imagination; and thirdly, their industry. Some of us might, perhaps, doubt the justice of attaching so much importance to
this last character, because we have all known clever men
who were indolent, and dull men who were industrious.
But though you may have known clever men who were
indolent, you never knew a *great* man who was so; and,
during such investigation as I have been able to give to the
lives of the artists whose works are in all points noblest,
no fact ever looms so large upon me—no law remains so
steadfast in the universality of its application—as the fact
and law that they are all great workers: nothing concerning them is matter of more astonishment than the quantity
they have accomplished in the given length of their life;
and when I hear a young man spoken of, as giving
promise of high genius, the first question I ask about him
is always—Does he work?

But though this quality of industry is essential to an
artist, it does not in any wise make an artist; many people
are busy, whose doings are little worth. Neither does
sensibility make an artist, since, as I hope, many can feel
strongly and nobly, who yet care nothing about art. But
the gifts which distinctly mark the artist—*without* which
he must be feeble in life, forgotten in death—*with* which
he may become one of the shakers of the earth, and one
of the single lights in heaven—are those of sympathy and

imagination. I will not occupy your time, nor incur the risk of your dissent, by endeavouring to give any close definition of this last word. We all have a general and sufficient idea of imagination, and of its work with our hands and in our hearts: we understand it, I suppose, as the imagining or picturing of new things in our thoughts; and we always show an involuntary respect for this power, wherever we can recognize it, acknowledging it to be a greater power than manipulation, or calculation, or observation, or any other human faculty. If we see an old woman spinning at the fireside, and distributing her thread dexterously from the distaff, we respect her for her manipulation—if we ask her how much she expects to make in a year, and she answers quickly, we respect her for her calculation—if she is watching at the same time that none of her grandchildren fall into the fire, we respect her for her observation—yet for this she may still be a commonplace old woman enough. But if she is all the time telling her grandchildren a fairy tale out of her head, we praise her for her imagination, and say, she must be a rather remarkable old woman.

Precisely in like manner, if an architect does his working-drawing well, we praise him for his manipulation—if he keeps closely within his contract, we praise him for his honest arithmetic—if he looks well to the laying of his beams, so that nobody shall drop through the floor, we praise him for his observation. But he must, somehow, tell us a fairy tale out of his head beside all this, else we cannot praise him for his imagination nor speak of him as we did of the old woman, as being in any wise out of the common way, a rather remarkable architect. It seemed to me, therefore, as if it might interest you to-night, if we were to consider together what fairy tales are, in and by architecture, to be told—what there is for you to do in this severe art of yours 'out of your heads', as well as by your hands.

Perhaps the first idea which a young architect is apt to be allured by, as a head-problem in these experimental days, is its being incumbent upon him to invent a 'new style' worthy of modern civilization in general, and of England in particular; a style worthy of our engines and telegraphs; as expansive as steam, and as sparkling as electricity. But, if there are any of my hearers who have been impressed with this sense of inventive duty, may I ask them, first, whether their plan is that every inventive architect amongst us shall invent a new style for himself, and have a county set aside for his conceptions, or a province for his practice? Or, must every architect invent a little piece of the new style, and all put it together at last like a dissected map? And if so, when the new style is invented, what is to be done next? I will grant you this Eldorado of imagination—but can you have more than one Columbus? Or, if you sail in company, and divide the prize of your discovery and the honour thereof, who is to come after your clustered Columbuses? To what fortunate islands of style are your architectural descendants to sail, avaricious of new lands? When our desired style is invented, will not the best we can all do be simply—to build in it?—and cannot you now do that in styles that are known? Observe, I grant, for the sake of your argument, what perhaps many of you know that I would not grant otherwise—that a new style *can* be invented. I grant you not only this, but that it shall be wholly different from any that was ever practised before. We will suppose that capitals are to be at the bottom of pillars instead of at the top; and that buttresses shall be on the tops of pinnacles instead of at the bottom; that you roof your apertures with stones which shall neither be arched nor horizontal; and that you compose your decoration of lines which shall neither be crooked nor straight. The furnace and the forge shall be at your service: you shall draw out your plates of glass and beat out your bars of iron till you have encompassed us all—if your style is of the practical kind—with endless perspective of black skeleton and blinding square— or if your style is to be of the ideal kind—you shall wreathe your streets with ductile leafage, and roof them with variegated crystal—you shall put, if you will, all London under one blazing dome of many colours that shall light the clouds round it with its flashing, as far as to the sea. And still, I ask you, What after this? Do you suppose those imaginations of yours will ever lie down there asleep beneath the shade of your iron leafage, or within the coloured light of your enchanted dome? Not so. Those souls, and fancies, and ambitions of yours, are wholly infinite; and, whatever may be done by others, you will still want to do something for yourselves; if you cannot rest content with Palladio, neither will you with Paxton; all the metal and glass that ever were melted have not so much weight in them as will clog the wings of one human spirit's aspiration.

If you will think over this quietly by yourselves, and can get the noise out of your ears of the perpetual, empty, idle, incomparably idiotic talk about the necessity of some novelty in architecture, you will soon see that the very essence of a Style, properly so called, is that it should be practised *for ages,* and applied to all purposes; and that so long as any given style is in practice, all that is left for individual imagination to accomplish must be within the scope of that style, not in the invention of a new one. If there are any here, therefore, who hope to obtain celebrity by the invention of some strange way of building which must convince all Europe into its adoption, to them, for the moment, I must not be understood to address myself, but only to those who would be content with that degree of celebrity which an artist may enjoy who works in the manner of his forefathers; which the builder of Salisbury Cathedral might enjoy in England, though he did not invent Gothic; and which Titian might enjoy at Venice, though he did not invent oil painting. Addressing myself then to those humbler, but wiser, or rather, only wise students who are content to avail themselves of some system of building already understood, let us consider together what room for the exercise of the imagination may be left to us under such conditions. And, first, I suppose it will be said, or thought, that the architect's principal field for exercise of his invention must be in the disposition of lines, mouldings, and masses, in agreeable proportions. Indeed, if you adopt some styles of architecture, you cannot exercise invention in any other way. And I admit that it requires genius and special gift to do this rightly. Not by rule, nor by study, can the gift of graceful proportionate design be obtained; only by the intuition of genius can so much as a single tier of façade be beautifully arranged; and the man has just cause for pride, as far as our gifts can ever be a cause for pride, who finds himself able, in a design of his own, to rival even the simplest arrangement of parts in one by Sanmicheli, Inigo Jones, or Christopher Wren.

Invention, then, and genius being granted, as necessary to accomplish this, let me ask you, What, after all, with this special gift and genius, you *have* accomplished, when you have arranged the lines of a building beautifully?

In the first place you will not, I think, tell me that the beauty there attained is of a touching or pathetic kind. A well-disposed group of notes in music will make you sometimes weep and sometimes laugh. You can express the depth of all affections by those dispositions of sound; you can give courage to the soldier, language to the lover, consolation to the mourner, more joy to the joyful, more humility to the devout. Can you do as much by your group of lines? Do you suppose the front of Whitehall, a singularly beautiful one, ever inspires the two Horse Guards, during the hour they sit opposite to it, with military ardour? Do you think that the lovers in our London walk down to the front of Whitehall for consolation when mistresses are unkind; or that any person wavering in duty, or feeble in faith, was ever confirmed in purpose or in creed by the pathetic appeal of those harmonious architraves? You will not say so. Then, if they cannot touch, or inspire, or comfort anyone, can your architectural proportions amuse anyone? Christmas is just over; you have doubtless been at many merry parties during the period. Can you remember any in which architectural proportions contributed to the entertainment of the evening? Proportions of notes in music were, I am sure, essential to your amusement; the setting of flowers in hair, and of ribands on dresses, were also subjects of frequent admiration with you, not inessential to your happiness. Among the juvenile members of your society the proportion of currants in cake, and sugar in comfits, became subjects of acute interest; and, when such proportions were harmonious, motives also of gratitude to cook and to confectioner. But, did you ever see young or old amused by the architrave of the door? Or otherwise interested in the proportions of the room than as they admitted more or fewer friendly faces? Nay, if all the amusement that there is in the best-proportioned architecture of London could be concentrated into one evening, and you were to issue tickets for nothing to this great proportional entertainment; how do you think it would stand between you and the Drury pantomime?

You are, then, remember, granted to be the people of genius—great and admirable; and you devote your lives to your art, but you admit that you cannot comfort anybody, you cannot encourage anybody, you cannot improve anybody, and you cannot amuse anybody. I proceed then further to ask, Can you inform anybody? Many sciences cannot be considered as highly touching or emotional; nay, perhaps not specially amusing; scientific men may sometimes, in these respects, stand on the same ground with you. As far as we can judge by the results of the late war, science helps our soldiers about as much as the front of Whitehall; and at the Christmas parties, the children wanted no geologists to tell them about the behaviour of bears and dragons in Queen Elizabeth's time. Still, your man of science teaches you something; he may be dull at a party, or helpless in a battle, he is not always that; but he can give you, at all events, knowledge of noble facts,

236

and open to you the secrets of the earth and air. Will your architectural proportions do as much? Your genius is granted, and your life is given, and what do you teach us?—Nothing, I believe, from one end of that life to the other, but that two and two make four, and that one is to two as three is to six.

You cannot, then, it is admitted, comfort anyone, serve or amuse anyone, nor teach anyone. Finally, I ask, Can you be of *Use* to anyone? 'Yes,' you reply; 'certainly we are of some use—we architects—in a climate like this, where it always rains.' You are of use, certainly; but, pardon me, only as builders—not as proportionalists. We are not talking of building as a protection, but only of that special work which your genius is to do; not of building substantial and comfortable houses like Mr. Cubitt, but of putting beautiful façades on them like Inigo Jones. And, again, I ask—Are you of use to anyone? Will your proportions of façade heal the sick, or clothe the naked? Supposing you devoted your lives to be merchants, you might reflect at the close of them, how many, fainting for want, you had brought corn to sustain; how many, infected with disease, you had brought balms to heal; how widely, among multitudes of far-away nations, you had scattered the first seeds of national power, and guided the first rays of sacred light. Had you been, in fine, *anything* else in the world *but* architectural designers, you might have been of some use or good to people. Content to be petty tradesmen, you would have saved the time of mankind; rough-handed daily labourers, you would have added to their stock of food or of clothing. But, being men of genius, and devoting your lives to the exquisite exposition of this genius, on what achievements do you think the memories of your old age are to fasten? Whose gratitude will surround you with its glow, or on what accomplished good, of that greatest kind for which men show *no* gratitude, will your life rest the contentment of its close? Truly, I fear that the ghosts of proportionate lines will be thin phantoms at your bedsides—very speechless to you; and that on all the emanations of your high genius you will look back with less delight than you might have done on a cup of cold water given to him who was thirsty, or to a single moment when you had 'prevented with your bread him that fled.'

Do not answer, nor think to answer, that with your great works and great payments of workmen in them, you would do this; I know you would and will, as Builders; but, I repeat, it is not your *building* that I am talking about, but your *brains;* it is your invention and your imagination of whose profit I am speaking. The good done through the building, observe, is done by your employers, not by you—you share in the benefit of it. The good that *you* personally must do is by your designing; and I compare you with musicians who do good by their pathetic composing, not as they do good by employing fiddlers in the orchestra; for it is the public who in reality do that, not the musicians. So clearly keeping to this one question, what good we architects are to do by our genius: and having found that on our proportionate system we can do no good to others, will you tell me, lastly, what good we can do to *ourselves?*

Observe, nearly every other liberal art or profession has some intense pleasure connected with it, irrespective of any good to others. As lawyers, or physicians, or clergymen, you would have the pleasure of investigation, and of historical reading, as part of your work: as men of science you would be rejoicing in curiosity perpetually gratified respecting the laws and facts of Nature: as artists you would have delight in watching the external forms of Nature: as day labourers or petty tradesmen, supposing you to undertake such work with as much intellect as you are going to devote to your designing, you would find continued subjects of interest in the manufacture or the agriculture which you helped to improve; or in the problems of commerce which bore your business. But your architectural designing leads you into no pleasant journeys —into no seeing of lovely things—no discerning of just laws—no warmth of compassion, no humilities of veneration, no progressive state of sight or soul. Our conclusion is—must be—that you will not amuse, nor inform, nor help anybody; you will not amuse, nor better, nor inform yourselves: you will sink into a state in which you can neither show, nor feel, nor see, anything, but that one is to two as three is to six. And in that state what should we call ourselves? Men? I think not. The right name for us would be—numerators and denominators. Vulgar Fractions.

Shall we, then, abandon this theory of the soul of architecture being in proportional lines, and look whether we can find anything better to exert our fancies upon?

May we not, to begin with, accept this great principle— that, as our bodies, to be in health, must be *generally* exercised, so our minds, to be in health, must be *generally* cultivated? You would not call a man healthy who had strong arms but was paralytic in his feet; nor one who

238

could walk well, but had no use of his hands; nor one who could see well, if he could not hear. You would not voluntarily reduce your bodies to any such partially developed state. Much more, then, you would not, if you could help it, reduce your minds to it. Now, your minds are endowed with a vast number of gifts of totally different uses—limbs of mind as it were, which, if you don't exercise, you cripple. One is curiosity; that is a gift, a capacity of pleasure in knowing; which, if you destroy, you make yourselves cold and dull. Another is sympathy; the power of sharing in the feelings of living creatures; which, if you destroy, you make yourselves hard and cruel. Another of your limbs of mind is admiration; the power of enjoying beauty or ingenuity; which, if you destroy, you make yourselves base and irreverent. Another is wit; or the power of playing with the lights on the many sides of truth; which, if you destroy, you make yourselves gloomy, and less useful and cheering to others than you might be. So that in choosing your way of work it should be your aim, as far as possible, to bring out all these faculties, as far as they exist in you; not one merely, nor another, but all of them. And the way to bring them out, is simply to concern yourselves attentively with the subjects of each faculty. To cultivate sympathy you must be among living creatures, and thinking about them; and to cultivate admiration, you must be among beautiful things and looking at them.

All this sounds much like truism, at least, I hope it does, for then you will surely not refuse to act upon it; and to consider further how, as architects, you are to keep yourselves in contemplation of living creatures and lovely things.

You all probably know the beautiful photographs which have been published within the last year or two of the porches of the Cathedral of Amiens. I hold one of these up to you (merely that you may know what I am talking about, as of course you cannot see the detail at this distance, but you will recognize the subject). Have you ever considered how much sympathy, and how much humour, are developed in filling this single doorway with these sculptures of the history of St. Honoré (and, by the way, considering how often we English are now driving up and down the Rue St. Honoré, we may as well know as much of the saint as the old architect cared to tell us). You know, in all legends of saints who ever were bishops, the first thing you are told of them is that they didn't want to be bishops. So here is St. Honoré, who doesn't want to be a bishop, sitting sulkingly in the corner, he hugs his book with both hands, and won't get up to take his crosier; and here are all the city aldermen of Amiens come to *poke* him up; and all the monks in the town in a great puzzle what they shall do for a bishop if St. Honoré won't be; and here's one of the monks in the opposite corner who is quite cool about it, and thinks they'll get on well enough without St. Honoré—you see that in his face quite perfectly. At last St. Honoré consents to be bishop, and here he sits in a throne, and has his book now grandly on a desk instead of his knees, and he directs one of his village curates how to find relics in a wood; here is the wood, and here is the village curate, and here are the tombs, with the bones of St. Victorien and Gentien in them.

After this St. Honoré performs grand mass, and the miracle occurs of the appearance of a hand blessing the wafer, which occurrence afterwards was painted for the arms of the abbey. Then St. Honoré dies; and here is his tomb with his statue on the top; and miracles are being performed at it—a deaf man having his ear touched, and a blind man groping his way up to the tomb with his dog. Then here is a great procession in honour of the relics of St. Honoré; and under his coffin are some cripples being healed; and the coffin itself is put above the bar which separates the cross from the lower subjects, because the tradition is that the figure on the crucifix of the Church of St. Firmin bowed its head in token of acceptance, as the relics of St. Honoré passed beneath.

Now just consider the amount of sympathy with human nature, and observance of it, shown in this one bas-relief; the sympathy with disputing monks, with puzzled aldermen, with melancholy recluse, with triumphant prelate, with palsy-stricken poverty, with ecclesiastical magnificence, or miracle-working faith. Consider how much intellect was needed in the architect, and how much observance of Nature, before he could give the expression to these rich and quaint fragments of tombs and altars— weave with perfect animation the entangled branches of the forest.

But you will answer me, all this is not architecture at all—it is sculpture. Will you then tell me precisely where the separation exists between one and the other? We will begin at the very beginning. I will show you a piece of what you will certainly admit to be a piece of pure architecture; it is drawn on the back of another photograph, another of those marvellous tympana from Notre

Dame, which you call, I suppose, impure. Well, look on this picture, and on this. Don't laugh; you must not laugh, that's very improper of you, this is classical architecture. I have taken it out of the essay on that subject in the *Encyclopaedia Britannica*.

Yet I suppose none of you would think yourselves particularly ingenious architects if you had designed nothing more than this; nay, I will even let you improve it into any grand proportion you choose, and add to it as many windows as you choose; the only thing I insist upon in our specimen of pure architecture is, that there should be no mouldings nor ornaments upon it. And I suspect you don't quite like your architecture so pure as this. We want a few mouldings, you will say—just a few. Those who want mouldings, hold up their hands. We are unanimous, I think. Will you, then, design profiles of these mouldings yourselves, or will you copy them? If you wish to copy them, and to copy them always, of course I leave you at once to your authorities, and your imaginations to their repose. But if you wish to design them yourselves, how do you do it? You draw the profile according to your taste, and you order your mason to cut it. Now, will you tell me the logical difference between drawing the profile of a moulding and giving *that* to be cut, and drawing the folds of the drapery of a statue and giving *those* to be cut? The last is much more difficult to do than the first; but degrees of difficulty constitute no specific difference, and you will not accept it, surely, as a definition of the difference between architecture and sculpture, that 'architecture is doing anything that is easy, and sculpture anything that is difficult.'

It is true, also, that the carved moulding represents nothing, and the carved drapery represents something; but you will not, I should think, accept, as an explanation of the difference between architecture and sculpture, this any more than the other, that 'sculpture is art which has meaning, and architecture art which has none.'

Where, then, is your difference? In this perhaps, you will say; that whatever ornaments we can direct ourselves, and get accurately cut to order, we consider architectural. The ornaments that we are obliged to leave to the pleasure of the workman, or the superintendence of some other designer, we consider sculptural, especially if they are more or less extraneous and incrusted—not an essential part of the building.

Accepting this definition, I am compelled to reply, that it is in effect nothing more than an amplification of my first one—that whatever is easy you call architecture, whatever is difficult you call sculpture. For you cannot suppose the arrangement of the place in which the sculpture is to be put is so difficult or so great a part of the design as the sculpture itself. For instance: you all know the pulpit of Niccolo Pisano, in the baptistery at Pisa. It is composed of seven rich *relievi*, surrounded by panel mouldings, and sustained on marble shafts. Do you suppose Niccolo Pisano's reputation—such part of it at least as rests on this pulpit (and much does)—depends on the panel mouldings or on the *relievi?* The panel mouldings are by his hand; he would have disdained to leave even them to a common workman; but do you think he found any difficulty in them, or thought there was any credit in them? Having once done the sculpture, those enclosing lines were mere child's play to him; the determination of the diameter of shafts and height of capitals was an affair of minutes; his *work* was in carving the Crucifixion and the Baptism.

Or, again, do you recollect Orcagna's tabernacle in the church of San Michele, at Florence? That, also, consists of rich and multitudinous bas-reliefs, enclosed in panel mouldings, with shafts of mosaic, and foliated arches sustaining the canopy. Do you think Orcagna, any more than Pisano, if his spirit could rise in the midst of us at this moment, would tell us that he had trusted his fame to the foliation, or had put his soul's pride into the paneling? Not so; he would tell you that his spirit was in the stooping figures that stand around the couch of the dying Virgin.

Or, lastly, do you think the man who designed the procession on the portal of Amiens was the subordinate workman? That there was an architect over *him*, restraining him within certain limits, and ordering of him his bishops at so much a mitre, and his cripples at so much a crutch? Not so. *Here*, on this sculptured shield, rests the Master's hand; *this* is the centre of the Master's thought: from this, and in subordination to this, waved the arch and sprang the pinnacle. Having done this, and being able to give human expression and action to the stone, all the rest—the rib, the niche, the foil, the shaft—were mere toys in his hand and accessories to his conception; and if once you also gain the gift of doing this, if once you can carve one fronton such as you have here, I tell you, you would be able—so far as it depended on your invention—to scatter cathedrals over England as fast as clouds rise from its streams after summer rain.

Nay, but perhaps you answer again, our sculptors at

present do not design cathedrals, and could not. No, they could not; but that is merely because we have made architecture so dull that they cannot take any interest in it, and, therefore, do not care to add to their higher knowledge the poor and common knowledge of principles of building. You have thus separated building from sculpture, and you have taken away the power of both; for the sculptor loses nearly as much by never having room for the development of a continuous work, as you do from having reduced your work to a continuity of mechanism. You are essentially, and should always be, the same body of men, admitting only such difference in operation as there is between the work of a painter at different times, who sometimes labours on a small picture, and sometimes on the frescoes of a palace gallery.

This conclusion, then, we arrive at, *must* arrive at; the fact being irrevocably so: that in order to give your imagination and the other powers of your souls full play, you must do as all the great architects of old time did— you must yourselves be your sculptors. Phideas, Michelangelo, Orcagna, Pisano, Giotto—which of these men, do you think, could not use his chisel? You say, 'It is difficult; quite out of your way.' I know it is; nothing that is great is easy; and nothing that is great, so long as you study building without sculpture, can be *in* your way. I want to put it in your way, and you find your way to it. But, on the other hand, do not shrink from the task as if the refined art of perfect sculpture were always required from you. For, though architecture and sculpture are not separate arts, there is an architectural *manner* of sculpture; and it is, in the majority of its applications, a comparatively easy one. Our great mistake at present, in dealing with stone at all, is requiring to have all our work too refined; it is just the same mistake as if we were to require all our book illustrations to be as fine work as Raphael's. John Leech does not sketch so well as Leonardo da Vinci; but do you think that the public could easily spare him; or that he is wrong in bringing out his talent in the way in which it is most effective? Would you advise him, if he asked your advice, to give up his wood-blocks and take to canvas? I know you would not; neither would you tell him, I believe, on the other hand, that, because he could not draw as well as Leonardo, therefore he ought to draw nothing but straight lines with a ruler, and circles with compasses, and no figure-subjects at all. That would be some loss to you; would it not? You would all be vexed if next week's *Punch* had nothing in it but proportionate lines. And yet, do not you see that you are doing precisely the same thing with *your* powers of sculptural design that he would be doing with his powers of pictorial design, if he gave you nothing but such lines? You feel that you cannot carve like Phideas; therefore you will not carve at all, but only draw mouldings; and thus all that intermediate power which is of especial value in modern days—that popular power of expression which is within the attainment of thousands, and would address itself to tens of thousands—is utterly lost to us in stone, though in ink and paper it has become one of the most important engines, and one of the most desired luxuries, of modern civilization.

Here, then, is one part of the subject to which I would especially invite your attention, namely, the distinctive character which may be wisely permitted to belong to architectual sculpture, as distinguished from perfect sculpture on one side, and from mere geometrical decoration on the other.

And first, observe what an indulgence we have in the distance at which most work is to be seen. Supposing we were able to carve eyes and lips with the most exquisite precision, it would all be of no use as soon as the work was put far above the eye; but, on the other hand, as beauties disappear by being far withdrawn, so will faults; and the mystery and confusion which are the natural consequence of distance, while they would often render your best skill but vain, will as often render your worst errors of little consequence; nay, more than this, often a deep cut, or a rude angle, will produce in certain positions an effect of expression both startling and true, which you never hoped for. Not that mere distance will give animation to the work, if it has none in itself; but if it has life at all, the distance will make that life more perceptible and powerful by softening the defects of execution. So that you are placed, as workmen, in this position of singular advantage, that you may give your fancies free play, and strike hard for the expression that you want, knowing that, if you miss it, no one will detect you; if you at all touch it, Nature herself will help you, and with every changing shadow and basking sunbeam bring forth new phases of your fancy.

But it is not merely this privilege of being imperfect which belongs to architectural sculpture. It has a true privilege of imagination, far excelling all that can be granted to the more finished work, which, for the sake of distinction, I will call—and I don't think we can have a much better term—'furniture sculpture'; sculpture, that is, which can be moved from place to place to furnish rooms.

For observe, to that sculpture the spectator is usually brought in a tranquil or prosaic state of mind; he sees it associated rather with what is sumptuous than sublime, and under circumstances which address themselves more to his comfort than his curiosity. The statue which is to be pathetic, seen between the flashes of footmen's livery round the dining-table, must have strong elements of pathos in itself: and the statue which is to be awful, in the midst of the gossip of the drawing-room, must have the elements of awe wholly in itself. But the spectator is brought to *your* work already in an excited and imaginative mood. He has been impressed by the cathedral wall as it loomed over the low streets, before he looks up to the carving of its porch—and his love of mystery has been touched by the silence and the shadows of the cloister, before he can set himself to decipher the bosses on its vaulting. So that when once he begins to observe your doings, he will ask nothing better from you, nothing kinder from you, than that you would meet this imaginative temper of his half-way; that you would further touch the sense of terror, or satisfy the expectation of things strange, which have been prompted by the mystery or the majesty of the surrounding scene. And thus, your leaving forms more or less undefined, or carrying out your fancies, however extravagant, in grotesqueness of shadow or shape, will be for the most part in accordance with the temper of the observer; and he is likely, therefore, much more willingly to use his fancy to help your meanings, than his judgment to detect your faults.

Again. Remember that when the imagination and feelings are strongly excited, they will not only bear with strange things but they will *look* into *minute* things with a delight quite unknown in hours of tranquillity. You surely must remember moments of your lives in which, under some strong excitement of feeling, all the details of visible objects presented themselves with a strange intensity and insistence [*sic*], whether you would or no; urging themselves upon the mind, and thrust upon the eye, with a force of fascination which you could not refuse. Now, to a certain extent, the senses get into this state whenever the imagination is strongly excited. Things trivial at other times assume a dignity or significance which we cannot explain; but which is only the more attractive because inexplicable: and the powers of attention, quickened by

245

the feverish excitement, fasten and feed upon the minutest circumstances of detail, and remotest traces of intention. So that what would at other times be felt as more or less mean or extraneous in a work of sculpture and which would assuredly be offensive to the perfect taste in its moments of languor, or of critical judgment, will be grateful, and even sublime, when it meets this frightened inquisitiveness, this fascinated watchfulness, or the roused imagination. And this is all for your advantage; for, in the beginnings of your sculpture, you will assuredly find it easier to imitate minute circumstances of costume or character, than to perfect the anatomy of simple forms or the flow of noble masses; and it will be encouraging to remember that the grace you cannot perfect, and the simplicity you cannot achieve, would be in great part vain, even if you could achieve them, in their appeal to the hasty curiosity of passionate fancy; but that the sympathy which would be refused to your science will be granted to your innocence; and that the mind of the general observer, though wholly unaffected by correctness of anatomy or propriety of gesture, will follow you with fond and pleased concurrence, as you carve the knots of the hair, and the patterns of the vesture.

Further yet. We are to remember that not only do the associated features of the larger architecture tend to excite the strength of fancy, but the architectural laws to which you are obliged to submit your decoration stimulate its *ingenuity*. Every crocket which you are to crest with sculpture—every foliation which you have to fill, presents itself to the spectator's fancy, not only as a pretty thing, but as a *problematic* thing. It contained, he perceives immediately, not only a beauty which you wished to display, but a necessity which you were forced to meet; and the problem, how to occupy such and such a space with organic form in any probable way, or how to turn such a boss or ridge into a conceivable image of life, becomes at once, to him as to you, a matter of amusement as much as of admiration. The ordinary conditions of perfection in form, gesture, or feature, are willingly dispensed with, when the ugly dwarf and ungainly goblin have only to gather themselves into angles, or crouch to carry corbeils; and the want of skill which, in other kinds of work, would have been required for the finishing of the parts, will at once be forgiven here, if you have only disposed ingeniously what you have executed roughly, and atoned for the rudeness of your hands by the quickness of your wits.

Hitherto, however, we have been considering only the circumstances in architecture favourable to the development of the *powers* of imagination. A yet more important point for us seems, to me, the place which it gives to all *objects* of imagination.

For, I suppose, you will not wish me to spend any time in proving that imagination must be vigorous in proportion to the quantity of material which it has to handle; and that, just as we increase the range of what we see, we increase the richness of what we can imagine. Granting this, consider what a field is open to your fancy merely in the subject-matter which architecture admits. Nearly every other art is severely limited in its subjects—the landscape painter, for instance, gets little help from the aspects of beautiful humanity; the historical painter, less, perhaps, than he ought, from the accidents of wild nature; and the pure sculptor, still less, from the minor details of common life. But is there anything within range of sight, or conception, which may not be of use to *you*, or in which your interest may not be excited with advantage to your art? From visions of angels, down to the last important gesture of a child at play, whatever may be conceived of Divine, or beheld of Human, may be dared or adopted by you; throughout the kingdom of animal life, no creature is so vast, or so minute, that you cannot deal with it, or bring it into service; the lion and the crocodile will crouch about your shafts; the moth and the bee will sun themselves upon your flowers; for you, the fawn will leap; for you, the snail be slow; for you, the dove smooth her bosom, and the hawk spread her wings towards the south. All the wide world of vegetation blooms and bends for you; the leaves tremble that you may bid them be still under the marble snow; the thorn and the thistle, which the earth casts forth as evil, are to you the kindliest servants; no dying petal, nor drooping tendril, is so feeble as to have no help for you; no robed pride of blossom so kingly, but it will lay aside its purple, to receive at your hands the pale immortality. Is there anything in common life too mean—in common things too trivial—to be ennobled by your touch? As there is nothing in life, so there is nothing in lifelessness which has not its lesson for you, or its gift; and when you are tired of watching the strength of the plume, and the tenderness of the leaf, you may walk down to your rough rivershore, or into the thickest markets of your thoroughfares; and there is not a piece of torn cable that will not twine into a perfect moulding; there is not a fragment of castaway matting, or shattered basket-work, that will not work into a chequer or a capital. Yes: and if you gather up the very sand, and break the stone on which you tread, among its fragments of all but invisible shells you will find forms that will take their place, and that proudly, among the starred traceries of your vaulting; and you, who can crown the mountain with its fortress, and the city with its towers, are thus able also to give beauty to ashes, and worthiness to dust.

Now, in that your art presents all this material to you, you have already much to rejoice in. But you have more to rejoice in, because all this is submitted to you, not to be dissected or analysed, but to be sympathized with, and to bring out, therefore, what may be accurately called the moral part of imagination. We saw that, if we kept ourselves among lines only, we should have cause to envy the naturalist, because he was conversant with facts; but you will have little to envy now, if you make yourselves conversant with the feelings that arise out of his facts. For instance, the naturalist, coming upon a block of marble, has to begin considering immediately how far its purple is owing to iron, or its whiteness to magnesia; he breaks his piece of marble, and at the close of his day, has nothing but a little sand in his crucible, and some data added to the theory of the elements. But *you* approach your marble to sympathize with it, and rejoice over its beauty. You cut at it a little indeed, but only to bring out its veins more perfectly; and at the end of your day's work you leave your marble shaft with joy and complacency in its perfectness, as marble. When you have to watch an animal instead of a stone, you differ from the naturalist in the same way. He may, perhaps, if he be an amiable naturalist, take delight in having living creatures round him; still the major part of his work is, or has been, in counting feathers, separating fibres, and analysing structures. But your work is always with the living creature; the thing you have to get at in him is his life, and ways of going about things. It does not matter to you how many cells there are in his bones, or how many filaments in his feathers; what you want is his moral character and way of behaving himself; it is just that which your imagination, if healthy, will first seize—just that which your chisel, if vigorous, will first cut. You must get the storm spirit into your eagles, and the lordliness into your lions, and the tripping fear into your fawns; and in order to do this, you must be in continual sympathy with every fawn of them; and be hand-in-glove with all the lions, and hand-in-claw with all the hawks. And don't fancy that you will occupy mind after mind of utterly countless multitudes, long after you are gone. You have not, like authors, to plead for a hearing, or to fear oblivion. Do but build large enough, and carve boldly enough, and all the world will hear you; they cannot choose but look.

I do not mean to awe you by this thought; I do not mean that, because you will have so many witnesses and watchers, you are never to jest, or do anything gaily or lightly; on the contrary, I have pleaded, from the beginning, for this art of yours, especially because it has room for the whole of your character: if jest is in you, let the jest be jested; if mathematical ingenuity is yours, let your problem be put, and your solution be worked out, as quaintly as you choose; above all, see that your work is easily and happily done, else it will never make anybody else happy; but while you thus give the rein to all your impulses see that those impulses be heeded and centred by one noble impulse; and let that be Love—triple love—for the art which you practise, the creation in which you move, and the creatures to whom you minister.

I say, first, Love for the art which you practise. Be assured that if ever any other motive becomes a leading one in your mind, as the principal one for exertion, except your love of art, that moment it is all over with your art. I do not say you are not to desire money, nor to desire fame, nor to desire position; you cannot but desire all three; nay, you may—if you are willing that I should use the word Love in a desecrated sense—love all three; that is, passionately covet them; yet you must not covet or love them in the first place. Men of strong passions and imaginations must always care a great deal for anything, but the whole question is one of first or second. Does your art lead you, or your gain lead you? You may like making money exceedingly; but if it comes to a fair question, whether you are to make five hundred pounds less by this business, or to spoil your building, and you choose to spoil your building, there's an end of you. So you may be as thirsty for fame as a cricket is for cream; but, if it comes to a fair question, whether you are to please the mob, or do the thing as you know it ought to be done; and you can't do both, and choose to please the mob—it's all over with you;—there's no hope for you; nothing that you can do will ever be worth a man's glance as he passes by. The test is absolute, inevitable—Is your art first with you? Then you are artists; you may be, after you have made your money, misers and usurers; you may be, after you have got your fame, jealous, and proud, and wretched,

249

and base: but yet, *as long as you won't spoil your work,* you are artists. On the other hand—Is your money first with you, and your fame first with you? Then, you may be very charitable with your money, and very magnificent with your money, and very graceful in the way you wear your reputation, and very courteous to those beneath you, and very acceptable to those above you; but you are *not artists.* You are mechanics, and drudges.

You must love the creation you work in the midst of. For wholly in proportion to the intensity of feeling which you bring to the subject you have chosen, will be the depth and justice of your perception of its character. And this depth of feeling is not to be gained on the instant, when you want to bring it to bear on this or that. It is the result of the general habit of striving to feel rightly; and, among thousands of various means of doing this, perhaps the one I ought specially to name to you, is the keeping yourselves clear of petty and mean cares. Whatever you do, don't be anxious, nor fill your heads with little chagrins and little desires. I have just said, that you may be great artists, and yet be miserly and jealous, and troubled about many things. So you may be; but I said also that the miserliness or trouble must not be in your hearts all day. It is possible that you may get a habit of saving money; or it is possible, at a time of great trial, you may yield to the temptation of speaking unjustly of a rival—and you will shorten your powers and dim your sight even by this; but the thing that you have to dread far more than any such unconscious habit, or any such momentary fall—is the *constancy of small emotions;* the anxiety whether Mr. So-and-so will like your work; whether such and such a workman will do all that you want of him; and so on; not wrong feelings or anxieties in themselves, but impertinent, and wholly incompatible with the full exercise of your imagination.

Keep yourselves, therefore, quiet, peaceful, with your eyes open. It doesn't matter at all what Mr. So-and-so thinks of your work; but it matters a great deal what that bird is doing up there in its nest, or how that vagabond child at the street corner is managing his game of knuckle-down. And remember, you cannot turn aside from your own interests, to the birds' and the children's interests, unless you have long before got into the habit of loving and watching birds and children; so that it all comes at last to the forgetting yourselves, and the living out of yourselves, in the calm of the great world, or if you will, in its agitation; but always in a calm of your own bringing. Do not think it wasted time to submit yourselves to any influence which may bring upon you any noble feeling. Rise early, always watch the sunrise, and the way the clouds break from the dawn; you will cast your statue-draperies in quite another than your common way, when the remembrance of that cloud motion is with you, and of the scarlet vesture of the morning. Live always in the springtime in the country; you do not know what leaf-form means, unless you have seen the buds burst, and the young leaves breathing low in the sunshine, and wondering at the first shower of rain. But above all, accustom yourselves to look for, and to love, all nobleness of gesture and feature in the human form; and remember that the highest nobleness is usually among the aged, the poor, and the infirm; you will find, in the end, that it is not the strong arm of the soldier, nor the laugh of the young beauty, that are the best studies for you. Look at them, and look at them reverently; but be assured that endurance is nobler than strength and patience than beauty; and that it is not in the high church pews, where the gay dresses are, but in the church free seats, where the widows' weeds are, that you may see the faces that will fit best between the angels' wings, in the church porch.

And therefore, lastly and chiefly, you must love the creatures to whom you minister, your fellow-men; for, if you do not love them, not only will you be little interested in the passing events of life, but in all your gazing at humanity, you will be apt to be struck only by outside form, and not by expression. It is only kindness and tenderness which will ever enable you to see what beauty there is in the dark eyes that are sunk with weeping, and in the paleness of those fixed faces which the earth's adversity has compassed about, till they shine in their patience like dying watchfires through twilight. But it is not this only which makes it needful for you, if you would be great, to be also kind; there is a most important and all-essential reason in the very nature of your own art. So soon as you desire to build largely, and with addition of noble sculpture, you will find that your work must be associative. You cannot carve a whole cathedral yourself—you can carve but few and simple parts of it. Either your own work must be disgraced in the mass of the collateral inferiority, or you must raise your fellow-designers to correspondence of power. If you have genius, you will yourselves take the lead in the building you design; you will carve its porch and direct its disposition. But for all subsequent advancement of its detail, you must trust to the agency and the invention of others; and it rests with you either to repress what faculties your workmen have, into cunning subordination to your own; or to rejoice in discovering even the powers that may rival you, and leading forth mind after mind into fellowship with your fancy, and association with your fame.

I need not tell you that if you do the first—if you endeavour to depress or disguise the talents of your subordinates—you are lost; for nothing could imply more darkly and decisively than this, that your art and your work were not beloved by you; that it was your own prosperity that you were seeking, and your own skill only that you cared to contemplate. I do not say that you must not be jealous at all: it is rarely in human nature to be wholly without jealousy; and you may be forgiven for going some day sadly home, when you find some youth, unpractised and unapproved, giving the life-stroke to his work which you, after years of training, perhaps, cannot reach: but your jealousy must not conquer—your love of your building must conquer, helped by your kindness of heart. See—I set no high or difficult standard before you. I do not say that you are to surrender your pre-eminence in *mere* unselfish generosity. But I do say that you must surrender your pre-eminence in your love of your building, helped by your kindness; and that whomsoever you find better able to do what will adorn it than you—that person you are to give place to: and to console yourselves for the humiliation, first, by your joy in seeing the edifice growing more beautiful under his chisel; and secondly, by your sense of having done kindly and justly. But if you are morally strong enough to make the kindness and justice the first motive, it will be better—best of all—if you do not consider it as kindness at all, but bare and stern justice; for, truly, such help as we can give each other in this world is a *debt* to each other; and the man who perceives a superiority or capacity in a subordinate, and neither confesses nor assists it, is not merely the withholder of kindness, but the committer of injury. But be the motive what you will, only see that you do the thing; and take the joy of the consciousness that, as your art embraces a wider field than all others—and addresses a vaster multitude than all others—and is surer of audience than all others—so it is profounder and holier in Fellowship than all others. The artist, when his pupil is perfect, must see him leave his side that he may declare his distinct, perhaps opponent skill. Man of science wrestles with man of science for priority of discovery, and pursues in pangs of jealous haste his solitary inquiry. You alone are called by kindness—by necessity—by equity, to fraternity of toil; and thus, in those misty and massive piles which rise above the domestic roofs of our ancient cities, there was—there may be again—a meaning more profound and true than any that fancy so commonly has attached to them. Men say their pinnacles point to heaven. Why, so does every tree that buds, and every bird that rises as it sings. Men say their aisles are good for worship. Why, so is every mountain glen, and rough sea-shore. But this they have, of distinct and indisputable glory—that their mighty walls were never raised and never shall be, but by men who love and aid each other in their weakness;—that all their interlacing strength of vaulted stone has its foundation upon the stronger arches of manly fellowship, and all their changing grace of depressed or lifted pinnacle owes its cadence and completeness to sweeter symmetries of human soul.

Modern Painters
(Volume V)
(1860)

These oscillations of temper, and progressions of discovery, extending over a period of seventeen years, ought not to diminish the reader's confidence in the book. Let him be assured of this, that unless important changes are occurring in his opinions continually, all his life long, not one of those opinions can be on any questionable subject true. All true opinions are living, and show their life by being capable of nourishment; therefore of change. But their change is that of a tree—not of a cloud.

In the main aim and principle of the book, there is no variation, from its first syllable to its last. It declares the perfectness and eternal beauty of the work of God; and tests all work of man by concurrence with, or subjection to that. And it differs from most books, and has a chance of being in some respects better for the difference, in that it has not been written either for fame, or for money, or for conscience-sake, but of necessity.

It has not been written for praise. Had I wished to gain present reputation, by a little flattery adroitly used in some places, a sharp word or two withheld in others, and the substitution of verbiage generally for investigation, I could have made the circulation of these volumes tenfold what it has been in modern society. Had I wished for future fame I should have written one volume, not five. Also, it has not been written for money. In this wealth-producing country, seventeen years' labour could hardly have been invested with less chance of equivalent return.

Also, it has not been written for conscience-sake. I had no definite hope in writing it; still less any sense of its being required of me as a duty. It seems to me, and seemed always, probable, that I might have done much more good in some other way. But it has been written of necessity. I saw an injustice done, and tried to remedy it. I heard falsehood taught, and was compelled to deny it. Nothing else was possible to me. I knew not how little or how much might come of the business, or whether I was fit for it; but here was the lie full set in front of me, and there was no way round it, but only over it. So that, as the work changed like a tree, it was also rooted like a tree— not where it would, but where need was; on which, if any fruit grow such as you can like, you are welcome to gather it without thanks; and so far as it is poor or bitter, it will be your justice to refuse it without reviling.

Modern Painters, Vol. V, Preface

Of the many marked adaptations of nature to the mind of man, it seems one of the most singular, that trees intended especially for the adornment of the wildest mountains should be in broad outline the most formal of trees. The vine, which is to be the companion of man, is waywardly docile in its growth, falling into festoons beside his cornfields, or roofing his garden-walks, or casting its shadow all summer upon his door. Associated always with the trimness of cultivation, it introduces all possible elements of sweet wildness. The pine, placed nearly always among scenes disordered and desolate, brings into them all possible elements of order and precision. Lowland trees may lean to this side and that, though it is but a meadow breeze that bends them, or a bank of cowslips from which their trunks lean aslope. But let storm and avalanche do their worst, and let the pine find only a ledge of vertical precipice to cling to, it will nevertheless grow straight. Thrust a rod from its last shoot down the stem; it shall point to the centre of the earth as long as the tree lives.

Also it may be well for lowland branches to reach hither and thither for what they need, and to take all kinds of irregular shape and extension. But the pine is trained to need nothing, and to endure everything. It is resolvedly whole, self-contained, desiring nothing but rightness, content with restricted completion. Tall or short, it will be straight. Small or large, it will be round. It may be permitted also to these soft lowland trees that they should make themselves gay with show of blossom, and glad with pretty charities of fruitfulness. We builders with the sword have harder work to do for man, and must do it in close-set troops. To stay the sliding of the mountain snows, which would bury him; to hold in divided drops, at our sword-points the rain which would sweep away him and his treasure-fields; to nurse in shade among our brown fallen leaves the tricklings that feed the brooks in drought; to give massive shield against the winter wind, which shrieks through the bare branches of the plain:—such service must we do him steadfastly while we live. Our bodies, also, are at his service: softer than the bodies of other trees, though our toil is harder than theirs. Let him take them as pleases him, for his houses and ships. So also it may be well for these timid lowland trees to tremble with all their leaves, or turn their paleness to the sky, if but a rush of rain passes by them; or to let fall their leaves at last, sick and sere. But we pines must live carelessly amidst the wrath of clouds. We only wave our branches to and fro when the storm pleads with us, as men toss their arms in a dream.

Modern Painters, Vol. V, Part 6, Ch. 9

I have watched them in such scenes with the deeper interest, because of all trees they have hitherto had most influence on human character. The effect of other vegetation, however great, has been divided by mingled species; elm and oak in England, poplar in France, birch in Scotland, olive in Italy and Spain, share their power with inferior trees, and with all the changing charm of successive agriculture. But the tremendous unity of the pine absorbs and moulds the life of a race. The pine shadows rest upon a nation. The Northern peoples, century after century, lived under one or other of the two great powers of the Pine and the Sea, both infinite. They dwelt amidst the forests, as they wandered on the waves and saw no end, nor any other horizon; still the dark green trees, or the dark green waters, jagged the dawn with their fringe or their foam. And whatever elements of imagination, or of warrior strength, or of domestic justice, were brought down by the Norwegian and the Goth against the dissoluteness or degradation of the South of Europe, were taught them under the green roofs and wild penetralia of the pine.

Modern Painters, Vol. V, Part 6, Ch. 9

Let us suppose that this ounce of mud is left in perfect rest, and that its elements gather together, like to like, so that their atoms may get into the closest relations possible.

Let the clay begin. Ridding itself of all foreign substance, it gradually becomes a white earth, already very beautiful; and fit, with help of congealing fire, to be made into finest porcelain, and painted on, and be kept in kings' palaces. But such artificial consistence is not its best. Leave it still quiet to follow its own instinct of unity, and it becomes not only white, but clear; not only clear, but hard; not only clear and hard, but so set that it can deal with light in a wonderful way, and gather out of it the loveliest blue rays only, refusing the rest. We call it then a sapphire.

Such being the consummation of the clay, we give similar permission of quiet to the sand. It also becomes, first, a white earth, then proceeds to grow clear and hard, and at last arranges itself in mysterious, infinitely fine parallel lines, which have the power of reflecting not merely the blue rays, but the blue, green, purple, and red rays in the greatest beauty in which they can be seen through any hard material whatsoever. We call it then an opal.

In next order the soot sets to work; it cannot make itself white at first, but instead of being discouraged, tries harder and harder, and comes out clear at last, and the hardest thing in the world; and for the blackness that it had, obtains in exchange the power of reflecting all the rays of the sun at once in the vividest blaze that any solid thing can shoot. We call it then a diamond.

Last of all the water purifies or unites itself, contented enough if it only reach the form of a dew-drop; but if we insist on its proceeding to a more perfect consistence, it crystallizes into the shape of a star.

And for the ounce of slime which we had by political economy of competition, we have by political economy of co-operation, a sapphire, an opal, and a diamond, set in the midst of a star of snow.

Modern Painters, Vol. V, Part 8, Ch. 1

The Lance of Pallas

All great art is the expression of man's delight in God's work, not in *his own*. But observe, he is not himself his own work: he is himself precisely the most wonderful piece of God's workmanship extant. In this best piece not only he is bound to take delight, but cannot, in a right state of thought, take delight in anything else, otherwise than through himself. Through himself, however, as the *sun* of creation, not as *the* creation. In himself, as the light of the world. Not as being the world. Let him stand in his due relation to other creatures, and to inanimate things— know them all and love them, as made for him, and he for them;—and he becomes himself the greatest and holiest of them. But let him cast off this relation, despise and forget the less creation round him, and instead of being the light of the world, he is a sun in space—a fiery ball, spotted with storm.

All the diseases of mind leading to fatallest ruin consist primarily in this isolation. They are the concentration of man upon himself, whether his heavenly interests or his worldly interests, matters not; it is the being *his own* interests which makes the regard of them so mortal. Every form of asceticism on one side, of sensualism on the other, is an isolation of his soul or of his body; the fixing his thoughts upon them alone; while every healthy state of nations and of individual minds consists in the unselfish presence of the human spirit everywhere, energizing over all things; speaking and living through all things.

Man being thus the crowning and ruling work of God, it will follow that all his best art must have something to tell about himself, as the soul of things, and ruler of creatures. It must also make this reference to himself under a true conception of his own nature. Therefore all art which involves no reference to man is inferior or nugatory. And all art which involves misconception of man, or base thought of him, is in that degree false and base.

Now the basest thought possible concerning him is, that he has no spiritual nature; and the foolishest misunderstanding of him possible is, that he has or should have, no animal nature. For his nature is nobly animal, nobly spiritual—coherently and irrevocably so; neither part of it may, but at its peril, expel, despise, or defy the other. All great art confesses and worships both.

The art which, since the writings of Rio and Lord Lindsay is specially known as "Christian," erred by pride in its denial of the animal nature of man;—and, in connection with all monkish and fanatical forms of religion, by looking always to another world instead of this. It wasted its strength in visions, and was therefore swept away, notwithstanding all its good and glory, by the strong truth of the naturalist art of the sixteenth century. But that naturalist art erred on the other side; denied at last the spiritual nature of man, and perished in corruption. . . .

Perhaps an accurate analysis of the schools of art of all time might show us that when the immortality of the soul was practically and completely believed, the elements of decay, danger, and grief in visible things were always disregarded. However this may be, it is assuredly so in the early Christian schools. The ideas of danger or decay seem not merely repugnant, but inconceivable to them; the expression of immortality and perpetuity is alone possible. I do not mean that they take no note of the absolute fact of corruption. This fact the early painters often compel themselves to look fuller in the front than any other men: as in the way they usually paint the Deluge (the raven feeding on the bodies), and in all the various triumphs and processions of the power of Death, which formed one great chapter of religious teaching and painting, from Orcagna's time to the close of the Purist epoch. But I mean that this external fact of corruption is separated in their minds from the main conditions of their work; and its horror enters no more into their general treatment of landscape than the fear of murder or martyrdom, both of which they had nevertheless continually to represent. None of these things appeared to them as affecting the general dealings of the Deity with His world. Death, pain, and decay were simply momentary accidents in the course of immortality, which never ought to exercise any depressing influence over the hearts of men, or in the life of Nature. God, in intense life, peace, and helping power, was always and everywhere. . . .

It may perhaps be thought that this is a very high and right state of mind.

Unfortunately, it appears that the attainment of it is never possible without inducing some form of intellectual weakness.

No painter belonging to the purist religious schools ever mastered his art. Perugino nearly did so; but it was because he was more rational—more a man of the world —than the rest. No literature exists of a high class produced by minds in the pure religious temper. On the contrary, a great deal of literature exists, produced by persons in that temper, which is markedly, and very far, below average literary work. . . . That result indeed follows naturally enough on its habit of assuming that things must be right, or must come right, when, probably, the fact is, that so far as we are concerned, they are entirely wrong; and going wrong: and also on its weak and false way of looking on what these religious persons call "the bright side of things," that is to say, on one side of them only, when God has given them two sides, and intended us to see both.

I was reading but the other day, in a book by a zealous, useful, and able Scotch clergyman, one of these rhapsodies, in which he described a scene in the Highlands to show (he said) the goodness of God. In this Highland scene there was nothing but sunshine, and fresh breezes, and bleating lambs, and clean tartans, and all manner of pleasantness. Now a Highland scene is, beyond dispute, pleasant enough in its own way; but, looked close at, has its shadows. Here, for instance, is the very fact of one, as pretty as I can remember—having seen many. It is a little valley of soft turf, enclosed in its narrow oval by jutting rocks and broad flakes of nodding fern. From one side of it to the other winds, serpentine, a clear brown stream, drooping into quicker ripple as it reaches the end of the oval field, and then, first islanding a purple and white rock with an amber pool, it dashes away into a narrow fall of foam under a thicket of mountain-ash and alder. The autumn sun, low but clear, shines on the scarlet ash-berries and on the golden birch-leaves, which, fallen here and there, when the breeze has not caught them, rest quiet in the crannies of the purple rock. Beside the rock, in the hollow under the thicket, the carcase of a ewe, drowned in the last flood, lies nearly bare to the bone, its white ribs protruding through the skin, raven-torn; and the rags of its wool still flickering from the branches that first stayed it as the stream swept it down. A little lower, the current plunges, roaring, into a circular chasm like a well, surrounded on three sides by a chimney-like hollowness of polished rock, down which the foam slips in detached snow-flakes. Round the edges of the pool beneath, the water circles slowly, like black oil; a little butterfly lies on its back, its wings glued to one of the eddies, its limbs feebly quivering; a fish rises, and it is gone. Lower down the stream, I can just see over a knoll, the green and damp turf roofs of four or five hovels, built at the edge of a morass, which is trodden by the cattle into a black Slough of Despond at their doors, and traversed by a few ill-set stepping-stones, with here and there a flat slab on the tops, where they have sunk out of sight, and at the turn of the brook I see a man fishing, with a boy and a dog—a picturesque and pretty group enough certainly, if they had not been there all day starving. I know them, and I know the dog's ribs also, which are nearly as bare as the dead ewe's; and the child's wasted shoulders, cutting his old tartan jacket through, so sharp are they. . . .

Truly, this Highland and English hill-scenery is fair enough; but has its shadows; and deeper colouring, here and there, than that of heath and rose.

Now, as far as I have watched the main powers of the human mind, they have risen first from the resolution to see fearlessly, pitifully, and to its very worst, what these deep colours mean, wheresoever they fall; not by any means to pass on the other side, looking pleasantly up to the sky, but to stoop to the horror, and let the sky, for the present, take care of its own clouds. However this may be in moral matters, with which I have nothing here to do, in my own field of inquiry the fact is so; and all great and beautiful work has come of first gazing without shrinking into the darkness. If, having done so, the human spirit can, by its courage and faith, conquer the evil, it rises into conceptions of victorious and consummated beauty. It is then the spirit of the highest Greek and Venetian Art. If unable to conquer the evil, but remaining in strong though melancholy war with it, not rising into supreme beauty, it is the spirit of the best northern art, typically represented by that of Holbein and Dürer. If, itself conquered by the evil, infected by the dragon breath of it, and at last brought into captivity, so as to take delight in evil for ever, it becomes the spirit of the dark, but still powerful sensualistic art, represented typically by that of Salvator. We must trace this fact briefly through Greek, Venetian, and Düreresque art; we shall then see how the art of decline came of avoiding the evil, and seeking pleasure only; and thus obtain, at last, some power of judging whether the tendency of our own contemplative art be right or ignoble.

The ruling purpose of Greek poetry is the assertion of victory, by heroism, over fate, sin, and death. The terror of these great enemies is dwelt upon chiefly by the tragedians. The victory over them, by Homer.

The adversary chiefly contemplated by the tragedians is Fate, or predestinate misfortune. And that under three principal forms.

(A) Blindness or ignorance; not in itself guilty, but inducing acts which otherwise would have been guilty; and leading, no less than guilt, to destruction.

(B) Visitation upon one person of the sin of another.

(c) Repression by brutal, or tyrannous strength, of a benevolent will.

In all these cases sorrow is much more definitely connected with sin by the Greek tragedians than by Shakspere. The "fate" of Shakspere is, indeed, a form of blindness, but it issues in little more than haste or indiscretion. It is, in the literal sense, "fatal," but hardly criminal.

The "I am fortune's fool" of Romeo, expresses Shakspere's primary idea of tragic circumstances. Often his victims are entirely innocent, swept away by mere current of strong encompassing calamity (Ophelia, Cordelia, Arthur, Queen Katherine). This is rarely so with the Greeks. The victim may indeed be innocent, as Antigone, but is in some way resolutely entangled with crime and destroyed by it, as if it struck by pollution, no less than participation.

The victory over sin and death is therefore also with the Greek tragedians more complete than with Shakspere. As the enemy has more direct moral personality,—as it is sinfulness more than mischance, it is met by a higher moral resolve, a greater preparation of heart, a more solemn patience and purposed self-sacrifice. At the close of a Shakspere tragedy, nothing remains but dead march and clothes of burial. At the close of a Greek tragedy there are far-off sounds of a divine triumph, and a glory as of resurrection.

The Homeric temper is wholly different. Far more tender, more practical, more cheerful; bent chiefly on present things and giving victory now, and here, rather than in hope, and hereafter. The enemies of mankind, in Homer's conception, are more distinctly conquerable; they are ungoverned passions, especially anger, and unreasonable impulse generally (ἀτη). Hence the anger of Achilles, misdirected by pride, but rightly directed by friendship, is the subject of the *Iliad*. The anger of Ulysses ('Οδυσσεὺς, "the angry"), misdirected at first into idle and irregular hostilities, directed at last to execution of sternest justice, is the subject of the *Odyssey*.

Though this is the central idea of the two poems, it is connected with general display of the evil of all unbridled passions, pride, sensuality, indolence, or curiosity. The pride of Atrides, the passion of Paris, the sluggishness of Elpenor, the curiosity of Ulysses himself about the Cyclops, the impatience of his sailors in untying the winds, and all other faults or follies down to that—(evidently no small one in Homer's mind)—of domestic disorderliness, are throughout shown in contrast with conditions of patient affection and household peace.

Also, the wild powers and mysteries of Nature are in the Homeric mind among the enemies of man; so that all the labours of Ulysses are an expression of the contest of manhood, not only with its own passions or with the folly of others, but with the merciless and mysterious powers of the natural world.

This is perhaps the chief signification of the seven years' stay with Calypso, "the concealer." Not, as vulgarly thought, the concealer of Ulysses, but the great concealer—the hidden power of natural things. She is the daughter of Atlas and the Sea (Atlas, the sustainer of heaven, and the Sea, the disturber of the Earth). She dwells in the island of Ogygia ("the ancient or venerable"). (Whenever Athens, or any other Greek city, is spoken of with any peculiar reverence, it is called "Ogygian.") Escaping from this goddess of secrets, and from other spirits, some of destructive natural force (Scylla), others signifying the enchantment of mere natural beauty (Circe, daughter of the Sun and Sea), he arrives at last at the Phæacian land, whose king is "strength with intellect," and whose queen "virtue." These restore him to his country.

Now observe that in their dealing with all these subjects the Greeks never shrink from horror; down to its uttermost depth, to its most appalling physical detail, they strive to sound the secrets of sorrow. For them there is no passing by on the other side, no turning away the eyes to vanity from pain. Literally, they have not "lifted up their souls unto vanity." Whether there be consolation for them or not, neither apathy nor blindness shall be their saviour; if, for them, thus knowing the facts of the grief of earth, any hope, relief, or triumph may hereafter seem possible,—well; but if not, still hopeless, reliefless, eternal, the sorrow shall be met face to face. This Hector, so righteous, so merciful, so brave, has, nevertheless, to look upon his dearest brother in miserablest death. His own soul passes away in hopeless sobs through the throat-wound of the Grecian spear. That is one aspect of things in this world, a fair world truly, but having, among its other aspects, this one, highly ambiguous.

Meeting it boldly as they may, gazing right into the skeleton face of it, the ambiguity remains; nay, in some sort gains upon them. We trusted in the gods;—we thought that wisdom and courage would save us. Our wisdom and courage themselves deceive us to our death. Athena had the aspect of Deiphobus—terror of the enemy. She has not terrified him, but left us, in our mortal need.

And beyond that mortality, what hope have we? Nothing is clear to us on that horizon, nor comforting. Funeral honours; perhaps also rest; perhaps a shadowy life—artless, joyless, loveless. No devices in that darkness of the grave, nor daring, nor delight. Neither marrying nor giving in marriage, nor casting of spears, nor rolling of chariots, nor voice of fame. Lapped in pale Elysian mist, chilling the forgetful heart and feeble frame, shall we waste on for ever? Can the dust of earth claim more of immortality than this? Or shall we have even so much as rest? May we, indeed, lie down again in the dust: or have not our sins hidden from us even the things that belong to that peace? May not chance and the whirl of passion govern us there: when there shall be no thought, nor work, nor wisdom, nor breathing of the soul?

Be it so. With no better reward, no brighter hope, we will be men while we may: men, just, and strong, and fearless, and up to our power, perfect. Athena herself, our wisdom and our strength, may betray us:—Phœbus, our sun, smite us with plague, or hide his face from us helpless;—Jove and all the powers of fate oppress us, or give us up to destruction. While we live, we will hold fast our integrity; no weak tears shall blind us, no untimely tremors abate our strength of arm nor swiftness of limb. The gods have given us at least this glorious body and this righteous conscience; these will we keep bright and pure to the end. So may we fall to misery, but not to baseness; so may we sink to sleep, but not to shame.

And herein was conquest. So defied, the betraying and accusing shadows shrank back; the mysterious horror subdued itself to majestic sorrow. Death was swallowed up in victory. Their blood, which seemed to be poured out upon the ground, rose into hyacinthine flowers. All the beauty of earth opened to them; they had ploughed into its darkness, and they reaped its gold; the gods, in whom they had trusted through all semblance of oppression, came down to love them and be their helpmates. All nature round them became divine—one harmony of power and peace. The sun hurt them not by day, nor the moon by night; the earth opened no more her jaws into the pit; the sea whitened no more against them the teeth of his devouring waves, Sun, and moon, and earth, and sea,—all melted into grace and love; the fatal arrows rang not now at the shoulders of Apollo, the healer, lord of life, and of the three great spirits of life—Care, Memory, and Melody. Great

Artemis guarded their flocks by night; Selene kissed in love the eyes of those who slept. And from all came the help of heaven to body and soul; a strange spirit lifting the lovely limbs; strange light glowing on the golden hair; and strangest comfort filling the trustful heart, so that they could put off their armour, and lie down to sleep,—their work well done, whether at the gates of their temples or of their mountains; accepting the death they once thought terrible, as the gift of Him who knew and granted what was best.

Modern Painters, Vol. V, Part 9, Ch. 2

Born half-way between the mountains and the sea— that young George of Castelfranco—of the Brave Castle:— Stout George they called him, George of Georges, so goodly a boy he was—Giorgione.

Have you ever thought what a world his eyes opened on—fair, searching eyes of youth? What a world of mighty life, from those mountain roots to the shore;—of loveliest life, when he went down, yet so young, to the marble city—and became himself as a fiery heart to it?

A city of marble, did I say? nay, rather a golden city, paved with emerald. For truly, every pinnacle and turret glanced or glowed, overlaid with gold, or bossed with jasper. Beneath, the unsullied sea drew in deep breathing, to and fro, its eddies of green wave. Deep-hearted, majestic, terrible as the sea,—the men of Venice moved in sway of power and war; pure as her pillars of alabaster, stood her mothers and maidens; from foot to brow, all noble, walked her knights; the low bronzed gleaming of sea-rusted armour shot angrily under their blood-red mantle-folds. Fearless, faithful, patient, impenetrable, implacable, —every word a fate—sat her senate. In hope and honour, lulled by flowing of wave around their isles of sacred sand, each with his name written and the cross graved at his side, lay her dead. A wonderful piece of world. Rather, itself a world. It lay along the face of the waters, no larger, as its captains saw it from their masts at evening, than a bar of sunset that could not pass away but for its power, it must have seemed to them as if they were sailing in the expanse of heaven, and this a great planet, whose orient edge widened through ether. A world from which all ignoble care and petty thoughts were banished, with all the common and poor elements of life.

No foulness, nor tumult, in those tremulous streets, that filled, or fell, beneath the moon; but rippled music of majestic change, or thrilling silence. No weak walls could rise above them; no low-roofed cottage, nor straw-built shed. Only the strength as of rock, and the finished setting of stones most precious. And around them, far as the eye could reach, still the soft moving of stainless waters, proudly pure; as not the flower, so neither the thorn nor the thistle, could grow in the glancing fields. Ethereal strength of Alps, dreamlike, vanishing in high procession beyond the Torcellan shore; blue islands of Paduan hills, poised in the golden west. Above, free winds and fiery clouds ranging at their will;—brightness out of the north, and balm from the south, and the stars of the evening and morning clear in the limitless light of arched heaven and circling sea.

Such was Giorgione's school—such Titian's home.

Near the south-west corner of Covent Garden, a square brick pit or well is formed by a close-set block of houses, to the back windows of which it admits a few rays of light. Access to the bottom of it is obtained out of Maiden Lane, through a low archway and an iron gate; and if you stand long enough under the archway to accustom your eyes to the darkness you may see on the left hand a narrow door, which formerly gave quiet access to a respectable barber's shop, of which the front window, looking into Maiden Lane, is still extant, filled, in this year (1860), with a row of bottles, connected, in some defunct manner, with a brewer's business. A more fashionable neighbourhood, it is said, eighty years ago than now—never certainly a cheerful one—wherein a boy being born on St. George's day, 1775, began soon after to take interest in the world of Covent Garden, and put to service such spectacles of life as it afforded.

No knights to be seen there, nor, I imagine, many beautiful ladies; their costume at least disadvantageous, depending much on incumbency of hat and feather, and short waists; the majesty of men founded similarly on shoebuckles and wigs;—impressive enough when Reynolds will do his best for it; but not suggestive of much ideal delight to a boy.

'Bello ovile dov' io dormii agnello'; of things beautiful, besides men and women, dusty sunbeams up or down the street on summer mornings; deep furrowed cabbage-leaves at the greengrocer's; magnificence of oranges in wheelbarrows round the corner; and Thames' shore within three minutes' race.

None of these things very glorious; the best, however, that England, it seems, was then able to provide for a boy of gift: who, such as they are, loves them—never, indeed, forgets them. The short waists modify to the last his visions of Greek ideal. His foregrounds had always a succulent cluster or two of greengrocery at the corners. Enchanted oranges gleam in Covent Gardens of the Hesperides; and great ships go to pieces in order to scatter chests of them on the waves. That mist of early sunbeams in the London dawn crosses, many and many a time, the clearness of Italian air; and by Thames' shore, with its stranded barges and glidings of red sail, dearer to us than Lucerne lake or Venetian lagoon,—by Thames' shore we will die.

With such circumstances round him in youth, let us note what necessary effects followed upon the boy. I assume him to have had Giorgione's sensibility (and more than Giorgione's, if that be possible) to colour and form. I tell you farther, and this fact you may receive trustfully, that his sensibility to human affection and distress was no less keen than even his sense for natural beauty—heart-sight deep as eyesight.

Consequently, he attaches himself with the faithfullest child-love to everything that bears an image of the place he was born in. No matter how ugly it is,—has it anything about it like Maiden Lane, or like Thames' shore? If so, it shall be painted for their sake. Hence, to the very close of life, Turner could endure ugliness which no one else, of the same sensibility, would have borne with for an instant. Dead brick walls, blank square windows, old clothes, market-womanly types of humanity—anything fishy and muddy, like Billingsgate or Hungerford Market, had great attraction for him; black barges, patched sails, and every possible condition of fog.

You will find these tolerations and affections guiding or sustaining him to the last hour of his life; the notablest of all such endurances being that of dirt. No Venetian ever draws anything foul; but Turner devoted picture after picture to the illustration of effects of dinginess, smoke, soot, dust, and dusty texture; old sides of boats, weedy roadside vegetation, dung-hills, straw-yards, and all the soilings and stains of every common labour.

And more than this, he not only could endure, but enjoyed and looked for *litter*, like Covent Garden wreck after the market. His pictures are often full of it, from side to side; their foregrounds differ from all others in the natural way that things have of lying about in them. Even his richest vegetation, in ideal work, is confused; and he delights in shingle, débris, and heaps of fallen stones. The last words he ever spoke to me about a picture were in gentle exultation about his St. Gothard: 'that *litter* of stones which I endeavoured to represent.'

The second great result of this Covent Garden training was, understanding of and regard for the poor, whom the Venetians, we saw, despised; whom, contrarily, Turner loved, and more than loved—understood. He got no romantic sight of them, but an infallible one, as he prowled about the end of his lane, watching night effects in the wintry streets; nor sight of the poor alone, but of the poor in direct relations with the rich. He knew, in good and evil, what both classes thought of, and how they dealt with, each other.

Reynolds and Gainsborough, bred in country villages, learned there the country boy's reverential theory of 'the squire,' and kept it. They painted the squire and the squire's lady as centres of the movements of the universe, to the end of their lives. But Turner perceived the younger squire in other aspects about his lane, occurring prominently in its night scenery, as a dark figure, or one of two, against the moonlight. He saw also the working of city commerce, from endless warehouse, towering over Thames, to the back shop in the lane, with its stale herrings—highly interesting these last; one of his father's best friends, whom he often afterwards visited affectionately at Bristol, being a fishmonger and glue-boiler; which gives us a friendly turn of mind towards herring-fishing, whaling, Calais poissardes, and many other of our choicest subjects in after-life; all this being connected with that mysterious forest below London Bridge on one side; and, on the other, with these masses of human power and national wealth which weigh upon us, at Covent Garden here, with strange compression, and crush us into narrow Hand Court.

'That mysterious forest below London Bridge'—better for the boy than wood of pine, or grove of myrtle. How he must have tormented the watermen, beseeching them to let him crouch anywhere in the bows, quiet as a log, so only that he might get floated down there among the ships, and round and round the ships, and with the ships, and by the ships, and under the ships, staring, and clambering;—these the only quite beautiful things he can see in all the world, except the sky; but these, when the sun is on their sails, filling or falling, endlessly disordered by sway of tide and stress of anchorage, beautiful unspeakably; which ships also are inhabited by glorious creatures—red-faced sailors, with pipes, appearing over the gunwhales, true knights, over their castle parapets—the most angelic beings in the whole compass of London world. And Trafalgar happening long before we can draw ships, we, nevertheless, coax all current stories out of the wounded sailors, do our best at present to show Nelson's funeral streaming up the Thames; and vow that Trafalgar shall have its tribute of memory some day. Which, accordingly, is accomplished—once, with all our might, for its death; twice, with all our might, for its victory; thrice, in pensive farewell to the old *Téméraire*, and with it, to that order of things.

Now this fond companying with sailors must have divided his time, it appears to me, pretty equally between Covent Garden and Wapping (allowing for incidental excursions to Chelsea on one side, and Greenwich on the other), which time he would spend pleasantly, but not magnificently, being limited in pocket-money, and leading a kind of 'Poor-Jack' life on the river.

In some respects, no life could be better for a lad. But it was not calculated to make his ear fine to the niceties of language, nor form his moralities on an entirely regular standard. Picking up his first scraps of vigorous English chiefly at Deptford and in the markets, and his first ideas of female tenderness and beauty among nymphs of the barge and the barrow,—another boy might, perhaps, have become what people usually term 'vulgar.' But the original make and frame of Turner's mind being not vulgar, but as nearly as possible a combination of the minds of Keats and Dante, joining capricious waywardness, and intense openness to every fine pleasure of sense, and hot defiance of formal precedent, with a quite infinite tenderness, generosity, and desire of justice and truth—this kind of mind did not become vulgar, but very tolerant of vulgarity, even fond of it in some forms; and on the outside, visibly infected by it, deeply enough; the curious result, in its combination of elements, being to most people wholly incomprehensible. It was as if a cable had been woven of blood-crimson silk, and then tarred on the outside. People handled it, and the tar came off on their hands; red gleams were seen through the black underneath, at the places where it had been strained. Was it ochre?—said the world—or red lead?

Schooled thus in manners, literature, and general moral principles at Chelsea and Wapping, we have finally to inquire concerning the most important point of all. We have seen the principal differences between this boy and Giorgione, as respects sight of the beautiful, understanding of poverty, of commerce, and of order of battle; then follows another cause of difference in our training—not slight,—the aspect of religion, namely, in the neighbourhood of Covent Garden. I say the aspect; for that was all the lad could judge by, disposed, for the most part, to learn chiefly by his eyes, in this special matter he finds there is really no other way of learning. His father taught him 'to lay one penny upon another.' Of mother's teaching, we hear of none; of parish pastoral teaching, the reader may guess how much.

I chose Giorgione rather than Veronese to help me in carrying out this parallel, because I do not find in Giorgione's work any of the early Venetian monarchist element. He seems to me to have belonged more to an abstract contemplative school. I may be wrong in this; it is no matter;—suppose it were so, and that he came down to Venice somewhat recusant or insentient, concerning the usual priestly doctrines of his day, how would the Venetian religion, from an outer intellectual standing-point, have *looked* to him?

He would have seen it to be a religion indisputably powerful in human affairs; often very harmfully so; sometimes devouring widows' houses, and consuming the strongest and fairest from among the young: freezing into merciless bigotry the policy of the old: also, on the other hand, animating national courage, and raising souls, otherwise sordid, into heroism: on the whole, always a real and great power; served with daily sacrifice of gold, time, and thought; putting forth its claims, if hypocritically, at least in bold hypocrisy, not waiving any atom of them in doubt or fear; and, assuredly, in large measure, sincere, believing in itself, and believed: a goodly system, moreover, in aspect; gorgeous, harmonious, mysterious;—a thing which had either to be obeyed or combated, but could not be scorned. A religion towering over all the city—many-buttressed—luminous in marble stateliness, as the dome of our Lady of Safety shines over the sea; many-voiced, also, giving, over all the eastern seas, to the sentinel his watch-word, to the soldier his war-cry; and, on the lips of all who died for Venice, shaping the whisper of death.

I suppose the boy Turner to have regarded the religion of his city also from an external intellectual standing-point.

What did he see in Maiden Lane?

Let not the reader be offended with me: I am willing to let him describe, at his own pleasure, what Turner saw there; but to me, it seems to have been this. A religion maintained occasionally, even the whole length of the lane, at point of constable's staff; but, at other times, placed under the custody of the beadle, within certain black and unstately iron railings of St. Paul's Covent Garden. Among the wheelbarrows and over the vegetables, no perceptible dominance of religion; in the narrow, disquieted streets, none; in the tongues, deeds, daily ways of Maiden Lane, little. Some honesty, indeed, and English industry, and kindness of heart, and general idea of justice; but faith, of any national kind, shut up from one Sunday to the next, not artistically beautiful even in those Sabbatical exhibitions; its paraphernalia being chiefly, of high pews, heavy elocution, and cold grimness of behaviour.

What chiaroscuro belongs to it—(dependent mostly on candlelight),—we will, however, draw, considerately; no goodliness of escutcheon, nor other respectability being omitted, and the best of their results confessed, a meek old woman and a child being let into a pew, for whom the reading by candlelight will be beneficial.

For the rest, this religion seems to him discreditable—discredited—not believing in itself: putting forth its authority in a cowardly way, watching how far it might be tolerated, continually shrinking, disclaiming, fencing, finessing; divided against itself, not by stormy rents, but by thin fissures, and splittings of plaster from the walls. Not to be either obeyed, or combated, by an ignorant, yet clear-sighted youth! only to be scorned. And scorned not one whit the less, though also the dome dedicated to *it* looms high over distant winding of the Thames; as St. Mark's campanile rose, for goodly land-mark, over mirage of lagoon. For St. Mark ruled over life; the Saint of London over death; St. Mark over St. Mark's Place, but St. Paul over St. Paul's Churchyard.

Under these influences pass away the first reflective hours of life, with such conclusion as they can reach. In consequence of a fit of illness, he was taken—I cannot ascertain in what year—to live with an aunt, at Brentford; and here, I believe, received some schooling, which he seems to have snatched vigorously; getting knowledge, at least by translation, of the more picturesque classical authors, which he turned presently to use, as we shall see. Hence also, walks about Putney and Twickenham in the summer time acquainted him with the look of English meadow-ground in its restricted states of paddock and park; and with some round-headed appearances of trees, and stately entrances to houses of mark: the avenue at

Bushey, and the iron gates and carved pillars of Hampton, impressing him apparently with great awe and admiration; so that in after-life his little country house is,—of all places in the world,—at Twickenham! Of swans and reedy shores he now learns the soft motion and the green mystery, in a way not to be forgotten.

And at last fortune wills that the lad's true life shall begin; and one summer's evening, after various wonderful stage-coach experiences on the north road, which gave him a love of stage-coaches ever after, he finds himself sitting alone among the Yorkshire hills. For the first time, the silence of Nature round him, her freedom sealed to him, her glory opened to him. Peace at last; no roll of cart-wheel, nor mutter of sullen voices in the back shop; but curlew-cry in space of heaven, and welling of bell-toned streamlet by its shadowy rock. Freedom at last. Dead-wall, dark railing, fenced field, gated garden, all passed away like the dream of a prisoner; and behold, far as foot or eye can race or range, the moor, and cloud. Loveliness at last. It is here then, among these deserted vales! Not among men. Those pale, poverty-struck, or cruel faces;—that multitudinous, marred humanity—are not the only things that God has made. Here is something He has made which no one has marred. Pride of purple rocks and river pools of blue, and tender wilderness of glittering trees, and misty lights of evening on immeasurable hills.

Beauty, and freedom, and peace; and yet another teacher, graver than these. Sound preaching at last here, in Kirkstall crypt, concerning fate and life. Here, where the dark pool reflects the chancel pillars, and the cattle lie in unhindered rest, the soft sunshine on their dappled bodies, instead of priests' vestments; their white furry hair ruffled a little, fitfully, by the evening wind deep-scented from the meadow thyme.

Consider deeply the import to him of this, his first sight of ruin, and compare it with the effect of the architecture that was around Giorgione. There were indeed aged buildings, at Venice, in his time, but none in decay. All ruin was removed, and its place filled as quickly as in our London; but filled always by architecture loftier, and more wonderful than that whose place it took, the boy himself happy to work upon the walls of it; so that the idea of the passing away of the strength of men and beauty of their works never could occur to him sternly. Brighter and brighter the cities of Italy had been rising and broadening on hill and plain, for three hundred years. He saw only strength and immortality, could not but paint both; conceived the form of man as deathless, calm with power, and fiery with life.

Turner saw the exact reverse of this. In the present work of men, meanness, aimlessness, unsightliness: thin-walled, lath-divided, narrow-garreted houses of clay; booths of a darksome Vanity Fair, busily base.

But on Whitby Hill, and by Bolton Brook, remained traces of other handiwork. Men who could build had been there; and who also had wrought, not merely for their own days. But to what purpose? Strong faith, and steady hands, and patient souls—can this, then, be all you have left? this the sum of your doing on the earth;—a nest whence the night-owl may whimper to the brook, and a ribbed skeleton of consumed arches, looming above the bleak banks of mist, from its cliff to the sea?

As the strength of men to Giorgione, to Turner their weakness and vileness, were alone visible. They themselves, unworthily or ephemeral; their work, despicable, or decayed. In the Venetian's eyes, all beauty depended on man's presence and pride; in Turner's, on the solitude he had left, and the humiliation he had suffered.

And thus the fate and issue of all his work were determined at once. He must be a painter of the strength of nature, there was no beauty elsewhere than in that; he must paint also the labour and sorrow and passing away of men: this was the great human truth visible to him.

Their labour, their sorrow, and their death. Mark the three. Labour; by sea and land, in field and city, at forge and furnace, helm and plough. No pastoral indolence nor classic pride shall stand between him and the troubling of the world; still less between him and the toil of his country,—blind, tormented, unwearied, marvellous England.

Also their Sorrow; Ruin of all their glorious work, passing away of their thoughts and their honour, mirage of pleasure, FALLACY OF HOPE; gathering of weed on temple step; gaining of wave on deserted strand; weeping of the mother for the children, desolate by her breathless first-born in the streets of the city, desolate by her last sons slain, among the beasts of the field.

And their Death. That old Greek question again;—yet unanswered. The unconquerable spectre still flitting among the forest trees at twilight; rising ribbed out of the sea-sand;—white, a strange Aphrodite,—out of the sea-foam; stretching its gray, cloven wings among the clouds; turning the light of their sunsets into blood. This has to be looked

273

upon, and in a more terrible shape than ever Salvator or Dürer saw it. The wreck of one guilty country does not infer the ruin of all countries, and need not cause general terror respecting the laws of the universe. Neither did the orderly and narrow succession of domestic joy and sorrow in a small German community bring the question in its breadth, or in any unresolvable shape, before the mind of Dürer. But the English death—the European death of the nineteenth century—was of another range and power; more terrible a thousand-fold in its merely physical grasp and grief; more terrible, incalculably, in its mystery and shame. What were the robber's casual pang, or the range of the flying skirmish, compared to the work of the axe, and the sword, and the famine, which was done during this man's youth on all the hills and plains of the Christian earth, from Moscow to Gibraltar? He was eighteen years old when Napoleon came down on Arcola. Look on the map of Europe and count the blood-stains on it, between Arcola and Waterloo.

Not alone those blood-stains on the Alpine snow and the blue of the Lombard plain. The English death was before his eyes also. No decent, calculable, consoled dying; no passing to rest like that of the aged burghers of Nuremberg town. No gentle processions to churchyards among the fields, the bronze crests bossed deep on the memorial tablets, and the skylark singing above them from among the corn. But the life trampled out in the slime of the street, crushed to dust amidst the roaring of the wheel, tossed countlessly away into howling winter wind along five hundred leagues of rock-fanged shore. Or, worst of all, rotted down to forgotten graves through years of ignorant patience, and vain seeking for help from man, for hope in God—infirm, imperfect yearning, as of motherless infants starving at the dawn; oppressed royalties of captive thought, vague ague-fits of bleak, amazed despair.

A goodly landscape this, for the lad to paint, and under a goodly light. Wide enough the light was, and clear; no more Salvator's lurid chasm on jagged horizon, nor Dürer's spotted rest of sunny gleam on hedgerow and field; but light over all the world. Full shone now its awful globe, one pallid charnel-house,—a ball strewn bright with human ashes, glaring in poised sway beneath the sun, all blinding-white with death from pole to pole,—death, not of myriads of poor bodies only, but of will, and mercy, and conscience; death, not once inflicted on the flesh, but daily fastening on the spirit; death, not silent or patient, waiting his appointed hour, but voiceful, venomous; death with the taunting word, and burning grasp, and infixed sting.

'Put ye in the sickle, for the harvest is ripe.' The word is spoken in our ears continually to other reapers than the angels,—to the busy skeletons that never tire for stooping. When the measure of iniquity is full, and it seems that another day might bring repentance and redemption,— 'Put ye in the sickle.' When the young life has been wasted all away, and the eyes are just opening upon the tracks of ruin, and faint resolution rising in the heart for nobler things,—'Put ye in the sickle.' When the roughest blows of fortune have been borne long and bravely, and the hand is just stretched to grasp its goal,—'Put ye in the sickle.' And when there are but a few in the midst of a nation, to save it, or to teach, or to cherish; and all its life is bound up in those few golden ears,—'Put ye in the sickle, pale reapers, and pour hemlock for your feast of harvest home.'

This was the sight which opened on the young eyes, this the watchword sounding within the heart of Turner in his youth.

So taught, and prepared for his life's labour, sate the boy at last alone among his fair English hills; and began to paint, with cautious toil, the rocks, and fields, and trickling brooks, and soft white clouds of heaven.

Modern Painters, Vol. V, Part 9, Ch. 9

Observe first that a great painter must necessarily be a man of strong and perfect physical constitution. He must be intensely sensitive, active, and vigorous in all powers whatever; gifted especially with a redundant nervous energy, able to sustain his eye and hand in unbroken continuousness of perception and effort. I do not stay to prove this. It will be found a fact by those who care to enquire into the matter. And this being so, your great painter can only under the most extraordinary circumstances be liable to fits of physical exhaustion or depression, and assuredly he is never liable to any morbid conditions of either; he may be healthily tired when he has worked hard, and will be all right again after he has rationally rested; he may be profoundly vexed, or thrown into fierce passion, but he will never mistake his own vexation for a gloomy state of the universe, nor expect to find consolation or calm by any supernatural help; he will set himself to forget his vexation, and conquer his passion, as small irksome pieces of entirely his own business, precisely in the way he would set himself to mend a hole in his canvas, or cool a pan of dangerously hot varnish. Farther, he is gifted by his exquisite sensibility with continual power of pleasure in eye, ear, and fancy; and his business consists, one half of it, in the pursuit of that pleasure, and the other half in the pursuit of facts, which pursuit is another kind of pleasure, as great, and besides sharp and refreshing when the other is at all deadened by repetition.

Farther, it not only is his business to seek this pleasure, but he has no trouble in seeking it, it is everywhere ready to his hand, as ever fruit was in Paradise. Nothing exists in the world about him that is not beautiful in his eyes, in one degree or another; so far as not beautiful it is serviceable to set off beauty; nothing can possibly present itself to him that is not either lovely, or tractable, and shapeable into loveliness; there is no Evil in his eyes;—only Good, and that which displays good. Light is lovely to him; but not a whit more precious than shadow—white is pleasant to him, as it is to you and me; but he differs from you and me in having no less delight in black, when black is where black should be. Graceful and soft forms are indeed a luxury to him; but he would not thank you for them unless you allowed him also rugged ones. Feasting is consolatory to his system, as to yours and mine, but he differs from us in feeling also an exquisite complacency in Fasting, and taking infinite satisfaction in Emptiness. You can excite his intense gratitude by the gift of Anything, and if you have Nothing to give him, you will find that Nothing is exactly the thing he most wants, and that he will immediately proceed to make half a picture out of it. How can you make such a man as this Discontented with the world? There are Three colours in it—he wants no fourth—finds three quite as much as he can manage. There's good firm ground to set easels on in it—he is not sure that they would stand so firm upon clouds, or that he could paint flying. But the world is a passing, dreamy, visionary state of things! Do you then want them to be always the same—how could one vary one's picture if that were so? But people lose their beauty and get old in the world! Then they have long beards, nothing can be more picturesque. But people die out of the world! How else would there be room for the Children in it, and how could one paint without children? But how unhappy people are in the world. It must be their own fault surely, I'm not. But how thin and ugly their grief makes them—don't you mourn for the departure of the bloom of youth? Not at all—like painting thin people as well as fat ones—one can see their skulls better. But how wicked people are in the world! is it not dreadful to see such wickedness? Not at all—it varies the expression of their faces; there would be no pleasure in painting if they all looked alike. . . .

What can be done with such a man? How are you to make him care about future things? Even if misfortunes fall upon him, such as would make other people religious, he will not seek for consolation in Heaven. He will seek it in his painting-room. So long as he can paint, nothing will crush him. Nothing short of blindness—nothing, that is, but his ceasing to be a painter, will enable him to contemplate futurity.

Nay;—it may be replied—may he not be led, without suffering, but in his own work and his own way to that happy religion which you have admitted to be possible, in which this world may be enjoyed without forgetting the next? No; by no manner of means—at least of means hitherto brought to bear in this world's history. As far as we have seen, hitherto, all happy religious life has consisted in the fulfilment of direct social duty—in pure and calm domestic relations—in active charity, or in simply useful occupations, trades, husbandry, such as leave the mind free to dwell on matters connected with the spiritual life. You may have religious shepherds, labourers, farmers, merchants, shopmen, manufacturers—and Religious painters, so far as they make themselves manufacturers—so far as they remain painters—no.

For consider the first business of a painter; half, as I said, of his business in this world must consist in simply seeking his own pleasure, and that, in the main, a sensual pleasure. I don't mean a degrading one, but a bodily not a spiritual pleasure. Seeing a fine red, or a beautiful line is a bodily and selfish pleasure, at least as compared with Gratitude or Love—or the other feelings called into play by social action. And moreover, this bodily pleasure must be sought for Itself and Himself. Not for anybody else's sake. Unless a painter works wholly to please himself, he will please nobody;—he must not be thinking while he is at work of any human creature's likings, but his own. He must not benevolently desire to please any more than ambitiously—neither in kindness, nor in pride, may he defer to other people's sensations. "I alone here, on my inch of earth, paint this thing for my own sole joy, and according to my own sole mind. So I should paint it, if no other human being existed but myself. Let who will get good or ill from this—I am not concerned therewith. Thus

277

I must do it, for thus I see it, and thus I like it, woe be to me if I paint as other people see or like.' This is the first law of the painter's being; ruthless and selfish—cutting him entirely away from all love of his fellow-creatures, till the work is done. When done he may open the door to them, saying calmly 'If you like this—well, I am glad. If you like it not, away with you, I've nothing for you." No great exertion of benevolence, even in this. But farther. In order to the pursuit of this beauty rightly, our great painter must not shrink in a timid way from any form of vice or ugliness. He must know them to the full, or he cannot understand the relations of beauty and virtue to them. . . .

And this being so, as the great painter is not allowed to be indignant or exclusive, it is not possible for him to nourish his (so called) spiritual desires, as it is to an ordinarily virtuous person. Your ordinarily good man absolutely avoids, either for fear of getting harm, or because he has no pleasure in such places or people, all scenes that foster vice, and all companies that delight in it. He spends his summer evenings on his own quiet lawn, listening to the blackbirds or singing hymns with his children. But you can't learn to paint of blackbirds, nor by singing hymns. You must be in the wildness of the midnight masque—in the misery of the dark street at dawn—in the crowd when it rages fiercest against law—in the council-chamber when it devises worst [   ] against the people—on the moor with the wanderer, or the robber—in the boudoir with the delicate recklessness of female guilt—and all this, without being angry at any of these things—without ever losing your temper so much as to make your hand shake, or getting so much of the mist of sorrow in your eyes, as will at all interfere with your matching of colours; never even allowing yourself to disapprove of anything that anybody enjoys, so far as not to enter into their enjoyment. Does a man get drunk, you must be ready to pledge him. Is he preparing to cut purses—you must go to Gadshill with him—nothing doubting—no wise thinking yourself bound to play the Justice, yet always cool yourself as you either look on, or take any necessary part in the play. Cool, and strong-willed—moveless in observant soul. Does a man die at your feet—your business is not to help him, but to note the colour of his lips; does a woman embrace her destruction before you, your business is not to save her, but to watch how she bends her arms. Not a specially religious or spiritual business this, it might appear.

And then, lastly. Not only is your painter thus concerned wholly and indiscriminately with the affairs of this world, but the mechanism of his own business is one which must occupy nearly all the thoughts of his leisure or seclusion. Whatever time others give to meditation, or other beneficial mental exercise, he must give to mere practice of touch, and study of hue. Painting cannot be learned in any other way. So many hours a day of steady practice—all your mind and nervous energy put into it—or no good painting. No genius will exempt you from this law of toil; a painter's genius especially signifies the love of beauty which will never let him rest in the effort to realize it. A man of science may, if he choose, rest content at any moment with the knowledge he has attained, for however much more he learns, he will be as far from knowing All, as ever he was; but to a painter, absolute perfectness of skill is an approachable, though not an attainable goal: every hour that he gives to his work, brings him nearer a conceivable faculty of laying on the exact colour he wants in the exact shape he wants; he feels himself every day able to do more and more as he would; and though he knows he can never be absolutely perfect, any more than a continually enlarging circle can become an infinite straight line, still, the straight line is before his eyes, and forces him for ever to strive to reach it more and more nearly. This continual mechanical toil, this fixed physical aim, occupies his intellect and energy at every spare moment—blunts his sorrows, restrains his enthusiasms, limits his speculations, takes away all common chances of his being affected by the feelings or imaginations which lead other men to religion.

Modern Painters, Vol. II, Appendix II

Unto This Last
(1860)

Essay I

The Roots of Honour

Among the delusions which at different periods have possessed themselves of the minds of large masses of the human race, perhaps the most curious—certainly the least creditable—is the modern *soi-disant* science of political economy, based on the idea that an advantageous code of social action may be determined irrespectively of the influence of social affection.

Of course, as in the instances of alchemy, astrology, witchcraft, and other such popular creeds, political economy has a plausible idea at the root of it. 'The social affections,' says the economist, 'are accidental and disturbing elements in human nature; but avarice and the desire of progress are constant elements. Let us eliminate the inconstants, and, considering the human being merely as a covetous machine, examine by what laws of labour, purchase, and sale, the greatest accumulative result in wealth is obtainable. Those laws once determined, it will be for each individual afterwards to introduce as much of the disturbing affectionate element as he chooses, and to determine for himself the result on the new conditions supposed.'

This would be a perfectly logical and successful method of analysis, if the accidentals afterwards to be introduced were of the same nature as the powers first examined. Supposing a body in motion to be influenced by constant and inconstant forces, it is usually the simplest way of examining its course to trace it first under the persistent conditions, and afterwards introduce the causes of variation. But the disturbing elements in the social problem are not of the same nature as the constant ones: they alter the essence of the creature under examination the moment they are added; they operate, not mathematically, but chemically, introducing conditions which render all our previous knowledge unavailable. We made learned experiments upon pure nitrogen, and have convinced ourselves that it is a very manageable gas: but, behold! the thing which we have practically to deal with is its chloride; and this, the moment we touch it on our established principles, sends us and our apparatus through the ceiling.

Observe, I neither impugn nor doubt the conclusion of the science if its terms are accepted. I am simply uninterested in them, as I should be in those of a science of gymnastics which assumed that men had no skeletons. It might be shown, on that supposition, that it would be advantageous to roll the students up into pellets, flatten them into cakes, or stretch them into cables; and that when these results were effected, the re-insertion of the skeleton would be attended with various inconveniences to their constitution. The reasoning might be admirable, the conclusions true, and the science deficient only in applicability. Modern political economy stands on a precisely similar basis. Assuming, not that the human being has no skeleton, but that it is all skeleton, it founds an ossifiant theory of progress on this negation of a soul; and having shown the utmost that may be made of bones, and constructed a number of interesting geometrical figures with death's-head and humeri, successfully proves the inconvenience of the reappearance of a soul among these corpuscular structures. I do not deny the truth of this theory: I simply deny its applicability to the present phase of the world.

This inapplicability has been curiously manifested during the embarrassment caused by the late strikes of our workmen. Here occurs one of the simplest cases, in a pertinent and positive form, of the first vital problem which political economy has to deal with (the relation between employer and employed); and, at a severe crisis, when lives in multitudes and wealth in masses are at stake, the political economists are helpless—practically mute: no demonstrable solution of the difficulty can be given by them, such as may convince or calm the opposing parties. Obstinately the masters take one view of the matter; obstinately the operatives another; and no political science can set them at one.

It would be strange if it could, it being not by "science" of any kind that men were ever intended to be set at one.

Disputant after disputant vainly strives to show that the interests of the masters are, or are not, antagonistic to those of the men: none of the pleaders ever seeming to remember that it does not absolutely or always follow that the persons must be antagonistic because their interests are. If there is only a crust of bread in the house, and mother and children are starving, their interests are not the same. If the mother eats it, the children want it; if the children eat it, the mother must go hungry to her work. Yet it does not necessarily follow that there will be "antagonism" between them, that they will fight for the crust, and that the mother, being the strongest, will get it, and eat it. Neither, in any other case, whatever the relations of the persons may be, can it be assumed for certain that, because their interests are diverse, they must necessarily regard each other with hostility, and use violence or cunning to obtain the advantage.

Even if this were so, and it were as just as it is convenient to consider men as actuated by no other moral influences than those which affect rats or swine, the logical conditions of the question are still indeterminable. It can never be shown generally either that the interests of master and labourer are alike, or that they are opposed; for, according to circumstances, they may be either. It is, indeed, always the interest of both that the work should be rightly done, and a just price obtained for it; but, in the division of profits, the gain of one may or may not be the loss of the other. It is not the master's interest to pay wages so low as to leave the men sickly and depressed, nor the workman's interest to be paid high wages if the smallness of the master's profit hinders him from enlarging his business, or conducting it in a sage and liberal way. A stoker ought not to desire high pay if the company is too poor to keep the engine-wheels in repair.

And the varieties of circumstances which influence these reciprocal interests are so endless, that all endeavour to deduce rules of action from balance of expediency is in vain. And it is meant to be in vain. For no human actions ever were intended by the Maker of men to be guided by balances of expediency, but by balances of justice. He has therefore rendered all endeavours to determine expediency futile for evermore. No man ever knew, or can know, what will be the ultimate result to himself, or to others, of any given line of conduct. But every man may know, and most of us do know, what is a just and unjust act. And all of us may know also, that the consequences of justice will be ultimately the best possible, both to others and ourselves, though we can neither say what *is* best, nor how it is likely to come to pass.

I have said balances of justice, meaning, in the term justice to include affection—such affection as one man *owes* to another. All right relations between master and operative, and all their best interests, ultimately depend on these.

We shall find the best and simplest illustration of the relations of master and operative in the position of domestic servants.

We will suppose that the master of a household desires only to get as much work out of his servants as he can, at the rate of wages he gives. He never allows them to be idle; feeds them as poorly and lodges them as ill as they will endure; and in all things pushes his requirements to the exact point beyond which he cannot go without forcing the servant to leave him. In doing this, there is no violation on his part of what is commonly called "justice." He agrees with the domestic for his whole time and service, and takes them—the limits of hardship in treatment being fixed by the practice of other masters in his neighbourhood; that is to say, by the current rate of wages for domestic labour. If the servant can get a better place, he is free to take one, and the master can only tell what is the real market value of his labour, by requiring as much as he will give.

This is the politico-economical view of the case, according to the doctors of that science; who assert by this procedure the greatest average of work will be obtained from the servant and therefore the greatest benefit to the community and through the community, by reversion, to the servant himself.

That, however, is not so. It would be so if the servant were an engine of which the motive power was steam, magnetism, gravitation, or any other agent of calculable force. But he being, on the contrary, an engine whose motive power is a Soul, the force of this very peculiar agent, as an unknown quantity, enters into all the political economists' equations without his knowledge, and falsifies every one of their results. The largest quantity of work will not be done by this curious engine for pay, or under pressure, or by help of any kind of fuel which may be supplied by the chaldron. It will be done only when the motive force, that is to say, the will or spirit of creature, is brought to its greatest strength by its own proper fuel: namely, by the affections.

It may indeed happen, and does happen often, that if

283

the master is a man of sense and energy, a large quantity of material work may be done under mechanical pressure, enforced by strong will and guided by wise method; also it may happen, and does happen often, that if the master is indolent and weak (however good-natured), a very small quantity of work and that bad, may be produced by the servant's undirected strength, and contemptuous gratitude. But the universal law of the matter is that, assuming any given quantity of energy and sense in master and servant, the greatest material result obtainable by them will be, not through antagonism to each other, but through affection for each other; and that, if the master, instead of endeavouring to get as much work as possible from the servant, seeks rather to render his appointed and necessary work beneficial to him, and to forward his interests in all just and wholesome ways, the real amount of work ultimately done, or of good rendered, by the person so cared for, will indeed be the greatest possible.

Observe, I say, "of good rendered," for a servant's work is not necessarily or always the best thing he can give his master. But good of all kinds, whether in material service, in protective watchfulness of his master's interest and credit, or in joyful readiness to seize unexpected and irregular occasions of help.

Nor is this one whit less generally true because indulgence will be frequently abused, and kindness met with ingratitude. For the servant, who gently treated, is ungrateful, treated ungently, will be revengeful; and the man who is dishonest to a liberal master will be injurious to an unjust one.

In any case, and with any person, this unselfish treatment will produce the most effective return. Observe, I am here considering the affections wholly as a motive power; not at all as things in themselves desirable or noble, or in any other way abstractedly good. I look at them simply as an anomalous force, rendering every one of the ordinary political economist's calculations nugatory; while, even if he desired to introduce this new element into his estimates, he has no power of dealing with it; for the affections only become a true motive power when they ignore every other motive and condition of political economy. Treat the servant kindly, with the idea of turning his gratitude to account, and you will get, as you deserve, no gratitude, nor any value for your kindness; but treat him kindly without any economical purpose, and all economical purposes will be answered; in this, as in all other

284

matters, whosoever will save his life shall lose it, who so loses it shall find it.

The next clearest and simplest example of relation between master and operative is that which exists between the commander of a regiment and his men.

Supposing the officer only desires to play the rules of discipline so as, with least trouble to himself, to make the regiment most effective, he will not be able, by any rules or administration of rules, on this selfish principle, to develop the full strength of his subordinates. If a man of sense and firmness, he may, as in the former instance, produce a better result than would be obtained by the irregular kindness of a weak officer; but let the sense and firmness be the same in both cases, and assuredly the officer who has the most direct personal relations with his men, the most care for their interests, and the most value for their lives, will develop their effective strength, through their affection for his own person, and trust in his character, to a degree wholly unattainable by other means. This law applies still more stringently as the numbers concerned are larger: a charge may often be successful, though the men dislike their officers; a battle has rarely been won, unless they loved their general.

Passing from these simple examples to the more complicated relations existing between a manufacturer and his workmen, we are met first by certain curious difficulties, resulting, apparently, from a harder and colder state of moral elements. It is easy to imagine an enthusiastic affection existing among soldiers for the colonel. Not so easy to imagine an enthusiastic affection among cotton-spinners for the proprietor of the mill. A body of men associated for purposes of robbery (as a Highland clan in ancient times) shall be animated by perfect affection, and every member of it be ready to lay down his life for the life of his chief. But a band of men associated for purposes of legal production and accumulation is usually animated, it appears, by no such emotions, and none of them are in any wise willing to give his life for the life of his chief. Not only are we met by this apparent anomaly, in moral matters, but by others connected with it, in administration of system. For a servant or a soldier is engaged at a definite rate of wages, for a definite period; but a workman at a rate of wages variable according to the demand for labour, and with the risk of being at any time thrown out of his situation by chances of trade. Now, as under these contingencies, no action of the affections can take place, but only an explosive action of *dis*affections, two points offer themselves for consideration in the matter.

The first—How far the rate of wages may be so regulated as not to vary with the demand for labour.

The second—How far it is possible that bodies of workmen may be engaged and maintained at such fixed rates of wages (whatever the state of trade may be), without enlarging or diminishing their number, so as to give them permanent interest in the establishment with which they are connected, like that of the domestic servants in an old family, or an *esprit de corps,* like that of the soldiers in a crack regiment.

The first question is, I say, how far it may be possible to fix the rate of wages, irrespectively of the demand for labour.

Perhaps one of the most curious facts in the history of human error is the denial by the common political economist of the possibility of thus regulating wages; while, for all the important, and much of the unimportant, labour, on the earth, wages are already so regulated.

We do not sell our prime-ministership by Dutch auction; nor, on the decease of a bishop, whatever may be the general advantages of simony, do we (yet) offer his diocese to the clergyman who will take the episcopacy at the lowest contract. We (with exquisite sagacity of political economy!) do indeed sell commissions; but not openly, generalships: sick, we do not inquire for a physician who takes less than a guinea; litigious, we never think of reducing six-and-eightpence to four-and-sixpence; caught in a shower, we do not canvass the cabmen, to find one who values his driving at less than sixpence a mile.

It is true that in all these cases there is, and in every conceivable case there must be, ultimate reference to the presumed difficulty of the work, or number of candidates for the office. If it were thought that the labour necessary to make a good physician would be gone through by a sufficient number of students with the prospect of only half-guinea fees, public consent would soon withdraw the unnecessary half-guinea. In this ultimate sense, the price of labour is indeed always regulated by the demand for it; but, so far as the practical and immediate administration of the matter is regarded, the best labour always has been, and is, as *all* labour ought to be, paid by an invariable standard.

"What!" the reader perhaps answers amazedly: "pay good and bad workmen alike?"

Certainly. The difference between one prelate's sermons

and his successor's—or between one physician's opinion and another's—is far greater, as respects the qualities of mind involved, and far more important in result to you personally, than the difference between good and bad laying of bricks (though that is greater than most people suppose). Yet you pay with equal fee, contentedly, the good and bad workmen upon your soul, and the good and bad workmen upon your body; much more may you pay, contentedly, with equal fees, the good and bad workmen upon your house.

"Nay, but I choose my physician, and (?) my clergyman, thus indicating my sense of the quality of their work." By all means, also, choose your bricklayer: that is the proper reward of the good workman, to be "chosen." The natural and right system respecting all labour is, that it should be paid at a fixed rate, but the good workman employed, and the bad workman unemployed. The false, unnatural, and destructive system is when the bad workman is allowed to offer his work at half-price, and either take the place of the good, or force him by his competition to work for an inadequate sum.

This equality of wages, then, being the first object towards which we have to discover the directest available road, the second is, as above stated, that of maintaining constant numbers of workmen in employment, whatever may be the accidental demand for the article they produce.

I believe the sudden and extensive inequalities of demand, which necessarily arise in the mercantile operations of an active nation, constitute the only essential difficulty which has to be overcome in a just organization of labour.

The subject opens into too many branches to admit of being investigated in a paper of this kind; but the following general facts bearing on it may be noted.

The wages which enable any workman to live are necessarily higher, if his work is liable to intermission, than if it is assured and continuous; and however severe the struggle for work may become, the general law will always hold, that men must get more daily pay if, on the average, they can only calculate on work three days a week than they would require if they were sure of work six days a week. Supposing that a man cannot live on less than a shilling a day, his seven shillings he must get, either for three days' violent work, or six days' deliberate work. The tendency of all modern mercantile operations is to throw both wages and trade into the form of a lottery, and to make the workman's pay depend on intermittent exertion, and the principal's profit on dexterously used chance.

In what partial degree, I repeat, this may be necessary in consequence of the activities of modern trade, I do not here investigate; contenting myself with the fact that in its fatallest aspects it is assuredly unnecessary, and results merely from love of gambling on the part of the masters, and from ignorance and sensuality in the men. The masters cannot bear to let any opportunity of gain escape them, and frantically rush at every gap and breach in the walls of Fortune, raging to be rich, and affronting, with impatient covetousness, every risk of ruin, while the men prefer three days of violent labour, and three days of drunkenness, to six days of moderate work and wise rest. There is no way in which a principal, who really desires to help his workmen, may do it more effectually than by checking these disorderly habits both in himself and them; keeping his own business operations on a scale which will enable him to pursue them securely; not yielding to temptations of precarious gain; and at the same time, leading his workmen into regular habits of labour and life, either by inducing them rather to take low wages, in the form of a fixed salary, than high wages, subject to the chance of their being thrown out of work; or, if this be impossible, by discouraging the system of violent exertion for nominally high day wages, and leading the men to take lower pay for more regular labour.

In effecting any radical changes of this kind, doubtless there would be great inconvenience and loss incurred by all the originators of the movement. That which can be done with perfect convenience and without loss, is not always the thing that most needs to be done, or which we are most imperatively required to do.

I have already alluded to the difference hitherto existing between regiments of men associated for purposes of violence, and for purposes of manufacture; in that the former appear capable of self-sacrifice—the latter, not; which singular fact is the real reason of the general lowness of estimate in which the profession of commerce is held, as compared with that of arms. Philosophically, it does not, at first sight, appear reasonable (many writers have endeavoured to prove it unreasonable) that a peaceable and rational person, whose trade is buying and selling, should be held in less honour than an unpeaceable and often irrational person, whose trade is slaying. Nevertheless, the consent of mankind has always, in spite of the philosophers, given precedence to the soldier.

And this is right.

For the soldier's trade, verily and essentially, is not slaying, but being slain. This, without well knowing its own meaning, the world honours it for. A bravo's trade is slaying; but the world has never respected bravos more than merchants: the reason it honours the soldier is, because he holds his life at the service of the State. Reckless he may be—fond of pleasure or of adventure— all kinds of by-motives and mean impulses may have determined the choice of his profession, and may affect (to all appearance exclusively) his daily conduct in it; but our estimate of him is based on this ultimate fact—of which we are well assured—that put him in a fortress breach, with all the pleasures of the world behind him, he will keep his face to the front; and he knows that his choice may be put to him at any moment—and has beforehand taken his part—virtually takes such part continually—does, in reality, die daily.

Not less is the respect we pay to the lawyer and physician, founded ultimately on their self-sacrifice. Whatever the learning or acuteness of a great lawyer, our chief respect for him depends on our belief that, set in a judge's seat, he will strive to judge justly, come of it what may. Could we suppose that he would take bribes, and use his acuteness and legal knowledge to give plausibility to iniquitous decisions, no degree of intellect would win for him our respect. Nothing will win it, short of our tacit conviction, that in all important acts of his life justice is first with him; his own interest second.

In the case of a physician, the ground of the honour we render him is clearer still. Whatever his science, we would shrink from him in horror if we found him regard his patients merely as subjects to experiment upon; much more, if we found that, receiving bribes from persons interested in their deaths, he was using his best skill to give poison in the mask of medicine.

Finally, the principle holds with utmost clearness as it respects clergymen. No goodness of disposition will excuse want of science in a physician, or of shrewdness in an advocate; but a clergyman, even though his power of intellect be small, is respected on the presumed ground of his unselfishness and serviceableness.

Now there can be no question but that the tact, foresight, decision, and other mental powers, required for the successful management of a large mercantile concern, if not such as could be compared with those of a great lawyer, general, or divine, would at least match the general conditions of mind required in the subordinate officers of a ship, or of a regiment, or in the curate of a country parish. If, therefore, all the efficient members of the so-called liberal professions are still, somehow, in public estimate of honour, preferred before the head of a commercial firm, the reason must lie deeper than in the measurement of their several powers of mind.

And the essential reason for such preference will be found to lie in the fact that the merchant is presumed to act always selfishly. His work may be very necessary to the community; but the motive of it is understood to be wholly personal. The merchant's first object in all his dealings must be (the public believe) to get as much for himself, and leave as little to his neighbour (or customer) as possible. Enforcing this upon him, by political statute, as the necessary principle of his action; recommending it to him on all occasions, and themselves reciprocally adopting it, proclaiming vociferously, for law of the universe, that a buyer's function is to cheapen, and a seller's to cheat—the public, nevertheless, involuntarily condemn the man of commerce for his compliance with their own statement, and stamp him for ever as belonging to an inferior grade of human personality.

This they will find, eventually, they must give up doing. They must not cease to condemn selfishness; but they will have to discover a kind of commerce which is not exclusively selfish. Or, rather, they will have to discover that there never was, or can be, any other kind of commerce; that this which they have called commerce was not commerce at all, but cozening; and that a true merchant differs as much from a merchant according to laws of modern political economy, as the hero of the "Excursion" from Autolycus. They will find that commerce is an occupation which gentlemen will every day see more need to engage in, rather than in the businesses of talking to men, or slaying them; that, in true commerce, as in true preaching, or true fighting, it is necessary to admit the idea of occasional voluntary loss; that sixpences have to be lost, as well as lives, under a sense of duty; that the market may have its martyrdoms as well as the pulpit; and trade its heroisms as well as war.

May have—in the final issue, must have—and only has not had yet, because men of heroic temper have always been misguided in their youth into other fields; not recognizing what is in our days, perhaps, the most important of all fields; so that, while many a zealous person loses his life in trying to teach the form of a gospel, very few will lose a hundred pounds in showing the practice of one.

The fact is, that people never have had clearly explained to them the true functions of a merchant with respect to other people. I should like the reader to be very clear about this.

Five great intellectual professions, relating to daily necessities of life, have hitherto existed—three exist necessarily, in every civilized nation.

The Soldier's profession is to *defend* it.

The Pastor's to *teach* it.

The Physician's to *keep it in health*.

The Lawyer's to *enforce justice* in it.

The Merchant's to *provide* for it.

And the duty of all these men is, on due occasion, to *die* for it.

'On due occasion,' namely:—

The Soldier, rather than leave his post in battle.

The Physician, rather than leave his post in plague.

The Pastor, rather than teach Falsehood.

The Lawyer, rather than countenance Injustice.

The Merchant—what is *his* "due occasion" of death?

It is the main question for the merchant, as for all of us. For, truly, the man who does not know when to die, does not know how to live.

Observe, the merchant's function (or manufacturer's, for in the broad sense in which it is here used the word must be understood to include both) is to provide for the nation. It is no more his function to get profit for himself out of that provision than it is a clergyman's function to get his stipend. This stipend is a due and necessary adjunct, but not the object of his life, if he be a true clergyman, any more than his fee (or honorarium) is the object of life to a true physician. Neither is his fee the object of life to a true merchant. All three, if true men, have a work to be done irrespective of fee—to be done even at any cost, or for quite the contrary of fee; the pastor's function being to teach, the physician's to heal, and the merchant's, as I have said, to provide. That is to say, he has to understand to their very root the qualities of the thing he deals in, and the means of obtaining or producing it; and he has to apply all his sagacity and energy to the producing or obtaining it in perfect state, and distributing it at the cheapest possible price where it is most needed.

And because the production or obtaining of any commodity involves necessarily the agency of many lives and hands, the merchant becomes in the course of his business the master and governor of large masses of men in a more direct, though less confessed way, than a military officer or pastor; so that on him falls, in great part, the responsibility for the kind of life they lead; and it becomes his duty, not only to be always considering how to produce what he sells, in the purest and cheapest forms, but how to make the various employments involved in the production, or transference of it, most beneficial to the men employed.

And as into these two functions, requiring for their right exercise the highest intelligence, as well as patience, kindness and tact, the merchant is bound to put all his energy, so for their just discharge he is bound, as soldier or physician is bound, to give up, if need be, his life, in such way as it may be demanded of him. Two main points he has in his providing function to maintain: first, his engagements (faithfulness to engagements being the real root of all possibilities, in commerce); and, secondly, the perfectness and purity of the thing provided; so that, rather than fail in any engagement, or consent to any deterioration, adulteration, or unjust and exorbitant price of that which he provides, he is bound to meet fearlessly any form of distress, poverty, or labour, which may, through maintenance of these points, come upon him.

Again: in his office as governor of the men employed by him, the merchant or manufacturer is invested with a distinctly paternal authority and responsibility. In most cases, a youth entering a commercial establishment is withdrawn altogether from home influence; his master must become his father, else he has, for practical and constant help, no father at hand: in all cases the master's authority, together with the general tone and atmosphere of his business, and the character of the men with whom the youth is compelled in the course of it to associate, have more immediate and pressing weight than the home influence, and will usually neutralize it either for good or evil; so that the only means which the master has of doing justice to the men employed by him is to ask himself sternly whether he is dealing with such subordinate as he would with his own son, if compelled by circumstances to take such a position.

Supposing the captain of a frigate saw it right, or were by any chance obliged, to place his own son in the position of a common sailor: as he would then treat his son, he is bound always to treat every one of the men under him. So, also, supposing the master of a manufactory saw it right, or were by any chance obliged, to place his own son in the position of an ordinary workman; as he would then treat his son, he is bound always to treat every one of his men. This is the only effective, true, or practical RULE which can be given on this point of political economy.

And as the captain of a ship is bound to be the last man to leave his ship in case of wreck, and to share his last crust with the sailors in case of famine, so the manufacturer, in any commercial crisis or distress, is bound to take the suffering of it with his men, and even to take more of it for himself than he allows his men to feel; as a father would in a famine, or battle, sacrifice himself for his son.

All which sounds very strange: the only real strangeness in the matter being, nevertheless, that it should so sound. For all that is true, and that not partially nor theoretically, but everlastingly and practically: all other doctrine than this respecting matters political being false in premises, absurd in deduction, and impossible in practice, consistently with any progressive state of national life; all the life which we now possess as a nation showing itself in the resolute denial and scorn, by a few strong minds and faithful hearts, of the economic principles taught to our multitudes, which principles, so far as accepted, lead straight to national destruction. Respecting the modes and forms of destruction to which they lead, and, on the other hand, respecting the further practical working of true polity, I hope to reason further in a following paper.

The Crown of Wild Olive
(1866)

Lecture **ii**

Traffic

(Delivered in the Town Hall, Bradford, April 21, 1864)

My good Yorkshire friends, you asked me down here among your hills that I might talk to you about this Exchange you are going to build: but, earnestly and seriously asking you to pardon me, I am going to do nothing of the kind. I cannot talk, or at least can say very little, about this same Exchange. I must talk of quite other things, though not willingly;—I could not deserve your pardon, if, when you invited me to speak on one subject, I *wilfully* spoke on another. But I cannot speak, to purpose, of anything about which I do not care; and most simply and sorrowfully I have to tell you, in the outset, that I do *not* care about this Exchange of yours.

If, however, when you sent me your invitation, I had answered, "I won't come, I don't care about the Exchange of Bradford," you would have been justly offended with me, not knowing the reasons of so blunt a carelessness. So I have come down, hoping that you will patiently let me tell you why, on this, and many other such occasions, I now remain silent, when formerly I should have caught at the opportunity of speaking to a gracious audience.

In a word, then, I do not care about this Exchange— because *you* don't; and because you know perfectly well I cannot make you. Look at the essential conditions of the case, which you, as business men, know perfectly well, though perhaps you think I forget them. You are going to spend £30,000, which to you, collectively, is nothing; the buying a new coat is, as to the cost of it, a much more important matter of consideration to me, than building a new Exchange is to you. But you think you may as well have the right thing for your money. You know there are a great many odd styles of architecture about; you don't want to do anything ridiculous; you hear of me, among others, as a respectable architectural man-milliner; and you send for me, that I may tell you the leading fashion; and what is, in our shops, for the moment, the newest and sweetest thing in pinnacles.

Now, pardon me for telling you frankly, you cannot have good architecture merely by asking people's advice on occasion. All good architecture is the expression of national life and character; and it is produced by a prevalent and eager national taste, or desire for beauty. And I want you to think a little of the deep significance of this word "taste"; for no statement of mine has been more earnestly or oftener controverted than that good taste is essentially a moral quality. "No," say many of my antagonists, "taste is one thing, morality is another. Tell us what is pretty: we shall be glad to know that; but we need no sermons—even were you able to preach them, which may be doubted."

Permit me, therefore, to fortify this old dogma of mine somewhat. Taste is not only a part and an index of morality;—it is the ONLY morality. The first, and last, and closest trial question to any living creature is, "What do you like?" Tell me what you like, and I'll tell you what you are. Go out into the street, and ask the first man or woman you meet, what their "taste" is; and if they answer candidly, you know them, body and soul. "You, my friend in the rags, with the unsteady gait, what do *you* like?" "A pipe, and a quartern of gin." I know you. "You, good woman, with the quick step and tidy bonnet, what do you like?" "A swept hearth, and a clean tea-table; and my husband opposite me, and a baby at my breast." Good, I know you also. "You, little girl with the golden hair and the soft eyes, what do you like?" "My canary, and a run among the wood hyacinths." "You, little boy with the dirty hands, and the low forehead, what do you like?" "A shy at the sparrows, and a game at pitch farthing." Good; we know them all now. What more need we ask?

"Nay," perhaps you answer; "we need rather to ask what these people and children do, than what they like. If they *do* right, it is no matter that they like what is wrong; and if they *do* wrong, it is no matter that they like what is right. Doing is the great thing; and it does not matter that the man likes drinking, so that he does not drink; nor that the little girl likes to be kind to her canary, if she will not learn her lessons, nor that the little boy likes throwing stones at the sparrows, if he goes to the Sunday school."

295

Indeed, for a short time, and in a provisional sense, this is true. For if, resolutely, people do what is right, in time to come they like doing it. But they only are in a right moral state when they *have* come to like doing it; and as long as they don't like it, they are still in a vicious state. The man is not in health of body who is always thinking of the bottle in the cupboard, though he bravely bears his thirst; but the man who heartily enjoys water in the morning, and wine in the evening, each in its proper quantity and time. And the entire object of true education is to make people not merely *do* the right things, but *enjoy* the right things:— not merely industrious, but to love industry—not merely learned, but to love knowledge—not merely pure, but to love purity—not merely just, but to hunger and thirst after justice.

But you may answer or think, "Is the liking for outside ornaments,—for pictures, or statues, or furniture, or architecture, a moral quality?" Yes, most surely, if a rightly set liking. Taste for *any* pictures or statues is not a moral quality, but taste for good ones is. Only here again we have to define the word "good." I don't mean by "good," clever—or learned—or difficult in the doing. Take a picture by Teniers, of sots quarrelling over their dice; it is an entirely clever picture; so clever that nothing in its kind has ever been done equal to it; but it is also an entirely base and evil picture. It is an expression of delight in the prolonged contemplation of a vile thing, and delight in that is an "unmannered," or "immoral" quality. It is "bad taste" in the profoundest sense—it is the taste of the devils. On the other hand, a picture of Titian's, or a Greek statue, or a Greek coin, or a Turner landscape, expresses delight in the perpetual contemplation of a good and perfect thing. That is an entirely moral quality—it is the taste of the angels. And all delight in fine art, and all love of it, resolve themselves into simple love of that which deserves love. That deserving is the quality which we call "loveliness"—(we ought to have an opposite word, hateliness, to be said of the things which deserve to be hated); and it is not an indifferent nor optional thing whether we love this or that; but it is just the vital function of all our being. What we *like* determines what we *are*, and is the sign of what we are; and to teach taste is inevitably to form character.

As I was thinking over this, in walking up Fleet Street the other day, my eye caught the title of a book standing open in a bookseller's window. It was—"On the necessity of the diffusion of taste among all classes." "Ah," I thought to myself, "my classifying friend, when you have diffused your taste, where will your classes be? The man who likes what you like, belongs to the same class with you, I think. Inevitably so. You may put him to other work if you choose; but, by the condition you have brought him into, he will dislike the work as much as you would yourself. You get hold of a scavenger or a coster-monger, who enjoyed the Newgate Calendar for litera-ture, and 'Pop goes the Weasel' for music. You think you can make him like Dante and Beethoven? I wish you joy of your lessons; but if you do, you have made a gentleman of him:—he won't like to go back to his costermonger-ing."

And so completely and unexceptionally is this so, that, if I had time to-night, I could show you that a nation cannot be affected by any vice, or weakness, without expressing it, legibly, and for ever, either in bad art, or by want of art; and that there is no national virtue, small or great, which is not manifestly expressed in all the art which circumstances enable the people possessing that virtue to produce. Take, for instance, your great English virtue of enduring and patient courage. You have at present in England only one art of any consequence—that is, iron-working. You know thoroughly well how to cast and hammer iron. Now, do you think, in those masses of lava which you build volcanic cones to melt, and which you forge at the mouths of the Infernos you have created; do you think, on those iron plates, your courage and endurance are not written for ever,—not merely with an iron pen, but on iron parchment? And take also your great English vice—European vice—vice of all the world—vice of all other worlds that roll or shine in heaven, bearing with them yet the atmosphere of hell—the vice of jealousy, which brings competition into your commerce, treachery into your councils, and dishonour into your wars—that vice which has rendered for you, and for your next neighbouring nation, the daily occupations of exis-tence no longer possible, but with the mail upon your breasts and the sword loose in its sheath; so that at last, you have realised for all the multitudes of the two great peoples who lead the so-called civilization of the earth,—you have realised for them all, I say, in person and in policy, what was once true only of the rough Border riders of your Cheviot hills—

"They carved at the meal
With gloves of steel,

And they drank the red wine through the helmet barr'd;"—

do you think that this national shame and dastardliness of heart are not written as legibly on every rivet of your iron armour as the strength of the right hands that forged it?

Friends, I know not whether this thing be the more ludicrous or the more melancholy. It is quite unspeakably both. Suppose, instead of being now sent for by you, I had been sent for by some private gentleman, living in a suburban house, with his garden separated only by a fruit wall from his next door neighbour's; and he had called me to consult with him on the furnishing of his drawing-room. I begin looking about me, and find the walls rather bare; I think such and such a paper might be desirable—perhaps a little fresco here and there on the ceiling—a damask curtain or so at the windows. "Ah," says my employer, "damask curtains, indeed! That's all very fine, but you know I can't afford that kind of thing just now!" "Yet the world credits you with a splendid income!" "Ah, yes," says my friend, "but do you know, at present I am obliged to spend it nearly all in steel-traps?" "Steel-traps! for whom?" "Why, for that fellow on the other side the wall, you know: we're very good friends, capital friends; but we are obliged to keep our traps set on both sides of the wall; we could not possibly keep on friendly terms without them, and our spring guns. The worst of it is, we are both clever fellows enough; and there's never a day passes that we don't find out a new trap, or a new gun-barrel, or something; we spend about fifteen millions a year each in our traps, take it altogether; and I don't see how we're to do with less." A highly comic state of life for two private gentlemen! but for two nations, it seems to me, not wholly comic. Bedlam would be comic, perhaps, if there were only one madman in it; and your Christmas pantomime is comic, when there is only one clown in it; but when the whole world turns clown, and paints itself red with its own heart's blood instead of vermilion, it is something else than comic, I think.

Mind, I know a great deal of this is play, and willingly allow for that. You don't know what to do with yourselves for a sensation: fox-hunting and cricketing will not carry you through the whole of this unendurably long mortal life: you liked pop-guns when you were schoolboys, and rifles and Armstrongs are only the same things better made: but then the worst of it is, that what was play to you when boys, was not play to the sparrows; and what is play to you now, is not play to the small birds of State neither; and for the black eagles, you are somewhat shy of taking shots at them, if I mistake not.

I must get back to the matter in hand, however. Believe me, without farther instance, I could show you, in all time, that every nation's vice, or virtue, was written in its art: the soldiership of early Greece; the sensuality of late Italy; the visionary religion of Tuscany; the splendid human energy of Venice. I have no time to do this to-night (I have done it elsewhere before now); but I proceed to apply the principle to ourselves in a more searching manner.

I notice that among all the new buildings which cover your once wild hills, churches and schools are mixed in due, that is to say, in large proportion, with your mills and mansions; and I notice also that the churches and schools are almost always Gothic, and the mansions and mills are never Gothic. May I ask the meaning of this? for, remember, it is peculiarly a modern phenomenon. When Gothic was invented, houses were Gothic as well as churches; and when the Italian style superseded the Gothic, churches were Italian as well as houses. If there is a Gothic spire to the cathedral of Antwerp, there is a Gothic belfry to the Hôtel de Ville at Brussels; if Inigo Jones builds an Italian Whitehall, Sir Christopher Wren builds an Italian St. Paul's. But now you live under one school of architecture, and worship under another. What do you mean by doing this? Am I to understand that you are thinking of changing your architecture back to Gothic; and that you treat your churches experimentally, because it does not matter what mistakes you make in a church? Or am I to understand that you consider Gothic a pre-eminently sacred and beautiful mode of building, which you think, like the fine frankincense, should be mixed for the tabernacle only, and reserved for your religious service? For if this be the feeling, though it may seem at first as if it were graceful and reverent, at the root of the matter, it signifies neither more nor less than that you have separated your religion from your life.

For consider what a wide significance this fact has; and remember that it is not you only, but all the people of England, who are behaving thus, just now.

You have all got into the habit of calling the church "the house of God." I have seen, over the doors of many churches, the legend actually carved, "*This* is the house of God and this is the gate of heaven." Now, note where that legend comes from, and of what place it was first spoken. A boy leaves his father's house to go on a long journey on foot, to visit his uncle: he has to cross a wild hill-desert; just as if one of your own boys had to cross the wilds to visit an uncle at Carlisle. The second or third day your boy finds himself somewhere between Hawes and Brough, in the midst of the moors, at sunset. It is stony ground, and boggy; he cannot go one foot farther that night. Down he lies, to sleep, on Wharnside, where best he may, gathering a few of the stones together to put under his head;—so wild the place is, he cannot get anything but stones. And there, lying under the broad night, he has a dream; and he sees a ladder set up on the earth, and the top of it reaches to heaven, and the angels of God are seen ascending and descending upon it. And when he wakes out of his sleep, he says, "How dreadful is this place; surely this is none other than the house of God, and this is the gate of heaven." This PLACE, observe; not this church; not this city; not this stone, even, which he puts up for a memorial—the piece of flint on which his head was lain. But this *place;* this windy slope of Wharnside; this moorland hollow, torrent-bitten, snow-blighted! this *any* place where God lets down the ladder. And how are you to know where that will be? or how are you to determine where it may be, but by being ready for it always? Do you know where the lightning is to fall next? You *do* know that, partly; you can guide the lightning; but you cannot guide the going forth of the Spirit, which is as that lightning when it shines from the east to the west.

But the perpetual and insolent warping of that strong verse to serve a merely ecclesiastical purpose, is only one of the thousand instances in which we sink back into gross Judaism. We call our churches "temples." Now, you know perfectly well they are *not* temples. They have never had, never can have, anything whatever to do with temples. They are "synagogues"—"gathering places"—where you gather yourselves together as an assembly; and by not calling them so, you again miss the force of another mighty text—"Thou, when thou prayest, shalt not be as the hypocrites are; for they love to pray standing in the *churches"* [we should translate it], "that they may be seen of men. But thou, when thou prayest, enter into thy closet, and when thou hast shut thy door, pray to thy Father,"—which is, not in chancel nor in aisle, but "in secret."

Now, you feel, as I say this to you—I know you feel—as if I were trying to take away the honour of your churches. Not so; I am trying to prove to you the honour of your houses and your hills; not that the Church is not sacred—but that the whole Earth is. I would have you feel what careless, what constant, what infectious sin there is in all modes of thought, whereby, in calling your churches only "holy," you call your hearths and homes "profane"; and have separated yourselves from the heathen by casting all your household gods to the ground, instead of recognizing, in the places of their many and feeble Lares, the presence of your One and Mighty Lord and Lar.

"But what has all this to do with our Exchange?" you ask me, impatiently. My dear friends, it has just everything to do with it; on these inner and great questions depend all the outer and little ones; and if you have asked me down here to speak to you, because you had before been interested in anything I have written, you must know that all I have yet said about architecture was to show this. The book I called *The Seven Lamps* was to show that certain right states of temper and moral feeling were the magic powers by which all good architecture, without exception, had been produced. *The Stones of Venice* had, from beginning to end, no other aim than to show that the Gothic architecture of Venice had arisen out of, and indicated in all its features, a state of pure national faith, and of domestic virtue; and that its Renaissance architecture had arisen out of, and in all its features indicated, a state of concealed national infidelity, and of domestic corruption. And now, you ask me what style is best to build in, and how can I answer, knowing the meaning of the two styles, but by another question—do you mean to build as Christians or as infidels? And still more—do you mean to build as honest Christians or as honest Infidels? as thoroughly and confessedly either one or the other? You don't like to be asked such rude questions. I cannot help it; they are of much more importance than this Exchange business; and if they can be at once answered, the Exchange business settles itself in a moment. But before I press them farther, I must ask leave to explain one point clearly.

In all my past work, my endeavour has been to show that good architecture is essentially religious—the production of a faithful and virtuous, not of an infidel and corrupted people. But in the course of doing this, I have had also to show that good architecture is not *ecclesiastical*. People are so apt to look upon religion as the business of the clergy, not their own, that the moment they hear of anything depending on "religion," they think it must also have depended on the priesthood; and I have had to take what place was to be occupied between these two errors, and fight both, often with seeming contradiction. Good architecture is the work of good and believing men; therefore, you say, at least some people say, "Good architecture must essentially have been the work of the clergy, not of the laity." No—a thousand times no; good architecture has always been the work of the commonalty, *not* of the clergy. "What," you say, "those glorious cathedrals—the pride of Europe—did their builders not form Gothic architecture?" No; they corrupted Gothic architecture. Gothic was formed in the baron's castle, and the burgher's street. It was formed by the thoughts, and hands, and powers of labouring citizens and warrior kings. By the monk it was used as an instrument for the aid of his superstition: when that superstition became a beautiful madness, and the best hearts of Europe vainly dreamed and pined in the cloister, and vainly raged and perished in the crusade,—through that fury of perverted faith and wasted war, the Gothic rose also to its loveliest, most fantastic, and, finally, most foolish dreams; and in those dreams was lost.

I hope, now, that there is no risk of your misunderstanding me when I come to the gist of what I want to say to-night;—when I repeat, that every great national architecture has been the result and exponent of a great national religion. You can't have bits of it here, bits there—you must have it everywhere or nowhere. It is not the monopoly of a clerical company—it is not the exponent of a theological dogma—it is not the hieroglyphic writing of an initiated priesthood; it is the manly language of a people inspired by resolute and common purpose, and rendering resolute and common fidelity to the legible laws of an undoubted God.

Now there have as yet been three distinct schools of European architecture. I say, European, because Asiatic and African architectures belong so entirely to other races and climates, that there is no question of them here; only, in passing, I will simply assure you that whatever is good or great in Egypt, and Syria, and India, is just good or great for the same reasons as the buildings on our side of the Bosphorus. We Europeans, then, have had three great religions: the Greek, which was the worship of the God of Wisdom and Power; the Mediæval, which was the worship of the God of Judgment and Consolation; the Renaissance, which was the worship of the God of Pride and Beauty: these three we have had—they are past,—and now, at last, we English have got a fourth religion, and a God of our own, about which I want to ask you. But I must explain these three old ones first.

I repeat, first, the Greeks essentially worshipped the God of Wisdom; so that whatever contended against their religion,—to the Jews a stumbling-block,—was, to the Greeks—*Foolishness*.

The first Greek idea of deity was that expressed in the word, of which we keep the remnant in our words "*Di*-urnal" and "*Di*-vine"—the god of *Day*, Jupiter and revealer. Athena is his daughter, but especially daughter of the Intellect, springing armed from the head. We are only with the help of recent investigation beginning to penetrate the depth of meaning couched under the Athenaic symbols: but I may note rapidly, that her ægis, the mantle with the serpent fringes, in which she often, in the best statues, is represented as folding up her left hand, for better guard; and the Gorgon, on her shield, are both representative mainly of the chilling horror and sadness (turning men to stone, as it were,) of the outmost and superficial spheres of knowledge—that knowledge which separates, in bitterness, hardness, and sorrow, the heart of the full-grown man from the heart of the child. For out of imperfect knowledge spring terror, dissension, danger, and disdain; but from perfect knowledge, given by the full-revealed Athena, strength and peace, in sign of which she is crowned with the olive spray, and bears the resistless spear.

This, then, was the Greek conception of purest Deity; and every habit of life, and every form of his art developed themselves from the seeking this bright, serene, resistless wisdom; and setting himself, as a man, to do things evermore rightly and strongly; not with any ardent affection or ultimate hope; but with a resolute and continent energy of will, as knowing that for failure there was no consolation, and for sin there was no remission. And the Greek architecture rose unerring, bright, clearly defined, and self-contained.

Next followed in Europe the great Christian faith, which was essentially the religion of Comfort. Its great doctrine is the remission of sins; for which cause, it happens, too often, in certain phases of Christianity, that sin and sickness themselves are partly glorified, as if, the more you had to be healed of, the more divine was the healing. The practical result of this doctrine, in art, is a continual contemplation of sin and disease, and of imaginary states of purification from them; thus we have an architecture conceived in a mingled sentiment of melancholy and aspiration, partly severe, partly luxuriant, which will bend itself to every one of our needs, and every one

of our fancies, and be strong or weak with us, as we are
strong or weak ourselves. It is, of all architecture, the
basest, when base people build it—of all, the noblest, when
built by the noble.

And now note that both these religions—Greek and
Mediæval—perished by falsehood in their own main purpose. The Greek religion of Wisdom perished in a false
philosophy—"Oppositions of science, falsely so called."
The Mediæval religion of Consolation perished in false
comfort; in remission of sins given lyingly. It was the
selling of absolution that ended the Mediæval faith; and
I can tell you more, it is the selling of absolution which, to
the end of time, will mark false Christianity. Pure Christianity gives her remission of sins only by *ending* them;
but false Christianity gets her remission of sins by *com-
pounding for* them. And there are many ways of com-
pounding for them. We English have beautiful little quiet
ways of buying absolution, whether in low Church or
high, far more cunning than any of Tetzel's trading.

Then, thirdly, there followed the religion of Pleasure, in
which all Europe gave itself to luxury, ending in death.
First, *bals masqués* in every saloon, and then guillotines
in every square. And all these three worships issue in vast
temple building. Your Greek worshipped Wisdom, and
built you the Parthenon—the Virgin's temple. The Mediæval worshipped Consolation, and built you Virgin temples also—but to our Lady of Salvation. Then the Revival-
ist worshipped beauty, of a sort, and built you Versailles
and the Vatican. Now lastly, will you tell me what *we*
worship, and what *we* build?

You know we are speaking always of the real, active,
continual, national worship; that by which men act, while
they live; not that which they talk of, when they die.
Now, we have, indeed, a nominal religion, to which we
pay tithes of property and sevenths of time; but we have
also a practical and earnest religion, to which we devote
nine-tenths of our property, and six-sevenths of our time.
And we dispute a great deal about the nominal religion:
but we are all unanimous about this practical one; of
which I think you will admit that the ruling goddess may
be best generally described as the "Goddess of Getting-
on," or "Britannia of the Market." The Athenians had an
"Athena Agoraia," or Athena of the Market; but she was
a subordinate type of their goddess, while our Britannia
Agoraia is the principal type of ours. And all your great
architectural works are, of course, built to her. It is long
since you built a great cathedral; and how you would

laugh at me if I proposed building a cathedral on the top of one of these hills of yours, to make it an Acropolis! But your railroad mounds, vaster than the walls of Babylon; your railroad stations, vaster than the temple of Ephesus, and innumerable; your chimneys, how much more mighty and costly than cathedral spires! your harbour-piers; your warehouses; your exchanges!—all these are built to your great Goddess of "Getting-on"; and she has formed, and will continue to form, your architecture, as long as you worship her; and it is quite vain to ask me to tell you how to build to *her;* you know far better than I.

There might, indeed, on some theories, be a conceivably good architecture for Exchanges—that is to say, if there were any heroism in the fact or deed of exchange, which might be typically carved on the outside of your building. For, you know, all beautiful architecture must be adorned with sculpture or painting; and for sculpture or painting, you must have a subject. And hitherto it has been a received opinion among the nations of the world that the only right subjects for either, were *heroisms* of some sort. Even on his pots and his flagons, the Greek put a Hercules slaying lions, or an Apollo slaying serpents, or Bacchus slaying melancholy giants, and earthborn despondencies. On his temples, the Greek put contests of great warriors in founding states, or of gods with evil spirits. On his houses and temples alike, the Christian put carvings of angels conquering devils; or of hero-martyrs exchanging this world for another: subject inappropriate, I think, to our direction of exchange here. And the Master of Christians not only left His followers without any orders as to the sculpture of affairs of exchange on the outside of buildings, but gave some strong evidence of His dislike of affairs of exchange within them. And yet there might surely be a heroism in such affairs; and all commerce become a kind of selling of doves, not impious. The wonder has always been great to me, that heroism has never been supposed to be in anywise consistent with the practice of supplying people with food, or clothes; but rather with that of quartering one's self upon them for food, and stripping them of their clothes. Spoiling of armour is an heroic deed in all ages; but the selling of clothes, old, or new, has never taken any colour of magnanimity. Yet one does not see why feeding the hungry and clothing the naked should ever become base businesses, even when engaged in on a large scale. If one could contrive to attach the notion of conquest to them anyhow! so that, supposing there were anywhere an

305

obstinate race, who refused to be comforted, one might take some pride in giving them compulsory comfort! and, as it were, *"occupying* a country" with one's gifts, instead of one's armies? If one could only consider it as much a victory to get a barren field sown, as to get an eared field stripped; and contend who should build villages, instead of who should "carry" them! Are not all forms of heroism conceivable in doing these serviceable deeds? You doubt who is strongest? It might be ascertained by push of spade, as well as push of sword. Who is wisest? There are witty things to be thought of in planning other business than campaigns. Who is bravest? There are always the elements to fight with, stronger than men; and nearly as merciless.

The only absolutely and unapproachably heroic element in the soldier's work seems to be—that he is paid little for it—and regularly: while you traffickers, and exchangers, and others occupied in presumably benevolent business, like to be paid much for it—and by chance. I never can make out how it is that a *knight*-errant does not expect to be paid for his trouble, but a *pedlar*-errant always does;— that people are willing to take hard knocks for nothing, but never to sell ribands cheap; that they are ready to go on fervent crusades, to recover the tomb of a buried God, but never on any travels to fulfil the orders of a living one;—that they will go anywhere barefoot to preach their faith, but must be well bribed to practise it, and are perfectly ready to give the Gospel gratis, but never the loaves and fishes.

If you chose to take the matter up on any such soldierly principle; to do your commerce, and your feeding of nations, for fixed salaries; and to be as particular about giving people the best food, and the best cloth, as soldiers are about giving them the best gunpowder, I could carve something for you on your exchange worth looking at. But I can only at present suggest decorating its frieze with pendant purses; and making its pillars broad at the base, for the sticking of bills. And in the innermost chambers of it there might be a statue of Britannia of the Market, who may have, perhaps advisably, a partridge for her crest, typical at once of her courage in fighting for noble ideas, and of her interest in game; and round its neck, the inscription in golden letters, "Perdix fovit quæ non peperit." Then, for her spear, she might have a weaver's beam; and on her shield, instead of St. George's Cross, the Milanese boar, semi-fleeced, with the town of Gennesaret proper, in the field; and the legend, "In the best market," and her corselet, of leather, folded over her heart in the shape of a purse, with thirty slits in it, for a piece of money to go in it, on each day of the month. And I doubt not but that people would come to see your exchange, and its goddess, with applause.

Nevertheless, I want to point out to you certain strange characters in this goddess of yours. She differs from the great Greek and Mediæval deities essentially in two things—first, as to the continuance of her presumed power; secondly, as to the extent of it.

1st, as to the Continuance.

The Greek Goddess of Wisdom gave continual increase of wisdom, as the Christian Spirit of Comfort (or Comforter) continual increase of comfort. There was no question, with these, of any limit or cessation of function. But with your Agora Goddess, that is just the most important question. Getting on—but where to? Gathering together—but how much? Do you mean to gather always—never to spend? If so, I wish you joy of your goddess, for I am just as well off as you, without the trouble of worshipping her at all. But if you do not spend, somebody else will—somebody else must. And it is because of this (among many other such errors) that I have fearlessly declared your so-called science of Political Economy to be no science; because, namely, it has omitted the study of exactly the most important branch of the business—the study of *spending*. For spend you must, and as much as you make, ultimately. You gather corn:—will you bury England under a heap of grain; or will you, when you have gathered, finally eat? You gather gold:—will you make your house-roofs of it, or pave your streets with it? That is still one way of spending it. But if you keep it, that you may get more, I'll give you more; I'll give you all the gold you want—all you can imagine—if you can tell me what you'll do with it. You shall have thousands of gold pieces;—thousands of thousands—millions—mountains, of gold: where will you keep them? Will you put an Olympus of silver upon a golden Pelion—make Ossa like a wart? Do you think the rain and dew would then come down to you, in the streams from such mountains, more blessedly than they will down the mountains which God has made for you, of moss and whinstone? But it is not gold that you want to gather! What is it? greenbacks? No; not those neither. What is it then—is it ciphers after a capital I? Cannot you practise writing ciphers, and write as many as you want! Write ciphers for an hour every morning, in a big book, and say every evening, I am worth all those noughts more than I was yesterday. Won't that do? Well, what in the name of Plutus is it you want? Not gold, not greenbacks, not ciphers after a capital I? You will have to answer, after all, "No; we want, somehow or other, money's *worth*." Well, what is that? Let your Goddess of Getting-on discover it, and let her learn to stay therein.

II. But there is yet another question to be asked respecting this Goddess of Getting-on. The first was of the continuance of her power; the second is of its extent.

Pallas and the Madonna were supposed to be all the world's Pallas, and all the world's Madonna. They could teach all men, and they could comfort all men. But, look strictly into the nature of the power of your Goddess of Getting on; and you will find she is the Goddess—not of everybody's getting on—but only of somebody's getting on. This is a vital, or rather deathful, distinction. Examine it in your own ideal of the state of national life which this Goddess is to evoke and maintain. I asked you what it was, when I was last here;—you have never told me. Now, shall I try to tell you?

Your ideal of human life then is, I think, that it should be passed in a pleasant undulating world, with iron and coal everywhere underneath it. On each pleasant bank of this world is to be a beautiful mansion, with two wings; and stables, and coach-houses; a moderately-sized park; a large garden and hot-houses; and pleasant carriage drives through the shrubberies. In this mansion are to live the favoured votaries of the Goddess; the English gentleman, with his gracious wife, and his beautiful family; he always able to have the boudoir and the jewels for the wife, and the beautiful ball dresses for the daughters, and hunters for the sons, and a shooting in the Highlands for himself. At the bottom of the bank, is to be the mill; not less than a quarter of a mile long, with one steam engine at each end, and two in the middle, and a chimney three hundred feet high. In this mill are to be in constant employment from eight hundred to a thousand workers, who never drink, never strike, always go to church on Sunday, and always express themselves in respectful language.

Is not that, broadly, and in the main features, the kind of thing you propose to yourselves? It is very pretty indeed, seen from above; not at all so pretty, seen from below. For, observe, while to one family this deity is indeed the Goddess of Getting-on, to a thousand families she is the Goddess of *not* Getting-on. "Nay," you say, "they have all their chance." Yes, so has every one in a lottery, but there must always be the same number of blanks. "Ah! but in a lottery it is not skill and intelligence which take the lead, but blind chance." What then! do you think the old practice, that "they should take who have the power, and they should keep who can," is less iniquitous, when the power has become power of brains instead of fist? and that, though we may not take advantage of a child's or a woman's weakness, we may of a man's foolishness? "Nay, but finally, work must be done, and some one must be at the top, some one at the bottom." Granted, my friends. Work must always be, and captains of work must always be; and if you in the least remember the tone of any of my writings, you must know that they are thought unfit for this age, because they are always insisting on need of government, and speaking with scorn of liberty. But I beg you to observe that there is a wide difference between being captains or governors of work, and taking the profits of it. It does not follow, because you are general of an army, that you are to take all the treasure, or land, it wins; (if it fight for treasure or land;) neither, because you are king of a nation, that you are to consume all the profits of the nation's work. Real kings, on the contrary, are known invariably by their doing quite the reverse of this,—by their taking the least possible quantity of the nation's work for themselves. There is no test of real kinghood so infallible as that. Does the crowned creature live simply, bravely, unostentatiously? probably he *is* a King. Does he cover his body with jewels, and his table with delicates? in all probability he is *not* a King. It is possible he may be, as Solomon was; but that is when the nation shares his splendour with him. Solomon made gold, not only to be in his own palace as stones, but to be in Jerusalem as stones. But, even so, for the most part, these splendid kinghoods expire in ruin, and only the true kinghoods live, which are of royal labourers governing loyal labourers; who, both leading rough lives, establish the true dynasties. Conclusively you will find that because you are king of a nation, it does not follow that you are to gather for yourself all the wealth of that nation; neither, because you are king of a small part of the nation, and lord over the means of its maintenance— over field, or mill, or mine,—are you to take all the produce of that piece of the foundation of national existence for yourself.

You will tell me I need not preach against these things, for I cannot mend them. No, good friends, I cannot; but you can, and you will; or something else can and will. Even good things have no abiding power—and shall these evil things persist in victorious evil? All history shows, on the contrary, that to be the exact thing they never can do. Change *must* come; but it is ours to determine whether change of growth, or change of death. Shall the Parthenon be in ruins on its rock, and Bolton priory in its meadow, but these mills of yours be the consummation of the buildings of the earth, and their wheels be as the wheels of eternity? Think you that "men may come, and men may go," but—mills—go on for ever? Not so; out of these, better or worse shall come; and it is for you to choose which.

I know that none of this wrong is done with deliberate purpose. I know, on the contrary, that you wish your workmen well; that you do much for them, and that you desire to do more for them, if you saw your way to such benevolence safely. I know that even all this wrong and misery are brought about by a warped sense of duty, each of you striving to do his best; but, unhappily, not knowing for whom this best should be done. And all our hearts have been betrayed by the plausible impiety of the modern economist, telling us that, "To do the best for ourselves, is finally to do the best for others." Friends, our great Master said not so; and most absolutely we shall find this world is not made so. Indeed, to do the best for others, is finally to do the best for ourselves; but it will not do to have our eyes fixed on that issue. The Pagans had got beyond that. Hear what a Pagan says of this matter; hear what were, perhaps, the last written words of Plato,—if not the last actually written (for this we cannot know), yet assuredly in fact and power his parting words—in which, endeavouring to give full crowning and harmonious close to all his thoughts, and to speak the sum of them by the imagined sentence of the Great Spirit, his strength and his heart fail him, and the words cease, broken off for ever.

They are at the close of the dialogue called *Critias,* in which he describes, partly from real tradition, partly in ideal dream, the early state of Athens; and the genesis, and order, and religion, of the fabled isle of Atlantis; in which genesis he conceives the same first perfection and final degeneracy of man, which in our own Scriptural tradition is expressed by saying that the Sons of God inter-married with the daughters of men, for he supposes the earliest race to have been indeed the children of God; and to have corrupted themselves, until "their spot was not the spot of his children." And this, he says, was the end; that indeed "through many generations, so long as the God's nature in them yet was full, they were submissive to the sacred laws, and carried themselves lovingly to all that had kindred with them in divineness; for their uttermost spirit was faithful and true, and in every wise great; so that, in *all meekness of wisdom, they dealt with each other,* and took all the chances of life; and despising all things except virtue, they cared little what happened day by day, and *bore lightly the burden* of gold and of possessions; for they saw that, if *only their common love and virtue increased, all these things would be increased together with them;* but to set their esteem and ardent pursuit upon material possession would be to lose that first, and their virtue and affection together with it. And by such reasoning, and what of the divine nature remained in them, they gained all this greatness of which we have already told; but when the God's part of them faded and became extinct, being mixed again and again, and effaced by the prevalent mortality; and the human nature at last exceeded, they then became unable to endure the courses of fortune; and fell into shapelessness of life, and baseness in the sight of him who could see, having lost everything that was fairest of their honour; while to the blind hearts which could not discern the true life, tending to happiness, it seemed that they were then chiefly noble and happy, being filled with all iniquity of inordinate possession and power. Whereupon, the God of Gods, whose Kinghood is in laws, beholding a once just nation thus cast into misery, and desiring to lay such punishment upon them as might make them repent into restraining, gathered together all the gods into his dwelling place, which from heaven's centre overlooks whatever has part in creation; and having assembled them, he said"——

The rest is silence. Last words of the chief wisdom of the heathen, spoken of this idol of riches; this idol of yours; this golden image, high by measureless cubits, set up where your green fields of England are furnace-burnt into the likeness of the plain of Dura: this idol, forbidden to us, first of all idols, by our own Master and faith; forbidden to us also by every human lip that has ever, in any age or people, been accounted of as able to speak according to the purposes of God. Continue to make that forbidden deity your principal one, and soon no more art, no more science, no more pleasure will be possible. Catastrophe will come; or, worse than catastrophe, slow mouldering and withering into Hades. But if you can fix some conception of a true human state of life to be striven for—life, good for all men, as for yourselves; if you can determine some honest and simple order of existence;

following those trodden ways of wisdom, which are pleasantness, and seeking her quiet and withdrawn paths, which are peace;—then, and so sanctifying wealth into "commonwealth," all your art, your literature, your daily labours, your domestic affection, and citizen's duty, will join and increase into one magnificent harmony. You will know then how to build, well enough; you will build with stone well, but with flesh better; temples not made with hands, but riveted of hearts; and that kind of marble, crimson-veined, is indeed eternal.

Time and Tide
(1867)

Letter iii

> *Of True Legislation.—That every Man*
> *may be a Law to himself.*
> *(February 17, 1867)*

No, I have not been much worse in health; but I was
asked by a friend to look over some work in which you
will all be deeply interested one day, so that I could not
write again till now. I was the more sorry, because there
were several things I wished to note in your last letter;
one especially leads me directly to what I in any case was
desirous of urging upon you. You say, "In vol. 6th of
'Frederick the Great' I find a great deal that I feel quite
certain, if our Queen or Government could make law,
thousands of our English workmen would hail with a
shout of joy and gladness." I do not remember to what
you especially allude, but whatever the rules you speak of
may be, unless there be anything in them contrary to the
rights of present English property, why should you care
whether the Government makes them law or not? Can
you not, you thousands of English workmen, simply make
them a law to yourselves, by practising them?

It is now some five or six years since I first had
occasion to speak to the members of the London Working
Men's College on the subject of Reform, and the substance of what I said to them was this: "You are all
agape, my friends, for this mighty privilege of having your
opinions represented in Parliament. The concession might
be desirable,—at all events courteous,—if only it were
quite certain you had got any opinions to represent. But

have you? Are you agreed on any single thing you systematically want? Less work and more wages, of course; but how much lessening of work do you suppose is possible? Do you think the time will ever come for everybody to have *no* work and *all* wages? Or have you yet taken the trouble so much as to think out the nature of the true connection between wages and work, and to determine, even approximately, the real quantity of the one, that can, according to the laws of God and nature, be given for the other; for, rely on it, make what laws you like, that quantity only can you at last get.

"Do you know how many mouths can be fed on an acre of land, or how fast those mouths multiply? and have you considered what is to be done finally with unfeedable mouths? 'Send them to be fed elsewhere,' do you say? Have you, then, formed any opinion as to the time at which emigration should begin, or the countries to which it should preferably take place, or the kind of population which should be left at home? Have you planned the permanent state which you would wish England to hold, emigrating over her edges, like a full well, constantly? How full would you have her be of people, first? and of what sort of people? Do you want her to be nothing but a large workshop and forge, so that the name of 'Englishman' shall be synonymous with 'ironmonger,' all over the world? or would you like to keep some of your lords and landed gentry still, and a few green fields and trees?

"You know well enough that there is not one of these questions, I do not say which you can answer, but which you have ever *thought* of answering; and yet you want to have voices in Parliament! Your voices are not worth a rat's squeak, either in Parliament or out of it, till you have some ideas to utter with them; and when you have the thoughts, you will not want to utter them, for you will see that your way to the fulfilling of them does not lie through speech. You think such matters need debating about? By all means debate about them; but debate among yourselves, and with such honest helpers of your thoughts as you can find; if by that way you cannot get at the truth, do you suppose you could get at it sooner in the House of Commons, where the only aim of many of the members would be to refute every word uttered in your favour; and where the settlement of any question whatever depends merely on the perturbations of the balance of conflicting interests?"

That was, in main particulars, what I then said to the men of the Working Men's College; and in this recurrent agitation about Reform, that is what I would steadfastly say again. Do you think it is only under the lacquered splendours of Westminster,—you working men of England,—that your affairs can be rationally talked over? You have perfect liberty and power to talk over, and establish for yourselves, whatever laws you please; so long as you do not interfere with other people's liberties or properties. Elect a parliament of your own. Choose the best men among you, the best at least you can find, by whatever system of election you think likeliest to secure such desirable result. Invite trustworthy persons of other classes to join your council; appoint time and place for its stated sittings, and let this parliament, chosen after your own hearts, deliberate upon the possible modes of the regulation of industry, and advisablest schemes for helpful discipline of life; and so lay before you the best laws they can devise, which such of you as were wise might submit to, and teach their children to obey. And if any of the laws thus determined appear to be inconsistent with the present circumstances or customs of trade, do not make a noise about them, nor try to enforce them suddenly on others, nor embroider them on flags, nor call meetings in parks about them, in spite of railings and police; but keep them in your thoughts and sights, as objects of patient purpose and future achievement by peaceful strength.

For you need not think that even if you obtained a majority of representatives in the existing parliament, you could immediately compel any system of business, broadly contrary to that now established by custom. If you could pass laws to-morrow, wholly favourable to yourselves, as you might think, because unfavourable to your masters, and to the upper classes of society,—the only result would be that the riches of the country would at once leave it, and you would perish in riot and famine. Be assured that no great change for the better can ever be easily accomplished, or quickly; nor by impulsive, ill-regulated effort, nor by bad men; nor even by good men, without much suffering. The suffering must, indeed, come, one way or another, in all greatly critical periods; the only question, for us, is whether we will reach our ends (if we ever reach them) through a chain of involuntary miseries, many of them useless, and all ignoble; or whether we will know the worst at once, and deal with it by the wisely sharp methods of Godsped courage.

This, I repeat to you, it is wholly in your own power to do, but it is in your power on one condition only, that of steadfast truth to yourselves, and to all men. If there is not, in the sum of it, honesty enough among you to teach you to frame, and strengthen you to obey, *just* laws of trade, there is no hope left for you. No political constitution can ennoble knaves; no privileges can assist them; no possessions enrich them. Their gains are occult curses; comfortless loss their truest blessing; failure and pain Nature's only mercy to them. Look to it, therefore, first, that you get some wholesome honesty for the foundation of all things. Without the resolution in your hearts to do good work, so long as your right hands have motion in them; and to do it whether the issue be that you die or live, no life worthy the name will ever be possible to you, while, in once forming the resolution that your work is to be well done, life is really won, here and for ever. And to make your children capable of such resolution, is the beginning of all true education, of which I have more to say in a future letter.

Letter xiii

The Proper Offices of the Bishop and Duke;
or, "Overseer" and "Leader"
(March 21, 1867)

I see, by your last letter, for which I heartily thank you, that you would not sympathise with me in my sorrow for the desertion of his own work by George Cruikshank, that he may fight in the front of the temperance ranks. But you do not know what work he has left undone, nor how much richer inheritance you might have received from his hand. It was no more *his* business to etch diagrams of drunkenness than it is mine at this moment to be writing these letters against anarchy. It is "the first mild day of March" (high time, I think, that it should be!), and by rights I ought to be out among the budding banks and hedges, outlining sprays of hawthorn and clusters of primrose. That is *my* right work; and it is not, in the inner gist and truth of it, right nor good, for you, or for anybody else, that Cruikshank with his great gift, and I with my weak, but yet thoroughly clear and definite one, should both of us be tormented by agony of indignation and compassion, till we are forced to give up our peace, and pleasure, and power; and rush down into the streets and lanes of the city, to do the little that is in the strength of our single hands against their uncleanliness and iniquity. But, as in a sorely besieged town, every man must to the ramparts, whatsoever business he leaves, so neither he nor I have had any choice but to leave our household stuff, and go on crusade, such as we are called to; not that I mean, if Fate may be anywise resisted, to give up the strength of my life as he has given his; for I think he was wrong in doing so; and that he should only have carried the fiery cross his appointed leagues, and then given it to another hand; and, for my own part, I mean these very letters to close my political work for many a day; and I write them, not in any hope of their being at present listened to, but to disburthen my heart of the witness I have to bear, that I may be free to go back to my garden lawns, and paint birds and flowers there.

For these same statutes which we are to consider to-day, have indeed been in my mind now these fourteen years, ever since I wrote the last volume of the *Stones of Venice*, in which you will find, in the long note on Modern Education, most of what I have been now in detail writing to you, hinted in abstract; and, at the close of it, this sentence, of which I solemnly now avouch (in thankfulness that I was permitted to write it), every word; "Finally, I hold it for indisputable, that the first duty of a State is to see that every child born therein shall be well housed, clothed, fed, and educated, till it attain years of discretion. But in order to the effecting this the Government must have an authority over the people of which we now do not so much as dream."

That authority I did not then endeavour to define, for I knew all such assertions would be useless, and that the necessarily resultant outcry would merely diminish my influence in other directions. But now I do not care about influence any more, it being only my concern to say truly that which I know, and, if it may be, get some quiet life, yet, among the fields in the evening shadow.

There is, I suppose, no word which men are prouder of the right to attach to their names, or more envious of others who bear it, when they themselves may not, than the word "noble." Do you know what it originally meant, and always, in the right use of it, means? It means a "known" person; one who has risen far enough above others to draw men's eyes to him, and to be known (honourably) for such and such an one. "Ignoble," on the other hand, is derived from the same root as the word

317

"ignorance." It means an unknown, inglorious person. And no more singular follies have been committed by weak human creatures than those which have been caused by the instinct, pure and simple, of escaping from this obscurity. Instinct, which, corrupted, will hesitate at no means, good or evil, of satisfying itself with notoriety—instinct, nevertheless, which, like all other natural ones, has a true and pure purpose, and ought always in a worthy way to be satisfied.

All men ought to be in this sense "noble"; known of each other, and desiring to be known. And the first law which a nation, desiring to conquer all the devices of the Father of Lies, should establish among its people, is that they *shall* be known.

Will you please now read § 22 of *Sesame and Lilies?* The reviewers in the ecclesiastical journals laughed at it, as a rhapsody, when the book came out; none having the slightest notion of what I meant: (nor, indeed, do I well see how it could be otherwise!). Nevertheless, I meant precisely and literally what is there said, namely, that a bishop's duty being to watch over the souls of his people, and *give* account of every one of them, it becomes practically necessary for him first to *get* some account of their bodies. Which he was wont to do in the early days of Christianity by help of a person called "deacon" or "ministering servant," whose name is still retained among preliminary ecclesiastical dignities, vainly enough! Putting, however, all question of forms and names aside, the thing actually needing to be done is this—that over every hundred (more or less) of the families composing a Christian State, there should be appointed an overseer, or bishop, to render account, to the State, of the life of every individual in those families; and to have care both of their interest and conduct to such an extent as they may be willing to admit, or as their faults may justify: so that it may be impossible for any person, however humble, to suffer from unknown want, or live in unrecognised crime;—such help and observance being rendered without officiousness either of interference or inquisition (the limits of both being determined by national law), but with the patient and gentle watchfulness which true Christian pastors now exercise over their flocks; only with a higher legal authority presently to be defined, of interference on due occasion.

And with this farther function, that such overseers shall be not only the pastors, but the biographers, of their people; a written statement of the principal events in the life of each family being annually required to be rendered

318

by them to a superior State Officer. These records, laid up in public offices, would soon furnish indications of the families whom it would be advantageous to the nation to advance in position, or distinguish with honour, and aid by such reward as it should be the object of every Government to distribute no less punctually, and far more frankly, than it distributes punishment: (compare *Munera Pulveris*, Essay IV., in paragraph on Critic Law), while the mere fact of permanent record being kept of every event of importance, whether disgraceful or worthy of praise, in each family, would of itself be a deterrent from crime, and a stimulant to well-deserving conduct, far beyond mere punishment or reward.

Nor need you think that there would be anything in such a system un-English, or tending to espionage. No uninvited visits should ever be made in any house, unless law had been violated; nothing recorded, against its will, of any family, but what was inevitably known of its publicly visible conduct, and the results of that conduct. What else was written should be only by the desire, and from the communications, of its head. And in a little while it would come to be felt that the true history of a nation was indeed not of its wars, but of its households; and the desire of men would rather be to obtain some conspicuous place in these honourable annals, than to shrink behind closed shutters from public sight. Until at last, George Herbert's grand word of command would hold not only on the conscience, but the actual system and outer economy of life,

"Think the King sees thee still, for *his* King does."

Secondly, above these bishops or pastors, who are only to be occupied in offices of familiar supervision and help, should be appointed higher officers of State, having executive authority over as large districts as might be conveniently (according to the number and circumstances of their inhabitants) committed to their care; officers who, according to the reports of the pastors, should enforce or mitigate the operation of too rigid general law, and determine measures exceptionally necessary for public advantage. For instance, the general law being that all children of the operative classes, at a certain age, should be sent to public schools, these superior officers should have power, on the report of the pastors, to dispense with the attendance of children who had sick parents to take charge of, or whose home-life seemed to be one of better advantage for them than that of the common schools; or who, for any other like cause, might justifiably claim remission. And it being the general law that the entire body of the public should contribute to the cost, and divide the profits, of all necessary public works and undertakings, as roads, mines, harbour protections, and the like, and that nothing of this kind should be permitted to be in the hands of private speculators, it should be the duty of the district officer to collect whatever information was accessible respecting such sources of public profit; and to represent the circumstances in Parliament: and then, with Parliamentary authority, but on his own sole personal responsibility, to see that such enterprises were conducted honestly, and with due energy and order.

The appointment to both these offices should be by election, and for life; by what forms of election shall be matter of inquiry, after we have determined some others of the necessary constitutional laws.

I do not doubt but that you are already beginning to think it was with good reason I held my peace these fourteen years,—and that, for any good likely to be done by speaking, I might as well have held it altogether!

It may be so: but merely to complete and explain my own work, it is necessary that I should say these things finally; and I believe that the imminent danger to which we are now in England exposed by the gradually accelerated fall of our aristocracy (wholly their own fault), and the substitution of money-power for their martial one; and by the correspondingly imminent prevalence of mob violence here, as in America; together with the continually increasing chances of insane war, founded on popular passion, whether of pride, fear, or acquisitiveness,—all these dangers being further darkened and degraded by the monstrous forms of vice and selfishness which the appliances of recent wealth, and of vulgar mechanical art, make possible to the million,—will soon bring us into a condition in which men will be glad to listen to almost any words but those of a demagogue, and to seek any means of safety rather than those in which they have lately trusted. So, with your good leave, I will say my say to the end, mock at it who may.

P.S.—I take due note of the regulations of trade proposed in your letter just received—all excellent. I shall come to them presently, "Cash payment" above all. You may write that on your trade-banners in letters of gold, wherever you would have them raised victoriously.

Letter xiv

The First Group of Essential Laws—Against Theft by False
Work, and by Bankruptcy.—Necessary
Publicity of Accounts
(March 26, 1867)

I feel much inclined to pause at this point, to answer
the kind of questions and objections which I know must be
rising in your mind, respecting the authority supposed to
be lodged in the persons of the officers just specified. But I
can neither define, nor justify to you, the powers I would
desire to see given to them, till I state to you the kind of
laws they would have to enforce: of which the first group
should be directed to the prevention of all kinds of thieving; but chiefly of the occult and polite methods of it; and,
of all occult methods, chiefly, the making and selling of
bad goods. No form of theft is so criminal as this—none
so deadly to the State. If you break into a man's house
and steal a hundred pounds' worth of plate, he knows his
loss, and there is an end (besides that you take your risk
of punishment for your gain, like a man). And if you do
it bravely and openly, and habitually live by such inroad,
you may retain nearly every moral and manly virtue, and
become a heroic rider and reiver, and hero of song. But if
you swindle me out of twenty shillings' worth of quality
on each of a hundred bargains, I lose my hundred pounds
all the same, and I get a hundred untrustworthy articles
besides, which will fail me and injure me in all manner of
ways, when I least expect it; and you, having done your
thieving basely, are corrupted by the guilt of it to the very
heart's core.

This is the first thing, therefore, which your general
laws must be set to punish, fiercely, immitigably, to the
utter prevention and extinction of it, or there is no hope
for you. No religion that ever was preached on this earth
of God's rounding ever proclaimed any salvation to sellers
of bad goods. If the Ghost that is in you, whatever the
essence of it, leaves your hand a juggler's, and your heart
a cheat's, it is not a Holy Ghost, be assured of that. And
for the rest, all political economy, as well as all higher
virtue, depends *first on sound work*.

Let your laws, then, I say, in the beginning, be set to
secure this. You cannot make punishment too stern for
subtle knavery. Keep no truce with this enemy, whatever

321

pardon you extend to more generous ones. For light weights and false measures, or for proved adulteration or dishonest manufacture of articles, the penalty should be simply confiscation of goods and sending out of the country. The kind of person who desires prosperity by such practices could not be made to "emigrate" too speedily. What to do with him in the place you appointed to be blessed by his presence, we will in time consider.

Under such penalty, however, and yet more under the pressure of such a right public opinion as could pronounce and enforce such penalty, I imagine that sham articles would become speedily as rare as sound ones are now. The chief difficulty in the matter would be to fix your standard. This would have to be done by the guild of every trade in its own manner, and within certain easily recognisable limits, and this fixing of standard would necessitate much simplicity in the forms and kinds of articles sold. You could only warrant a certain kind of glazing or painting in china, a certain quality of leather or cloth, bricks of a certain clay, loaves of a defined mixture of meal. Advisable improvements or varieties in manufacture would have to be examined and accepted by the trade guild: when so accepted, they would be announced in public reports; and all puffery and self-proclamation, on the part of tradesmen, absolutely forbidden, as much as the making of any other kind of noise or disturbance.

But observe, this law is only to have force over tradesmen whom I suppose to have joined voluntarily in carrying out a better system of commerce. Outside of their guild, they would have to leave the rogue to puff and cheat as he chose, and the public to be gulled as they chose. All that is necessary is that the said public should clearly know the shops in which they could get warranted articles; and, as clearly, those in which they bought at their own risk.

And the above-named penalty of confiscation of goods should of course be enforced only against dishonest members of the trade guild. If people chose to buy of those who had openly refused to join an honest society, they should be permitted to do so, at their pleasure, and peril: and this for two reasons,—the first, that it is always necessary, in enacting strict law, to leave some safety valve for outlet of irrepressible vice (nearly all the stern lawgivers of old time erred by oversight in this; so that the morbid elements of the State, which it should be allowed to get rid of in a cutaneous and openly curable manner, were thrown inwards, and corrupted its constitution, and

322

broke all down);—the second, that operations of trade and manufacture conducted under, and guarded by, severe law, ought always to be subject to the stimulus of such erratic external ingenuity as cannot be tested by law, or would be hindered from its full exercise by the dread of it; not to speak of the farther need of extending all possible indulgence to foreign traders who might wish to exercise their industries here without liability to the surveillance of our trade guilds.

Farther, while for all articles warranted by the guild (as above supposed) the prices should be annually fixed for the trade throughout the kingdom; and the producing workman's wages fixed, so as to define the master's profits within limits admitting only such variation as the nature of the given article of sale rendered inevitable; yet, in the production of other classes of articles, whether by skill of applied handicraft, or fineness of material above the standard of the guild, attaining, necessarily, values above its assigned prices, every firm should be left free to make its own independent efforts and arrangements with its workmen, subject always to the same penalty, if it could be proved to have consistently described, or offered, anything to the public for what it was not: and finally, the state of the affairs of every firm should be annually reported to the guild, and its books laid open to inspection, for guidance in the regulation of prices in the subsequent year; and any firm whose liabilities exceeded its assets by a hundred pounds should be forthwith declared bankrupt. And I will anticipate what I have to say in succeeding letters so far as to tell you that I would have this condition extend to every firm in the country, large or small, and of whatever rank in business. And thus you perceive, my friend, I shall not have to trouble you or myself much with deliberations respecting commercial "panics," nor to propose legislative cures for *them*, by any laxatives or purgatives of paper currency, or any other change of pecuniary diet.

English Art
(1870)

... Within certain limits I believe [the efforts to improve the designs of our manufactures] may indeed take effect: so that we may no more humour momentary fashions by ugly results of chance instead of design; and may produce both good tissues, of harmonious colours, and good forms and substance of pottery and glass. But we shall never excel in decorative design. Such design is usually produced by people of great natural powers of mind, who have no variety of subjects to employ themselves on, no oppressive anxieties, and are in circumstances either of natural scenery or of daily life, which cause pleasurable excitement. *We* cannot design, because we have too much to think of, and we think of it too anxiously. It has long been observed how little real anxiety exists in the minds of the partly savage races which excel in decorative art; and we must not suppose that the temper of the Middle Ages was a troubled one, because every day brought its danger or its change. The very eventfulness of the life rendered it careless, as generally is still the case with soldiers and sailors. Now, when there are great powers of thought, and little to think of, all the waste energy and fancy are thrown into the manual work, and you have so much intellect as would direct the affairs of a large mercantile concern for a day, spent all at once, quite unconsciously, in drawing an ingenious spiral.

Also, powers of doing fine ornamental work are only to be reached by a perpetual discipline of the hand as well as of the fancy; discipline as attentive and painful as that which a juggler has to put himself through, to overcome the more palpable difficulties of his profession. The execution of the best artists is always a splendid tour-de-force; and much that in painting is supposed to be dependent on material is indeed only a lovely and quite inimitable legerdemain. Now, when powers of fancy, stimulated by this triumphant precision of manual dexterity, descend uninterruptedly from generation to generation, you have at last, what is not so much a trained artist, as a new species of animal, with whose instinctive gifts you have no chance of contending. And thus all our imitations of other people's work are futile. We must learn first to make honest English wares, and afterwards to decorate them as may please the then approving Graces.

Secondly—and this is an incapacity of a graver kind, yet having its own good in it also—we shall never be successful in the highest fields of ideal or theological art.

For there is one strange, but quite essential, character in us—ever since the Conquest, if not earlier—a delight in the forms of burlesque which are connected in some degree with the foulness of evil. I think the most perfect type of a true English mind in its best possible temper, is that of Chaucer; and you will find that, while it is for the most part full of thoughts of beauty, pure and wild like that of an April morning, there are, even in the midst of this, sometimes momentarily jesting passages which stoop to play with evil—while the power of listening to and enjoying the jesting of entirely gross persons, whatever the feeling may be which permits it, afterwards degenerates into forms of humour which render some of quite the greatest, wisest, and most moral of English writers now almost useless for our youth. And yet you will find that whenever Englishmen are wholly without this instinct, their genius is comparatively weak and restricted.

Now, the first necessity for the doing of any great work in ideal art, is the looking upon all foulness with horror, as a contemptible though dreadful enemy. You may easily understand what I mean, by comparing the feelings with which Dante regards any form of obscenity or of base jest, with the temper in which the same things are regarded by Shakespeare. And this strange earthly instinct of ours, coupled as it is, in our good men, with great simplicity and common sense, renders them shrewd and perfect observers and delineators of actual nature, low or high; but precludes them from that speciality of art which is properly called sublime. If ever we try anything in the manner of Michael Angelo or of Dante, we catch a fall, even in literature, as Milton in the battle of the angels, spoiled from Hesiod; while in art, every attempt in this style has hitherto been the sign either of the presumptuous egotism of persons who had never really learned to be workmen, or it has been connected with very tragic forms of the contemplation of death,—it has always been partly insane, and never once wholly successful.

But we need not feel any discomfort in these limitations of our capacity. We can do much that others cannot, and more than we have ever yet ourselves completely done. Our first great gift is in the portraiture of living people— a power already so accomplished in both Reynolds and Gainsborough that nothing is left for future masters but to add the calm of perfect workmanship to their vigour and felicity of perception. And of what value a true school of portraiture may become in the future, when worthy men will desire only to be known, and others will not fear to know them, for what they truly were, we cannot from any past records of art influence yet conceive. But in my next address it will be partly my endeavour to show you how much more useful, because more humble, the labour of great masters might have been, had they been content to bear record of the souls that were dwelling with them on earth, instead of striving to give a deceptive glory to those they dreamed of in heaven.

Secondly, we have an intense power of invention and expression in domestic drama (King Lear and Hamlet being essentially domestic in their strongest motives of interest). There is a tendency at this moment towards a noble development of our art in this direction, checked by many adverse conditions, which may be summed in one,— the insufficiency of generous civic or patriotic passion in the heart of the English people; a fault which makes its domestic affection selfish, contracted, and, therefore, frivolous.

Thirdly, in connection with our simplicity and good-humour, and partly with that very love of the grotesque which debases our ideal, we have a sympathy with the lower animals which is peculiarly our own; and which, though it has already found some exquisite expression in the works of Bewick and Landseer, is yet quite undeveloped. This sympathy, with the aid of our now authoritative science of physiology, and in association with our British love of adventure, will, I hope, enable us to give to the future inhabitants of the globe an almost perfect record of the present forms of animal life upon it, of which many are on the point of being extinguished.

Lastly, and not the least important of our special powers, I have to note our skill in landscape. . . .

Inaugural Lecture as Slade Professor of Fine Art at Oxford, 1870, Vol. XX

The Eagle's Nest
(1872)

The other day, as I was calling on the ornithologist
whose collection of birds is, I suppose, altogether un-
rivalled in Europe,—(at once a monument of unwearied
love of science, and an example, in its treatment, of the
most delicate and patient art)—Mr. Gould—he showed
me the nest of a common English bird; a nest which,
notwithstanding his knowledge of the dexterous building
of birds in all the world, was not without interest even to
him, and was altogether amazing and delightful to me. It
was a bullfinch's nest, which had been set in the fork of a
sapling tree, where it needed an extended foundation. And
the bird had built this first story of her nest with withered
stalks of clematis blossom; and with nothing else. These
twigs it had interwoven lightly, leaving the branched heads
all at the outside, producing an intricate Gothic boss of
extreme grace and quaintness, apparently arranged both
with triumphant pleasure in the art of basket-making, and
with definite purpose of obtaining ornamental form.

I fear there is no occasion to tell you that the bird had
no purpose of the kind. I say that I *fear* this, because I
would much rather have to undeceive you in attributing
too much intellect to the lower animals, than too little.
But I suppose the only error which, in the present condition of natural history, you are likely to fall into, is that
of supposing that a bullfinch is merely a mechanical arrangement of nervous fibre, covered with feathers by a
chronic cutaneous eruption; and impelled by a galvanic
stimulus to the collection of clematis.

You would be in much greater, as well as in a more
shameful, error, in supposing this, than if you attributed to
the bullfinch the most deliberate rivalship with Mr. Street's
prettiest Gothic designs. The bird has exactly the degree

of emotion, the extent of science, and the command of art, which are necessary for its happiness; it had felt the clematis twigs to be lighter and tougher than any others within its reach, and probably found the forked branches of them convenient for reticulation. It had naturally placed these outside, because it wanted a smooth surface for the bottom of its nest; and the beauty of the result was more dependent on the blossoms than the bird.

Nevertheless, I am sure that if you had seen the nest,—much more, if you had stood beside the architect at work upon it,—you would have greatly desired to express your admiration to her; and that if Wordsworth, or any other simple and kindly person, could even wish, for a little flower's sake,

> "That to this mountain daisy's self were known
> The Beauty of its star-shaped shadow, thrown
> On the smooth surface of this naked stone,"

much more you would have yearned to inform the bright little nest-builder of your sympathy; and to explain to her, on art principles, what a pretty thing she was making.

Does it never occur to you, then, that to some of the best and wisest artists among ourselves, it may not be always possible to explain what pretty things they are making; and that, perhaps, the very perfection of their art is in their knowing so little about it?

Whether it has occurred to you or not, I assure you that it is so. The greatest artists, indeed, will condescend, occasionally, to be scientific;—will labour, somewhat systematically, about what they are doing, as vulgar persons do; and are privileged, also, to enjoy what they have made more than birds do; yet seldom, observe you, as being beautiful, but very much in the sort of feeling which we may fancy the bullfinch had also,—that the thing, whether pretty or ugly, could not have been better done; that they could not have made it otherwise, and are thankful it is no worse.

The Eagle's Nest, Lecture III

Fors Clavigera
(1872 and 1873)

Carpaccio's Princess and the American Girls

The bed is a broad four-poster, the posts being beautifully wrought golden or gilded rods, variously wreathed and branched, carrying a canopy of warm red. The princess's shield is at the head of it, and the feet are raised entirely above the floor of the room, on a dais which projects at the lower end so as to form a seat, on which the child has laid her crown. Her little blue slippers lie at the side of the bed,—her white dog beside them. The coverlid is scarlet, the white sheet folded half-way back over it; the young girl lies straight, bending neither at the waist or knee, the sheet rising and falling over her in a narrow unbroken wave, like the shape of the coverlid of the last sleep, when the turf scarcely rises. She is some seventeen or eighteen years old, her head is turned towards us on the pillow, the cheek resting on her hand, as if she were thinking, yet utterly calm in sleep, and almost colourless. Her hair is tied with a narrow riband, and divided into two wreaths, which encircle her head like a double crown. The white nightgown hides the arm raised on the pillow, down to the wrist.

At the door of the room an angel enters (the little dog, though lying awake, vigilant, takes no notice). He is a very small angel, his head just rises a little above the shelf round the room, and would only reach as high as the princess's chin, if she were standing up He has soft grey wings, lustreless; and his dress, of subdued blue, has violet sleeves, open above the elbow, and showing white sleeves below. He comes in without haste, his body, like a mortal one, casting shadow from the light through the door behind, his face perfectly quiet; a palm-branch in his right hand—a scroll in his left.

So dreams the princess, with blessed eyes, that need no earthly dawn. It is very pretty of Carpaccio to make her dream out the angel's dress so particularly, and notice the slashed sleeves; and to dream so little an angel—very nearly a doll angel,—bringing her the branch of palm, and message. But the lovely characteristic of all is the evident delight of her continual life. Royal power over herself, and happiness in her flowers, her books, her sleeping, and waking, her prayers, her dreams, her earth, her heaven.

After I had spent my morning over this picture, I had to go to Verona by the afternoon train. In the carriage with me were two American girls with their father and mother, people of the class which has lately made so much money, suddenly, and does not know what to do with it: and these two girls, of about fifteen and eighteen, had evidently been indulged in everything (since they had had the means) which western civilization could imagine. And here they were, specimens of the utmost which the money and invention of the nineteenth century could produce in maidenhood,—children of its most progressive race,—enjoying the full advantages of political liberty, of enlightened philosophical education, of cheap pilfered literature, and of luxury at any cost. Whatever money, machinery, or freedom of thought could do for these two children, had been done. No superstition had deceived, no restraint degraded them:—types, they could not but be, of maidenly wisdom and felicity, as conceived by the forwardest intellects of our time.

And they were travelling through a district which, if any in the world, should touch the hearts and delight the eyes of young girls. Between Venice and Verona! Portia's villa perhaps in sight upon the Brenta, Juliet's tomb to be visited in the evening,—blue against the southern sky, the hills of Petrarch's home. Exquisite midsummer sunshine, with low rays, glanced through the vine-leaves; all the Alps were clear, from the Lake of Garda to Cadore, and to farthest Tyrol. What a princess's chamber, this, if these are princesses, and what dreams might they not dream, therein!

But the two American girls were neither princesses, nor seers, nor dreamers. By infinite self-indulgence, they had reduced themselves simply to two pieces of white putty that could feel pain. The flies and the dust stuck to them as to clay, and they perceived, between Venice and Verona, nothing but the flies and the dust. They pulled

330

down the blinds the moment they entered the carriage, and then sprawled, and writhed, and tossed among the cushions of it, in vain contest, during the whole fifty miles, with every miserable sensation of bodily affliction that could make time intolerable.

Fors Clavigera, Letter 20, August 1872

The road from the village of Shirley, near Addington, where my father and mother are buried, to the house they lived in when I was four years old, lay, at that time, through a quite secluded district of field and wood, traversed here and there by winding lanes, and by one or two smooth mail-coach roads, beside which, at intervals of a mile or two, stood some gentleman's house, with its lawn, gardens, offices, and attached fields, indicating a country life of long continuance and quiet respectability. Except such an one here and there, one saw no dwellings above the size of cottages or small farmsteads; these, wood-built usually, and thatched, their porches embroidered with honeysuckle, and their gardens with daisies, their doors mostly ajar, or with one half shut to keep in the children, and a bricked or tiled footway from it to the wicket gate,—all neatly kept, and vivid with a sense of the quiet energies of their contented tenants,—made the lane-turnings cheerful, and gleamed in half-hidden clusters beneath the slopes of the wood-lands at Sydenham and Penge. There were no signs of distress, of effort, or of change; many of enjoyment, and not a few of wealth beyond the daily needs of life.

That same district is now covered by, literally, many thousands of houses built within the last ten years, of rotten brick, with various iron devices to hold it together. They, every one, have a drawing-room and dining-room, transparent from back to front, so that from the road one sees the people's heads inside, clear against the light. They have a second story of bedrooms, and an underground one of kitchen. They are fastened in a Siamese twin manner together by their sides, and each couple has a Greek or Gothic portico shared between them, with magnificent steps, and highly ornamented capitals. Attached to every double block are exactly similar double parallelograms of garden, laid out in new gravel and scanty turf, on the model of the pleasure grounds in the Crystal Palace, and enclosed by high, thin, and pale brick walls. The gardens in front are fenced from the road with an immense weight

331

of cast iron, and entered between two square gate-posts, with projecting stucco cornices, bearing the information that the eligible residence within is Mortimer House or Montague Villa.

Fors Clavigera, Vol. II, Letter 29, April 1873

You have, I hope, noticed that throughout these letters addressed to you as workmen and labourers,—though I have once or twice ventured to call myself your fellow-workman, I have oftener spoken as belonging to, and sharing main modes of thought with, those who are not labourers, but either live in various ways by their wits—as lawyers, authors, reviewers, clergymen, parliamentary orators, and the like—or absolutely in idleness on the labour of others,—as the representative Squire. And, broadly speaking, I address you as workers, and speak in the names of the rest as idlers, thus not estimating the mere wit-work as work at all; it is always play, when it is good.

Speaking to you, then, as workers, and of myself as an idler, tell me honestly whether you consider me as addressing my betters or my worses? Let us give ourselves no airs on either side. Which of us, do you seriously think, you or I, are leading the more honourable life? Would you like to lead my life rather than your own; or, if you couldn't help finding it pleasanter, would you be ashamed of yourselves for leading it? Is your place, or mine, considered as cure and sinecure, the better? And are either of us legitimately in it? I would fain know your own real opinion on these things.

But note further; there is another relation between us than of idler and labourer; the much more direct one of Master and Servant. I can set you to any kind of work I like, whether it be good for you or bad, pleasant to you or painful. Consider, for instance, what I am doing at this very instant—half-past seven, morning, 25th February, 1873. It is a bitter black frost, the ground deep in snow, and more falling. I am writing comfortable in a perfectly warm room; some of my servants were up in the cold at half-past five to get it ready for me; others, a few days ago, were digging my coals near Durham, at the risk of their lives; an old woman brought me my watercresses through the snow for breakfast yesterday; another old woman is going two miles through it to-day to fetch me my letters at ten o'clock. Half-a-dozen men are building a wall for me to keep the sheep out of my garden, and a railroad stoker is holding his own against the north wind, to fetch me some Brobdingnag raspberry plants to put in it. Somebody in the east end of London is making boots for me, for I can't wear those I have much longer; a washerwoman is in suds, somewhere, to get me a clean shirt for to-morrow; a fisherman is in dangerous weather somewhere, catching me some fish for Lent; and my cook will soon be making me pancakes, for it is Shrove Tuesday. Having written this sentence, I go to the fire, warm my fingers, saunter a little, listlessly, about the room, and grumble because I can't see to the other side of the lake.

And all these people, my serfs or menials, who are undergoing any quantity or kind of hardship I choose to put on them,—all these people, nevertheless, are more contented than I am: I can't be happy, not I,—for one thing, because I haven't got the MS. Additional, (never mind what number) in the British Museum, which they bought in 1848, for two hundred pounds, and I never saw it! And have never been easy in my mind, since. . . .

But I used another terrible word just now—"menial." The modern English vulgar mind has a wonderful dread of doing anything of that sort!

I suppose there is scarcely another word in the language which people more dislike having applied to them, or of which they less understand the application. It comes from a beautiful old Chaucerian word, "menie," or many, signifying the attendant company of any one worth attending to; the disciples of a master, scholars of a teacher, soldiers of a leader, lords of a King. Chaucer says the God of Love came, in the garden of the Rose, with "his many";—in the court of the King of Persia spoke a Lord, one "of his many." Therefore there is nothing in itself dishonourable in being menial: the only question is—*whose* many you belong to, and whether he is a person worth belonging to, or even safe to be belonged to; also, there is somewhat in the cause of your following: if you follow for love, it is good to be menial—if for honour, good also;—if for ten per cent.—as a railroad company follows its Director, it is not good to be menial. Also there is somewhat in the manner of following: if you obey your Taskmaster's eye, it is well;—if only his whip, still, well; but not so well:— but, above all, or below all, if you have to obey the whip as a bad hound, because you have no nose, like the members of the present House of Commons, it is a very humble form of menial service indeed.

But even as to the quite literal form of it, in house or

domestic service, are you sure it is so very disgraceful a state to live in?

Among the people whom one must miss out of one's life, dead, or worse than dead, by the time one is fifty-four, I can only say, for my own part, that the one I practically and truly miss most, next to father and mother (and putting losses of imaginary good out of the question), was a "menial," my father's nurse, and mine. She was one of our many—(our many being always but few), and from her girlhood to her old age, the entire ability of her life was given to serving us. She had a natural gift and specialty for doing disagreeable things; above all, the service of a sick room; so that she was never quite in her glory unless some of us were ill. She had also some parallel specialty for *saying* disagreeable things; and might be relied upon to give the extremely darkest view of any subject, before proceeding to ameliorative action upon it. And she had a very creditable and republican aversion to doing immediately, or in set terms, as she was bid; so that when my mother and she got old together, and my mother became very imperative and particular about having her teacup set on one side of her little round table, Anne would observantly and punctiliously put it always on the other; which caused my mother to state to me, every morning after breakfast, gravely, that, if ever a woman in this world was possessed by the Devil, Anne was that woman. But in spite of these momentary and petulant aspirations to liberality and independence of character, poor Anne remained verily servile in soul, all her days; and was altogether occupied from the age of fifteen to seventy-two in doing other people's wills instead of her own, and seeking other people's good instead of her own; nor did I ever hear on any occasion of her doing harm to a human being, except by saving two hundred and some odd pounds for her relations; in consequence of which some of them, after her funeral, did not speak to the rest for several months.

Two hundred and odd pounds;—it might have been more; but I used to hear of little loans to the relations occasionally; and besides, Anne would sometimes buy a quite unjustifiably expensive silk gown. People in her station of life are always so improvident. Two hundred odd pounds at all events she had laid by, in her fifty-seven years of unselfish labour. Actually twenty ten-pound notes.

Fors Clavigera, Vol. II, Letter 28, February 1873

Notes on Prout and Hunt
(1879)

Middle-Class Patronage

It is especially to be remembered that drawings of this
simple character were made [sixty years since] for [the]
middle classes, exclusively; and even for the second order
of the middle classes, more accurately expressed by the
term *bourgeoisie*. The great people always bought Canaletto, not Prout, and Van Huysum, not Hunt. There
was indeed no quality in the bright little water-colours
which could look other than pert in ghostly corridors, and
petty in halls of state; but they gave an unquestionable
tone of liberal-mindedness to a suburban villa, and were
the cheerfullest possible decorations for a moderate-sized
breakfast-parlour opening on a nicely mown lawn. Their
loveliness even rose, on occasion, to the charity of beauti-
fying the narrow chambers of those whom business or
fixed habit still retained in the obscurity of London itself;
and I remember with peculiar respect the pride of a
benevolent physician, who never would exchange his
neighbourhood to the poor of St. Giles's for the lucrative
lustre of a West End square, in wreathing his tiny little
front drawing-room with Hunt's loveliest apple-blossom,
and taking the patients for whom he had prescribed fresh
air the next instant on a little visit to the country.

Nor was this adaptation to the tastes and circumstances
of the London citizen a constrained or obsequious compliance on the part of the kindly artists. They were themselves, in mind, as in habits of life, completely a part of
the characteristic metropolitan population whom an occasional visit to the Continent always thrilled with surprise
on finding themselves again among persons who familiarly
spoke French; and whose summer holidays, though more
customary, amused them nevertheless with the adventure,

and beguiled them with the pastoral charm, of an uninterrupted picnic. Mr. Prout lived at Brixton, just at the rural extremity of Cold Harbour Lane, where the spire of Brixton Church, the principal architectural ornament of the neighbourhood, could not but greatly exalt, by comparison, the impressions received from that of Strasburg Cathedral, or the Hôtel de Ville of Bruxelles; and Mr. Hunt, though often in the spring and summer luxuriating in country lodgings, was only properly at home in the Hampstead Road, and never painted a cluster of nuts without some expression, visible enough by the manner of their presentation, of the pleasure it was to him to see them in the shell, instead of in a bag at the greengrocer's.

The lightly rippled level of this civic life lay, as will be easily imagined, far beneath the distractions, while it maintained itself meekly, yet severely, independent of the advantages, held out by the social system of what is most reverently called "Town." Neither the disposition, the health, nor the means of either artist admitted of their spending their evenings, in general, elsewhere than by their own firesides; nor could a spring leveé of English peeresses and foreign ambassadors be invited by the modest painter whose only studio was his little back-parlour, commanding a partial view of the scullery steps and the water-butt. The fluctuations of moral and aesthetic sentiment in the public mind were of small moment to the humble colourists, who depended only on the consistency of its views on the subject of early strawberries; and the thrilling subjects presented by the events or politics of the day were equally indifferent to the designer who invited interest to nothing later than the architecture of the fifteenth century. Even the treasures of scientific instruction, and marvels of physical discovery, were without material influence on the tranquility of the two native painters' uneducated skill. Prout drew every lovely street in Europe, without troubling himself to learn a single rule of perspective; while Hunt painted mossy banks for five-and-twenty years, without ever caring to know a sphagnum from a polypody, and embossed or embowered his birds' eggs to a perfection, which Greek connoisseurs would have assured us the mother had unsuspectingly sat on, without enlarging his range of ornithological experience beyond the rarities of tomtit and hedge-sparrow.

This uncomplaining resignation of patronage, and unblushing blindness to instruction, were allied, in both painters, with a steady consistency in technical practice, which, from the first, and to the last, precluded both from all hope of promotion to the honours, as it withheld them from the peril of entanglement in the rivalries, connected with the system of exhibition in the Royal Academy. Mr. Prout's method of work was entirely founded on the quite elementary qualities of white paper and black Cumberland lead; and expressly terminated within the narrow range of prismatic effects producible by a brown or blue outline, with a wash of ochre or cobalt. Mr. Hunt's early drawings depended for their peculiar charm on the most open and simple management of transparent colour; and his later ones, for their highest attainments, on the flexibility of a pigment which yielded to the slightest touch and softest motion of a hand always more sensitive than firm. The skill which unceasing practice, within limits thus modestly unrelaxed, and with facilities of instrument thus openly confessed, enabled each draughtsman in his special path to attain, was exerted with a vividness of instinct somewhat resembling that of animals, only in the slightest degree conscious of praiseworthiness, but animated by a healthy complacency, as little anxious for external sympathy as the self-content of a bee in the translucent symmetry of its cell, or of a chaffinch in the silver tracery of her nest—and uniting, through the course of their uneventful and active lives, the frankness of the bird with the industry of the insect.

Notes on Prout and Hunt, Vol. XI

Praeterita

(1885-89)

I never had heard my father's or mother's voice once raised in any question with each other; nor seen an angry, or even slightly hurt or offended, glance in the eyes of either. I had never heard a servant scolded; nor even suddenly, passionately, or in any severe manner, blamed. I had never seen a moment's trouble or disorder in any household matter; nor anything whatever either done in a hurry or undone in due time. I had no conception of such a feeling as anxiety; my father's occasional vexation in the afternoons, when he had only got an order for twelve butts after expecting one for fifteen, as I have just stated, was never manifested to *me;* and itself related only to the question whether his name would be a step higher or lower in the year's list of sherry exporters; for he never spent more than half his income, and therefore found himself little incommoded by occasional variations in the total of it. I had never done any wrong that I knew of— beyond occasionally delaying the commitment to heart of some improving sentence, that I might watch a wasp on the window pane, or a bird in the cherry tree; and I had never seen any grief.

Next to this quite priceless gift of Peace, I had received the perfect understanding of the natures of Obedience and Faith. I obeyed word, or lifted finger, of father or mother, simply as a ship her helm; not only without idea of resistance, but receiving the direction as a part of my own life and force, and helpful law, as necessary to me in every moral action as the law of gravity in leaping. And my practice in Faith was soon complete: nothing was ever promised me that was not given; nothing ever threatened me that was not inflicted, and nothing ever told me that was not true.

Peace, obedience, faith; these three for chief good; next to these, the habit of fixed attention with both eyes and mind—on which I will not further enlarge at this moment, this being the main practical faculty of my life, causing Mazzini to say of me, in conversation authentically reported, a year or two before his death, that I had "the most analytic mind in Europe." An opinion in which, so far as I am acquainted with Europe, I am myself entirely disposed to concur.

Lastly, an extreme perfection in palate and all other bodily senses, given by the utter prohibition of cake, wine comfits, or, except in carefullest restriction, fruit; and by fine preparation of what food was given me. Such I esteem the main blessings of my childhood;—next, let me count the equally dominant calamities.

First, that I had nothing to love.

My parents were—in a sort—visible powers of nature to me, no more loved than the sun and the moon: only I should have been annoyed and puzzled if either of them had gone out; (how much, now, when both are darkened.)—still less did I love God; not that I had any quarrel with Him, or fear of Him; but simply found what people told me was His service, disagreeable; and what people told me was His book, not entertaining. I had no companions to quarrel with, neither; nobody to assist, and nobody to thank. Not a servant was ever allowed to do anything for me, but what it was their duty to do; and why should I have been grateful to the cook for cooking, or the gardener for gardening,—when the one dared not give me a baked potato without asking leave, and the other would not let my ants' nests alone, because they made the walks untidy? The evil consequence of all this was not, however, what might perhaps have been expected, that I grew up selfish or unaffectionate; but that, when affection did come, it came with violence utterly rampant and unmanageable, at least by me, who never before had anything to manage.

For (second of chief calamities) I had nothing to endure. Danger or pain of any kind I knew not: my strength was never exercised, my patience never tried, and my courage never fortified. Not that I was ever afraid of anything,—either ghosts, thunder or beasts; and one of the nearest approaches to insubordination which I was ever tempted into as a child, was in passionate effort to get leave to play with the lion's cubs in Wombwell's menagerie.

Thirdly. I was taught no precision nor etiquette of manners; it was enough if, in the little society we saw, I remained unobtrusive, and replied to a question without shyness: but the shyness came later, and increased as I grew conscious of the rudeness arising from the want of social discipline, and found it impossible to acquire, in advanced life, dexterity in any bodily exercise, skill in any pleasing accomplishment, or ease and tact in ordinary behaviour.

Lastly, and chief of evils. My judgment of right and wrong, and powers of independent action were left entirely undeveloped; because the bridle and blinkers were never taken off me. Children should have their times of being off duty, like soldiers; and when once the obedience, if required, is certain, the little creature should be very early put for periods of practice in complete command of itself; set on the barebacked horse of its own will, and left to break it by its own strength. But the ceaseless authority exercised over my youth left me, when cast out at last into the world, unable for some time to do more than drift with its vortices.

My present verdict, therefore, on the general tenor of my education at that time, must be, that it was at once too formal and too luxurious; leaving my character, at the most important moment for its construction, cramped indeed, but not disciplined; and only by protection innocent, instead of by practice virtuous. My mother saw this herself, and but too clearly, in later years; and whenever I did anything wrong, stupid, or hard-hearted,—(and I have done many things that were all three,)—always said, "It is because you were too much indulged."

The poor modern slaves and simpletons who let themselves be dragged like cattle, or felled timber, through the countries they imagine themselves visiting, can have no conception whatever of the complex joys and ingenious hopes, connected with the choice and arrangement of the travelling carriage in old times. The mechanical questions first, of strength—easy rolling—steady and safe poise of persons and luggage; the general stateliness of effect to be obtained for the abashing of plebeian beholders; the cunning design and distribution of store-cellars under the seats, secret drawers under front windows, invisible pockets under padded lining, safe from dust, and accessible only by insidious slits, or necromantic valves like Aladdin's trapdoor; the fitting of cushions where they would not slip, the rounding of corners for more delicate repose; the prudent attachments and springs of blinds; the perfect fitting of windows, on which one-half the comfort of a travelling carriage really depends; and the adaptation of all these concentrated luxuries to the probabilities of who would sit where, in the little apartment which was to be virtually one's home for five or six months;—all this was an imaginary journey in itself, with every pleasure, and none of the discomfort, of practical travelling. . . .

For a family carriage of this solid construction, with its luggage, and load of six or more persons, four horses were of course necessary to get any sufficient way on it; and half-a-dozen such teams were kept at every post-house. . . .

The French horses, and more or less those on all the great lines of European travelling, were properly stout trotting cart-horses, well up to their work and over it; untrimmed, long-tailed, good-humouredly licentious, whinneying and frolicking with each other when they had a chance; sagaciously steady to their work; obedient to the voice mostly, to the rein only for more explicitness; never touched by the whip, which was used merely to express the driver's exultation in himself and them,—signal obstructive vehicles in front out of the way, and advise all the inhabitants of the villages and towns traversed on the day's journey, that persons of distinction were honouring them by their transitory presence.

And then, with Salvador was held council in the inn-parlour of Strasburg, whether—it was then the Friday afternoon—we should push on to-morrow for our Sunday's rest to Basle, or to Shaffhausen.

How much depended—if ever anything "depends" on anything else,—on the issue of that debate! Salvador inclined to the straight and level Rhine-side road, with the luxury of the "Three Kings" attainable by sunset. But at Basle, it had to be admitted, there were no Alps in sight, no cataract within hearing, and Salvador honourably laid before us the splendid alternative possibility of reaching, by traverse of the hilly road of the Black Forest, the gates of Schaffhausen itself, before they closed for the night.

The Black Forest! The fall of Schaffhausen! The chain of the Alps! within one's grasp for Sunday! What a Sunday, instead of customary Walworth and the Dulwich fields! My impassioned petition at last carried it, and the earliest morning saw us trotting over the bridge of boats to Kehl, and in the eastern light I well remember watching the line of the Black Forest hills enlarge and rise, as we crossed the plain of the Rhine. "Gates of the hills"; opening for me to a new life—to cease no more, except at the Gates of the Hills whence one returns not.

And so, we reached the base of the Schwarzwald, and entered an ascending dingle; and scarcely, I think, a quarter of an hour after entering, saw our first "Swiss cottage." How much it meant to all of us,—how much prophesied to me, no modern traveller could the least conceive, if I spent days in trying to tell him. A sort of triumphant shriek—like all the railway whistles going off at once at Clapham Junction—has gone up from the Fooldom of Europe at the destruction of the myth of William Tell. To us, every word of it was true—but mythically luminous with more than mortal truth; and here, under the black woods, glowed the visible, beautiful, tangible testimony to it in the purple larch timber, carved to exquisiteness by the joy of peasant life, continuous, motionless there in the pine shadow on its ancestral turf, —unassailed and unassailing, in the blessedness of righteous poverty, of religious peace.

The myth of William Tell is destroyed forsooth? and you have tunnelled Gothard, and filled, it may be, the Bay of Uri;—and it was all for you and your sake that the grapes dropped blood from the press of St. Jacob, and the pine club struck down horse and helm in Morgarten Glen?

Difficult enough for you to imagine, that old travellers' time when Switzerland was yet the land of the Swiss, and the Alps had never been trod by foot of man. Steam, never heard of yet, but for short fair weather crossing at sea (were there paddle-packets across Atlantic? I forget). Any way, the roads by land were safe; and entered once into this mountain Paradise, we wound on through its balmy glens, past cottage after cottage on their lawns, still glistening in the dew.

The road got into more barren heights by the mid-day, the hills arduous; once or twice we had to wait for horses, and we were still twenty miles from Schaffhausen at sunset; it was past midnight when we reached her closed gates. The disturbed porter had the grace to open them— not quite wide enough; we carried away one of our lamps in collision with the slanting bar as we drove through the arch. How much happier the privilege of dreamily entering a mediæval city, though with the loss of a lamp, than the free ingress of being jammed between a dray and a tramcar at a railroad station.

It is strange that I but dimly recollect the following morning; I fancy we must have gone to some sort of church or other; and certainly, part of the day went in admiring the bow-windows projecting into the clean streets. None of us seem to have thought the Alps would be visible without profane exertion in climbing hills. We dined at four, as usual, and the evening being entirely fine, went out to walk, all of us,—my father and mother and Mary and I.

We must have still spent some time in town-seeing, for it was drawing towards sunset when we got up to some sort of garden promenade—west of the town, I believe; and high above the Rhine, so as to command the open country across it to the south and west. At which open country of low undulation, far into blue,—gazing as at one of our own distances from Malvern of Worcester-shire, or Dorking of Kent,—suddenly—behold—beyond!

There was no thought in any of us for a moment of their being clouds. They were clear as crystal, sharp on the pure horizon sky, and already tinged with rose by the sinking sun. Infinitely beyond all that we had ever thought or dreamed,—the seen walls of lost Eden could not have been more beautiful to us; not more awful, round heaven, the walls of sacred Death. . . . [Oxford]

It was an institution of the college that every week the undergraduates should write an essay on a philosophical subject, explicatory of some brief Latin text of Horace, Juvenal, or other accredited and pithy writer; and, I suppose, as a sort of guarantee to the men that what they wrote was really looked at, the essay pronounced the best was read aloud in hall on Saturday afternoon, with en-forced attendance of the other undergraduates. Here, at least, was something in which I felt that my little faculties had some scope, and both conscientiously, and with real interest in the task, I wrote my weekly essay with all the sagacity and eloquence I possessed. And therefore, though much flattered, I was not surprised when a few weeks after coming up, my tutor announced to me, with a look of approval, that I was to read my essay in hall next Saturday.

Serenely, and on good grounds, confident in my powers of reading rightly, and with a decent gravity which I felt to be becoming on this my first occasion of public distinc-tion, I read my essay, I have reason to believe, not ungracefully; and descended from the rostrum to receive—as I doubted not—the thanks of the gentlemen-commoners for this creditable presentment of the wisdom of the body. But poor Clara, after her first ball, receiving her cousin's compliments in the cloak-room, was less surprised than I by my welcome from my cousins of the long-table. Not in envy, truly, but in fiery disdain, varied in expression through every form and manner of English language, from the Olympian sarcasm of Charteris to the level-delivered volley of Grimston, they explained to me that I had committed groosest *lèse-majesté* against the order of gentlemen-commoners; that no gentleman-commoner's essay ought ever to contain more than twelve lines, with four words in each; and that even indulging to my folly, and conceit, and want of *savoir faire,* the impropriety of writing an essay with any meaning in it, like vulgar students,—the thoughtlessness and audacity of writing one that would take at least a quarter of an hour to read, and then reading it all, might for this once be forgiven to such a greenhorn, but that Coventry wasn't the word for the place I should be sent to if ever I did such a thing again. I am happy at least in remembering that I bore my fall from the clouds without much hurt, or even too ridiculous astonishment. I at once admitted the justice of these representations, yet I do not remember that I modified the style of my future essays materially in consequence, neither do I remember what line of conduct I had proposed to myself in the event of again obtaining the privilege of edifying the Saturday's congregation. Perhaps my essays really diminished in value, or perhaps even the tutors had enough of them. All I know is, I was never asked to.

I am amused, as I look back, in now perceiving what an æsthetic view I had of all my tutors and companions,—how consistently they took to me the aspect of pictures, and how I from the first declined giving any attention to those which were not well painted enough. My ideal of a tutor was founded on what Holbein or Dürer had represented in Erasmus or Melanchthon, or, even more solemnly, on Titian's Magnificoes or Bonifazio's Bishops. No presences of that kind appeared either in Tom or Peckwater; and even Doctor Pusey (who also never spoke to me) was not in the least a picturesque or tremendous figure, but only a sickly and rather ill put together English clerical gentleman, who never looked one in the face, or appeared aware of the state of the weather.

My own tutor was a dark-eyed, animated, pleasant, but not in the least impressive person, who walked with an unconscious air of assumption, noticeable by us juniors not to his advantage. Kynaston was ludicrously like a fat schoolboy. Hussey, grim and brown as I said, somewhat lank, incapable of jest, equally incapable of enthusiasm; for the rest doing his duty thoroughly, and a most estimable member of the college and university,—but to me, a resident calamity far greater than I knew, whose malefic influence I recognize in memory only.

Finally, the Dean himself, though venerable to me from the first, in his evident honesty, self-respect, and real power of a rough kind, was yet in his general aspect too much like the sign of the Red Pig which I afterwards saw set up in pudding raisins, with black currants for eyes, by an imaginative grocer in Chartres fair; and in the total bodily and ghostly presence of him was to me only a rotundly progressive terror, or sternly enthroned and niched Anathema.

There was one tutor, however, out of my sphere, who reached my ideal, but disappointed my hope, then,—as perhaps his own, since;—a man sorrowfully under the dominion of the Greek *anangke*—the present Dean. He was, and is, one of the rarest types of nobly-presenced Englishmen, but I fancy it was his adverse star that made him an Englishman at all—the prosaic and practical element in him having prevailed over the sensitive one. He was the only man in Oxford among the masters of my day who knew anything of art; and his keen saying of Turner, that he "had got hold of a false ideal," would have been infinitely helpful to me at that time, had he explained and enforced it. But I suppose he did not see enough in me to make him take trouble with me,—and, what was much more serious, he saw not enough in himself to take trouble, in that field, with himself.

There was a more humane and more living spirit, however, inhabitant of the north-west angle of the Cardinal's Square: and a great many of the mischances which were only harmful to me through my own folly may be justly held, and to the full, counterbalanced by that one piece of good fortune, of which I had the wit to take advantage. Dr. Buckland was a Canon of the Cathedral, and he, with his wife and family, were all sensible and good-natured, with originality enough in the sense of them to give sap and savour to the whole college.

Originality—passing slightly into grotesqueness, and a little diminishing their effective power. The Doctor had too much humour ever to follow far enough the dull side of a subject. Frank was too fond of his bear cub to give attention enough to the training of the cubbish element in himself; and a day scarcely passed without Mit's committing herself in some manner disapproved by the statelier college demoiselles. But all were frank, kind, and clever, vital in the highest degree; to me, medicinal and saving.

Dr. Buckland was extremely like Sydney Smith in his staple of character; no rival with him in wit, but like him in humour, common sense, and benevolently cheerful doctrine of Divinity. At his breakfast-table I met the leading scientific men of the day, from Herschel downwards, and often intelligent and courteous foreigners,—with whom my stutter of French, refined by Adèle into some precision of accent, was sometimes useful. Every one was at ease and amused at that breakfast-table,—the menu and service of it usually in themselves interesting. I have always regretted a day of unlucky engagement on which I missed a delicate toast of mice; and remembered, with delight, being waited upon one hot summer morning by two graceful and polite little Carolina lizards, who kept off the flies.

On the journey of 1837, when I was eighteen, I felt, for the last time, the pure childish love of nature which Wordsworth so idly takes for an intimation of immortality. We went down by the North Road, as usual; and on the fourth day arrived at Catterick Bridge, where there is a clear pebble-bedded stream, and both west and east some rising of hills, foretelling the moorlands and dells of upland Yorkshire; and there the feeling came back to me—as it could never return more.

It is a feeling only possible to youth, for all care, regret, or knowledge of evil destroys it; and it requires also the full sensibility of nerve and blood, the conscious strength of heart, and hope; not but that I suppose the purity of youth may feel what is best of it even through sickness and the waiting for death; but only in thinking death itself God's sending.

346

In myself, it has always been quite exclusively confined to *wild,* that is to say, wholly natural places, and especially to scenery animated by streams, or by the sea. The sense of the freedom, spontaneous, unpolluted power of nature was essential in it. I enjoyed a lawn, a garden, a daisied field, a quiet pond, as other children do; but by the side of Wandel, or on the downs of Sandgate, or by a Yorkshire stream under a cliff, I was different from other children, that ever I have noticed: but the feeling cannot be described by any of us that have it. Wordsworth's "haunted me like a passion" is no description of it, for it is not *like,* but *is,* a passion; the point is to define how it *differs* from other passions,—what sort of human, pre-eminently human, feeling it is that loves a stone for a stone's sake, and a cloud for a cloud's. A monkey loves a monkey for a monkey's sake, and a nut for the kernel's, but not a stone for a stone's. I took stones for bread, but not certainly at the Devil's bidding.

I was different, be it once more said, from other children even of my own type, not so much in the actual nature of the feeling, but in the mixture of it. I had, in my little clay pitcher, vialfuls, as it were, of Wordsworth's reverence, Shelley's sensitiveness, Turner's accuracy, all in one. A snowdrop was to me, as to Wordsworth, part of the Sermon on the Mount; but I never should have written sonnets to the celandine, because it is of a coarse yellow, and imperfect form. With Shelley, I loved blue sky and blue eyes, but never in the least confused the heavens with my own poor little Psychidion. And the reverence and passion were alike kept in their places by the constructive Turnerian element; and I did not weary myself in wishing that a daisy could see the beauty of its shadow, but in trying to draw the shadow rightly, myself.

But so stubborn and chemically inalterable the laws of the prescription were, that now, looking back from 1886 to that brook shore of 1837, whence I could see the whole of my youth, I find myself in nothing whatsoever *changed.* Some of me is dead, more of me stronger; I have learned a few things, forgotten many; in the total of me, I am but the same youth, disappointed and rheumatic.

Virtually there was no other jeweller in Geneva, in the great times. There were some respectable, uncompetitive shops, not dazzling, in the main street; and smaller ones, with an average supply of miniature watches, that would go well for ten years; and uncostly, but honest, trinketry. But one went to Mr Bautte's with awe, and of necessity, as one did to one's bankers. There was scarcely any external sign of Bautte whatever—a small brass plate at the side of a narrow arched door, into an alley—into a secluded alley—leading into a monastic courtyard, out of which—or rather out of the alley, where it opened to the court, you ascended a winding stair, wide enough for two only, and came to a green door, swinging, at the top of it; and there you paused to summon courage to enter.

A not large room, with a single counter at the further side. Nothing shown on the counter. Two confidential attendants behind it, and—it might possibly be Mr. Bautte! —or his son—or his partner—or anyhow the Ruling power—at his desk beside the back window. You told what you wanted: it was necessary to know your mind, and to be sure you *did* want it; there was no showing of things for temptation at Bautte's. You wanted a bracelet, a brooch, a watch—plain or enamelled. Choice of what was wanted was quietly given. There were no big stones, nor blinding galaxies of wealth. Entirely sound workmanship in the purest gold that could be worked; fine enamel for the most part, for colour, rather than jewels; and a certain Bauttesque subtlety of linked and wreathed design, which the experienced eye recognized when worn in Paris or London. Absolutely just and moderate price; wear,—to the end of your days. You came away with a sense of duty fulfilled, of treasure possessed, and of a new foundation to the respectability of your family.

You returned into the light of the open street with a blissful sense of a parcel being made up to be sent after you, and in the consequently calm expiation of mind, went usually to watch the Rhône.

Bautte's was in the main street, out of which one caught glimpses down the short cross-ones, of the passing water; as at Sandgate, or the like fishing towns, one got peeps of the sea. With twenty steps you were beside it.

For all other rivers there is a surface, and an underneath, and a vaguely displeasing idea of the bottom. But the Rhône flows like one lambent jewel; its surface is nowhere, its ethereal self is everywhere, the iridescent rush and translucent strength of it blue to the shore, and radiant to the depth.

Fifteen feet thick, of not flowing, but flying water; not

348

water, neither,—melted glacier, rather, one should call it; the force of the ice is with it, and the wreathing of the clouds, the gladness of the sky, and the continuance of Time.

Waves of clear sea are, indeed, lovely to watch, but they are always coming or gone, never in any taken shape to be seen for a second. But here was one mighty wave that was always itself, and every fluted swirl of it, constant as the wreathing of a shell. No wasting away of the fallen foam, no pause for gathering of power, no helpless ebb of discouraged recoil; but alike through bright day and lulling night, the never-pausing plunge, and never-fading flash, and never-hushing whisper, and, while the sun was up, the ever-answering glow of unearthly aquamarine, ultramarine, violet-blue, gentian-blue, peacock-blue, river-of-paradise blue, glass of a painted window melted in the sun, and the witch of the Alps flinging the spun tresses of it for ever from her snow.

The innocent way, too, in which the river used to stop to look into every little corner. Great torrents always seem angry, and great rivers too often sullen; but there is no anger, no disdain, in the Rhône. It seemed as if the mountain stream was in mere bliss at recovering itself again out of the lake-sleep, and raced because it rejoiced in racing, fain yet to return and stay. There were pieces of wave that danced all day as if Perdita were looking on to learn; there were little streams that skipped like lambs and leaped like chamois; there were pools that shook the sunshine all through them, and were rippled in layers of overlaid ripples, like crystal sand; there were currents that twisted the light into golden braids, and inlaid the threads with turquoise enamel; there were strips of stream that had certainly above the lake been millstreams, and were looking busily for mills to turn again; there were shoots of stream that had once shot fearfully into the air, and now sprang up again laughing that they had only fallen a foot or two;—and in the midst of all the gay glittering and eddied lingering, the noble bearing by of the midmost depth, so mighty, yet so terrorless and harmless, with its swallows skimming instead of petrels, and the dear old decrepit town as safe in the embracing sweep of it as if it were set in a brooch of sapphire.

I draw back to my own home, twenty years ago, permitted to thank Heaven once more for the peace, and hope, and loveliness of it, and the Elysian walks with

Joanie, and Paradisiacal with Rosie, under the peach-blossom branches by the little glittering stream which I had paved with crystal for them. I had built behind the highest cluster of laurels a reservoir, from which, on sunny afternoons, I could let a quite rippling film of water run for a couple of hours down behind the hayfield, where the grass in spring still grew fresh and deep. There used to be always a corncrake or two in it. Twilight after twilight I have hunted that bird, and never once got glimpse of it: the voice was always at the other side of the field, or in the inscrutable air or earth. And the little stream had its falls, and pools, and imaginary lakes. Here and there it laid for itself lines of graceful sand; there and here it lost itself under beads of chalcedony. It wasn't the Liffey, nor the Nith, nor the Wandel; but the two girls were surely a little cruel to call it "The Gutter"! Happiest times, for all of us, that ever were to be; not but that Joanie and her Arthur are giddy enough, both of them yet, with their five little ones, but they have been sorely anxious about me, and I have been sorrowful enough for myself, since ever I lost sight of that peach-blossom avenue. "Eden-land" Rosie calls it sometimes in her letters. Whether its tiny river were of the waters of Abana, or Euphrates, or Thamesis, I know not, but they were sweeter to my thirst than the fountains of Trevi or Branda.

How things bind and blend themselves together! The last time I saw the Fountain of Trevi, it was from Arthur's father's room—Joseph Severn's, where we both took Joanie to see him in 1872, and the old man made a sweet drawing of his pretty daughter-in-law, now in her schoolroom; he himself then eager in finishing his last picture of the Marriage in Cana, which he had caused to take place under a vine trellis, and delighted himself by painting the crystal and ruby glittering of the changing rivulet of water out of the Greek vase, glowing into wine. Fonte Branda I last saw with Charles Norton, under the same arches where Dante saw it. We drank of it together, and walked together that evening on the hills above, where the fireflies among the scented thickets shone fitfully in the still undarkened air. *How* they shone! moving like fine-broken starlight through the purple leaves. How they shone! through the sunset that faded into thunderous night as I entered Siena three days before, the white edges of the mountainous clouds still lighted from the west, and the openly golden sky calm behind the Gate of Siena's heart, with its still golden words, "Cor magis tibi Sena pandit," and the fireflies everywhere in sky and cloud rising and falling, mixed with the lightning, and more intense than the stars.

BRANTWOOD,
June 19th, 1889.

𝒞

Other SIGNET CLASSICS You Will Enjoy